ON WRONG AND RIGHT

An Introduction to Moral and Political Philosophy through Classic Texts

Joseph R. Kirkland, J.D.
University of Michigan Dearborn

Kendall Hunt
publishing company

Cover image © Shutterstock, Inc.

Kendall Hunt
publishing company

www.kendallhunt.com
Send all inquiries to:
4050 Westmark Drive
Dubuque, IA 52004-1840

ISBN 978-1-5249-0264-3

Printed in the United States of America

For Robert and Carol Kirkland, who made everything possible,
and for Kerri Kirkland, who makes everything worth it.

Contents

CHAPTER ONE

On Wrong and Right

In a memorable scene from the 1990 Tim Burton film *Edward Scissorhands*, the title character—a kind, innocent orphan with the unusual predicament of possessing giant metal shears where one ordinarily finds hands—joins his adoptive family, The Bogs, for dinner. Bill Bogs is the gruff patriarch of the family. Peg, his kindly wife, is the person responsible for inviting Edward into their home. Kevin is the bratty younger brother, while Kim is the sweet older sister who—spoiler alert—falls in love with Edward. The conversation turns to ethics:

Bill: All right . . . A little ethics, Edward. You're walking down the street. You find a suitcase of money. Nobody's around. There is no obvious owner. What do you do? (A) Keep the money? (B) Spend it on gifts for your loved ones? (C) Give it to the poor? (D) Turn it in to the police?

Kim: Dad. This is stupid . . .

Kevin: I'd keep the money!

Peg: (glares at Kevin) Simmer down.

Bill: Edward?

Kim: (tries to change the subject) I think we should all do something after dinner. Like go bowling together or—

Peg: You're not seeing Jim tonight?

Kim: No.

Kevin: We had the coolest "show and tell" today. This kid brought in a box of baby opossums, maybe ten of them or twelve. They were totally naked, no hair at all, and—

Peg: Quiet, Kev. Your father's not finished.

Bill: Edward? Which one?

Edward: (timidly) I'd rather spend it on my loved ones.

(Bill drops his head into his hands.)

Peg: But, Edward, that would be wrong.

Kevin: You dope, everybody knows that you're supposed to give it to the police.

Bill: Good boy, Kevin.

Kim: Come on you guys, think about it. Buying presents would be much nicer. That's what I'd want to do.

Bill: Kim! We're trying to help Edward, not confuse him more. Can't you be serious, just for once?

Kim: I am being serious. I thought it was a nice idea.

Bill: We're not talking nice, we're talking right and wrong.[i]

This exchange reveals a great deal about each character, but it also raises a series of intriguing questions. What does it mean to do the right thing? What does it mean to be a good person? As children, we were likely told to keep our promises, to refrain from lying, to "treat others as we would like to be treated," to dutifully return the briefcase full of cash to the police, and so forth. Yet what or who determines the nature or content of concepts like *goodness* or *rightness*? Truisms are one thing, but what is really going on in our language and in our judgments when we invoke values like *good* and *bad*, or *right* and *wrong*? What do these concepts even mean, and what force—if any—do or should they have? You may have very strong beliefs and/or feelings concerning the right thing to do in Bill Bogs' hypothetical scenario, but how can we determine if our beliefs and/or feelings on this or any ethical matter or in line with what morality actually requires of us?

Ethics is the branch of philosophy dedicated to the examination of questions such as these. What, then, is philosophy? To philosophize in the proper sense of the word is not merely to exhibit a perfunctory curiosity about things or simply to engage in idle speculation about matters abstruse. Nor is it to adopt a general approach to a particular field or endeavor. Thus, while we may speak loosely in other contexts of having a "philosophy of this" or a "philosophy of that," as an academic discipline, **philosophy** involves the rigorous and critical analysis of fundamental problems, concepts, and values, as well as the analysis of our reasons for accepting some positions while rejecting others concerning these matters. Thus, philosophical ethics (i.e., **moral philosophy**) involves the rigorous, critical analysis of fundamental concepts, values, and problems that pertain to morality—that is, the nature of right and wrong. Philosophy, of course, is not the only domain of inquiry to address fundamental values. Art and theology, for example, most certainly tackle aspects of the nature and import of values. What distinguishes philosophical ethics from other ways of broaching moral value is its methods, which emphasize reasoned argument.

Philosophy in the Western world emerged in Ancient Greece and from Ancient Greek mythology. The ancient Greek word for "reason"—in this sense of a rational account or explanation—is *logos*. Whereas a *mythos* represents a story or tale (think here of the English word "fable"), *logos* for the ancient Greeks referred to (among other things) both a rational account or explanation of something and the distinctively human ability to engage in reasoned discourse on a variety of matters. Aristotle, one of the most influential philosophers who ever lived, characterized this particular conception of *logos* thusly:

> In Aristotle's view, human beings are set apart from the other animals not by their capacity for self-expression, but rather by their capacity for rational speech (*logos*). Man possesses more than mere voice (*phone*); he can do more than just intimate that he feels pleasure or pain. Thus his humanity is in no way constituted by his ability to speak out, to get a load off his chest, to give vent to his spleen. He could just as well accomplish a purge of emotion by the inarticulate utterance of the beast. For Aristotle, *logos* is something more refined than the capacity to make private feelings public: it enables the human being to perform as no other animal can; it makes it possible for him to perceive and make clear to others through reasoned discourse the difference between what is advantageous and what is harmful, between what is just and what is unjust, and between what is good and what is evil.[ii]

Thus, one way to characterize the gradual emergence of Greek philosophy from Greek myth is to frame it as the gradual triumph of *logos* over *mythos*, of a slow but steady transition from a concern with the transmission of fables (*mythoi*) claiming divine warrant to the pursuit of a knowledge of fundamental concepts and values based on reasoned arguments (*logoi*). Etymologically speaking, our English word "logic" stems from the Greek *logos*, and one could argue that logic is the native tongue of philosophy itself. Relatedly, our common English suffix for "the science or the study of" something ("-ology") comes from the selfsame root. Thus, moral philosophy is characterized by its emphasis on the weighing and assessment of various logical arguments for and against various positions on moral matters. We see this in the exchange of arguments between the earliest philosophers in the Western tradition, and we see it in contemporary philosophical inquiry and discourse as well. For further information on the nature of logical arguments and how best to assess them, please consult *Appendix A: An Introduction to Logical Argument*.

Ethics is not the only branch of philosophy, however. We can identify at least four major areas of specialization ("branches of philosophy") in terms of some of the major concepts and values addressed in each:

- METAPHYSICS → reality / existence / being, etc.
- EPISTEMOLOGY → knowledge / truth / evidence / belief, etc.
- ETHICS → goodness / rightness / virtue, etc.
- POLITICAL PHILOSOPHY → justice / fairness / equality, etc.

There are other areas of specialization within philosophy beyond these four main branches. They include **aesthetics** (the philosophy of art and beauty) and the aforementioned **logic** (the study of correct reasoning)—though many Western philosophers would be more prone to describe logic not so much as just another branch on the metaphorical tree, but so much as the very trunk or roots of philosophy. Moreover, there are various branches in philosophy wherein other particular fields or areas of intellectual inquiry are subjected to philosophical analysis. These include the **philosophy of law**, the **philosophy of religion**, the **philosophy of science**, and the **philosophy of language**, for example. What unites these diverse forms of specialization is a shared methodology that focuses on the assessment of reasoned arguments concerning whatever particular issue is being analyzed, discussed, or debated, that is, to seek for those accounts or explanations that are supported in turn by the strongest *logoi*.

If you carefully surveyed the list of central concepts addressed in the respective branches of philosophy, above, you may have detected something interesting. Whereas metaphysical and epistemological questions deal with the way things *are* (i.e., "What is reality?" or "What is knowledge?"), ethical and politically philosophical questions deal with the way things *should be* (i.e., "What should I do?" or "How ought we live?"). This is an illustration of an important conceptual distinction: *description* versus *prescription*. Descriptive fields, claims, theories, and so forth are concerned with what we could call matters of *fact*. Prescriptive endeavors, on the other hand, are concerned with judgments of *value*. The verbs employed here are illuminating: "is" versus "ought." Thus, unsurprisingly, moral philosophy and political philosophy are intimately linked. We could frame this link with an analogy: as ethical questions are to the individual person (i.e., "How should *I* live?" or "What ought *I* do?"), politically philosophical questions are to humans socially or collectively understood (i.e., "How should *we* live?" or "How ought *our society* be organized?"). Whereas moral philosophy addresses values such as *goodness*, *rightness*, and *virtue*, political philosophy addresses values such as *justice*, *equality*, and *fairness*, among others.

Moral Relativism

Maybe you believe that values such as these are relative. The term for this view, appropriately, is **moral relativism**. The famous ancient philosopher and sophist **Protagoras** of Abdera (490–420 BCE) seemed to defend this view in his infamous quip: "Man is the measure of all things." But note the ambiguity of the noun "man." The word is ambiguous because we could either parse "man" as "the individual person," or parse "man" in the collective sense. Astronaut Neil Armstrong played on this ambiguity when, as he became the first member of our species to step foot on an alien world, he proclaimed: "That's one small step for [a] man, one giant leap for mankind." If we read "man" in the Protagorean aphorism as referring to the individual, then we could read it as a proclamation of **individual relativism**: the claim that moral values are relative to the preferences of the individual. If, however, we read "man" as "persons, generally or collectively," then his statement becomes a defense of **cultural relativism**: the claim that moral values are relative to the conventions or norms of a particular culture. Most, though not all, philosophers have rejected both forms of relativism for a variety of reasons, and we will begin our exploration of ethics with an analysis of the debate between relativists and nonrelativists.

- **Individual Relativism:** The theory that moral values are ultimately reducible to individual preference.
- **Cultural Relativism:** The theory that moral values are ultimately reducible to cultural convention.

Divine Command Theory

One possible way to avoid moral relativism is to try and ground moral values in the will of a divine authority. The **Divine Command Theory** is a moral theory that holds that morality is a function of divine commands and prohibitions. On this view, if God commands us to do something, then that conduct is right. Conversely, if God commands us to refrain from doing something, then that conduct is wrong. The debate over the strengths and weaknesses of this particular moral theory is the topic of the *Euthyphro*, a dialogue composed by **Plato** of Athens (c. 428–348 BCE), which features a discussion between the titular Euthyphro and Plato's mentor and teacher **Socrates** of Athens (470–399 BCE). The name of this dialogue and that of its main Socratic interlocutor in turn gives name to a fundamental challenge to the divine command theory: the **Euthyphro Dilemma**, namely, are good actions good *because God commands them*, or does God command them *because they are good*? Careful reasoning reveals that this is no merely trivial or semantic question. The first "horn" of the dilemma potentially reduces moral values such as goodness to ultimately nothing more than the sheer exercise of arbitrary power (i.e., "Because I said so!"), and the second "horn" potentially places something beyond even the power of God to alter: namely, the nature of morality itself. Reading and discussing the *Euthyphro* will give us a perfect opportunity to wrestle with this dilemma and its implications for the fate of the divine command theory as an ethical theory.

- **The Divine Command Theory:** Theory that holds that morality is a function of divine commands: morally good actions are those commanded by God, while morally bad actions are those prohibited by God.
- **The Euthyphro Dilemma:** Dilemma proposed by Socrates in Plato's dialogue *Euthyphro*. The dilemma arises for proponents of the Divine Command Theory. Are good actions good because God commands them, or does God command certain actions because they are inherently good?

Virtue Ethics

The word "ethics" itself is derived from the Ancient Greek *ethikos*, which in turn is derived from the Ancient Greek *ethos*, meaning "habit." Another way to approach the study of how we ought to live is to focus on what sorts of habits we ought to cultivate and what sort of person we should strive to become. This approach is called **aretaic** or **virtue ethics**, from the Greek *arete* meaning "virtue." In this sense, a virtue is a positive trait of character, exhibited in habitual action, that is good for anyone to have. Some typical moral virtues include traits such as honesty, courage, generosity, compassion, and so forth. Under this approach, ethics becomes a question of which character traits and habits we should develop (i.e., the virtues) and which should be avoided (i.e., the vices). **Aristotle** (384–322 BCE) was and remains one of the most influential aretaic thinkers, and his treatise *The Nicomachean Ethics* presents moral virtue as the reasonable mean between two extremes: a deficient extreme on the one hand and an excessive extreme on the other. True virtue involves "hitting the mark" of rational control and self-moderation (*sophrosyne*) both in our actions (*praxis*) and in our emotional reactions (*pathos*) to things. Intriguingly, Aristotle argues that a morally virtuous character is a necessary (though not a sufficient) condition for a truly happy human life, what Aristotle deems *eudaimonia*.

- **Moral virtues:** Traits of character, exhibited in habitual action, that are good for anyone to have.

Consequentialist Ethics

Perhaps you've heard of the familiar cliché, "The road to hell is paved with good intentions." Some moral philosophers have agreed, arguing that, while we may act with the best of intentions, if our actions actually cause more harm than good, then our noble intentions are morally irrelevant. What matters, morally speaking, to philosophers of this persuasion are the actual consequences of our actions, and thus we call this particular theoretical approach **consequentialism**. A diagram may be helpful here.

Intention / Will → Action → CONSEQUENCES

As human beings, we can deliberate before we act and seize on particular intentions for acting. Another way to put that is that human beings "act from a will"—that is, we intend certain things to happen before we act. We then are free to choose to act on our intentions, and, when we act in the world, consequences—intended or no—follow. For the consequentialist, morally good actions are those that produce the best outcomes, our intentions notwithstanding. In general, then, the consequentialist holds that good actions are those that produce more positive than negative consequences. The most influential consequentialist moral theory is **Utilitarianism**. Proposed by **Jeremy Bentham** (1748–1832) and then subsequently refined and popularized by his protégé (and godson) **John Stuart Mill** (1806–1873), utilitarianism is the doctrine that we ought to act so as to maximize the amount of happiness in the world. For the utilitarian, positive outcomes are equated with an increase in happiness, whereas negative outcomes are equated with an increase in unhappiness. Bentham framed this in terms of "The Principle of Utility," whereas Mill framed this in terms of his "Greatest Happiness Principle." Intriguingly (and importantly), utilitarians do not emphasize one's own happiness at the expense of others. Indeed, what made and makes the utilitarian approach quite radical to some is its insistence that *everyone's* interest in being happy is morally relevant. The utilitarian, then, is no **egoist**: that is, a person who argues that we have moral obligations to no one but oneself. Rather, utilitarianism emphasizes that our actions are to be assessed ethically in terms of the extent to which they impact the happiness of *everyone* affected thereby.

Emotivism and the Moral Sentiments

Others have argued that traditional moral philosophy has typically underestimated the important role played by our emotions (or "moral sentiments") when it comes to moral matters. **Emotivism** is the moral theory that holds that our moral judgments (e.g., "Lying is wrong. You should not lie.") are themselves either principally the product of our emotions or even ultimately an expression of emotion itself. The Scottish historian and philosopher **David Hume** (1711–1776) and his good friend and economist **Adam Smith** (1723–1790) were two of the more influential thinkers to emphasize the role of moral sentiments (e.g., sympathy, and feelings of approval or disapproval) when it comes to making sense of moral matters. Hume challenged the longstanding assumption in Western philosophy that our moral judgments are principally the product of reason. Beginning with the ancient Greeks, it had long been presumed that there is an intimate connection between behaving rationally (or reasonably) and behaving well. Hume turned this presumption on its head, infamously quipping that "reason is, and ought to be, the slave to our passions." For Hume, reason is ultimately *instrumental* in nature: that is, our rational faculties permit us to calculate more or less efficient *means* to attaining our various ends, but—critically—reason does not and cannot supply us with *ends*. As Hume somewhat dramatically puts it, "'tis not contrary to reason to prefer the destruction of the whole world to the scratching of my finger." Instead, Hume contends that morality is to be grounded in our emotional and not our rational faculties.

- **Emotivism**: The moral theory that holds that moral judgments are ultimately the product of our emotions and/or expressions of our emotional states or attitudes.

Deontological Ethics

We have seen that some philosophers defend a consequentialist approach to moral questions. This approach is not without its critics, however. **Deontological ethics** represents the major nonconsequentialist competitor to utilitarianism in ethical theory. From the ancient Greek *deon* meaning "duty," deontologists argue that some actions are in and of themselves morally obligatory or morally impermissible. Whereas the utilitarian argues that consequences alone matter, and that our intentions are (in a certain sense) morally irrelevant, the deontologist will argue that we cannot ignore our reasons for acting in assessing the moral worth of said actions.

INTENTION / WILL → ACTION → Consequences

The most influential deontological ethicist was and is **Immanuel Kant** (1724–1804). An epoch-shaping and epoch-shaking philosopher in a host of areas, Kant also revolutionized ethical theory in arguing that there is an objective, universal "moral law" that applies to all rational, and therefore autonomous, beings. Kant strenuously disagreed with Hume's emphasis on the moral sentiments, suggesting that an emotivist approach in ethics raises the specter of a collapse into, among other things, moral relativism, if not outright moral nihilism. Instead, Kant argued that morality is a function of rationality through and through, for reason *both* imposes moral duties upon us *and* reveals what we are morally obligated to do in a given situation. Every rational being is duty-bound to behave in some ways and refrain from behaving in others, and thus the consequences of our actions are not, themselves, morally relevant. It may be expedient for me to tell a lie or take a life—it may even make a great many people happy—but that does not thereby make it right. Kant grounded his deontological ethic in a single, supreme moral principle which, in turn, is the source of all of our more specific duties: The Categorical Imperative. While Kant argues there is but one such supreme moral principle, he nonetheless held that it may be formulated in a handful of ways. One such formulation of the Categorical Imperative—the "Universal Law Formulation"—holds that we are to act only on those maxims (i.e., principles) that we can consistently will apply to everyone. The Categorical Imperative in its various formulations has been massively influential both in and beyond moral philosophy, though precise interpretation of it remains the subject of much philosophical dispute.

Political Philosophy

Our text closes with a selection of wildly influential classic texts in the field of political philosophy. We have already seen how and why moral philosophy and political philosophy are linked: not least of all in their shared commitment to the analysis of *values*. The political philosopher raises questions about, among other things, the origin and legitimacy of civil society and the state (i.e., government), and various competing conceptions of justice, fairness, and so forth. **John Locke** (1632–1704) in his *Second Treatise of Civil Government* and **Thomas Hobbes** (1588–1679) in his *Leviathan* tackle (among other things) the so-called "state of nature" before the rise of civil society, a phenomenon that itself becomes possible ultimately and only through the establishment of a "social contract." Their respective perspectives on both the origins and the nature of states of nature and social contracts, as we shall see, differ in critical ways. We have seen that **John Stuart Mill** (1806–1873) played a critical role in revising and popularizing the utilitarian moral philosophy. Mill's seminal political treatise *On Liberty* has also played a massive role in shaping the debate over, among other things, the proper limits of government interference in our personal lives, and the dangerous "tyranny of the majority" that can occur when a statistical majority impose their preferences and values on minorities within the same society. In *On Liberty*, Mill defends a principle for determining when intrusion into our personal lives is warranted and thus permissible: The Harm Principle. Our text closes with a document whose brevity is inversely proportional to its influence on world history: *The Manifesto of the Communist Party*. Authored by philosopher and economist **Karl Marx** (1818–1883) and his friend and collaborator **Friedrich Engels** (1820–1895) in 1848, the *Manifesto* collects and distills a series of their criticisms of the capitalist mode of production. It also serves as a brief introduction to Marx's political philosophy and his philosophy of history and society: "The history of all hitherto existing society is the history of class struggles."

Concluding Remarks

This text, then, is an introduction to both moral and political philosophy through classic texts in the Western philosophical tradition. The readings contained herein survey a broad range of concerns and questions both moral and political, and they afford you a rare and special opportunity to observe and engage with some of the most influential philosophers of all time. It will not always be an easy read. Much of the language is technical in nature and densely composed. But as philosopher **Baruch Spinoza** (1632–1677) once wrote, "All things excellent are as difficult as they are rare." Let us begin.

Notes

i *Edward Scissorhands* (1990), pp. 87–88.

ii Paul Rahe. *Republics Ancient and Modern: The Ancient Regime in Classical Greece*. The University of North Carolina Press (1994).

Homework Assignment #1a

Name: ______________________________ Section: ______________________________

Name and briefly *define* the four major branches of philosophy. Then, *provide examples* of the kinds of questions we may expect to find in each of these areas of philosophy.

Homework Assignment #1b

Name: ______________________________ Section: ______________________________

Explain the main difference between *descriptive* claims and *prescriptive* claims. Provide your own examples of each.

Homework Assignment #1c

Name: ______________________________ Section: ______________________________

Based on this chapter's brief summaries of some of the major theoretical approaches in philosophical ethics (e.g., Relativism, Divine Command Theory, Virtue Ethics, etc.) which – if any – strike you as the most accurate account of right and wrong? Explain your reasoning.

CHAPTER TWO

Cultural Relativism

William Graham Sumner (1840–1910)

SELECTED READINGS

- *Folkways*—William Graham Sumner
- "Who's to Judge?"—Louis Pojman

Folkways

William Graham Sumner

There is a right way to catch game, to win a wife, to make one's self appear, to cure disease, to honor ghosts, to treat comrades or strangers, to behave when a child is born, on the warpath, in council, and so on in all cases which can arise. The ways are defined on the negative side, that is, by taboos. The "right" way is the way which the ancestors used and which has been handed down. The tradition is its own warrant. It is not held subject to verification by experience. The notion of right is in the folkways. It is not outside of them, of independent origin, and brought to them to test them. In the folkways, whatever is, is right. This is because they are traditional, and therefore contain in themselves the authority of the ancestral ghosts. When we come to the folkways we are at the end of our analysis. The notion of right and ought is the same in regard to all the folkways. . . .

The morality of a group at a time is the sum of the taboos and prescriptions in the folkways by which right conduct is defined. Therefore morals can never be intuitive. They are historical, institutional, and empirical. World philosophy, life policy, right, rights, and morality are all products of the folkways. They are reflections on, and generalizations from, the experience of the pleasure and pain which is won in efforts to carry on the struggle for existence under actual life conditions. The generalizations are very crude and vague in their germinal forms. They are all embodied in folklore, and all our philosophy and science have been developed out of them.

MORES ARE A DIRECTIVE FORCE

Of course the view which has been stated is antagonistic to the view that philosophy and ethics furnish creative and determining forces in society and history. That view comes down to us from the Greek philosophy and it has now prevailed so long that all current discussion conforms to it. Philosophy and ethics are pursued as independent disciplines, and the results are brought to the science of society and to statesmanship and legislation as authoritative dicta. We also have *Völkerpsychologie*, *Sozialpolitik*, and other intermediate forms which show the struggle of metaphysics to retain control of the science of society. The "historic sense," the *Zeitgeist*, and other terms of similar import are partial recognitions of the mores and their importance in the science of society. It can be seen also that philosophy and ethics are products of the folkways. They are taken out of the mores, but are never original and creative; they are secondary and derived. They often interfere in the second stage of the sequence,—act, thought, act. Then they produce harm, but some ground is furnished for the claim that they are creative or at least regulative. In fact, the real process in great bodies of men is not one of deduction from any great principle of philosophy or ethics. It is one of minute efforts to live well under existing conditions, which efforts are repeated indefinitely by great numbers, getting strength from habit and from the fellowship of united action. The resultant folkways become coercive. All are forced to conform, and the folkways dominate the societal life. Then they seem true and right, and arise into mores as the norm of welfare. Thence are produced faiths, ideas, doctrines, religions, and philosophies, according to the stage of civilization and the fashions of reflection and generalization.

WHAT IS GOODNESS OR BADNESS OF THE MORES?

It is most important to notice that, for the people of a time and place, their own mores are always good, or rather that for them there can be no question of the goodness or badness of their mores. The reason is because the standards of good and right are in the mores. If the life conditions change, the traditional folkways may produce pain and loss, or fail to produce the same good as formerly. Then the loss of comfort and ease brings doubt into the judgment of welfare (causing doubt of the pleasure of the gods, or of war power, or of health), and thus disturbs the unconscious philosophy of the mores. Then a later time will pass judgment on the mores. Another society may also pass judgment on the mores. In our literary and historical study of the mores we want to get from them their educational value, which consists in the stimulus or warning as to what is, in its effects, societally good or bad. This may lead us to reject or neglect a phenomenon like infanticide, slavery, or witchcraft, as an old "abuse" and "evil," or to pass by the crusades as a folly which cannot recur. Such a course would be a great error. Everything in the mores of a time and place must be regarded as justified with regard to that time and place. "Good" mores are those which are well adapted to the situation. "Bad" mores are those which are not so adapted. The mores are not so stereotyped and changeless as might appear, because they are forever moving towards more complete adaptation to conditions and interests, and also towards more complete adjustment to each other. People in mass have never made or kept up a custom in order to hurt their own interests. They have made innumerable errors as to what their interests were and how to satisfy them, but they have always aimed to serve their interests as well as they could. This gives the standpoint for the student of the mores. All things in them come before him on the same plane. They all bring instruction and warning. They all have the same relation to power and welfare. The mistakes in them are component parts of them. We do not study them in order to approve some of them and condemn others. They are all equally worthy of attention from the fact that they existed and were used. The chief object of study in them is their adjustment to interests, their relation to welfare, and their coordination in a harmonious system of life policy. For the men of the time there are no "bad" mores. What is traditional and current is the standard of what ought to be. The masses never raise any question about such things. If a few raise doubts and questions, this proves that the folkways have already begun to lose firmness and the regulative element in the mores has begun to lose authority. This indicates that the folkways are on their way to a new adjustment. The extreme of folly, wickedness, and absurdity in the mores is witch persecutions, but the best men of the seventeenth century had no doubt that witches existed, and that they ought to be burned. The religion, statecraft, jurisprudence, philosophy, and social system of that age all contributed to maintain that belief. It was rather a culmination than a contradiction of the current faiths and convictions, just as the dogma that all men are equal and that one ought to have as much political power in the state as another was the culmination of the political dogmatism and social philosophy of the nineteenth century. Hence our judgments of the good or evil consequences of folkways are to be kept separate from our study of the historical phenomena of them, and of their strength and the reasons for it. The judgments have their place in plans and doctrines for the future, not in a retrospect.

THE MORES HAVE THE AUTHORITY OF FACTS

The mores come down to us from the past. Each individual is born into them as he is born into the atmosphere, and he does not reflect on them, or criticize them any more than a baby analyzes the atmosphere before he begins to breathe it. Each one is subjected to the influence of the mores, and formed by them, before he is capable of reasoning about them. It may be objected that nowadays, at least, we criticize all traditions, and accept none just because they are handed down to us. If we take up cases of things which are still entirely or almost entirely in the mores, we shall see that this is not so. There are sects of free-lovers amongst us who want to discuss pair marriage. They are not simply people of evil life. They invite us to discuss rationally our inherited customs and ideas as to marriage, which, they say, are by no means so excellent and elevated as we believe. They have never won any serious attention. Some others want to argue in favor of polygamy on grounds of expediency. They fail to obtain a hearing. Others want to discuss property. In spite of some literary activity on their part, no discussion of property, bequest, and inheritance has ever been opened. Property and marriage are in the mores. Nothing can ever change them but the unconscious and imperceptible movement of the mores. Religion was originally a matter of the mores. It became a societal institution and a function of the state. It has now to a great extent been put back into the mores. Since laws with penalties to enforce religious creeds or practices have gone out of use any one may think and act as he pleases about religion. Therefore it is not now "good form" to attack religion. Infidel publications are now tabooed by the mores, and are more effectually repressed than ever before. They produce no controversy. Democracy is in our American mores. It is a product of our physical and economic conditions. It is impossible to discuss or criticize it. It is glorified for popularity, and is a subject of dithyrambic rhetoric. No one treats it with complete candor and sincerity. No one dares to analyze it as he would aristocracy or autocracy. He would get no hearing and would only incur abuse. The thing to be noticed in all these cases is that the masses oppose a deaf ear to every argument against the mores. It is only in so far as things have been transferred from the mores into laws and positive institutions that there is discussion about them or rationalizing upon them. The mores contain the norm by which, if we should discuss the mores, we should have to judge the mores. We learn the mores as unconsciously as we learn to walk and eat and breathe. The masses never learn how we walk, and eat, and breathe, and they never know any reason why the mores are what they are. The justification of them is that when we wake to consciousness of life we find them facts which already hold us in the bonds of tradition, custom, and habit. The mores contain embodied in them notions, doctrines, and maxims, but they are facts. They are in the present tense. They have nothing to do with what ought to be, will be, may be, or once was, if it is not now.

MORES AND MORALS/SOCIAL CODE

For every one the mores give the notion of what ought to be. This includes the notion of what ought to be done, for all should cooperate to bring to pass, in the order of life, what ought to be. All notions of propriety, decency, chastity, politeness, order, duty, right, rights, discipline, respect, reverence, cooperation, and fellowship, especially all things in regard to which good and ill depend entirely on the point at which the line is drawn, are in the mores. The mores can make things seem right and good to one group or one age which to another seem antagonistic to every instinct of human nature. The thirteenth century bred in every heart such a sentiment in regard to heretics that inquisitors had no more misgivings in their proceedings than men would have now if they should attempt to exterminate rattlesnakes. The sixteenth century gave to all such notions about witches that witch persecutors thought they were waging war on enemies of God and man. Of course the inquisitors and witch persecutors constantly developed the notions of heretics and witches. They exaggerated the notions and then gave them back again to the mores, in their expanded form, to inflame the hearts of men with terror and hate and to become, in the next stage, so much more fantastic and ferocious motives. Such is the reaction between the mores and the acts of the living generation. The world philosophy of the age is never anything but the reflection on the mental horizon, which is formed out of the mores, of the ruling ideas which are in the mores themselves. It is from a failure to recognize the to and fro in this reaction that the current notion arises that mores are produced by doctrines. The "morals" of an age are never anything but the consonance between what is done and what the mores of the age require. The whole revolves on itself, in the relation of the specific to the general, within the horizon formed by the mores. Every attempt to win an outside standpoint from which to reduce the whole to an absolute philosophy of truth and right, based on an unalterable principle, is a delusion. New elements are brought in only by new conquests of nature through science and art. The new conquests change the conditions of life and the interests of the members of the society. Then the mores change by adaptation to new conditions and interests. The philosophy and ethics then follow to account for and justify the changes in the mores; often, also, to claim that they have caused the changes. They never do anything but draw new lines of bearing between the parts of the mores and the horizon of thought within which they are enclosed, and which is a deduction from the mores. The horizon is widened by more knowledge, but for one age it is just as much a generalization from the mores as for another. It is always unreal. It is only a product of thought. The ethical philosophers select points on this horizon from which to take their bearings, and they think that they have won some authority for their systems when they travel back again from the generalization to the specific custom out of which it was deduced. The cases of the inquisitors and witch persecutors who toiled arduously and continually for their chosen ends, for little or no reward, show us the relation between mores on the one side and philosophy, ethics, and religion on the other. . . .

[from *Folkways* by William Graham Sumner]

"Who's to Judge?"

Louis Pojman

In an ancient writing, the Greek historian Herodotus (485–430 BCE) relates that the Persian King Darius once called into his presence some Greeks and asked them what he should pay them to eat the bodies of their fathers when they died. They replied that no sum of money would tempt them to do such a terrible deed; whereupon Darius sent for certain people of the Callatian tribe, who eat their fathers, and asked them in the presence of the Greeks what he should give them to burn the bodies of their fathers at their decease [as the Greeks do]. The Callatians were horrified at the thought and bid him desist in such terrible talk. So Herodotus concludes, "Culture is King o'er all."

Today we condemn ethnocentrism, the uncritical belief in the inherent superiority of one's own culture, as a variety of prejudice tantamount to racism and sexism. What is right in one culture may be wrong in another, what is good east of the river may be bad west of the same river, what is a virtue in one nation may be seen as a vice in another, so it behooves us not to judge others but to be tolerant of diversity.

This rejection of ethnocentrism in the West has contributed to a general shift in public opinion about morality, so that for a growing number of Westerners, consciousness raising about the validity of other ways of life has led to a gradual erosion of belief in moral *objectivism*, the view that there are universal moral principles, valid for all people at all times and climes. For example, in polls taken in my ethics and introduction to philosophy classes over the past several years (in three different universities in three areas of the country) students by a two-to-one ratio affirmed a version of moral relativism over *moral absolutism* with hardly 3 percent seeing something in between these two polar opposites. Of course, I'm not suggesting that all of these students have a clear understanding of what relativism entails, for many of those who say that they are ethical relativists also state on the same questionnaire that "abortion except to save the mother's life is always wrong," that "capital punishment is always morally wrong," or that "suicide is never morally permissible." The apparent contradictions signal an apparent confusion on the matter.

In this essay I want to examine the central notions of ethical relativism and look at the implications that seem to follow from it. After this I want to set forth the outlines of a very modest objectivism, which holds to the objective validity of moral principles but takes into account many of the insights of relativism.

1. AN ANALYSIS OF RELATIVISM

Ethical relativism is the theory that there are no universally valid moral principles, but that all moral principles are valid relative to culture or individual choice. It is to be distinguished from moral skepticism, the view that there are no valid moral principles at all (or at least we cannot know whether there are any), and from all forms of moral objectivism or absolutism. The following statement by the relativist philosopher John Ladd is a good characterization of the theory:

> Ethical relativism is the doctrine that the moral rightness and wrongness of actions varies from society to society and that there are no absolute universal moral standards binding on all men at all times. Accordingly, it holds that whether or not it is right for an individual to act in a certain way depends on or is relative to the society to which he belongs. (John Ladd, *Ethical Relativism*)

If we analyze this passage, we derive the following argument:

1. What is considered morally right and wrong varies from society to society, so that there are no moral principles accepted by all societies.
2. All moral principles derive their validity from cultural acceptance.
3. Therefore, there are no universally valid moral principles, objective standards which apply to all people everywhere and at all times.

1. The first thesis, which may be called the *Diversity Thesis* and identified with *Cultural Relativism*, is simply an anthropological thesis, which registers the fact that moral rules differ from society to society. As we noted in the introduction of this essay, there is enormous variety in what may count as a moral

principle in a given society. The human condition is malleable in the extreme, allowing any number of folkways or moral codes. As Ruth Benedict has written:

> The cultural pattern of any civilization makes use of a certain segment of the great arc of potential human purposes and motivations . . . [A]ny culture makes use of certain selected material techniques or cultural traits. The great arc along which all the possible human behaviors are distributed is far too immense and too full of contradictions for any one culture to utilize even any considerable portion of it. Selection is the first requirement. (*Patterns of Culture*, New York, 1934, p. 219)

It may or may not be the case that there is not a single moral principle held in common by every society, but if there are any, they seem to be few, at best. Certainly, it would be very hard to derive one single "true" morality on the basis of observation of various societies' moral standards.

2. The second thesis, the *Dependency Thesis*, asserts that individual acts are right or wrong depending on the nature of the society from which they emanate. Morality does not occur in a vacuum, but what is considered morally right or wrong must be seen in a context, depending on the goals, wants, beliefs, history, and environment of the society in question. As William Graham Sumner says, "We learn the [morals] as unconsciously as we learn to walk and hear and breathe, and they never know any reason why the [morals] are what they are. The justification of them is that when we wake to consciousness of life we find them facts which already hold us in the bonds of tradition, custom, and habit." Trying to see things from an independent, non-cultural point of view would be like taking out our eyes in order to examine their contours and qualities. We are simply culturally determined beings.

We could, of course, distinguish a weak and a strong thesis of dependency. The nonrelativist can accept a certain relativity in the way moral principles are applied in various cultures, depending on beliefs, history, and environment. For example, Orientals show respect by covering the head and uncovering the feet, whereas Occidentals do the opposite, but both adhere to a principle of respect for deserving people. They just apply the principle of respect differently. Drivers in Great Britain drive on the left side of the road, while those in the rest of Europe and the United States drive on the right side, but both adhere to a principle of orderly progression of traffic. The application of the rule is different but the principle in question is the same principle in both cases. But the ethical relativist must maintain a stronger thesis, one that insists that the very validity of the principles is a product of the culture and that different cultures will invent different valid principles. The ethical relativist maintains that even beyond the environmental factors and differences in beliefs, there is a fundamental disagreement between societies.

In a sense, we all live in radically different worlds. Each person has a different set of beliefs and experiences, a particular perspective that colors all of his or her perceptions. Do the farmer, the real estate dealer, and the artist, looking at the same spatio-temporal field, see the *same* field? Not likely. Their different orientations, values, and expectations govern their perceptions, so that different aspects of the field are highlighted and some features are missed. Even as our individual values arise from personal experience, so social values are grounded in the peculiar history of the community. Morality, then, is just the set of common rules, habits, and customs which have won social approval over time, so that they seem part of the nature of things, as facts. There is nothing mysterious or transcendent about these codes of behavior. They are the outcomes of our social history.

There is something conventional about *any* morality, so that every morality really depends on a level of social acceptance. Not only do various societies adhere to different moral systems, but the very same society could (and often does) change its moral views over time and place. For example, the Southern USA now views slavery as immoral whereas just over one hundred years ago, it did not. We have greatly altered our views on abortion, divorce, and sexuality as well.

3. The conclusion that there are no absolute or objective moral standards binding on all people follows from the first two propositions. Cultural relativism (the Diversity Thesis) plus the Dependency Thesis yields ethical relativism in its classic form. If there are different moral principles from culture to culture and if all morality is rooted in culture, then it follows that there are no universal moral principles valid for all cultures and people at all times.

2. SUBJECTIVE ETHICAL RELATIVISM (SUBJECTIVISM)

Some people think that even this conclusion is too tame and maintain that morality is not dependent on the society but on the individual him or herself. As students sometimes maintain, "Morality is in the eye of the beholder." Ernest Hemingway wrote, "So far, about morals, I know only that what is moral is what you feel good after and what is immoral is what you feel bad after and judged by these moral standards, which I do not defend, the bullfight is very moral to me because I feel very fine while it is going on and have a feeling of life and death and mortality and immortality, and after it is over I feel very sad but very fine."

This form of moral subjectivism has the sorry consequence that it makes morality a useless concept, for, on its premises, little or no interpersonal criticism or judgment is logically possible. Heming-way may feel good about killing bulls in a bull fight, while Albert Schweitzer or Mother Teresa may feel the opposite. No argument about the matter is possible. The only basis for judging Hemingway or anyone else wrong would be if he failed to live up to his own principles, but, of course, one of Hemingway's principles could be that hypocrisy is morally permissible (he feels good about it), so that it would be impossible for him to do wrong. For Hemingway hypocrisy and non-hypocrisy are both morally permissible. On the basis of Subjectivism it could very easily turn out that Adolf Hitler is as moral as Gandhi, so long as each believes he is living by his chosen principles. Notions of moral good and bad, right or wrong, cease to have interpersonal evaluative meaning.

In the opening days of my philosophy classes, I often find students vehemently defending subjective relativism. I then give them their first test of the reading material – which is really a test of their relativism. The next class period I return all the tests, marked with the grade "F" even though my comments show that most of them are of very high quality. When the students explode with outrage (some of them have never before seen this letter on their papers) at this "injustice," I explain that I too have accepted subjectivism for purposes of marking exams, in which case the principle of justice has no objective validity and their complaint is without merit.

You may not like it when your teacher gives you an F on your test paper, while she gives your neighbor an A for one exactly similar, but there is no way to criticize her for injustice, since justice is not one of her elected principles.

Absurd consequences follow from Subjective Ethical Relativism. If it is correct, then morality reduces to aesthetic tastes over which there can be no argument nor interpersonal judgment. Although many students say that they hold this position, there seems to be a conflict between it and other of their moral views (e.g., that Hitler is really morally bad or capital punishment is always wrong). There seems to be a contradiction between Subjectivism and the very concept of morality, which it is supposed to characterize, for morality has to do with "proper" resolution of interpersonal conflict and the amelioration of the human predicament. Whatever else it does, it has a minimal aim of preventing a state of chaos where life is "solitary, poor, nasty, brutish, and short." But if so, Subjectivism is no help at all in doing this, for it doesn't rest on social *agreement* of principle (as the conventionalist maintains) or on an objectively independent set of norms that bind all people for the common good.

Subjectivism treats individuals as billiard balls on a societal pool table where they meet only in radical collisions, each aiming for its own goal and striving to do the other fellow in before he does you. This atomistic view of personality is belied by the fact that we develop in families and mutually dependent communities, in which we share a common language, common institutions, and habits, and that we often feel each other's joys and sorrows. As John Donne said, "No man is an island, entire of itself; every man is a piece of the continent."

Radical individualistic relativism seems incoherent. If so, it follows that the only plausible view of ethical relativism must be one that grounds morality in the group or culture. This form of relativism is called "conventionalism," and to it we now turn.

3. CONVENTIONAL ETHICAL RELATIVISM (CONVENTIONALISM)

Conventional Ethical Relativism, the view that there are no objective moral principles but that all valid moral principles are justified by virtue of their cultural acceptance, recognizes the social nature of morality. That is precisely its power and virtue. It does not seem subject to the same absurd consequences which plague Subjectivism. Recognizing the importance of our social environment in generating customs and beliefs, many people suppose that ethical relativism is the correct ethical theory. Furthermore, they are drawn to it for its liberal philosophical stance. It seems to be an enlightened response to the sin of ethnocentricity, and it seems to entail or strongly imply an attitude of tolerance towards other cultures. As Benedict says, in recognizing ethical relativity "we shall arrive at a more realistic social faith, accepting as grounds of hope and as new bases for tolerance the coexisting and equally valid patterns of life which mankind has created for itself from the raw materials of existence." The most famous of those holding this position is the anthropologist Melville Herskovits, who argues even more explicitly than Benedict that ethical relativism entails intercultural tolerance:

1. If Morality is relative to its culture, then there is no independent basis for criticizing the morality of any other culture but one's own.
2. If there is no independent way of criticizing any other culture, we ought to be *tolerant* of the moralities of other cultures.
3. Morality is relative to its culture.

   Therefore

4. we ought to be tolerant of the moralities of other cultures.

Tolerance is certainly a virtue, but is this a good argument for it? I think not. If morality simply is relative to each culture then if the culture does not have a principle of tolerance, its members have no obligation to be tolerant. Herskovits seems to be treating the *principle of tolerance* as the one exception to his relativism. He seems to be treating it as an absolute moral principle. But from a relativistic point of view there is no more reason to be tolerant than to be intolerant, and neither stance is objectively morally better than the other.

Not only do relativists fail to offer a basis for criticizing those who are intolerant, but they cannot rationally criticize anyone who espouses what they might regard as a heinous principle. If, as seems to be the case, valid criticism supposes an objective or impartial standard, relativists cannot morally criticize anyone outside their own culture. Adolf Hitler's genocidal actions, so long as they are culturally accepted, are as morally legitimate as Mother Teresa's works of mercy. If Conventional Relativism is accepted, racism, genocide of unpopular minorities, oppression of the poor, slavery, and even the advocacy of war for its own sake are as equally moral as their opposites. And if a subculture decided that starting a nuclear war was somehow morally acceptable, we could not morally criticize these people.

Any actual morality, whatever its content, is as valid as every other, and more valid than ideal moralities-since the latter aren't adhered to by any culture.

There are other disturbing consequences of ethical relativism. It seems to entail that reformers are always (morally) wrong since they go against the tide of cultural standards. William Wilberforce was wrong in the eighteenth century to oppose slavery; the British were immoral in opposing suttee in India (the burning of widows, which is now illegal in India). The Early Christians were wrong in refusing to serve in the Roman army or bow down to Caesar, since the majority in the Roman Empire believed that these two acts were moral duties. In fact, Jesus himself was immoral in breaking the law of his day by healing on the Sabbath day and by advocating the principles of the Sermon on the Mount, since it is clear that few in his time (or in ours) accepted them.

Yet we normally feel just the opposite, that the reformer is the courageous innovator who is right, who has the truth, against the mindless majority. Sometimes the individual must stand alone with the truth, risking social censure and persecution. As Dr. Stockman says in Ibsen's *Enemy of the People*, after he loses the battle to declare his town's profitable polluted tourist spa unsanitary, "The most dangerous enemy of the truth and freedom among us-is the compact majority. Yes, the damned, compact, and liberal majority. The majority has *might* – unfortunately – but *right* it is not. Right are I and a few others." Yet if relativism is correct, the opposite is necessarily the case. Truth is with the crowd and error with the individual. . . .

There is an even more basic problem with the notion that morality is dependent on cultural acceptance for its validity. The problem is that the notion of a culture or society is notoriously difficult to define. This is especially so in a pluralistic society like our own where the notion seems to be vague with unclear boundary lines. One person may belong to several societies (subcultures) with different value emphases and arrangements of principles. A person may belong to the nation as a single society with certain values of patriotism, honor, courage, laws (including some which are controversial but have majority acceptance, such as the law on abortion). But he or she may also belong to a church which opposes some of the laws of the State. He may also be an integral member of a socially mixed community where different principles hold sway, and he may belong to clubs and a family where still other rules are adhered to. Relativism would seem to tell us that where he is a member of societies with conflicting moralities he must be judged both wrong and not-wrong whatever he does. For example, if Mary is a U.S. citizen and a member of the Roman Catholic Church, she is wrong (qua Catholic) if she chooses to have an abortion and not-wrong (qua citizen of the U.S.A.) if she acts against the teaching of the Church on abortion. As a member of a racist university fraternity, KKK, John has no obligation to treat his fellow Black student as an equal, but as a member of the University community itself (where the principle of equal rights is accepted) he does have the obligation; but as a member of the surrounding community (which may reject the principle of equal rights) he again has no such obligation; but then again as a member of the nation at large (which accepts the principle) he is obligated to treat his fellow with respect. What is the morally right thing for John to do? The question no longer makes much sense in this moral Babel. It has lost its action-guiding function.

Perhaps the relativist would adhere to a principle which says that in such cases the individual may choose which group to belong to as primary. If Mary chooses to have an abortion, she is choosing to belong to the general society relative to that principle. And John must likewise choose between groups. The trouble with this option is that it seems to lead back to counter-intuitive results. If Gangland Gus of Murder, Incorporated, feels like killing Bank President Ortcutt and wants to feel good about it, he identifies with the Murder, Incorporated society rather than the general public morality. Does this justify the killing? In fact, couldn't one justify anything simply by forming a small subculture that approved of it? Charles Manson would be morally pure in killing innocents simply by virtue of forming a little coterie. How large must the group be in order to be a legitimate sub culture or society? Does it need ten or fifteen people? How about just three? Come to think about it, why can't my burglary partner and I found our own society with a morality of its own? Of course, if my partner dies, I could still claim that I was acting from an originally social set of norms. But why can't I dispense with the interpersonal agreements altogether and invent my own morality – since morality, on this view, is only an invention anyway? Conventionalist Relativism seems to reduce to Subjectivism. And Subjectivism leads, as we have seen, to the demise of morality altogether.

However, while we may fear the demise of morality, as we have known it, this in itself may not be a good reason for rejecting relativism; that is, for judging it false. Alas, truth may not always be edifying. But the consequences of this position are sufficiently alarming to prompt us to look carefully for some weakness in the relativist's argument. So let us examine the premises and conclusion listed at the beginning of this essay as the three theses of relativism.

1. *The Diversity Thesis*: What is considered morally right and wrong varies from society to society, so that there are no moral principles accepted by all societies.
2. *The Dependency Thesis*: All moral principles derive their validity from cultural acceptance.
3. *Ethical Relativism*: Therefore, there are no universally valid moral principles, objective standards which apply to all people everywhere and at all times.

Does any one of these seem problematic? Let us consider the first thesis, the Diversity Thesis, which we have also called Cultural Relativism. Perhaps there is not as much diversity as anthropologists like Sumner and Benedict suppose. One can also see great similarities between the moral codes of various cultures. E. O. Wilson has identified over a score of common features, and before him Clyde Kluckhohn has noted some significant common ground:

Every culture has a concept of murder, distinguishing this from execution, killing in war, and other "justifiable homicides." The notions of incest and other regulations upon sexual behavior, the prohibitions upon untruth under defined circumstances, of restitution and reciprocity, of mutual obligations between parents and children – these and many other moral concepts are altogether universal. ("Ethical Relativity: Sic et Non," *Journal of Philosophy*, LII, 1955)

And Colin Turnbull, whose description of the sadistic, semi-displaced Ik in Northern Uganda, was seen as evidence of a people without principles of kindness and cooperation, has produced evidence that underneath the surface of this dying society, there is a deeper moral code from a time when the tribe flourished, which occasionally surfaces and shows its nobler face.

On the other hand, there is enormous cultural diversity and many societies have radically different moral codes. Cultural Relativism seems to be a fact, but, even if it is, it does not by itself establish the truth of Ethical Relativism. Cultural diversity in itself is neutral be tween theories. For the objectivist could concede complete cultural relativism, but still defend a form of universalism; for he or she could argue that some cultures simply lack correct moral principles.

On the other hand, a denial of complete Cultural Relativism (i.e., an admission of some universal principles) does not disprove Ethical Relativism. For even if we did find one or more universal principles, this would not prove that they had any objective status. We could still *imagine* a culture that was an exception to the rule and be unable to criticize it. So the first premise doesn't by itself imply Ethical Relativism and its denial doesn't disprove Ethical Relativism.

We turn to the crucial second thesis, the Dependency Thesis. Morality does not occur in a vacuum, but what is considered morally right or wrong must be seen in a context, depending on the goals, wants, beliefs, history, and environment of the society in question. We distinguished a weak and a strong thesis of dependency. The weak thesis says that the application of principles depends on the particular cultural predicament, whereas the strong thesis affirms that the principles themselves depend on that predicament. The nonrelativist can accept a certain relativity in the way moral principles are *applied* in various cultures, depending on beliefs, history, and environment. For example, a raw environment with scarce natural resources may justify the Eskimos' brand of euthanasia to the objectivist, who in another environment would consistently reject that practice. The members of a tribe in the Sudan throw their deformed children into the river because of their belief that such infants *belong* to the hippopotamus, the god of the river. We believe that they have a false belief about this, but the point is that the same principles of respect for property and respect for human life are operative in these contrary practices. They differ with us only in belief, not in substantive moral principle. This is an illustration of how nonmoral beliefs (e.g., deformed children belong to the hippopotamus) when applied to common moral principles (e.g., give to each his due) generate different actions in different cultures. In our own culture the difference in the nonmoral belief about the status of a fetus generates opposite moral prescriptions. So the fact that moral principles are weakly dependent doesn't show that Ethical Relativism is valid. In spite of this weak dependency on nonmoral factors, there could still be a set of general moral norms applicable to all cultures and even recognized in most, which are disregarded at a culture's own expense.

What the relativist needs is a strong thesis of dependency, that somehow all principles are essentially cultural inventions. But why should we choose to view morality this way? Is there anything to recommend the strong thesis over the weak thesis of dependency? The relativist may argue that in fact we don't have an obvious impartial standard from which to judge. "Who's to say which culture is right and which is wrong?" But this seems to be dubious. We can reason and perform thought experiments in order to make a case for one system over another. We may not be able to *know* with certainty that our moral beliefs are closer to the truth than those of another culture or those of others within our own culture, but we may be *justified* in believing that they are. If we can be closer to the truth regarding factual or scientific matters, why can't we be closer to the truth on moral matters? Why can't a culture simply be confused or wrong about its moral perceptions? Why can't we say that the society like the Ik which sees nothing wrong with enjoying watching its own children fall into fires is less moral in that regard than the culture that cherishes children and grants them protection and equal rights? To take such a stand is not to commit the fallacy of ethnocentrism, for we are seeking to derive principles through critical reason, not simply uncritical acceptance of one's own mores . . .

In conclusion I have argued (1) that Cultural Relativism (the fact that there are cultural differences regarding moral principles) does not entail Ethical Relativism (the thesis that there are no objectively valid universal moral principles); (2) that the Dependency Thesis (that morality derives its legitimacy from individual cultural acceptance) is mistaken; and (3) that there are universal moral principles based on a common human nature and a need to solve conflicts of interest and flourish.

So, returning to the question asked at the beginning of this essay, "Who's to judge what's right or wrong?" the answer is: *We are*. We are to do so on the basis of the best reasoning we can bring forth and with sympathy and understanding.

Key Terms and Concepts

folkways
mores
ethnocentrism
moral objectivism
ethical relativism
the Diversity Thesis
the Dependency Thesis
"weak" vs. "strong" Dependency Thesis
Subjective Ethical Relativism
Conventional Ethical Relativism

Questions for Further Reflection

1. Why does Sumner conclude that "for the people of a time and place, their own mores are always good"? Do you agree? Why or why not?
2. What is ethnocentrism and why does Pojman introduce the concept in his essay? Do you agree with his assessment? Why or why not?
3. What is the main difference between subjectivism and conventionalism?
4. What does Pojman mean when he describes the Diversity Thesis as "simply an anthropological thesis"?
5. What is the main difference between the Diversity Thesis and the Dependency Thesis? What is the main difference between the weak and strong versions of the Dependency Thesis?
6. What are some of the criticisms of subjectivism identified by Pojman? What are some of the criticisms of conventionalism identified by Pojman? Do you find any of them persuasive? Why or why not?
7. Explain the significance of the title of Pojman's essay in light of his conclusion.

Homework Assignment #2a

Name: ______________________________ Section: ______________________________

Explain how William Graham Sumner's "Folkways" can be read as a defense of what Louis Pojman calls Conventionalism.

Homework Assignment #2b

Name: ______________________________ Section: ______________________________

Explain the main difference between what Pojman calls the Diversity Thesis and the Dependency Thesis. Then, *explain* the main difference between the Weak Diversity Thesis and the Strong Diversity Thesis.

Homework Assignment #2c

Name: ______________________________ Section: ______________________________

Define ethnocentrism, and *explain* why Pojman introduces the concept of ethnocentrism in his essay. What claim does he make about the link between ethnocentrism and moral relativism?

Homework Assignment #2d

Name: ______________________________ Section: ______________________________

Louis Pojman is critical of both Subjectivism and Conventionalism. *Explain* at least two of the critiques he makes against both theories. Do you find any of his criticisms persuasive? Why or why not?

CHAPTER THREE

Divine Command Theory and the Euthyphro Dilemma

© Anastasios71/Shutterstock.com

Socrates (470–399 BCE)

© Dimitrios/Shutterstock.com

Plato (428–347 BCE)

SELECTED READINGS

- *Euthyphro*—Plato

Euthyphro

Plato

(Translated by Benjamin Jowett)

PERSONS OF THE DIALOGUE: Socrates, Euthyphro
SCENE: The Porch of the King Archon

EUTHYPHRO: Why have you left the Lyceum, Socrates? and what are you doing in the Porch of the King Archon? Surely you cannot be concerned in a suit before the King, like myself?

SOCRATES: Not in a suit, Euthyphro; impeachment is the word which the Athenians use.

EUTHYPHRO: What! I suppose that someone has been prosecuting you, for I cannot believe that you are the prosecutor of another.

SOCRATES: Certainly not.

EUTHYPHRO: Then someone else has been prosecuting you?

SOCRATES: Yes.

EUTHYPHRO: And who is he?

SOCRATES: A young man who is little known, Euthyphro; and I hardly know him: his name is Meletus, and he is of the deme of Pitthis. Perhaps you may remember his appearance; he has a beak, and long straight hair, and a beard which is ill grown.

EUTHYPHRO: No, I do not remember him, Socrates. But what is the charge which he brings against you?

SOCRATES: What is the charge? Well, a very serious charge, which shows a good deal of character in the young man, and for which he is certainly not to be despised. He says he knows how the youth are corrupted and who are their corruptors. I fancy that he must be a wise man, and seeing that I am the reverse of a wise man, he has found me out, and is going to accuse me of corrupting his young friends. And of this our mother the state is to be the judge. Of all our political men he is the only one who seems to me to begin in the right way, with the cultivation of virtue in youth; like a good husbandman, he makes the young shoots his first care, and clears away us who are the destroyers of them. This is only the first step; he will afterwards attend to the elder branches; and if he goes on as he has begun, he will be a very great public benefactor.

EUTHYPHRO: I hope that he may; but I rather fear, Socrates, that the opposite will turn out to be the truth. My opinion is that in attacking you he is simply aiming a blow at the foundation of the state. But in what way does he say that you corrupt the young?

SOCRATES: He brings a wonderful accusation against me, which at first hearing excites surprise: he says that I am a poet or maker of gods, and that I invent new gods and deny the existence of old ones; this is the ground of his indictment.

EUTHYPHRO: I understand, Socrates; he means to attack you about the familiar sign which occasionally, as you say, comes to you. He thinks that you are a neologian, and he is going to have you up before the court for this. He knows that such a charge is readily received by the world, as I myself know too well; for when I speak in the assembly about divine things, and foretell the future to them, they laugh at me and think me a madman. Yet every word that I say is true. But they are jealous of us all; and we must be brave and go at them.

SOCRATES: Their laughter, friend Euthyphro, is not a matter of much consequence. For a man may be thought wise; but the Athenians, I suspect, do not much trouble themselves about him until he begins to impart his wisdom to others, and then for some reason or other, perhaps, as you say, from jealousy, they are angry.

EUTHYPHRO: I am never likely to try their temper in this way.

SOCRATES: I dare say not, for you are reserved in your behavior, and seldom impart your wisdom. But I have a benevolent habit of pouring out myself to everybody, and would even pay for a listener, and I am afraid that the Athenians may think me too talkative. Now if, as I was saying, they would only laugh at me, as you say that they laugh at you, the time might pass gaily enough in the court; but perhaps they may be in earnest, and then what the end will be you soothsayers only can predict.

EUTHYPHRO: I dare say that the affair will end in nothing, Socrates, and that you will win your cause; and I think that I shall win my own.

SOCRATES: And what is your suit, Euthyphro? Are you the pursuer or the defendant?

EUTHYPHRO: I am the pursuer.

SOCRATES: Of whom?

EUTHYPHRO: You will think me mad when I tell you.

SOCRATES: Why, has the fugitive wings?

EUTHYPHRO: Nay, he is not very volatile at his time of life.

SOCRATES: Who is he?

EUTHYPHRO: My father.

SOCRATES: Your *father*, my good man!?

EUTHYPHRO: Yes.

SOCRATES: And of what is he accused?

EUTHYPHRO: Of murder, Socrates.

SOCRATES: By the powers, Euthyphro! how little does the common herd know of the nature of right and truth. A man must be an extraordinary man, and have made great strides in wisdom, before he could have seen his way to bring such an action.

EUTHYPHRO: Indeed, Socrates, he must.

SOCRATES: I suppose that the man whom your father murdered was one of your relatives—clearly he was; for if he had been a stranger you would never have thought of prosecuting him.

EUTHYPHRO: I am amused, Socrates, at your making a distinction between one who is a relation and one who is not a relation; for surely the pollution is the same in either case, if you knowingly associate with the murderer when you ought to clear yourself and him by proceeding against him. The real question is whether the murdered man has been justly slain. If justly, then your duty is to let the matter alone; but if unjustly, then even if the murderer lives under the same roof with you and eats at the same table, proceed against him. Now the man who is dead was a poor dependent of mine who worked for us as a field laborer on our farm in Naxos, and one day in a fit of drunken passion he got into a quarrel with one of our domestic servants and slew him. My father bound him hand and foot and threw him into a ditch, and then sent to Athens to ask of a diviner what he should do with him. Meanwhile he never attended to him and took no care about him, for he regarded him as a murderer; and thought that no great harm would be done even if he did die. Now this was just what happened. For such was the effect of cold and hunger and chains upon him, that before the messenger returned from the diviner, he was dead. And my father and family are angry with me for taking the part of the murderer and prosecuting my father. They say that he did not kill him, and that if he did, the dead man was but a murderer, and I ought not to take any notice, for that a son is impious who prosecutes a father. Which shows, Socrates, how little they know what the gods think about piety and impiety.

SOCRATES: Good heavens, Euthyphro! And is your knowledge of religion and of things pious and impious so very exact, that, supposing the circumstances to be as you state them, you are not afraid lest you too may be doing an impious thing in bringing an action against your father?

EUTHYPHRO: The best of Euthyphro, and that which distinguishes him, Socrates, from other men, is his exact knowledge of all such matters. What should I be good for without it?

SOCRATES: Rare friend! I think that I cannot do better than be your disciple. Then before the trial with Meletus comes on I shall challenge him, and say that I have always had a great interest in religious questions, and now, as he charges me with rash imaginations and innovations in religion, I have become your disciple. You, Meletus, as I shall say to him, acknowledge Euthyphro to be a great theologian, and sound in his opinions; and if you approve of him you ought to approve of me, and not have me into court; but if you disapprove, you should begin by indicting him who is my teacher, and who will be the ruin, not of the young, but of the old; that is to say, of myself whom he instructs, and of his old father whom he admonishes and chastises. And if Meletus refuses to listen to me, but will go on, and will not shift the indictment from me to you, I cannot do better than repeat this challenge in the court.

EUTHYPHRO: Yes, indeed, Socrates; and if he attempts to indict me I am mistaken if I do not find a flaw in him; the court shall have a great deal more to say to him than to me.

SOCRATES: And I, my dear friend, knowing this, am desirous of becoming your disciple. For I observe that no one appears to notice you—not even this Meletus; but his sharp eyes have found me out at once, and he has indicted me for impiety. And therefore, I adjure you to tell me the nature of piety and impiety, which you said that you knew so well, and of murder, and of other offences against the gods. What are they? Is not piety in every action always the same? And impiety, again—is it not always the opposite of piety, and also the same with itself, having, as impiety, one notion which includes whatever is impious?

EUTHYPHRO: To be sure, Socrates.

SOCRATES: And what is piety, and what is impiety?

EUTHYPHRO: Piety is doing as I am doing; that is to say, prosecuting anyone who is guilty of murder, sacrilege, or of any similar crime—whether he be your father or mother, or whoever he may be—that makes no difference; and not to prosecute them is impiety. And please to consider, Socrates, what a notable proof I will give you of the truth of my words, a proof which I have already given to others:—of the principle, I mean, that the impious, whoever he may be, ought not to go unpunished. For do not men regard Zeus as the best and most righteous of the gods?—and yet they admit that he bound his father (Cronos) because he wickedly devoured his sons, and that he too had punished his own father (Uranus) for a similar reason, in a nameless manner. And yet when I proceed against my father, they are angry with me. So inconsistent are they in their way of talking when the gods are concerned, and when I am concerned.

SOCRATES: May not this be the reason, Euthyphro, why I am charged with impiety—that I cannot away with these stories about the gods? and therefore I suppose that people think me wrong. But, as you who are well informed about them approve of them, I cannot do better than assent to your superior wisdom. What else can I say, confessing as I do, that I know nothing about them? Tell me, for the love of Zeus, whether you really believe that they are true.

EUTHYPHRO: Yes, Socrates; and things more wonderful still, of which the world is in ignorance.

SOCRATES: And do you really believe that the gods fought with one another, and had dire quarrels, battles, and the like, as the poets say, and as you may see represented in the works of great artists? The temples are full of them; and notably the robe of Athene, which is carried up to the Acropolis at the great Panathenaea, is embroidered with them. Are all these tales of the gods true, Euthyphro?

EUTHYPHRO: Yes, Socrates; and, as I was saying, I can tell you, if you would like to hear them, many other things about the gods which would quite amaze you.

SOCRATES: I dare say; and you shall tell me them at some other time when I have leisure. But just at present I would rather hear from you a more precise answer, which you have not as yet given, my friend, to the question: What is 'piety'? When asked, you only replied, Doing as you do, charging your father with murder.

EUTHYPHRO: And what I said was true, Socrates.

SOCRATES: No doubt, Euthyphro; but you would admit that there are many other pious acts?

EUTHYPHRO: There are.

SOCRATES: Remember that I did not ask you to give me two or three examples of piety, but to explain the general idea which makes all pious things to be pious. Do you not recollect that there was one idea which made the impious impious, and the pious pious?

EUTHYPHRO: I remember.

SOCRATES: Tell me what is the nature of this idea, and then I shall have a standard to which I may look, and by which I may measure actions, whether yours or those of any one else, and then I shall be able to say that such and such an action is pious, such another impious.

EUTHYPHRO: I will tell you, if you like.

SOCRATES: I should very much like.

EUTHYPHRO: Piety, then, is that which is dear to the gods, and impiety is that which is not dear to them.

SOCRATES: Very good, Euthyphro; you have now given me the sort of answer which I wanted. But whether what you say is true or not I cannot as yet tell, although I make no doubt that you will prove the truth of your words.

EUTHYPHRO: Of course.

SOCRATES: Come, then, and let us examine what we are saying. That thing or person which is dear to the gods is pious, and that thing or person which is hateful to the gods is impious, these two being the extreme opposites of one another. Was not that said?

EUTHYPHRO: It was.

SOCRATES: And well said?

EUTHYPHRO: Yes, Socrates, I thought so; it was certainly said.

SOCRATES: And further, Euthyphro, the gods were admitted to have enmities and hatreds and differences?

EUTHYPHRO: Yes, that was also said.

SOCRATES: And what sort of difference creates enmity and anger? Suppose for example that you and I, my good friend, differ about a number; do differences of this sort make us enemies and set us at variance with one another? Do we not go at once to arithmetic, and put an end to them by a sum?

EUTHYPHRO: True.

SOCRATES: Or suppose that we differ about magnitudes, do we not quickly end the differences by measuring?

EUTHYPHRO: Very true.

SOCRATES: And we end a controversy about heavy and light by resorting to a weighing machine?

EUTHYPHRO: To be sure.

SOCRATES: But what differences are there which cannot be thus decided, and which therefore make us angry and set us at enmity with one another? I dare say the answer does not occur to you at the moment, and therefore I will suggest that these enmities arise when the matters of difference are the just and unjust, good and evil, honorable and dishonorable. Are not these the points about which men differ, and about which when we are unable satisfactorily to decide our differences, you and I and all of us quarrel, when we do quarrel?

EUTHYPHRO: Yes, Socrates, the nature of the differences about which we quarrel is such as you describe.

SOCRATES: And the quarrels of the gods, noble Euthyphro, when they occur, are of a like nature?

EUTHYPHRO: Certainly they are.

SOCRATES: They have differences of opinion, as you say, about good and evil, just and unjust, honorable and dishonorable: there would have been no quarrels among them, if there had been no such differences—would there now?

EUTHYPHRO: You are quite right.

SOCRATES: Does not every man love that which he deems noble and just and good, and hate the opposite of them?

EUTHYPHRO: Very true.

SOCRATES: But, as you say, people regard the same things, some as just and others as unjust,—about these they dispute; and so there arise wars and fighting among them.

EUTHYPHRO: Very true.

SOCRATES: Then the same things are hated by the gods and loved by the gods, and are both hateful and dear to them?

EUTHYPHRO: True.

SOCRATES: And upon this view the same things, Euthyphro, will be pious and also impious?

EUTHYPHRO: So I should suppose.

SOCRATES: Then, my friend, I remark with surprise that you have not answered the question which I asked. For I certainly did not ask you to tell me what action is both pious and impious: but now it would seem that what is loved by the gods is also hated by them. And therefore, Euthyphro, in thus chastising your father you may very likely be doing what is agreeable to Zeus but disagreeable to Cronos or Uranus, and what is acceptable to Hephaestus but unacceptable to Hera, and there may be other gods who have similar differences of opinion.

EUTHYPHRO: But I believe, Socrates, that all the gods would be agreed as to the propriety of punishing a murderer: there would be no difference of opinion about that.

SOCRATES: Well, but speaking of men, Euthyphro, did you ever hear any one arguing that a murderer or any sort of evil-doer ought to be let off?

EUTHYPHRO: I should rather say that these are the questions which they are always arguing, especially in courts of law: they commit all sorts of crimes, and there is nothing which they will not do or say in their own defense.

SOCRATES: But do they admit their guilt, Euthyphro, and yet say that they ought not to be punished?

EUTHYPHRO: No; they do not.

SOCRATES: Then there are some things which they do not venture to say and do: for they do not venture to argue that the guilty are to be unpunished, but they deny their guilt, do they not?

EUTHYPHRO: Yes.

SOCRATES: Then they do not argue that the evil-doer should not be punished, but they argue about the fact of who the evil-doer is, and what he did and when?

EUTHYPHRO: True.

SOCRATES: And the gods are in the same case, if as you assert they quarrel about just and unjust, and some of them say while others deny that injustice is done among them. For surely neither God nor man will ever venture to say that the doer of injustice is not to be punished?

EUTHYPHRO: That is true, Socrates, in the main.

SOCRATES: But they join issue about the particulars—gods and men alike; and, if they dispute at all, they dispute about some act which is called in question, and which by some is affirmed to be just, by others to be unjust. Is not that true?

EUTHYPHRO: Quite true.

SOCRATES: Well then, my dear friend Euthyphro, do tell me, for my better instruction and information, what proof have you that in the opinion of all the gods a servant who is guilty of murder, and is put in chains by the master of the dead man, and dies because he is put in chains before he who bound him can learn from the interpreters of the gods what he ought to do with him, dies unjustly; and that on behalf of such an one a son ought to proceed against his father and accuse him of murder. How would you show that all the gods absolutely agree in approving of his act? Prove to me that they do, and I will applaud your wisdom as long as I live.

EUTHYPHRO: It will be a difficult task; but I could make the matter very clear indeed to you.

SOCRATES: I understand; you mean to say that I am not so quick of apprehension as the judges: for to them you will be sure to prove that the act is unjust, and hateful to the gods.

EUTHYPHRO: Yes indeed, Socrates; at least if they will listen to me.

SOCRATES: But they will be sure to listen if they find that you are a good speaker. There was a notion that came into my mind while you were speaking; I said to myself: 'Well, and what if Euthyphro does prove to me that all the gods regarded the death of the serf as unjust, how do I know anything more of the nature of piety and impiety? for granting that this action may be hateful to the gods, still piety and impiety are not adequately defined by these distinctions, for that which is hateful to the gods has been shown to be also pleasing and dear to them.' And therefore, Euthyphro, I do not ask you to prove this; I will suppose, if you like, that all the gods condemn and abominate such an action. But I will amend the definition so far as to say that what all the gods hate is impious, and what they love pious or holy; and what some of them love and others hate is both or neither. Shall this be our definition of piety and impiety?

EUTHYPHRO: Why not, Socrates?

SOCRATES: Why not! certainly, as far as I am concerned, Euthyphro, there is no reason why not. But whether this admission will greatly assist you in the task of instructing me as you promised, is a matter for you to consider.

EUTHYPHRO: Yes, I should say that what all the gods love is pious and holy, and the opposite which they all hate, impious.

SOCRATES: Ought we to enquire into the truth of this, Euthyphro, or simply to accept the mere statement on our own authority and that of others? What do you say?

EUTHYPHRO: We should enquire; and I believe that the statement will stand the test of enquiry.

SOCRATES: We shall know better, my good friend, in a little while. The point which I should first wish to understand is whether the pious or holy is beloved by the gods because it is holy, or holy because it is beloved of the gods.

EUTHYPHRO: I do not understand your meaning, Socrates.

SOCRATES: I will endeavor to explain: we, speak of carrying and we speak of being carried, of leading and being led, seeing and being seen. You know that in all such cases there is a difference, and you know also in what the difference lies?

EUTHYPHRO: I think that I understand.

SOCRATES: And is not that which is beloved distinct from that which loves?

EUTHYPHRO: Certainly.

SOCRATES: Well; and now tell me, is that which is carried in this state of carrying because it is carried, or for some other reason?

EUTHYPHRO: No; that is the reason.

SOCRATES: And the same is true of what is led and of what is seen?

EUTHYPHRO: True.

SOCRATES: And a thing is not seen because it is visible, but conversely, visible because it is seen; nor is a thing led because it is in the state of being led, or carried because it is in the state of being carried, but the converse of this. And now I think, Euthyphro, that my meaning will be intelligible; and my meaning is, that any state of action or passion implies previous action or passion. It does not become because it is becoming, but it is in a state of becoming because it becomes; neither does it suffer because it is in a state of suffering, but it is in a state of suffering because it suffers. Do you not agree?

EUTHYPHRO: Yes.

SOCRATES: Is not that which is loved in some state either of becoming or suffering?

EUTHYPHRO: Yes.

SOCRATES: And the same holds as in the previous instances; the state of being loved follows the act of being loved, and not the act the state.

EUTHYPHRO: Certainly.

SOCRATES: And what do you say of piety, Euthyphro: is not piety, according to your definition, loved by all the gods?

EUTHYPHRO: Yes.

SOCRATES: Because it is pious or holy, or for some other reason?

EUTHYPHRO: No, that is the reason.

SOCRATES: It is loved because it is holy, not holy because it is loved?

EUTHYPHRO: Yes.

SOCRATES: And that which is dear to the gods is loved by them, and is in a state to be loved of them because it is loved of them?

EUTHYPHRO: Certainly.

SOCRATES: Then that which is dear to the gods, Euthyphro, is not holy, nor is that which is holy loved of God, as you affirm; but they are two different things.

EUTHYPHRO: How do you mean, Socrates?

SOCRATES: I mean to say that the holy has been acknowledged by us to be loved of God because it is holy, not to be holy because it is loved.

EUTHYPHRO: Yes.

SOCRATES: But that which is dear to the gods is dear to them because it is loved by them, not loved by them because it is dear to them.

EUTHYPHRO: True.

SOCRATES: But, friend Euthyphro, if that which is holy is the same with that which is dear to God, and is loved because it is holy, then that which is dear to God would have been loved as being dear to God; but if that which is dear to God is dear to him because loved by him, then that which is holy would have been holy because loved by him. But now you see that the reverse is the case, and that they are quite different from one another. For one (i.e., *theophiles*) is of a kind to be loved cause it is loved, and the other (i.e., *osion*) is loved because it is of a kind to be loved. Thus you appear to me, Euthyphro, when I ask you what is the essence of holiness, to offer an attribute only, and not the essence—the attribute of being loved by all the gods. But you still refuse to explain to me the nature of holiness. And therefore, if you please, I will ask you not to hide your treasure, but to tell me once more what holiness or piety really is, whether dear to the gods or not (for that is a matter about which we will not quarrel); and what is impiety?

EUTHYPHRO: I really do not know, Socrates, how to express what I mean. For somehow or other our arguments, on whatever ground we rest them, seem to turn round and walk away from us.

SOCRATES: Your words, Euthyphro, are like the handiwork of my ancestor Daedalus; and if I were the sayer or propounder of them, you might say that my arguments walk away and will not remain fixed where they are placed because I am a descendant of his. But now, since these notions are your own, you must find some other gibe, for they certainly, as you yourself allow, show an inclination to be on the move.

EUTHYPHRO: Nay, Socrates, I shall still say that you are the Daedalus who sets arguments in motion; not I, certainly, but you make them move or go round, for they would never have stirred, as far as I am concerned.

SOCRATES: Then I must be a greater than Daedalus: for whereas he only made his own inventions to move, I move those of other people as well. And the beauty of it is, that I would rather not. For I would give the wisdom of Daedalus, and the wealth of Tantalus, to be able to detain them and keep them fixed. But enough of this. As I perceive that you are lazy, I will myself endeavor to show you how you might instruct me in the nature of piety; and I hope that you will not grudge your labor. Tell me, then—Is not that which is pious necessarily just?

EUTHYPHRO: Yes.

SOCRATES: And is, then, all which is just pious? Or is that which is pious all just, but that which is just, only in part and not all, pious?

EUTHYPHRO: I do not understand you, Socrates.

SOCRATES: And yet I know that you are as much wiser than I am, as you are younger. But, as I was saying, revered friend, the abundance of your wisdom makes you lazy. Please to exert yourself, for there is no real difficulty in understanding me. What I mean I may explain by an illustration of what I do not mean. The poet [Stasinus] sings—

"Of Zeus, the author and creator of all these things, You will not tell: for where there is fear there is also reverence."

Now I disagree with this poet. Shall I tell you in what respect?

EUTHYPHRO: By all means.

SOCRATES: I should not say that where there is fear there is also reverence; for I am sure that many persons fear poverty and disease, and the like evils, but I do not perceive that they reverence the objects of their fear.

EUTHYPHRO: Very true.

SOCRATES: But where reverence is, there is fear; for he who has a feeling of reverence and shame about the commission of any action, fears and is afraid of an ill reputation.

EUTHYPHRO: No doubt.

SOCRATES: Then we are wrong in saying that where there is fear there is also reverence; and we should say, where there is reverence there is also fear. But there is not always reverence where there is fear; for fear is a more extended notion, and reverence is a part of fear, just as the odd is a part of number, and number is a more extended notion than the odd. I suppose that you follow me now?

EUTHYPHRO: Quite well.

SOCRATES: That was the sort of question which I meant to raise when I asked whether the just is always the pious, or the pious always the just; and whether there may not be justice where there is not piety; for justice is the more extended notion of which piety is only a part. Do you dissent?

EUTHYPHRO: No, I think that you are quite right.

SOCRATES: Then, if piety is a part of justice, I suppose that we should enquire what part? If you had pursued the enquiry in the previous cases; for instance, if you had asked me what is an even number, and what part of number the even is, I should have had no difficulty in replying, a number which represents a figure having two equal sides. Do you not agree?

EUTHYPHRO: Yes, I quite agree.

SOCRATES: In like manner, I want you to tell me what part of justice is piety or holiness, that I may be able to tell Meletus not to do me injustice, or indict me for impiety, as I am now adequately instructed by you in the nature of piety or holiness, and their opposites.

EUTHYPHRO: Piety or holiness, Socrates, appears to me to be that part of justice which attends to the gods, as there is the other part of justice which attends to men.

SOCRATES: That is good, Euthyphro; yet still there is a little point about which I should like to have further information: What is the meaning of "attention"? For attention can hardly be used in the same sense when applied to the gods as when applied to other things. For instance, horses are said to require attention, and not every person is able to attend to them, but only a person skilled in horsemanship. Is it not so?

EUTHYPHRO: Certainly.

SOCRATES: I should suppose that the art of horsemanship is the art of attending to horses?

EUTHYPHRO: Yes.

SOCRATES: Nor is every one qualified to attend to dogs, but only the huntsman?

EUTHYPHRO: True.

SOCRATES: And I should also conceive that the art of the huntsman is the art of attending to dogs?

EUTHYPHRO: Yes.

SOCRATES: As the art of the ox-herd is the art of attending to oxen?

EUTHYPHRO: Very true.

SOCRATES: In like manner holiness or piety is the art of attending to the gods?—that would be your meaning, Euthyphro?

EUTHYPHRO: Yes.

SOCRATES: And is not attention always designed for the good or benefit of that to which the attention is given? As in the case of horses, you may observe that when attended to by the horseman's art they are benefited and improved, are they not?

EUTHYPHRO: True.

SOCRATES: As the dogs are benefited by the huntsman's art, and the oxen by the art of the ox-herd, and all other things are tended or attended for their good and not for their hurt?

EUTHYPHRO: Certainly, not for their hurt.

SOCRATES: But for their good?

EUTHYPHRO: Of course.

SOCRATES: And does piety or holiness, which has been defined to be the art of attending to the gods, benefit or improve them? Would you say that when you do a holy act you make any of the gods better?

EUTHYPHRO: No, no; that was certainly not what I meant.

SOCRATES: And I, Euthyphro, never supposed that you did. I asked you the question about the nature of the attention, because I thought that you did not.

EUTHYPHRO: You do me justice, Socrates; that is not the sort of attention which I mean.

SOCRATES: Good: but I must still ask: what is this attention to the gods which is called piety?

EUTHYPHRO: It is such, Socrates, as servants show to their masters.

SOCRATES: I understand—a sort of ministration to the gods.

EUTHYPHRO: Exactly.

SOCRATES: Medicine is also a sort of ministration or service, having in view the attainment of some object—would you not say of health?

EUTHYPHRO: I should.

SOCRATES: Again, there is an art which ministers to the ship-builder with a view to the attainment of some result?

EUTHYPHRO: Yes, Socrates, with a view to the building of a ship.

SOCRATES: As there is an art which ministers to the house-builder with a view to the building of a house?

EUTHYPHRO: Yes.

SOCRATES: And now tell me, my good friend, about the art which ministers to the gods: what work does that help to accomplish? For you must surely know if, as you say, you are of all men living the one who is best instructed in religion.

EUTHYPHRO: And I speak the truth, Socrates.

SOCRATES: Tell me then, oh tell me—what is that fair work which the gods do by the help of our ministrations?

EUTHYPHRO: Many and fair, Socrates, are the works which they do.

SOCRATES: Why, my friend, and so are those of a general. But the chief of them is easily told. Would you not say that victory in war is the chief of them?

EUTHYPHRO: Certainly.

SOCRATES: Many and fair, too, are the works of the husbandman, if I am not mistaken; but his chief work is the production of food from the earth?

EUTHYPHRO: Exactly.

SOCRATES: And of the many and fair things done by the gods, which is the chief or principal one?

EUTHYPHRO: I have told you already, Socrates, that to learn all these things accurately will be very tiresome. Let me simply say that piety or holiness is learning how to please the gods in word and deed, by prayers and sacrifices. Such piety is the salvation of families and states, just as the impious, which is unpleasing to the gods, is their ruin and destruction.

SOCRATES: I think that you could have answered in much fewer words the chief question which I asked, Euthyphro, if you had chosen. But I see plainly that you are not disposed to instruct me—clearly not: else why, when we reached the point, did you turn aside? Had you only answered me I should have truly learned of you by this time the nature of piety. Now, as the asker of a question is necessarily dependent on the answerer, whither he leads I must follow; and can only ask again, what is the pious, and what is piety? Do you mean that they are a sort of science of praying and sacrificing?

EUTHYPHRO: Yes, I do.

SOCRATES: And sacrificing is giving to the gods, and prayer is asking of the gods?

EUTHYPHRO: Yes, Socrates.

SOCRATES: Upon this view, then, piety is a science of asking and giving?

EUTHYPHRO: You understand me capitally, Socrates.

SOCRATES: Yes, my friend; the reason is that I am a votary of your science, and give my mind to it, and therefore nothing which you say will be thrown away upon me. Please then to tell me, what is the nature of this service to the gods? Do you mean that we prefer requests and give gifts to them?

EUTHYPHRO: Yes, I do.

SOCRATES: Is not the right way of asking to ask of them what we want?

EUTHYPHRO: Certainly.

SOCRATES: And the right way of giving is to give to them in return what they want of us. There would be no meaning in an art which gives to any one that which he does not want.

EUTHYPHRO: Very true, Socrates.

SOCRATES: Then piety, Euthyphro, is an art which gods and men have of doing business with one another?

EUTHYPHRO: That is an expression which you may use, if you like.

SOCRATES: But I have no particular liking for anything but the truth. I wish, however, that you would tell me what benefit accrues to the gods from our gifts. There is no doubt about what they give to us; for there is no good thing which they do not give; but how we can give any good thing to them in return is far from being equally clear. If they give everything and we give nothing, that must be an affair of business in which we have very greatly the advantage of them.

EUTHYPHRO: And do you imagine, Socrates, that any benefit accrues to the gods from our gifts?

SOCRATES: But if not, Euthyphro, what is the meaning of gifts which are conferred by us upon the gods?

EUTHYPHRO: What else, but tributes of honor; and, as I was just now saying, what pleases them?

SOCRATES: Piety, then, is pleasing to the gods, but not beneficial or dear to them?

EUTHYPHRO: I should say that nothing could be dearer.

SOCRATES: Then once more the assertion is repeated that piety is dear to the gods?

EUTHYPHRO: Certainly.

SOCRATES: And when you say this, can you wonder at your words not standing firm, but walking away? Will you accuse me of being the Daedalus who makes them walk away, not perceiving that there is another and far greater artist than Daedalus who makes them go round in a circle, and he is yourself; for the argument, as you will perceive, comes round to the same point. Were we not saying that the holy or pious was not the same with that which is loved of the gods? Have you forgotten?

EUTHYPHRO: I quite remember.

SOCRATES: And are you not saying that what is loved of the gods is holy; and is not this the same as what is dear to them—do you see?

EUTHYPHRO: True.

SOCRATES: Then either we were wrong in our former assertion; or, if we were right then, we are wrong now.

EUTHYPHRO: One of the two must be true.

SOCRATES: Then we must begin again and ask: What is piety? That is an enquiry which I shall never be weary of pursuing as far as in me lies; and I entreat you not to scorn me, but to apply your mind to the utmost, and tell me the truth. For, if any man knows, you are he; and therefore I must detain you, like Proteus, until you tell. If you had not certainly known the nature of piety and impiety, I am confident that you would never, on behalf of a serf, have charged your aged father with murder. You would not have run such a risk of doing wrong in the sight of the gods, and you would have had too much respect for the opinions of men. I am sure, therefore, that you know the nature of piety and impiety. Speak out then, my dear Euthyphro, and do not hide your knowledge.

EUTHYPHRO: Another time, Socrates; for I am in a hurry, and must go now.

SOCRATES: Alas! My companion, and will you leave me in despair? I was hoping that you would instruct me in the nature of piety and impiety; and then I might have cleared myself of Meletus and his indictment. I would have told him that I had been enlightened by Euthyphro, and had given up rash innovations and speculations, in which I indulged only through ignorance, and that now I am about to lead a better life.

[*The Dialogues of Plato. Trans.* By Benjamin Jowett (London: Macmillan, 1891).]

Key Terms and Concepts

Socrates
Socratic Method
Socratic Irony
Socratic Ignorance
The Divine Command Theory
The Euthyphro Dilemma
piety
impiety

Questions for Further Reflection

1. What brings Socrates and Euthyphro to court on the same day? Why does their conversation turn to the meaning of piety?
2. How does Euthyphro initially define piety? How does his definition change as the dialogue unfolds? How does the dialogue conclude?
3. Explain, in your own words, the Euthyphro Dilemma. What are the two "horns" of this dilemma and how are they distinct? What are some implications of this dilemma?
4. How is the Euthyphro Dilemma related to the Divine Command Theory in ethics?

Homework Assignment #3b

Name: ______________________________ Section: ______________________________

Explain specifically how the Euthyphro Dilemma is related to the Divine Command Theory in ethics.

[illegible] Homework [illegible] Thus [illegible]

Homework Assignment 2.1[illegible]

[illegible]

[illegible] specifically [illegible] Conceptual [illegible]

CHAPTER FOUR

Aristotle on Virtue, Habit, and Happiness

© Panos Karas/Shutterstock.com

Aristotle (384–322 BCE)

SELECTED READINGS

- *Nicomachean Ethics*—Aristotle
  - Books I-III

Nicomachean Ethics

Aristotle

(Translated by W.D. Ross)

BOOK ONE

1.

Every art and every inquiry, and similarly every action and pursuit, is thought to aim at some good; and for this reason the good has rightly been declared to be that at which all things aim. But a certain difference is found among ends; some are activities, others are products apart from the activities that produce them. Where there are ends apart from the actions, it is the nature of the products to be better than the activities. Now, as there are many actions, arts, and sciences, their ends also are many; the end of the medical art is health, that of shipbuilding a vessel, that of strategy victory, that of economics wealth. But where such arts fall under a single capacity – as bridle-making and the other arts concerned with the equipment of horses fall under the art of riding, and this and every military action under strategy, in the same way other arts fall under yet others – in all of these the ends of the master arts are to be preferred to all the subordinate ends; for it is for the sake of the former that the latter are pursued. It makes no difference whether the activities themselves are the ends of the actions, or something else apart from the activities, as in the case of the sciences just mentioned.

2.

If, then, there is some end of the things we do, which we desire for its own sake (everything else being desired for the sake of this), and if we do not choose everything for the sake of something else (for at that rate the process would go on to infinity, so that our desire would be empty and vain), clearly this must be the good and the chief good. Will not the knowledge of it, then, have a great influence on life? Shall we not, like archers who have a mark to aim at, be more likely to hit upon what is right? If so, we must try, in outline at least, to determine what it is, and of which of the sciences or capacities it is the object. It would seem to belong to the most authoritative art and that which is most truly the master art. And politics appears to be of this nature; for it is this that ordains which of the sciences should be studied in a state, and which each class of citizens should learn and up to what point they should learn them; and we see even the most highly esteemed of capacities to fall under this, *e.g.* strategy, economics, rhetoric; now, since politics uses the rest of the sciences, and since, again, it legislates as to what we are to do and what we are to abstain from, the end of this science must include those of the others, so that this end must be the good for man. For even if the end is the same for a single man and for a state, that of the state seems at all events something greater and more complete whether to attain or to preserve; though it is worthwhile to attain the end merely for one man, it is finer and more godlike to attain it for a nation or for city-states. These, then, are the ends at which our inquiry aims, since it is political science, in one sense of that term.

3.

Our discussion will be adequate if it has as much clearness as the subject-matter admits of, for precision is not to be sought for alike in all discussions, any more than in all the products of the crafts. Now fine and just actions, which political science investigates, admit of much variety and fluctuation of opinion, so that they may be thought to exist only by convention, and not by nature. And goods also give rise to a similar fluctuation because they bring harm to many people; for before now men have been undone by reason of their wealth, and others by reason of their courage. We must be content, then, in speaking of such subjects and with such premises to indicate the truth roughly and in outline, and in speaking about things which are only for the most part true and with premises of the same kind to reach conclusions that are no better. In the same spirit, therefore, should each type of statement be received; for it is the mark of an educated man to look for precision in each class of things just so far as the nature of the subject admits; it is evidently equally foolish to accept probable reasoning from a mathematician and to demand from a rhetorician scientific proofs.

Now each man judges well the things he knows, and of these he is a good judge. And so the man who has been educated in a subject is a good judge of that subject, and the man who has received an all-round education is a good judge in general. Hence a young man is not a proper hearer of lectures on political science; for he is inexperienced in the actions that occur in life, but its discussions start from these and are about these; and, further, since he tends to follow his passions, his study will be vain and unprofitable, because the end aimed at is not knowledge but action. And it makes no difference whether he is young in years or youthful in character; the defect does not depend on time, but on his living, and pursuing each successive object, as passion directs. For to such persons, as to the incontinent, knowledge brings no profit; but to those who desire and act in accordance with a rational principle knowledge about such matters will be of great benefit.

These remarks about the student, the sort of treatment to be expected, and the purpose of the inquiry, may be taken as our preface.

4.

Let us resume our inquiry and state, in view of the fact that all knowledge and every pursuit aims at some good, what it is that we say political science aims at and what is the highest of all goods achievable by action. Verbally there is very general agreement; for both the general run of men and people of superior refinement say that it is happiness, and identify living well and doing well with being happy; but with regard to what happiness is they differ, and the many do not give the same account as the wise. For the former think it is some plain and obvious thing, like pleasure, wealth, or honor; they differ, however, from one another- and often even the same man identifies it with different things, with health when he is ill, with wealth when he is poor; but, conscious of their ignorance, they admire those who proclaim some great ideal that is above their comprehension. Now some thought that apart from these many goods there is another which is self-subsistent and causes the goodness of all these as well. To examine all the opinions that have been held were perhaps somewhat fruitless; enough to examine those that are most prevalent or that seem to be arguable.

Let us not fail to notice, however, that there is a difference between arguments from and those to the first principles. For Plato, too, was right in raising this question and asking, as he used to do, 'are we on the way from or to the first principles?' There is a difference, as there is in a race-course between the course from the judges to the turning-point and the way back. For, while we must begin with what is known, things are objects of knowledge in two senses- some to us, some without qualification. Presumably, then, we must begin with things known to us. Hence anyone who is to listen intelligently to lectures about what is noble and just, and generally, about the subjects of political science must have been brought up in good habits. For the fact is the starting-point, and if this is sufficiently plain to him, he will not at the start need the reason as well; and the man who has been well brought up has or can easily get starting points. And as for him who neither has nor can get them, let him hear the words of Hesiod:

> Far best is he who knows all things himself;
> Good, he that hearkens when men counsel right;
> But he who neither knows, nor lays to heart
> Another's wisdom, is a useless wight.

5.

Let us, however, resume our discussion from the point at which we digressed. To judge from the lives that men lead, most men, and men of the most vulgar type, seem (not without some ground) to identify the good, or happiness, with pleasure; which is the reason why they love the life of enjoyment. For there are, we may say, three prominent types of life- that just mentioned, the political, and thirdly the contemplative life. Now the mass of mankind are evidently quite slavish in their tastes, preferring a life suitable to beasts, but they get some ground for their view from the fact that many of those in high places share the tastes of Sardanapallus. A consideration of the prominent types of life shows that people of superior refinement and of active disposition identify happiness with honor; for this is, roughly speaking, the end of the political life. But it seems too superficial to be what we are looking for, since it is thought to depend on those who bestow honor rather than on him who receives it, but the good we divine to be something proper to a man and not easily taken from him. Further, men seem to pursue honor in order that they may be assured of their goodness; at least it is by men of practical wisdom that they seek to be honored, and among those who know them, and on the ground of their virtue; clearly, then, according to them, at any rate, virtue is better. And perhaps one might even suppose this to be, rather than honor, the end of the political life. But even this appears somewhat incomplete; for possession of virtue seems actually compatible with being asleep, or with lifelong inactivity, and, further, with the greatest sufferings and misfortunes; but a man who was living so no one would call happy, unless he were maintaining a thesis at all costs. But enough of this; for the subject has been sufficiently treated even in the current discussions. Third comes the contemplative life, which we shall consider later.

The life of money-making is one undertaken under compulsion, and wealth is evidently not the good we are seeking; for it is merely useful and for the sake of something else. And so one might rather take the aforementioned objects to be ends; for they are loved for themselves. But it is evident that not even these are ends; yet many arguments have been thrown away in support of them. Let us leave this subject, then.

6.

We had perhaps better consider the universal good and discuss thoroughly what is meant by it, although such an inquiry is made an uphill one by the fact that the Forms have been introduced by friends of our own. Yet it would perhaps be thought to be better, indeed to be our duty, for the sake of maintaining the truth even to destroy what touches us closely, especially as we are philosophers or lovers of wisdom; for, while both are dear, piety requires us to honor truth above our friends.

The men who introduced this doctrine did not posit Ideas of classes within which they recognized priority and posteriority (which is the reason why they did not maintain the existence of an Idea embracing all numbers); but the term 'good' is used both in the category of substance and in that of quality and in that of relation, and that which is per se, *i.e.* substance, is prior in nature to the relative (for the latter is like an off shoot and accident of being); so that there could not be a common Idea set over all these goods. Further, since 'good' has as many senses as 'being' (for it is predicated both in the category of substance, as of God and of reason, and in quality, *i.e.* of the virtues, and in quantity, *i.e.* of that which is moderate, and in relation, *i.e.* of the useful, and in time, *i.e.* of the right opportunity, and in place, *i.e.* of the right locality and the like), clearly it cannot be something universally present in all cases and single; for then it could not have been predicated in all the categories but in one only. Further, since of the things answering to one Idea there is one science, there would have been one science of all the goods; but as it is there are many sciences even of the things that fall under one category, *e.g.* of opportunity, for opportunity in war is studied by strategics and in disease by medicine, and the moderate in food is studied by medicine and in exercise by the science of gymnastics. And one might ask the question, what in the world they mean by 'a thing itself', is (as is the case) in 'man himself' and in a particular man the account of man is one and the same. For in so far as they are man, they will in no respect differ; and if this is so, neither will 'good itself' and particular goods, in so far as they are good. But again it will not be good any the more for being eternal, since that which lasts long is no whiter than that which perishes in a day. The Pythagoreans seem to give a more plausible account of the good, when they place the one in the column of goods; and it is they that Speusippus seems to have followed.

But let us discuss these matters elsewhere; an objection to what we have said, however, may be discerned in the fact that the Platonists have not been speaking about all goods, and that the goods that are pursued and loved for themselves are called good by reference to a single Form, while those which tend to produce or to preserve these somehow or to prevent their contraries are called so by reference to these, and in a secondary sense. Clearly, then, goods must be spoken of in two ways, and some must be good in themselves, the others by reason of these. Let us separate, then, things good in themselves from things useful, and consider whether the former are called good by reference to a single Idea. What sort of goods would one call good in themselves? Is it those that are pursued even when isolated from others, such as intelligence, sight, and certain pleasures and honors? Certainly, if we pursue these also for the sake of something else, yet one would place them among things good in themselves. Or is nothing other than the Idea of good good in itself? In that case the Form will be empty. But if the things we have named are also things good in themselves, the account of the good will have to appear as something identical in them all, as that of whiteness is identical in snow and in white lead. But of honor, wisdom, and pleasure, just in respect of their goodness, the accounts are distinct and diverse. The good, therefore, is not some common element answering to one Idea.

But what then do we mean by the good? It is surely not like the things that only chance to have the same name. Are goods one, then, by being derived from one good or by all contributing to one good, or are they rather one by analogy? Certainly as sight is in the body, so is reason in the soul, and so on in other cases. But perhaps these subjects had better be dismissed for the present; for perfect precision about them would be more appropriate to another branch of philosophy. And similarly with regard to the Idea; even if there is some one good which is universally predicable of goods or is capable of separate and independent existence, clearly it could not be achieved or attained by man; but we are now seeking something attainable. Perhaps, however, some one might think it worthwhile to recognize this with a view to the goods that are attainable and achievable; for having this as a sort of pattern we shall know better the goods that are good for us, and if we know them shall attain them. This argument has some plausibility, but seems to clash with the procedure of the sciences; for all of these, though they aim at some good and seek to supply the deficiency of it, leave on one side the knowledge of the good. Yet that all the exponents of the arts should be ignorant of, and should not even seek, so great an aid is not probable. It is hard, too, to see how a weaver or a carpenter will be benefited in regard to his own craft by knowing this 'good itself', or how the man who has viewed the Idea itself will be a better doctor or general thereby. For a doctor seems not even to study health in this way, but the health of man, or perhaps rather the health of a particular man; it is individuals that he is healing. But enough of these topics.

7.

Let us again return to the good we are seeking, and ask what it can be. It seems different in different actions and arts; it is different in medicine, in strategy, and in the other arts likewise. What then is the good of each? Surely that for whose sake everything else is done. In medicine this is health, in strategy victory, in architecture a house, in any other sphere something else, and in every action and pursuit the end; for it is for the sake of this that all men do whatever else they do. Therefore, if there is an end for all that we do, this will be the good achievable by action, and if there are more than one, these will be the goods achievable by action.

So the argument has by a different course reached the same point; but we must try to state this even more clearly. Since there are evidently more than one end, and we choose some of these (*e.g.*, wealth, flutes, and in general instruments) for the sake of something else, clearly not all ends are final ends; but the chief good is evidently something final. Therefore, if there is only one final end, this will be what we are seeking, and if there are more than one, the most final of these will be what we are seeking. Now we call that which is in itself worthy of pursuit more final than that which is worthy of pursuit for the sake of something else, and that which is never desirable for the sake of something else more final than the things that are desirable both in themselves and for the sake of that other thing, and therefore we call final without qualification that which is always desirable in itself and never for the sake of something else.

Now such a thing happiness, above all else, is held to be; for this we choose always for self and never for the sake of something else, but honor, pleasure, reason, and every virtue we choose indeed for themselves (for if nothing resulted from them we should still choose each of them), but we choose them also for the sake of happiness, judging that by means of them we shall be happy. Happiness, on the other hand, no one chooses for the sake of these, nor, in general, for anything other than itself.

From the point of view of self-sufficiency the same result seems to follow; for the final good is thought to be self-sufficient. Now by self-sufficient we do not mean that which is sufficient for a man by himself, for one who lives a solitary life, but also for parents, children, wife, and in general for his friends and fellow citizens, since man is born for citizenship. But some limit must be set to this; for if we extend our requirement to ancestors and descendants and friends' friends we are in for an infinite series. Let us examine this question, however, on another occasion; the self-sufficient we now define as that which when isolated makes life desirable and lacking in nothing; and such we think happiness to be; and further we think it most desirable of all things, without being counted as one good thing among others- if it were so counted it would clearly be made more desirable by the addition of even the least of goods; for that which is added becomes an excess of goods, and of goods the greater is always more desirable. Happiness, then, is something final and self-sufficient, and is the end of action.

Presumably, however, to say that happiness is the chief good seems a platitude, and a clearer account of what it is still desired. This might perhaps be given, if we could first ascertain the function of man. For just as for a flute-player, a sculptor, or an artist, and, in general, for all things that have a function or activity, the good and the 'well' is thought to reside in the function, so would it seem to be for man, if he has a function. Have the carpenter, then, and the tanner certain functions or activities, and has man none? Is he born without a function? Or as eye, hand, foot, and in general each of the parts evidently has a function, may one lay it down that man similarly has a function apart from all these? What then can this be? Life seems to be common even to plants, but we are seeking what is peculiar to man. Let us exclude, therefore, the life of nutrition and growth. Next there would be a life of perception, but it also seems to be common even to the horse, the ox, and every animal. There remains, then, an active life of the element that has a rational principle; of this, one part has such a principle in the sense of being obedient to one, the other in the sense of possessing one and exercising thought. And, as 'life of the rational element' also has two meanings, we must state that life in the sense of activity is what we mean; for this seems to be the more proper sense of the term. Now if the function of man is an activity of soul which follows or implies a rational principle, and if we say 'so-and-so-and 'a good so-and-so' have a function which is the same in kind, *e.g.* a lyre, and a good lyre-player, and so without qualification in all cases, eminence in respect of goodness being added to the name of the function (for the function of a lyre-player is to play the lyre, and that of a good lyre-player is to do so well): if this is the case, and we state the function of man to be a certain kind of life, and this to be an activity or actions of the soul implying a rational principle, and the function of a good man to be the good and noble performance of these, and if any action is well performed when it is performed in accordance with the appropriate excellence: if this is the case, human good turns out to be activity of soul in accordance with virtue, and if there are more than one virtue, in accordance with the best and most complete.

But we must add 'in a complete life.' For one swallow does not make a summer, nor does one day; and so too one day, or a short time, does not make a man blessed and happy.

Let this serve as an outline of the good; for we must presumably first sketch it roughly, and then later fill in the details. But it would seem that any one is capable of carrying on and articulating what has once been well outlined, and that time is a good discoverer or partner in such a work; to which facts the advances of the arts are due; for any one can add what is lacking. And we must also remember what has been said before, and not look for precision in all things alike, but in each class of things such precision as accords with the subject-matter, and so much as is appropriate to the inquiry. For a carpenter and a geometer investigate the right angle in different ways; the former does so in so far as the right angle is useful for his work, while the latter inquires what it is or what sort of thing it is; for he is a spectator of the truth. We must act in the same way, then, in all other matters as well, that our main task may not be subordinated to minor questions. Nor must we demand the cause in all matters alike; it is enough in some cases that the fact be well established, as in the case of the first principles; the fact is the primary thing or first principle. Now of first principles we see some by induction, some by perception, some by a certain habituation, and others too in other ways. But each set of principles we must try to investigate in the natural way, and we must take pains to state them definitely, since they have a great influence on what follows. For the beginning is thought to be more than half of the whole, and many of the questions we ask are cleared up by it.

8.

We must consider it, however, in the light not only of our conclusion and our premises, but also of what is commonly said about it; for with a true view all the data harmonize, but with a false one the facts soon clash. Now goods have been divided into three classes, and some are described as external, others as relating to soul or to body; we call those that relate to soul most properly and truly goods, and psychical actions and activities we class as relating to soul. Therefore our account must be sound, at least according to this view, which is an old one and agreed on by philosophers. It is correct also in that we identify the end with certain actions and activities; for thus it falls among goods of the soul and not among external goods. Another belief which harmonizes with our account is that the happy man lives well and does well; for we have practically defined happiness as a sort of good life and good action. The characteristics that are looked for in happiness seem also, all of them, to belong to what we have defined happiness as being. For some identify happiness with virtue, some with practical wisdom, others with a kind of philosophic wisdom, others with these, or one of these, accompanied by pleasure or not without pleasure; while others include also external prosperity. Now some of these views have been held by many men and men of old, others by a few eminent persons; and it is not probable that either of these should be entirely mistaken, but rather that they should be right in at least some one respect or even in most respects.

With those who identify happiness with virtue or some one virtue our account is in harmony; for to virtue belongs virtuous activity. But it makes, perhaps, no small difference whether we place the chief good in possession or in use, in state of mind or in activity. For the state of mind may exist without producing any good result, as in a man who is asleep or in some other way quite inactive, but the activity cannot; for one who has the activity will of necessity be acting, and acting well. And as in the Olympic Games it is not the most beautiful and the strongest that are crowned but those who compete (for it is some of these that are victorious), so those who act win, and rightly win, the noble and good things in life.

Their life is also in itself pleasant. For pleasure is a state of soul, and to each man that which he is said to be a lover of is pleasant; *e.g.* not only is a horse pleasant to the lover of horses, and a spectacle to the lover of sights, but also in the same way just acts are pleasant to the lover of justice and in general virtuous acts to the lover of virtue. Now for most men their pleasures are in conflict with one another because these are not by nature pleasant, but the lovers of what is noble find pleasant the things that are by nature pleasant; and virtuous actions are such, so that these are pleasant for such men as well as in their own nature. Their life, therefore, has no further need of pleasure as a sort of adventitious charm, but has its pleasure in itself. For, besides what we have said, the man who does not rejoice in noble actions is not even good; since no one would call a man just who did not enjoy acting justly, nor any man liberal who did not enjoy liberal actions; and similarly in all other cases. If this is so, virtuous actions must be in themselves pleasant. But they are also good and noble, and have each of these attributes in the highest degree, since the good man judges well about these attributes; his judgment is such as we have described. Happiness then is the best, noblest, and most pleasant thing in the world, and these attributes are not severed as in the inscription at Delos:

Most noble is that which is most just, and best is health/But most pleasant is it to win what we love.

For all these properties belong to the best activities; and these, or one - the best - of these, we identify with happiness.

Yet evidently, as we said, it needs the external goods as well; for it is impossible, or not easy, to do noble acts without the proper equipment. In many actions we use friends and riches and political power as instruments; and there are some things the lack of which takes the luster from happiness, as good birth, goodly children, beauty; for the man who is very ugly in appearance or ill-born or solitary and childless is not very likely to be happy, and perhaps a man would be still less likely if he had thoroughly bad children or friends or had lost good children or friends by death. As we said, then, happiness seems to need this sort of prosperity in addition; for which reason some identify happiness with good fortune, though others identify it with virtue.

9.

For this reason also the question is asked, whether happiness is to be acquired by learning or by habituation or some other sort of training, or comes in virtue of some divine providence or again by chance. Now if there is any gift of the gods to men, it is reasonable that happiness should be given by the gods, and most surely gods-given of all human things inasmuch as it is the best. But this question would perhaps be more appropriate to another inquiry; happiness seems, however, even if it is not god-sent but comes as a result of virtue and some process of learning or training, to be among the most godlike things; for that which is the prize and end of virtue seems to be the best thing in the world, and something godlike and blessed.

It will also on this view be very generally shared; for all who are not maimed as regards their potentiality for virtue may win it by a certain kind of study and care. But if it is better to be happy thus than by chance, it is reasonable that the facts should be so, since everything that depends on the action of nature is by nature as good as it can be, and similarly everything that depends on art or any rational cause, and especially if it depends on the best of all causes. To entrust to chance what is greatest and most noble would be a very defective arrangement.

The answer to the question we are asking is plain also from the definition of happiness; for it has been said to be a virtuous activity of soul, of a certain kind. Of the remaining goods, some must necessarily pre-exist as conditions of happiness, and others are naturally cooperative and useful as instruments. And this will be found to agree with what we said at the outset; for we stated the end of political science to be the best end, and political science spends most of its pains on making the citizens to be of a certain character, viz. good and capable of noble acts.

It is natural, then, that we call neither ox nor horse nor any other of the animals happy; for none of them is capable of sharing in such activity. For this reason also a boy is not happy; for he is not yet capable of such acts, owing to his age; and boys who are called happy are being congratulated by reason of the hopes we have for them. For there is required, as we said, not only complete virtue but also a complete life, since many changes occur in life, and all manner of chances, and the most prosperous may fall into great misfortunes in old age, as is told of Priam in the Trojan Cycle; and one who has experienced such chances and has ended wretchedly no one calls happy.

10.

Must no one at all, then, be called happy while he lives; must we, as Solon says, see the end? Even if we are to lay down this doctrine, is it also the case that a man is happy when he is dead? Or is not this quite absurd, especially for us who say that happiness is an activity? But if we do not call the dead man happy, and if Solon does not mean this, but that one can then safely call a man blessed as being at last beyond evils and misfortunes, this also affords matter for discussion; for both evil and good are thought to exist for a dead man, as much as for one who is alive but not aware of them; *e.g.* honors and dishonors and the good or bad fortunes of children and in general of descendants. And this also presents a problem; for though a man has lived happily up to old age and has had a death worthy of his life, many reverses may befall his descendants- some of them may be good and attain the life they deserve, while with others the opposite may be the case; and clearly too the degrees of relationship between them and their ancestors may vary indefinitely. It would be odd, then, if the dead man were to share in these changes and become at one time happy, at another wretched; while it would also be odd if the fortunes of the descendants did not for some time have some effect on the happiness of their ancestors.

But we must return to our first difficulty; for perhaps by a consideration of it our present problem might be solved. Now if we must see the end and only then call a man happy, not as being happy but as having been so before, surely this is a paradox, that when he is happy the attribute that belongs to him is not to be truly predicated of him because we do not wish to call living men happy, on account of the changes that may befall them, and because we have assumed happiness to be something permanent and by no means easily changed, while a single man may suffer many turns of fortune's wheel. For clearly if we were to keep pace with his fortunes, we should often call the same man happy and again wretched, making the happy man out to be chameleon and insecurely based. Or is this keeping pace with his fortunes quite wrong? Success or failure in life does not depend on these, but human life, as we said, needs these as mere additions, while virtuous activities or their opposites are what constitute happiness or the reverse.

The question we have now discussed confirms our definition. For no function of man has so much permanence as virtuous activities (these are thought to be more durable even than knowledge of the sciences), and of these themselves the most valuable are more durable because those who are happy spend their life most readily and most continuously in these; for this seems to be the reason why we do not forget them. The attribute in question, then, will belong to the happy man, and he will be happy throughout his life; for always, or by preference to everything else, he will be engaged in virtuous action and contemplation, and he will bear the chances of life most nobly and altogether decorously, if he is 'truly good' and 'foursquare beyond reproach'.

Now many events happen by chance, and events differing in importance; small pieces of good fortune or of its opposite clearly do not weigh down the scales of life one way or the other, but a multitude of great events if they turn out well will make life happier (for not only are they themselves such as to add beauty to life, but the way a man deals with them may be noble and good), while if they turn out ill they crush and maim happiness; for they both bring pain with them and hinder many activities. Yet even in these nobility shines through, when a man bears with resignation many great misfortunes, not through insensibility to pain but through nobility and greatness of soul.

If activities are, as we said, what gives life its character, no happy man can become miserable; for he will never do the acts that are hateful and mean. For the man who is truly good and wise, we think, bears all the chances life becomingly and always makes the best of circumstances, as a good general makes the best military use of the army at his command and a good shoemaker makes the best shoes out of the hides that are given him; and so with all other craftsmen. And if this is the case, the happy man can never become miserable; though he will not reach blessedness, if he meet with fortunes like those of Priam.

Nor, again, is he many-colored and changeable; for neither will he be moved from his happy state easily or by any ordinary misadventures, but only by many great ones, nor, if he has had many great misadventures, will he recover his happiness in a short time, but if at all, only in a long and complete one in which he has attained many splendid successes.

When then should we not say that he is happy who is active in accordance with complete virtue and is sufficiently equipped with external goods, not for some chance period but throughout a complete life? Or must we add 'and who is destined to live thus and die as befits his life'? Certainly the future is obscure to us, while happiness, we claim, is an end and something in every way final. If so, we shall call happy those among living men in whom these conditions are, and are to be, fulfilled- but happy men. So much for these questions.

11.

That the fortunes of descendants and of all a man's friends should not affect his happiness at all seems a very unfriendly doctrine, and one opposed to the opinions men hold; but since the events that happen are numerous and admit of all sorts of difference, and some come more near to us and others less so, it seems a long - nay, an infinite - task to discuss each in detail; a general outline will perhaps suffice. If, then, as some of a man's own misadventures have a certain weight and influence on life while others are, as it were, lighter, so too there are differences among the misadventures of our friends taken as a whole, and it makes a difference whether the various suffering befall the living or the dead (much more even than whether lawless and terrible deeds are presupposed in a tragedy or done on the stage), this difference also must be taken into account; or rather, perhaps, the fact that doubt is felt whether the dead share in any good or evil. For it seems, from these considerations, that even if anything whether good or evil penetrates to them, it must be something weak and negligible, either in itself or for them, or if not, at least it must be such in degree and kind as not to make happy those who are not happy nor to take away their blessedness from those who are. The good or bad fortunes of friends, then, seem to have some effects on the dead, but effects of such a kind and degree as neither to make the happy unhappy nor to produce any other change of the kind.

12.

These questions having been definitely answered, let us consider whether happiness is among the things that are praised or rather among the things that are prized; for clearly it is not to be placed among potentialities. Everything that is praised seems to be praised because it is of a certain kind and is related somehow to something else; for we praise the just or brave man and in general both the good man and virtue itself because of the actions and functions involved, and we praise the strong man, the good runner, and so on, because he is of a certain kind and is related in a certain way to something good and important. This is clear also from the praises of the gods; for it seems absurd that the gods should be referred to our standard, but this is done because praise involves a reference, to something else. But if if praise is for things such as we have described, clearly what applies to the best things is not praise, but something greater and better, as is indeed obvious; for what we do to the gods and the most godlike of men is to call them blessed and happy. And so too with good things; no one praises happiness as he does justice, but rather calls it blessed, as being something more divine and better.

Eudoxus also seems to have been right in his method of advocating the supremacy of pleasure; he thought that the fact that, though a good, it is not praised indicated it to be better than the things that are praised, and that this is what God and the good are; for by reference to these all other things are judged. Praise is appropriate to virtue, for as a result of virtue men tend to do noble deeds, but encomia are bestowed on acts, whether of the body or of the soul. But perhaps nicety in these matters is more proper to those who have made a study of encomia; to us it is clear from what has been said that happiness is among the things that are prized and perfect. It seems to be so also from the fact that it is a first principle; for it is for the sake of this that we all do all that we do, and the first principle and cause of goods is, we claim, something prized and divine.

13.

Since happiness is an activity of soul in accordance with perfect virtue, we must consider the nature of virtue; for perhaps we shall thus see better the nature of happiness. The true student of politics, too, is thought to have studied virtue above all things; for he wishes to make his fellow citizens good and obedient to the laws. As an example of this we have the lawgivers of the Cretans and the Spartans, and any others of the kind that there may have been. And if this inquiry belongs to political science, clearly the pursuit of it will be in accordance with our original plan. But clearly the virtue we must study is human virtue; for the good we were seeking was human good and the happiness human happiness. By human virtue we mean not that of the body but that of the soul; and happiness also we call an activity of soul. But if this is so, clearly the student of politics must know somehow the facts about soul, as the man who is to heal the eyes or the body as a whole must know about the eyes or the body; and all the more since politics is more prized and better than medicine; but even among doctors the best educated spend much labor on acquiring knowledge of the body. The student of politics, then, must study the soul, and must study it with these objects in view, and do so just to the extent which is sufficient for the questions we are discussing; for further precision is perhaps something more laborious than our purposes require.

Some things are said about it, adequately enough, even in the discussions outside our school, and we must use these; *e.g.* that one element in the soul is irrational and one has a rational principle. Whether these are separated as the parts of the body or of anything divisible are, or are distinct by definition but by nature inseparable, like convex and concave in the circumference of a circle, does not affect the present question.

Of the irrational element one division seems to be widely distributed, and vegetative in its nature, I mean that which causes nutrition and growth; for it is this kind of power of the soul that one must assign to all nurslings and to embryos, and this same power to full-grown creatures; this is more reasonable than to assign some different power to them. Now the excellence of this seems to be common to all species and not specifically human; for this part or faculty seems to function most in sleep, while goodness and badness are least manifest in sleep (whence comes the saying that the happy are not better off than the wretched for half their lives; and this happens naturally enough, since sleep is an inactivity of the soul in that respect in which it is called good or bad), unless perhaps to a small extent some of the movements actually penetrate to the soul, and in this respect the dreams of good men are better than those of ordinary people. Enough of this subject, however; let us leave the nutritive faculty alone, since it has by its nature no share in human excellence.

There seems to be also another irrational element in the soul-one which in a sense, however, shares in a rational principle. For we praise the rational principle of the continent man and of the incontinent, and the part of their soul that has such a principle, since it urges them aright and towards the best objects; but there is found in them also another element naturally opposed to the rational principle, which fights against and resists that principle. For exactly as paralyzed limbs when we intend to move them to the right turn on the contrary to the left, so is it with the soul; the impulses of incontinent people move in contrary directions. But while in the body we see that which moves astray, in the soul we do not. No doubt, however, we must none the less suppose that in the soul too there is something contrary to the rational principle, resisting and opposing it. In what sense it is distinct from the other elements does not concern us. Now even this seems to have a share in a rational principle, as we said; at any rate in the continent man it obeys the rational principle and presumably in the temperate and brave man it is still more obedient; for in him it speaks, on all matters, with the same voice as the rational principle.

Therefore the irrational element also appears to be two-fold. For the vegetative element in no way shares in a rational principle, but the appetitive and in general the desiring element in a sense shares in it, in so far as it listens to and obeys it; this is the sense in which we speak of 'taking account' of one's father or one's friends, not that in which we speak of 'accounting for a mathematical property. That the irrational element is in some sense persuaded by a rational principle is indicated also by the giving of advice and by all reproof and exhortation. And if this element also must be said to have a rational principle, that which has a rational principle (as well as that which has not) will be two-fold, one subdivision having it in the strict sense and in itself, and the other having a tendency to obey as one does one's father.

Virtue too is distinguished into kinds in accordance with this difference; for we say that some of the virtues are intellectual and others moral, philosophic wisdom and understanding and practical wisdom being intellectual, liberality and temperance moral. For in speaking about a man's character we do not say that he is wise or has understanding but that he is good-tempered or temperate; yet we praise the wise man also with respect to his state of mind; and of states of mind we call those which merit praise virtues.

[*Nicomachean Ethics.* Translated by W.D. Ross. (Oxford: Clarendon Press, 1908).]

Nicomachean Ethics

Aristotle

(Translated by W.D. Ross)

BOOK TWO

1.

Virtue, then, is of two kinds: intellectual and moral. Intellectual virtue mainly owes both its birth and its growth to teaching (for which reason it requires experience and time), while moral virtue comes about as a result of habit, whence also its name (*ethike*) is one that is formed by a slight variation from the word *ethos* (habit). From this it is also plain that none of the moral virtues arises in us by nature; for nothing that exists by nature can form a habit contrary to its nature. For instance the stone which by nature moves downwards cannot be habituated to move upwards, not even if one tries to train it by throwing it up ten thousand times; nor can fire be habituated to move downwards, nor can anything else that by nature behaves in one way be trained to behave in another. Neither by nature, then, nor contrary to nature do the virtues arise in us; rather we are adapted by nature to receive them, and are made perfect by habit.

Again, of all the things that come to us by nature we first acquire the potentiality and later exhibit the activity (this is plain in the case of the senses; for it was not by often seeing or often hearing that we got these senses, but on the contrary we had them before we used them, and did not come to have them by using them); but the virtues we get by first exercising them, as also happens in the case of the arts as well. For the things we have to learn before we can do them, we learn by doing them, *e.g.* men become builders by building and lyre-players by playing the lyre; so too we become just by doing just acts, temperate by doing temperate acts, brave by doing brave acts.

This is confirmed by what happens in states; for legislators make the citizens good by forming habits in them, and this is the wish of every legislator, and those who do not effect it miss their mark, and it is in this that a good constitution differs from a bad one.

Again, it is from the same causes and by the same means that every virtue is both produced and destroyed, and similarly every art; for it is from playing the lyre that both good and bad lyre-players are produced. And the corresponding statement is true of builders and of all the rest; men will be good or bad builders as a result of building well or badly. For if this were not so, there would have been no need of a teacher, but all men would have been born good or bad at their craft. This, then, is the case with the virtues also; by doing the acts that we do in our transactions with other men we become just or unjust, and by doing the acts that we do in the presence of danger, and being habituated to feel fear or confidence, we become brave or cowardly. The same is true of appetites and feelings of anger; some men become temperate and good-tempered, others self-indulgent and irascible, by behaving in one way or the other in the appropriate circumstances. Thus, in one word, states of character arise out of like activities. This is why the activities we exhibit must be of a certain kind; it is because the states of character correspond to the differences between these. It makes no small difference, then, whether we form habits of one kind or of another from our very youth; it makes a very great difference, or rather all the difference.

2.

Since, then, the present inquiry does not aim at theoretical knowledge like the others (for we are inquiring not in order to know what virtue is, but in order to become good, since otherwise our inquiry would have been of no use), we must examine the nature of actions, namely how we ought to do them; for these determine also the nature of the states of character that are produced, as we have said. Now, that we must act according to the right rule is a common principle and must be assumed-it will be discussed later, *i.e.* both what the right rule is, and how it is related to the other virtues. But this must be agreed upon beforehand, that the whole account of matters of conduct must be given in outline and not precisely, as we said at the very beginning that the accounts we demand must be in accordance with the subject-matter; matters concerned with conduct and questions of what is good for us have no fixity, any more than matters of health. The general account being of this nature, the account of particular cases is yet more lacking in exactness; for they do not fall under any art or precept but the agents themselves must in each case consider what is appropriate to the occasion, as happens also in the art of medicine or of navigation.

But though our present account is of this nature we must give what help we can. First, then, let us consider this, that it is the nature of such things to be destroyed by defect and excess, as we see in the case of strength and of health (for to gain light on things imperceptible we must use the evidence of sensible things); both excessive and defective exercise destroys the strength, and similarly drink or food which is above or below a certain amount destroys the health, while that which is proportionate both produces and increases and preserves it. So too is it, then, in the case of temperance and courage and the other virtues. For the man who flies from and fears everything and does not stand his ground against anything becomes a coward, and the man who fears nothing at all but goes to meet every danger becomes rash; and similarly the man who indulges in every pleasure and abstains from none becomes self-indulgent, while the man who shuns every pleasure, as boors do, becomes in a way insensible; temperance and courage, then, are destroyed by excess and defect, and preserved by the mean.

But not only are the sources and causes of their origination and growth the same as those of their destruction, but also the sphere of their actualization will be the same; for this is also true of the things which are more evident to sense, *e.g.* of strength; it is produced by taking much food and undergoing much exertion, and it is the strong man that will be most able to do these things. So too is it with the virtues; by abstaining from pleasures we become temperate, and it is when we have become so that we are most able to abstain from them; and similarly too in the case of courage; for by being habituated to despise things that are terrible and to stand our ground against them we become brave, and it is when we have become so that we shall be most able to stand our ground against them.

3.

We must take as a sign of states of character the pleasure or pain that ensues on acts; for the man who abstains from bodily pleasures and delights in this very fact is temperate, while the man who is annoyed at it is self-indulgent, and he who stands his ground against things that are terrible and delights in this or at least is not pained is brave, while the man who is pained is a coward. For moral excellence is concerned with pleasures and pains; it is on account of the pleasure that we do bad things, and on account of the pain that we abstain from noble ones. Hence we ought to have been brought up in a particular way from our very youth, as Plato says, so as both to delight in and to be pained by the things that we ought; for this is the right education.

Again, if the virtues are concerned with actions and passions, and every passion and every action is accompanied by pleasure and pain, for this reason also virtue will be concerned with pleasures and pains. This is indicated also by the fact that punishment is inflicted by these means; for it is a kind of cure, and it is the nature of cures to be effected by contraries.

Again, as we said but lately, every state of soul has a nature relative to and concerned with the kind of things by which it tends to be made worse or better; but it is by reason of pleasures and pains that men become bad, by pursuing and avoiding these- either the pleasures and pains they ought not or when they ought not or as they ought not, or by going wrong in one of the other similar ways that may be distinguished. Hence men even define the virtues as certain states of impassivity and rest; not well, however, because they speak absolutely, and do not say 'as one ought' and 'as one ought not' and 'when one ought or ought not', and the other things that may be added. We assume, then, that this kind of excellence tends to do what is best with regard to pleasures and pains, and vice does the contrary.

The following facts also may show us that virtue and vice are concerned with these same things. There being three objects of choice and three of avoidance, the noble, the advantageous, the pleasant, and their contraries, the base, the injurious, the painful, about all of these the good man tends to go right and the bad man to go wrong, and especially about pleasure; for this is common to the animals, and also it accompanies all objects of choice; for even the noble and the advantageous appear pleasant.

Again, it has grown up with us all from our infancy; this is why it is difficult to rub off this passion, engrained as it is in our life. And we measure even our actions, some of us more and others less, by the rule of pleasure and pain. For this reason, then, our whole inquiry must be about these; for to feel delight and pain rightly or wrongly has no small effect on our actions.

Again, it is harder to fight with pleasure than with anger, to use Heraclitus' phrase, but both art and virtue are always concerned with what is harder; for even the good is better when it is harder. Therefore for this reason also the whole concern both of virtue and of political science is with pleasures and pains; for the man who uses these well will be good, he who uses them badly bad.

That virtue, then, is concerned with pleasures and pains, and that by the acts from which it arises it is both increased and, if they are done differently, destroyed, and that the acts from which it arose are those in which it actualizes itself- let this be taken as said.

4.

The question might be asked,; what we mean by saying that we must become just by doing just acts, and temperate by doing temperate acts; for if men do just and temperate acts, they are already just and temperate, exactly as, if they do what is in accordance with the laws of grammar and of music, they are grammarians and musicians.

Or is this not true even of the arts? It is possible to do something that is in accordance with the laws of grammar, either by chance or at the suggestion of another. A man will be a grammarian, then, only when he has both done something grammatical and done it grammatically; and this means doing it in accordance with the grammatical knowledge in himself.

Again, the case of the arts and that of the virtues are not similar; for the products of the arts have their goodness in themselves, so that it is enough that they should have a certain character, but if the acts that are in accordance with the virtues have themselves a certain character it does not follow that they are done justly or temperately. The agent also must be in a certain condition when he does them; in the first place he must have knowledge, secondly he must choose the acts, and choose them for their own sakes, and thirdly his action must proceed from a firm and unchangeable character. These are not reckoned in as conditions of the possession of the arts, except the bare knowledge; but as a condition of the possession of the virtues knowledge has little or no weight, while the other conditions count not for a little but for everything, *i.e.* the very conditions which result from often doing just and temperate acts.

Actions, then, are called just and temperate when they are such as the just or the temperate man would do; but it is not the man who does these that is just and temperate, but the man who also does them as just and temperate men do them. It is well said, then, that it is by doing just acts that the just man is produced, and by doing temperate acts the temperate man; without doing these no one would have even a prospect of becoming good. But most people do not do these, but take refuge in theory and think they are being philosophers and will become good in this way, behaving somewhat like patients who listen attentively to their doctors, but do none of the things they are ordered to do. As the latter will not be made well in body by such a course of treatment, the former will not be made well in soul by such a course of philosophy.

5.

Next we must consider what virtue is. Since things that are found in the soul are of three kinds- passions, faculties, states of character, virtue must be one of these. By passions I mean appetite, anger, fear, confidence, envy, joy, friendly feeling, hatred, longing, emulation, pity, and in general the feelings that are accompanied by pleasure or pain; by faculties the things in virtue of which we are said to be capable of feeling these, *e.g.* of becoming angry or being pained or feeling pity; by states of character the things in virtue of which we stand well or badly with reference to the passions, *e.g.* with reference to anger we stand badly if we feel it violently or too weakly, and well if we feel it moderately; and similarly with reference to the other passions.

Now neither the virtues nor the vices are passions, because we are not called good or bad on the ground of our passions, but are so called on the ground of our virtues and our vices, and because we are neither praised nor blamed for our passions (for the man who feels fear or anger is not praised, nor is the man who simply feels anger blamed, but the man who feels it in a certain way), but for our virtues and our vices we are praised or blamed.

Again, we feel anger and fear without choice, but the virtues are modes of choice or involve choice. Further, in respect of the passions we are said to be moved, but in respect of the virtues and the vices we are said not to be moved but to be disposed in a particular way.

For these reasons also they are not faculties; for we are neither called good nor bad, nor praised nor blamed, for the simple capacity of feeling the passions; again, we have the faculties by nature, but we are not made good or bad by nature; we have spoken of this before. If, then, the virtues are neither passions nor faculties, all that remains is that they should be states of character.

Thus we have stated what virtue is in respect of its genus.

6.

We must, however, not only describe virtue as a state of character, but also say what sort of state it is. We may remark, then, that every virtue or excellence both brings into good condition the thing of which it is the excellence and makes the work of that thing be done well; *e.g.* the excellence of the eye makes both the eye and its work good; for it is by the excellence of the eye that we see well. Similarly the excellence of the horse makes a horse both good in itself and good at running and at carrying its rider and at awaiting the attack of the enemy. Therefore, if this is true in every case, the virtue of man also will be the state of character which makes a man good and which makes him do his own work well.

How this is to happen we have stated already, but it will be made plain also by the following consideration of the specific nature of virtue. In everything that is continuous and divisible it is possible to take more, less, or an equal amount, and that either in terms of the thing itself or relatively to us; and the equal is an intermediate between excess and defect. By the intermediate in the object I mean that which is equidistant from each of the extremes, which is one and the same for all men; by the intermediate relatively to us that which is neither too much nor too little- and this is not one, nor the same for all. For instance, if ten is many and two is few, six is the intermediate, taken in terms of the object; for it exceeds and is exceeded by an equal amount; this is intermediate according to arithmetical proportion. But the intermediate relatively to us is not to be taken so; if ten pounds are too much for a particular person to eat and two too little, it does not follow that the trainer will order six pounds; for this also is perhaps too much for the person who is to take it, or too little- too little for Milo, too much for the beginner in athletic exercises. The same is true of running and wrestling. Thus a master of any art avoids excess and defect, but seeks the intermediate and chooses this- the intermediate not in the object but relatively to us.

If it is thus, then, that every art does its work well- by looking to the intermediate and judging its works by this standard (so that we often say of good works of art that it is not possible either to take away or to add anything, implying that excess and defect destroy the goodness of works of art, while the mean preserves it; and good artists, as we say, look to this in their work), and if, further, virtue is more exact and better than any art, as nature also is, then virtue must have the quality of aiming at the intermediate. I mean moral virtue; for it is this that is concerned with passions and actions, and in these there is excess, defect, and the intermediate. For instance, both fear and confidence and appetite and anger and pity and in general pleasure and pain may be felt both too much and too little, and in both cases not well; but to feel them at the right times, with reference to the right objects, towards the right people, with the right motive, and in the right way, is what is both intermediate and best, and this is characteristic of virtue. Similarly with regard to actions also there is excess, defect, and the intermediate. Now virtue is concerned with passions and actions, in which excess is a form of failure, and so is defect, while the intermediate is praised and is a form of success; and being praised and being successful are both characteristics of virtue. Therefore virtue is a kind of mean, since, as we have seen, it aims at what is intermediate.

Again, it is possible to fail in many ways (for evil belongs to the class of the unlimited, as the Pythagoreans conjectured, and good to that of the limited), while to succeed is possible only in one way (for which reason also one is easy and the other difficult- to miss the mark easy, to hit it difficult); for these reasons also, then, excess and defect are characteristic of vice, and the mean of virtue;

For men are good in but one way, but bad in many.

Virtue, then, is a state of character concerned with choice, lying in a mean, *i.e.* the mean relative to us, this being determined by a rational principle, and by that principle by which the man of practical wisdom would determine it. Now it is a mean between two vices, that which depends on excess and that which depends on defect; and again it is a mean because the vices respectively fall short of or exceed what is right in both passions and actions, while virtue both finds and chooses that which is intermediate. Hence in respect of its substance and the definition which states its essence virtue is a mean, with regard to what is best and right an extreme.

But not every action nor every passion admits of a mean; for some have names that already imply badness, *e.g.* spite, shamelessness, envy, and in the case of actions adultery, theft, murder; for all of these and suchlike things imply by their names that they are themselves bad, and not the excesses or deficiencies of them. It is not possible, then, ever to be right with regard to them; one must always be wrong. Nor does goodness or badness with regard to such things depend on committing adultery with the right woman, at the right time, and in the right way, but simply to do any of them is to go wrong. It would be equally absurd, then, to expect that in unjust, cowardly, and voluptuous action there should be a mean, an excess, and a deficiency; for at that rate there would be a mean of excess and of deficiency, an excess of excess, and a deficiency of deficiency. But as there is no excess and deficiency of temperance and courage because what is intermediate is in a sense an extreme, so too of the actions we have mentioned there is no mean nor any excess and deficiency, but however they are done they are wrong; for in general there is neither a mean of excess and deficiency, nor excess and deficiency of a mean.

7.

We must, however, not only make this general statement, but also apply it to the individual facts. For among statements about conduct those which are general apply more widely, but those which are particular are more genuine, since conduct has to do with individual cases, and our statements must harmonize with the facts in these cases. We may take these cases from our table. With regard to feelings of fear and confidence courage is the mean; of the people who exceed, he who exceeds in fearlessness has no name (many of the states have no name), while the man who exceeds in confidence is rash, and he who exceeds in fear and falls short in confidence is a coward. With regard to pleasures and pains - not all of them, and not so much with regard to the pains - the mean is temperance, the excess self-indulgence. Persons deficient with regard to the pleasures are not often found; hence such persons also have received no name. But let us call them 'insensible'.

With regard to giving and taking of money the mean is liberality, the excess and the defect prodigality and meanness. In these actions people exceed and fall short in contrary ways; the prodigal exceeds in spending and falls short in taking, while the mean man exceeds in taking and falls short in spending. (At present we are giving a mere outline or summary, and are satisfied with this; later these states will be more exactly determined.) With regard to money there are also other dispositions- a mean, magnificence (for the magnificent man differs from the liberal man; the former deals with large sums, the latter with small ones), an excess, tastelessness and vulgarity, and a deficiency, stinginess; these differ from the states opposed to liberality, and the mode of their difference will be stated later. With regard to honor and dishonor the mean is proper pride, the excess is known as a sort of 'empty vanity', and the deficiency is undue humility; and as we said liberality was related to magnificence, differing from it by dealing with small sums, so there is a state similarly related to proper pride, being concerned with small honors while that is concerned with great. For it is possible to desire honor as one ought, and more than one ought, and less, and the man who exceeds in his desires is called ambitious, the man who falls short unambitious, while the intermediate person has no name. The dispositions also are nameless, except that that of the ambitious man is called ambition. Hence the people who are at the extremes lay claim to the middle place; and we ourselves sometimes call the intermediate person ambitious and sometimes unambitious, and sometimes praise the ambitious man and sometimes the unambitious. The reason of our doing this will be stated in what follows; but now let us speak of the remaining states according to the method which has been indicated.

With regard to anger also there is an excess, a deficiency, and a mean. Although they can scarcely be said to have names, yet since we call the intermediate person good-tempered let us call the mean good temper; of the persons at the extremes let the one who exceeds be called irascible, and his vice irascibility, and the man who falls short an inirascible sort of person, and the deficiency inirascibility.

There are also three other means, which have a certain likeness to one another, but differ from one another: for they are all concerned with intercourse in words and actions, but differ in that one is concerned with truth in this sphere, the other two with pleasantness; and of this one kind is exhibited in giving amusement, the other in all the circumstances of life. We must therefore speak of these too, that we may the better see that in all things the mean is praise-worthy, and the extremes neither praiseworthy nor right, but worthy of blame. Now most of these states also have no names, but we must try, as in the other cases, to invent names ourselves so that we may be clear and easy to follow. With regard to truth, then, the intermediate is a truthful sort of person and the mean may be called truthfulness, while the pretense which exaggerates is boastfulness and the person characterized by it a boaster, and that which understates is mock modesty and the person characterized by it mock-modest. With regard to pleasantness in the giving of amusement the intermediate person is ready-witted and the disposition ready wit, the excess is buffoonery and the person characterized by it a buffoon, while the man who falls short is a sort of boor and his state is boorishness. With regard to the remaining kind of pleasantness, that which is exhibited in life in general, the man who is pleasant in the right way is friendly and the mean is friendliness, while the man who exceeds is an obsequious person if he has no end in view, a flatterer if he is aiming at his own advantage, and the man who falls short and is unpleasant in all circumstances is a quarrelsome and surly sort of person.

There are also means in the passions and concerned with the passions; since shame is not a virtue, and yet praise is extended to the modest man. For even in these matters one man is said to be intermediate, and another to exceed, as for instance the bashful man who is ashamed of everything; while he who falls short or is not ashamed of anything at all is shameless, and the intermediate person is modest. Righteous indignation is a mean between envy and spite, and these states are concerned with the pain and pleasure that are felt at the fortunes of our neighbors; the man who is characterized by righteous indignation is pained at undeserved good fortune, the envious man, going beyond him, is pained at all good fortune, and the spiteful man falls so far short of being pained that he even rejoices. But these states there will be an opportunity of describing elsewhere; with regard to justice, since it has not one simple meaning, we shall, after describing the other states, distinguish its two kinds and say how each of them is a mean; and similarly we shall treat also of the rational virtues.

8.

There are three kinds of disposition, then, two of them vices, involving excess and deficiency respectively, and one a virtue, viz. the mean, and all are in a sense opposed to all; for the extreme states are contrary both to the intermediate state and to each other, and the intermediate to the extremes; as the equal is greater relatively to the less, less relatively to the greater, so the middle states are excessive relatively to the deficiencies, deficient relatively to the excesses, both in passions and in actions. For the brave man appears rash relatively to the coward, and cowardly relatively to the rash man; and similarly the temperate man appears self-indulgent relatively to the insensible man, insensible relatively to the self-indulgent, and the liberal man prodigal relatively to the mean man, mean relatively to the prodigal. Hence also the people at the extremes push the intermediate man each over to the other, and the brave man is called rash by the coward, cowardly by the rash man, and correspondingly in the other cases.

These states being thus opposed to one another, the greatest contrariety is that of the extremes to each other, rather than to the intermediate; for these are further from each other than from the intermediate, as the great is further from the small and the small from the great than both are from the equal. Again, to the intermediate some extremes show a certain likeness, as that of rashness to courage and that of prodigality to liberality; but the extremes show the greatest unlikeness to each other; now contraries are defined as the things that are furthest from each other, so that things that are further apart are more contrary.

To the mean in some cases the deficiency, in some the excess is more opposed; *e.g.* it is not rashness, which is an excess, but cowardice, which is a deficiency, that is more opposed to courage, and not insensibility, which is a deficiency, but self-indulgence, which is an excess, that is more opposed to temperance. This happens from two reasons, one being drawn from the thing itself; for because one extreme is nearer and liker to the intermediate, we oppose not this but rather its contrary to the intermediate. *E.g.* since rashness is thought more like and nearer to courage, and cowardice more unlike, we oppose rather the latter to courage; for things that are further from the intermediate are thought more contrary to it. This, then, is one cause, drawn from the thing itself; another is drawn from ourselves; for the things to which we ourselves more naturally tend seem more contrary to the intermediate. For instance, we ourselves tend more naturally to pleasures, and hence are more easily carried away towards self-indulgence than towards propriety. We describe as contrary to the mean, then, rather the directions in which we more often go to great lengths; and therefore self-indulgence, which is an excess, is the more contrary to temperance.

9.

That moral virtue is a mean, then, and in what sense it is so, and that it is a mean between two vices, the one involving excess, the other deficiency, and that it is such because its character is to aim at what is intermediate in passions and in actions, has been sufficiently stated. Hence also it is no easy task to be good. For in everything it is no easy task to find the middle, *e.g.* to find the middle of a circle is not for everyone but for him who knows; so, too, anyone can get angry - that is easy - or give or spend money; but to do this to the right person, to the right extent, at the right time, with the right motive, and in the right way, that is not for everyone, nor is it easy; wherefore goodness is both rare and laudable and noble.

Hence he who aims at the intermediate must first depart from what is the more contrary to it, as Calypso advises:

Hold the ship out beyond that surf and spray.

For of the extremes one is more erroneous, one less so; therefore, since to hit the mean is hard in the extreme, we must as a second best, as people say, take the least of the evils; and this will be done best in the way we describe. But we must consider the things towards which we ourselves also are easily carried away; for some of us tend to one thing, some to another; and this will be recognizable from the pleasure and the pain we feel. We must drag ourselves away to the contrary extreme; for we shall get into the intermediate state by drawing well away from error, as people do in straightening sticks that are bent.

Now in everything the pleasant or pleasure is most to be guarded against; for we do not judge it impartially. We ought, then, to feel towards pleasure as the elders of the people felt towards Helen, and in all circumstances repeat their saying; for if we dismiss pleasure thus we are less likely to go astray. It is by doing this, then, (to sum the matter up) that we shall best be able to hit the mean.

But this is no doubt difficult, and especially in individual cases; for it is not easy to determine both how and with whom and on what provocation and how long one should be angry; for we too sometimes praise those who fall short and call them good-tempered, but sometimes we praise those who get angry and call them manly. The man, however, who deviates little from goodness is not blamed, whether he do so in the direction of the more or of the less, but only the man who deviates more widely; for he does not fail to be noticed. But up to what point and to what extent a man must deviate before he becomes blameworthy it is not easy to determine by reasoning, any more than anything else that is perceived by the senses; such things depend on particular facts, and the decision rests with perception. So much, then, is plain, that the intermediate state is in all things to be praised, but that we must incline sometimes towards the excess, sometimes towards the deficiency; for so shall we most easily hit the mean and what is right.

[*Nicomachean Ethics.* Translated by W.D. Ross. (Oxford: Clarendon Press, 1908).]

Nicomachean Ethics

Aristotle
(Translated by W.D. Ross)

BOOK THREE

I.

Since virtue is concerned with passions and actions, and on voluntary passions and actions praise and blame are bestowed, on those that are involuntary pardon, and sometimes also pity, to distinguish the voluntary and the involuntary is presumably necessary for those who are studying the nature of virtue, and useful also for legislators with a view to the assigning both of honors and of punishments. Those things, then, are thought-involuntary, which take place under compulsion or owing to ignorance; and that is compulsory of which the moving principle is outside, being a principle in which nothing is contributed by the person who is acting or is feeling the passion, *e.g.* if he were to be carried somewhere by a wind, or by men who had him in their power.

But with regard to the things that are done from fear of greater evils or for some noble object (*e.g.* if a tyrant were to order one to do something base, having one's parents and children in his power, and if one did the action they were to be saved, but otherwise would be put to death), it may be debated whether such actions are involuntary or voluntary. Something of the sort happens also with regard to the throwing of goods overboard in a storm; for in the abstract no one throws goods away voluntarily, but on condition of its securing the safety of himself and his crew any sensible man does so. Such actions, then, are mixed, but are more like voluntary actions; for they are worthy of choice at the time when they are done, and the end of an action is relative to the occasion. Both the terms, then, 'voluntary' and 'involuntary', must be used with reference to the moment of action. Now the man acts voluntarily; for the principle that moves the instrumental parts of the body in such actions is in him, and the things of which the moving principle is in a man himself are in his power to do or not to do. Such actions, therefore, are voluntary, but in the abstract perhaps involuntary; for no one would choose any such act in itself.

For such actions men are sometimes even praised, when they endure something base or painful in return for great and noble objects gained; in the opposite case they are blamed, since to endure the greatest indignities for no noble end or for a trifling end is the mark of an inferior person. On some actions praise indeed is not bestowed, but pardon is, when one does what he ought not under pressure which overstrains human nature and which no one could withstand. But some acts, perhaps, we cannot be forced to do, but ought rather to face death after the most fearful sufferings; for the things that 'forced' Euripides Alcmaeon to slay his mother seem absurd. It is difficult sometimes to determine what should be chosen at what cost, and what should be endured in return for what gain, and yet more difficult to abide by our decisions; for as a rule what is expected is painful, and what we are forced to do is base, whence praise and blame are bestowed on those who have been compelled or have not.

What sort of acts, then, should be called compulsory? We answer that without qualification actions are so when the cause is in the external circumstances and the agent contributes nothing. But the things that in themselves are involuntary, but now and in return for these gains are worthy of choice, and whose moving principle is in the agent, are in themselves involuntary, but now and in return for these gains voluntary. They are more like voluntary acts; for actions are in the class of particulars, and the particular acts here are voluntary. What sort of things are to be chosen, and in return for what, it is not easy to state; for there are many differences in the particular cases.

But if someone were to say that pleasant and noble objects have a compelling power, forcing us from without, all acts would be for him compulsory; for it is for these objects that all men do everything they do. And those who act under compulsion and unwillingly act with pain, but those who do acts for their pleasantness and nobility do them with pleasure; it is absurd to make external circumstances responsible, and not oneself, as being easily caught by such attractions, and to make oneself responsible for noble acts but the pleasant objects responsible for base acts. The compulsory, then, seems to be that whose moving principle is outside, the person compelled contributing nothing.

Everything that is done by reason of ignorance is not voluntary; it is only what produces pain and repentance that is involuntary. For the man who has done something owing to ignorance, and feels not the least vexation at his action, has not acted voluntarily, since he did not know what he was doing, nor yet involuntarily, since he is not pained. Of people, then, who act by reason of ignorance he who repents is thought an involuntary agent, and the man who does not repent may, since he is different, be called a not voluntary agent; for, since he differs from the other, it is better that he should have a name of his own.

Acting by reason of ignorance seems also to be different from acting in ignorance; for the man who is drunk or in a rage is thought to act as a result not of ignorance but of one of the causes mentioned, yet not knowingly but in ignorance.

Now every wicked man is ignorant of what he ought to do and what he ought to abstain from, and it is by reason of error of this kind that men become unjust and in general bad; but the term 'involuntary' tends to be used not if a man is ignorant of what is to his advantage- for it is not mistaken purpose that causes involuntary action (it leads rather to wickedness), nor ignorance of the universal (for that men are blamed), but ignorance of particulars, *i.e.* of the circumstances of the action and the objects with which it is concerned. For it is on these that both pity and pardon depend, since the person who is ignorant of any of these acts involuntarily.

Perhaps it is just as well, therefore, to determine their nature and number. A man may be ignorant, then, of who he is, what he is doing, what or whom he is acting on, and sometimes also what (*e.g.* what instrument) he is doing it with, and to what end (*e.g.* he may think his act will conduce to some one's safety), and how he is doing it (*e.g.* whether gently or violently). Now of all of these no one could be ignorant unless he were mad, and evidently also he could not be ignorant of the agent; for how could he not know himself? But of what he is doing a man might be ignorant, as for instance people say 'it slipped out of their mouths as they were speaking', or 'they did not know it was a secret', as Aeschylus said of the mysteries, or a man might say he 'let it go off when he merely wanted to show its working', as the man did with the catapult. Again, one might think one's son was an enemy, as Merope did, or that a pointed spear had a button on it, or that a stone was pumice-stone; or one might give a man a draught to save him, and really kill him; or one might want to touch a man, as people do in sparring, and really wound him. The ignorance may relate, then, to any of these things, *i.e.* of the circumstances of the action, and the man who was ignorant of any of these is thought to have acted involuntarily, and especially if he was ignorant on the most important points; and these are thought to be the circumstances of the action and its end. Further, the doing of an act that is called involuntary in virtue of ignorance of this sort must be painful and involve repentance.

Since that which is done under compulsion or by reason of ignorance is involuntary, the voluntary would seem to be that of which the moving principle is in the agent himself, he being aware of the particular circumstances of the action. Presumably acts done by reason of anger or appetite are not rightly called involuntary. For in the first place, on that showing none of the other animals will act voluntarily, nor will children; and secondly, is it meant that we do not do voluntarily any of the acts that are due to appetite or anger, or that we do the noble acts voluntarily and the base acts involuntarily? Is not this absurd, when one and the same thing is the cause? But it would surely be odd to describe as involuntary the things one ought to desire; and we ought both to be angry at certain things and to have an appetite for certain things, *e.g.* for health and for learning. Also what is involuntary is thought to be painful, but what is in accordance with appetite is thought to be pleasant. Again, what is the difference in respect of involuntariness between errors committed upon calculation and those committed in anger? Both are to be avoided, but the irrational passions are thought not less human than reason is, and therefore also the actions which proceed from anger or appetite are the man's actions. It would be odd, then, to treat them as involuntary.

2.

Both the voluntary and the involuntary having been delimited, we must next discuss choice; for it is thought to be most closely bound up with virtue and to discriminate characters better than actions do.

Choice, then, seems to be voluntary, but not the same thing as the voluntary; the latter extends more widely. For both children and the lower animals share in voluntary action, but not in choice, and acts done on the spur of the moment we describe as voluntary, but not as chosen.

Those who say it is appetite or anger or wish or a kind of opinion do not seem to be right. For choice is not common to irrational creatures as well, but appetite and anger are. Again, the incontinent man acts with appetite, but not with choice; while the continent man on the contrary acts with choice, but not with appetite. Again, appetite is contrary to choice, but not appetite to appetite. Again, appetite relates to the pleasant and the painful, choice neither to the painful nor to the pleasant.

Still less is it anger; for acts due to anger are thought to be less than any others objects of choice.

But neither is it wish, though it seems near to it; for choice cannot relate to what is impossible, and if any one said he chose them he would be thought silly; but there may be a wish even for what is impossible, *e.g.* for immortality. And wish may relate to things that could in no way be brought about by one's own efforts, *e.g.* that a particular actor or athlete should win in a competition; but no one chooses such things, but only the things that he thinks could be brought about by his own efforts. Again, wish relates rather to the end, choice to the means; for instance, we wish to be healthy, but we choose the acts which will make us healthy, and we wish to be happy and say we do, but we cannot well say we choose to be so; for, in general, choice seems to relate to the things that are in our own power.

For this reason, too, it cannot be opinion; for opinion is thought to relate to all kinds of things, no less to eternal things and impossible things than to things in our own power; and it is distinguished by its falsity or truth, not by its badness or goodness, while choice is distinguished rather by these.

Now with opinion in general perhaps no one even says it is identical. But it is not identical even with any kind of opinion; for by choosing what is good or bad we are men of a certain character, which we are not by holding certain opinions. And we choose to get or avoid something good or bad, but we have opinions about what a thing is or whom it is good for or how it is good for him; we can hardly be said to opine to get or avoid anything. And choice is praised for being related to the right object rather than for being rightly related to it, opinion for being truly related to its object. And we choose what we best know to be good, but we opine what we do not quite know; and it is not the same people that are thought to make the best choices and to have the best opinions, but some are thought to have fairly good opinions, but by reason of vice to choose what they should not. If opinion precedes choice or accompanies it, that makes no difference; for it is not this that we are considering, but whether it is identical with some kind of opinion.

What, then, or what kind of thing is it, since it is none of the things we have mentioned? It seems to be voluntary, but not all that is voluntary to be an object of choice. Is it, then, what has been decided on by previous deliberation? At any rate choice involves a rational principle and thought. Even the name seems to suggest that it is what is chosen before other things.

3.

Do we deliberate about everything, and is everything a possible subject of deliberation, or is deliberation impossible about some things? We ought presumably to call not what a fool or a madman would deliberate about, but what a sensible man would deliberate about, a subject of deliberation. Now about eternal things no one deliberates, *e.g.* about the material universe or the incommensurability of the diagonal and the side of a square. But no more do we deliberate about the things that involve movement but always happen in the same way, whether of necessity or by nature or from any other cause, *e.g.* the solstices and the risings of the stars; nor about things that happen now in one way, now in another, *e.g.* droughts and rains; nor about chance events, like the finding of treasure. But we do not deliberate even about all human affairs; for instance, no Spartan deliberates about the best constitution for the Scythians. For none of these things can be brought about by our own efforts.

We deliberate about things that are in our power and can be done; and these are in fact what is left. For nature, necessity, and chance are thought to be causes, and also reason and everything that depends on man. Now every class of men deliberates about the things that can be done by their own efforts. And in the case of exact and self-contained sciences there is no deliberation, *e.g.* about the letters of the alphabet (for we have no doubt how they should be written); but the things that are brought about by our own efforts, but not always in the same way, are the things about which we deliberate, *e.g.* questions of medical treatment or of money-making. And we do so more in the case of the art of navigation than in that of gymnastics, inasmuch as it has been less exactly worked out, and again about other things in the same ratio, and more also in the case of the arts than in that of the sciences; for we have more doubt about the former. Deliberation is concerned with things that happen in a certain way for the most part, but in which the event is obscure, and with things in which it is indeterminate. We call in others to aid us in deliberation on important questions, distrusting ourselves as not being equal to deciding.

We deliberate not about ends but about means. For a doctor does not deliberate whether he shall heal, nor an orator whether he shall persuade, nor a statesman whether he shall produce law and order, nor does anyone else deliberate about his end. They assume the end and consider how and by what means it is to be attained; and if it seems to be produced by several means they consider by which it is most easily and best produced, while if it is achieved by one only they consider how it will be achieved by this and by what means this will be achieved, till they come to the first cause, which in the order of discovery is last. For the person who deliberates seems to investigate and analyze in the way described as though he were analyzing a geometrical construction (not all investigation appears to be deliberation - for instance mathematical investigations - but all deliberation is investigation), and what is last in the order of analysis seems to be first in the order of becoming. And if we come on an impossibility, we give up the search, *e.g.* if we need money and this cannot be got; but if a thing appears possible we try to do it. By 'possible' things I mean things that might be brought about by our own efforts; and these in a sense include things that can be brought about by the efforts of our friends, since the moving principle is in ourselves. The subject of investigation is sometimes the instruments, sometimes the use of them; and similarly in the other cases- sometimes the means, sometimes the mode of using it or the means of bringing it about. It seems, then, as has been said, that man is a moving principle of actions; now deliberation is about the things to be done by the agent himself, and actions are for the sake of things other than themselves. For the end cannot be a subject of deliberation, but only the means; nor indeed can the particular facts be a subject of it, as whether this is bread or has been baked as it should; for these are matters of perception. If we are to be always deliberating, we shall have to go on to infinity.

The same thing is deliberated upon and is chosen, except that the object of choice is already determinate, since it is that which has been decided upon as a result of deliberation that is the object of choice. For every one ceases to inquire how he is to act when he has brought the moving principle back to himself and to the ruling part of himself; for this is what chooses. This is plain also from the ancient constitutions, which Homer represented; for the kings announced their choices to the people. The object of choice being one of the things in our own power which is desired after deliberation, choice will be deliberate desire of things in our own power; for when we have decided as a result of deliberation, we desire in accordance with our deliberation.

We may take it, then, that we have described choice in outline, and stated the nature of its objects and the fact that it is concerned with means.

4.

That wish is for the end has already been stated; some think it is for the good, others for the apparent good. Now those who say that the good is the object of wish must admit in consequence that that which the man who does not choose aright wishes for is not an object of wish (for if it is to be so, it must also be good; but it was, if it so happened, bad); while those who say the apparent good is the object of wish must admit that there is no natural object of wish, but only what seems good to each man. Now different things appear good to different people, and, if it so happens, even contrary things.

If these consequences are unpleasing, are we to say that absolutely and in truth the good is the object of wish, but for each person the apparent good; that that which is in truth an object of wish is an object of wish to the good man, while any chance thing may be so the bad man, as in the case of bodies also the things that are in truth wholesome are wholesome for bodies which are in good condition, while for those that are diseased other things are wholesome- or bitter or sweet or hot or heavy, and so on; since the good man judges each class of things rightly, and in each the truth appears to him? For each state of character has its own ideas of the noble and the pleasant, and perhaps the good man differs from others most by seeing the truth in each class of things, being as it were the norm and measure of them. In most things the error seems to be due to pleasure; for it appears a good when it is not. We therefore choose the pleasant as a good, and avoid pain as an evil.

5.

The end, then, being what we wish for, the means what we deliberate about and choose, actions concerning means must be according to choice and voluntary. Now the exercise of the virtues is concerned with means. Therefore virtue also is in our own power, and so too vice. For where it is in our power to act it is also in our power not to act, and vice versa; so that, if to act, where this is noble, is in our power, not to act, which will be base, will also be in our power, and if not to act, where this is noble, is in our power, to act, which will be base, will also be in our power. Now if it is in our power to do noble or base acts, and likewise in our power not to do them, and this was what being good or bad meant, then it is in our power to be virtuous or vicious.

The saying that 'no one is voluntarily wicked nor involuntarily happy' seems to be partly false and partly true; for no one is involuntarily happy, but wickedness is voluntary. Or else we shall have to dispute what has just been said, at any rate, and deny that man is a moving principle or begetter of his actions as of children. But if these facts are evident and we cannot refer actions to moving principles other than those in ourselves, the acts whose moving principles are in us must themselves also be in our power and voluntary.

Witness seems to be borne to this both by individuals in their private capacity and by legislators themselves; for these punish and take vengeance on those who do wicked acts (unless they have acted under compulsion or as a result of ignorance for which they are not themselves responsible), while they honor those who do noble acts, as though they meant to encourage the latter and deter the former. But no one is encouraged to do the things that are neither in our power nor voluntary; it is assumed that there is no gain in being persuaded not to be hot or in pain or hungry or the like, since we shall experience these feelings none the less. Indeed, we punish a man for his very ignorance, if he is thought responsible for the ignorance, as when penalties are doubled in the case of drunkenness; for the moving principle is in the man himself, since he had the power of not getting drunk and his getting drunk was the cause of his ignorance. And we punish those who are ignorant of anything in the laws that they ought to know and that is not difficult, and so too in the case of anything else that they are thought to be ignorant of through carelessness; we assume that it is in their power not to be ignorant, since they have the power of taking care.

But perhaps a man is the kind of man not to take care. Still they are themselves by their slack lives responsible for becoming men of that kind, and men make themselves responsible for being unjust or self-indulgent, in the one case by cheating and in the other by spending their time in drinking bouts and the like; for it is activities exercised on particular objects that make the corresponding character. This is plain from the case of people training for any contest or action; they practice the activity the whole time. Now not to know that it is from the exercise of activities on particular objects that states of character are produced is the mark of a thoroughly senseless person. Again, it is irrational to suppose that a man who acts unjustly does not wish to be unjust or a man who acts self-indulgently to be self-indulgent. But if without being ignorant a man does the things which will make him unjust, he will be unjust voluntarily. Yet it does not follow that if he wishes he will cease to be unjust and will be just. For neither does the man who is ill become well on those terms. We may suppose a case in which he is ill voluntarily, through living incontinently and disobeying his doctors. In that case it was then open to him not to be ill, but not now, when he has thrown away his chance, just as when you have let a stone go it is too late to recover it; but yet it was in your power to throw it, since the moving principle was in you. So, too, to the unjust and to the self-indulgent man it was open at the beginning not to become men of this kind, and so they are unjust and self-indulgent voluntarily; but now that they have become so it is not possible for them not to be so.

But not only are the vices of the soul voluntary, but those of the body also for some men, whom we accordingly blame; while no one blames those who are ugly by nature, we blame those who are so owing to want of exercise and care. So it is, too, with respect to weakness and infirmity; no one would reproach a man blind from birth or by disease or from a blow, but rather pity him, while everyone would blame a man who was blind from drunkenness or some other form of self-indulgence. Of vices of the body, then, those in our own power are blamed, those not in our power are not. And if this be so, in the other cases also the vices that are blamed must be in our own power.

Now some one may say that all men desire the apparent good, but have no control over the appearance, but the end appears to each man in a form answering to his character. We reply that if each man is somehow responsible for his state of mind, he will also be himself somehow responsible for the appearance; but if not, no one is responsible for his own evildoing, but everyone does evil acts through ignorance of the end, thinking that by these he will get what is best, and the aiming at the end is not self-chosen but one must be born with an eye, as it were, by which to judge rightly and choose what is truly good, and he is well endowed by nature who is well endowed with this. For it is what is greatest and most noble, and what we cannot get or learn from another, but must have just such as it was when given us at birth, and to be well and nobly endowed with this will be perfect and true excellence of natural endowment. If this is true, then, how will virtue be more voluntary than vice? To both men alike, the good and the bad, the end appears and is fixed by nature or however it may be, and it is by referring everything else to this that men do whatever they do.

Whether, then, it is not by nature that the end appears to each man such as it does appear, but something also depends on him, or the end is natural but because the good man adopts the means voluntarily virtue is voluntary, vice also will be none the less voluntary; for in the case of the bad man there is equally present that which depends on himself in his actions even if not in his end. If, then, as is asserted, the virtues are voluntary (for we are ourselves somehow partly responsible for our states of character, and it is by being persons of a certain kind that we assume the end to be so and so), the vices also will be voluntary; for the same is true of them.

With regard to the virtues in general we have stated their genus in outline, viz. that they are means and that they are states of character, and that they tend, and by their own nature, to the doing of the acts by which they are produced, and that they are in our power and voluntary, and act as the right rule prescribes. But actions and states of character are not voluntary in the same way; for we are masters of our actions from the beginning right to the end, if we know the particular facts, but though we control the beginning of our states of character the gradual progress is not obvious any more than it is in illnesses; because it was in our power, however, to act in this way or not in this way, therefore the states are voluntary.

Let us take up the several virtues, however, and say which they are and what sort of things they are concerned with and how they are concerned with them; at the same time it will become plain how many they are. And first let us speak of courage.

6.

That courage is a mean with regard to feelings of fear and confidence has already been made evident; and plainly the things we fear are terrible things, and these are, to speak without qualification, evils; for which reason people even define fear as expectation of evil. Now we fear all evils, *e.g.* disgrace, poverty, disease, friendlessness, death, but the brave man is not thought to be concerned with all; for to fear some things is even right and noble, and it is base not to fear them - *e.g.* disgrace; he who fears this is good and modest, and he who does not is shameless. He is, however, by some people called brave, by a transference of the word to a new meaning; for he has in him something which is like the brave man, since the brave man also is a fearless person. Poverty and disease we perhaps ought not to fear, nor in general the things that do not proceed from vice and are not due to a man himself. But not even the man who is fearless of these is brave. Yet we apply the word to him also in virtue of a similarity; for some who in the dangers of war are cowards are liberal and are confident in face of the loss of money. Nor is a man a coward if he fears insult to his wife and children or envy or anything of the kind; nor brave if he is confident when he is about to be flogged. With what sort of terrible things, then, is the brave man concerned? Surely with the greatest; for no one is more likely than he to stand his ground against what is awe-inspiring. Now death is the most terrible of all things; for it is the end, and nothing is thought to be any longer either good or bad for the dead. But the brave man would not seem to be concerned even with death in all circumstances, *e.g.* at sea or in disease. In what circumstances, then? Surely in the noblest. Now such deaths are those in battle; for these take place in the greatest and noblest danger. And these are correspondingly honored in city-states and at the courts of monarchs. Properly, then, he will be called brave who is fearless in face of a noble death, and of all emergencies that involve death; and the emergencies of war are in the highest degree of this kind. Yet at sea also, and in disease, the brave man is fearless, but not in the same way as the seaman; for he has given up hope of safety, and is disliking the thought of death in this shape, while they are hopeful because of their experience. At the same time, we show courage in situations where there is the opportunity of showing prowess or where death is noble; but in these forms of death neither of these conditions is fulfilled.

7.

What is terrible is not the same for all men; but we say there are things terrible even beyond human strength. These, then, are terrible to every one- at least to every sensible man; but the terrible things that are not beyond human strength differ in magnitude and degree, and so too do the things that inspire confidence. Now the brave man is as dauntless as man may be. Therefore, while he will fear even the things that are not beyond human strength, he will face them as he ought and as the rule directs, for honor's sake; for this is the end of virtue. But it is possible to fear these more, or less, and again to fear things that are not terrible as if they were. Of the faults that are committed one consists in fearing what one should not, another in fearing as we should not, another in fearing when we should not, and so on; and so too with respect to the things that inspire confidence. The man, then, who faces and who fears the right things and from the right motive, in the right way and from the right time, and who feels confidence under the corresponding conditions, is brave; for the brave man feels and acts according to the merits of the case and in whatever way the rule directs. Now the end of every activity is conformity to the corresponding state of character. This is true, therefore, of the brave man as well as of others. But courage is noble. Therefore the end also is noble; for each thing is defined by its end. Therefore it is for a noble end that the brave man endures and acts as courage directs.

Of those who go to excess he who exceeds in fearlessness has no name (we have said previously that many states of character have no names), but he would be a sort of madman or insensible person if he feared nothing, neither earthquakes nor the waves, as they say the Celts do not; while the man who exceeds in confidence about what really is terrible is rash. The rash man, however, is also thought to be boastful and only a pretender to courage; at all events, as the brave man is with regard to what is terrible, so the rash man wishes to appear; and so he imitates him in situations where he can. Hence also most of them are a mixture of rashness and cowardice; for, while in these situations they display confidence, they do not hold their ground against what is really terrible. The man who exceeds in fear is a coward; for he fears both what he ought not and as he ought not, and all the similar characterizations attach to him. He is lacking also in confidence; but he is more conspicuous for his excess of fear in painful situations. The coward, then, is a despairing sort of person; for he fears everything. The brave man, on the other hand, has the opposite disposition; for confidence is the mark of a hopeful disposition. The coward, the rash man, and the brave man, then, are concerned with the same objects but are differently disposed towards them; for the first two exceed and fall short, while the third holds the middle, which is the right, position; and rash men are precipitate, and wish for dangers beforehand but draw back when they are in them, while brave men are keen in the moment of action, but quiet beforehand.

As we have said, then, courage is a mean with respect to things that inspire confidence or fear, in the circumstances that have been stated; and it chooses or endures things because it is noble to do so, or because it is base not to do so. But to die to escape from poverty or love or anything painful is not the mark of a brave man, but rather of a coward; for it is softness to fly from what is troublesome, and such a man endures death not because it is noble but to fly from evil.

8.

Courage, then, is something of this sort, but the name is also applied to five other kinds.

(1) First comes the courage of the citizen-soldier; for this is most like true courage. Citizen-soldiers seem to face dangers because of the penalties imposed by the laws and the reproaches they would otherwise incur, and because of the honors they win by such action; and therefore those peoples seem to be bravest among whom cowards are held in dishonor and brave men in honor. . . .

This kind of courage is most like to that which we described earlier, because it is due to virtue; for it is due to shame and to desire of a noble object (*i.e.* honor) and avoidance of disgrace, which is ignoble. One might rank in the same class even those who are compelled by their rulers; but they are inferior, inasmuch as they do what they do not from shame but from fear, and to avoid not what is disgraceful but what is painful; for their masters compel them, as Hector does:

> But if I shall spy any dastard that cowers far from the fight,
>
> Vainly will such an one hope to escape from the dogs.

And those who give them their posts, and beat them if they retreat, do the same, and so do those who draw them up with trenches or something of the sort behind them; all of these apply compulsion. But one ought to be brave not under compulsion but because it is noble to be so.

(2) Experience with regard to particular facts is also thought to be courage; this is indeed the reason why Socrates thought courage was knowledge. Other people exhibit this quality in other dangers, and professional soldiers exhibit it in the dangers of war; for there seem to be many empty alarms in war, of which these have had the most comprehensive experience; therefore they seem brave, because the others do not know the nature of the facts. Again, their experience makes them most capable in attack and in defense, since they

can use their arms and have the kind that are likely to be best both for attack and for defense; therefore they fight like armed men against unarmed or like trained athletes against amateurs; for in such contests too it is not the bravest men that fight best, but those who are strongest and have their bodies in the best condition. Professional soldiers turn cowards, however, when the danger puts too great a strain on them and they are inferior in numbers and equipment; for they are the first to fly, while citizen-forces die at their posts, as in fact happened at the temple of Hermes. For to the latter flight is disgraceful and death is preferable to safety on those terms; while the former from the very beginning faced the danger on the assumption that they were stronger, and when they know the facts they fly, fearing death more than disgrace; but the brave man is not that sort of person.

(3) Passion also is sometimes reckoned as courage; those who act from passion, like wild beasts rushing at those who have wounded them, are thought to be brave, because brave men also are passionate; for passion above all things is eager to rush on danger, and hence Homer's 'put strength into his passion' and 'aroused their spirit and passion and 'hard he breathed panting' and 'his blood boiled'. For all such expressions seem to indicate the stirring and onset of passion. Now brave men act for honor's sake, but passion aids them; while wild beasts act under the influence of pain; for they attack because they have been wounded or because they are afraid, since if they are in a forest they do not come near one. Thus they are not brave because, driven by pain and passion, they rush on danger without foreseeing any of the perils, since at that rate even asses would be brave when they are hungry; for blows will not drive them from their food; and lust also makes adulterers do many daring things. (Those creatures are not brave, then, which are driven on to danger by pain or passion.) The 'courage' that is due to passion seems to be the most natural, and to be courage if choice and motive be added.

Men, then, as well as beasts, suffer pain when they are angry, and are pleased when they exact their revenge; those who fight for these reasons, however, are pugnacious but not brave; for they do not act for honor's sake nor as the rule directs, but from strength of feeling; they have, however, something akin to courage.

(4) Nor are sanguine people brave; for they are confident in danger only because they have conquered often and against many foes. Yet they closely resemble brave men, because both are confident; but brave men are confident for the reasons stated earlier, while these are so because they think they are the strongest and can suffer nothing. (Drunken men also behave in this way; they become sanguine). When their adventures do not succeed, however, they run away; but it was the mark of a brave man to face things that are, and seem, terrible for a man, because it is noble to do so and disgraceful not to do so. Hence also it is thought the mark of a braver man to be fearless and undisturbed in sudden alarms than to be so in those that are foreseen; for it must have proceeded more from a state of character, because less from preparation; acts that are foreseen may be chosen by calculation and rule, but sudden actions must be in accordance with one's state of character.

(5) People who are ignorant of the danger also appear brave, and they are not far removed from those of a sanguine temper, but are inferior inasmuch as they have no self-reliance while these have. Hence also the sanguine hold their ground for a time; but those who have been deceived about the facts fly if they know or suspect that these are different from what they supposed, as happened to the Argives when they fell in with the Spartans and took them for Sicyonians.

We have, then, described the character both of brave men and of those who are thought to be brave.

9.

Though courage is concerned with feelings of confidence and of fear, it is not concerned with both alike, but more with the things that inspire fear; for he who is undisturbed in face of these and bears himself as he should towards these is more truly brave than the man who does so towards the things that inspire confidence. It is for facing what is painful, then, as has been said, that men are called brave. Hence also courage involves pain, and is justly praised; for it is harder to face what is painful than to abstain from what is pleasant.

Yet the end which courage sets before it would seem to be pleasant, but to be concealed by the attending circumstances, as happens also in athletic contests; for the end at which boxers aim is pleasant- the crown and the honors - but the blows they take are distressing to flesh and blood, and painful, and so is their whole exertion; and because the blows and the exertions are many the end, which is but small, appears to have nothing pleasant in it. And so, if the case of courage is similar, death and wounds will be painful to the brave man and against his will, but he will face them because it is noble to do so or because it is base not to do so. And the more he is possessed of virtue in its entirety and the happier he is, the more he will be pained at the thought of death; for life is best worth living for such a man, and he is knowingly losing the greatest goods, and this is painful. But he is none the less brave, and perhaps all the more so, because he chooses noble deeds of war at that cost. It is not the case, then, with all the virtues that the exercise of them is pleasant, except in so far as it reaches its end. But it is quite possible that the best soldiers may be not men of this sort but those who are less brave but have no other good; for these are ready to face danger, and they sell their life for trifling gains.

So much, then, for courage; it is not difficult to grasp its nature in outline, at any rate, from what has been said.

10.

After courage let us speak of temperance; for these seem to be the virtues of the irrational parts. We have said that temperance is a mean with regard to pleasures (for it is less, and not in the same way, concerned with pains); self-indulgence also is manifested in the same sphere. Now, therefore, let us determine with what sort of pleasures they are concerned. We may assume the distinction between bodily pleasures and those of the soul, such as love of honor and love of learning; for the lover of each of these delights in that of which he is a lover, the body being in no way affected, but rather the mind; but men who are concerned with such pleasures are called neither temperate nor self-indulgent. Nor, again, are those who are concerned with the other pleasures that are not bodily; for those who are fond of hearing and telling stories and who spend their days on anything that turns up are called gossips, but not self-indulgent, nor are those who are pained at the loss of money or of friends.

Temperance must be concerned with bodily pleasures, but not all even of these; for those who delight in objects of vision, such as colors and shapes and painting, are called neither temperate nor self-indulgent; yet it would seem possible to delight even in these either as one should or to excess or to a deficient degree.

And so too is it with objects of hearing; no one calls those who delight extravagantly in music or acting self-indulgent, nor those who do so as they ought temperate.

Nor do we apply these names to those who delight in odor, unless it be incidentally; we do not call those self-indulgent who delight in the odor of apples or roses or incense, but rather those who delight in the odor of unguents or of dainty dishes; for self-indulgent people delight in these because these remind them of the objects of their appetite. And one may see even other people, when they are hungry, delighting in the smell of food; but to delight in this kind of thing is the mark of the self-indulgent man; for these are objects of appetite to him.

Nor is there in animals other than man any pleasure connected with these senses, except incidentally. For dogs do not delight in the scent of hares, but in the eating of them, but the scent told them the hares were there; nor does the lion delight in the lowing of the ox, but in eating it; but he perceived by the lowing that it was near, and therefore appears to delight in the lowing; and similarly he does not delight because he sees 'a stag or a wild goat', but because he is going to make a meal of it. Temperance and self-indulgence, however, are concerned with the kind of pleasures that the other animals share in, which therefore appear slavish and brutish; these are touch and taste. But even of taste they appear to make little or no use; for the business of taste is the discriminating of flavors, which is done by wine-tasters and people who season dishes; but they hardly take pleasure in making these discriminations, or at least self-indulgent people do not, but in the actual enjoyment, which in all cases comes through touch, both in the case of food and in that of drink and in that of sexual intercourse. This is why a certain gourmand prayed that his throat might become longer than a crane's, implying that it was the contact that he took pleasure in. Thus the sense with which self-indulgence is connected is the most widely shared of the senses; and self-indulgence would seem to be justly a matter of reproach, because it attaches to us not as men but as animals. To delight in such things, then, and to love them above all others, is brutish. For even of the pleasures of touch the most liberal have been eliminated, *e.g.* those produced in the gymnasium by rubbing and by the consequent heat; for the contact characteristic of the self-indulgent man does not affect the whole body but only certain parts.

11.

Of the appetites some seem to be common, others to be peculiar to individuals and acquired; *e.g.* the appetite for food is natural, since everyone who is without it craves for food or drink, and sometimes for both, and for love also (as Homer says) if he is young and lusty; but not everyone craves for this or that kind of nourishment or love, nor for the same things. Hence such craving appears to be our very own. Yet it has of course something natural about it; for different things are pleasant to different kinds of people, and some things are more pleasant to everyone than chance objects. Now in the natural appetites few go wrong, and only in one direction, that of excess; for to eat or drink whatever offers itself till one is surfeited is to exceed the natural amount, since natural appetite is the replenishment of one's deficiency. Hence these people are called belly-gods, this implying that they fill their belly beyond what is right. It is people of entirely slavish character that become like this. But with regard to the pleasures peculiar to individuals many people go wrong and in many ways. For while the people who are 'fond of so and so' are so called because they delight either in the wrong things, or more than most people do, or in the wrong way, the self-indulgent exceed in all three ways; they both delight in some things that they ought not to delight in (since they are hateful), and if one ought to delight in some of the things they delight in, they do so more than one ought and more than most men do.

Plainly, then, excess with regard to pleasures is self-indulgence and is culpable; with regard to pains one is not, as in the case of courage, called temperate for facing them or self-indulgent for not doing so, but the self-indulgent man is so called because he is pained more than he ought at not getting pleasant things (even his pain being caused by pleasure), and the temperate man is so called because he is not pained at the absence of what is pleasant and at his abstinence from it.

The self-indulgent man, then, craves for all pleasant things or those that are most pleasant, and is led by his appetite to choose these at the cost of everything else; hence he is pained both when he fails to get them and when he is merely craving for them (for appetite involves pain); but it seems absurd to be pained for the sake of pleasure. People who fall short with regard to pleasures and delight in them less than they should are hardly found; for such insensibility is not human. Even the other animals distinguish different kinds of food and enjoy some and not others; and if there is anyone who finds nothing pleasant and nothing more attractive than anything else, he must be something quite different from a man; this sort of person has not received a name because he hardly occurs. The temperate man occupies a middle position with regard to these objects. For he neither enjoys the things that the self-indulgent man enjoys most-but rather dislikes them-nor in general the things that he should not, nor anything of this sort to excess, nor does he feel pain or craving when they are absent, or does so only to a moderate degree, and not more than he should, nor when he should not, and so on; but the things that, being pleasant, make for health or for good condition, he will desire moderately and as he should, and also other pleasant things if they are not hindrances to these ends, or contrary to what is noble, or beyond his means. For he who neglects these conditions loves such pleasures more than they are worth, but the temperate man is not that sort of person, but the sort of person that the right rule prescribes.

12.

Self-indulgence is more like a voluntary state than cowardice. For the former is actuated by pleasure, the latter by pain, of which the one is to be chosen and the other to be avoided; and pain upsets and destroys the nature of the person who feels it, while pleasure does nothing of the sort. Therefore self-indulgence is more voluntary. Hence also it is more a matter of reproach; for it is easier to become accustomed to its objects, since there are many things of this sort in life, and the process of habituation to them is free from danger, while with terrible objects the reverse is the case. But cowardice would seem to be voluntary in a different degree from its particular manifestations; for it is itself painless, but in these we are upset by pain, so that we even throw down our arms and disgrace ourselves in other ways; hence our acts are even thought to be done under compulsion. For the self-indulgent man, on the other hand, the particular acts are voluntary (for he does them with craving and desire), but the whole state is less so; for no one craves to be self-indulgent.

The name self-indulgence is applied also to childish faults; for they bear a certain resemblance to what we have been considering. Which is called after which, makes no difference to our present purpose; plainly, however, the later is called after the earlier. The transference of the name seems not a bad one; for that which desires what is base and which develops quickly ought to be kept in a chastened condition, and these characteristics belong above all to appetite and to the child, since children in fact live at the beck and call of appetite, and it is in them that the desire for what is pleasant is strongest. If, then, it is not going to be obedient and subject to the ruling principle, it will go to great lengths; for in an irrational being the desire for pleasure is insatiable even if it tries every source of gratification, and the exercise of appetite increases its innate force, and if appetites are strong and violent they even expel the power of calculation. Hence they should be moderate and few, and should in no way oppose the rational principle-and this is what we call an obedient and chastened state-and as the child should live according to the direction of his tutor, so the appetitive element should live according to rational principle. Hence the appetitive element in a temperate man should harmonize with the rational principle; for the noble is the mark at which both aim, and the temperate man craves for the things he ought, as he ought, as when he ought; and when he ought; and this is what rational principle directs.

Here we conclude our account of temperance.

[*Nicomachean Ethics.* Translated by W.D. Ross. (Oxford: Clarendon Press, 1908).]

Key Terms and Concepts

(Aristotelian) form
(Aristotelian) matter
material cause
formal cause
efficient cause
final cause
telos
teleology
arête
eudaimonia
sophrosyne
The Golden Mean
praxis
pathos
habit
character
courage
temperance

Questions for Further Reflection

1. What does Aristotle mean by "the chief good" of life? What does he conclude is the chief good? Do you agree or disagree with his assessment? Why or why not?
2. Summarize Aristotle's analysis of pleasure, honor, and wealth in Book One. Why does he reject each as the "chief good" of life? Do you agree with his analysis? Why or why not?
3. How does Aristotle characterize happiness? How is his definition of happiness different from some other possible conceptions of happiness?
4. How does Aristotle distinguish between moral virtue and intellectual virtue?
5. Explain the connection between habit and character for Aristotle. Provide some examples.
6. Provide three of your own examples of (moral) virtues understood as a mean (*i.e.*, intermediate) between the extremes of excess and deficiency.
7. According to Aristotle, does every (moral) virtue admit of a mean? Why or why not?
8. Why does Aristotle argue that some virtues are "more opposed" to their excess instead of to their deficiency, and vice versa?
9. How does Aristotle link the concepts of voluntary action, choice, and deliberation?
10. How are habits and happiness related according to Aristotle? Do you agree with his assessment? Why or why not?

Homework Assignment #4a

Name: ______________________________ Section: ______________________________

Summarize Aristotle's analysis of pleasure, honor, and wealth in Book One of *Nicomachean Ethics*. Why does he reject each as being identical with "the chief good" of human life? Do you agree with his assessment? Why or why not?

Homework Assignment #4b

Name: Muhamed Zorabi Section: ____________

Explain how Aristotle characterizes "happiness." How is his definition of happiness different from some other possible conceptions of happiness? Do you agree with his assessment? Why or why not?

Happiness is an end that ultimately comes from worldly means. These means are often confused with happiness. Many people think that happiness is money, honor, and pleasure. All of these supposed examples of happiness lack telos of human. Aristotle characterizes happiness as Eudamonia, in a nutshell it means for one to be flourishing or living well. A great example of this is self actualization from mazlow's heirarchy needs, or achieving one's full potential/ having fulfillment. Aristotle's definition is not a mental state like many people initially think of.

I think his assesment of achieving human purpose is very valid, but I do not think it should be translated to happiness. It maybe a lost in translation kind of moment, but it doesn't take away from Aristotle's ideas about what the purpose of human life is.

Homework Assignment #4c

Name: ______________________________ Section: ______________________________

Provide three of your own examples of moral virtues (i.e., positive character traits) understood as the mean (or "intermediate") between the extremes of excess and deficiency. Be sure to describe the two vices that correspond to each of the three virtues that you provide.

CHAPTER FIVE

The Stoic and Epicurean Philosophies of Life

Epictetus (55–135 CE)

Epicurus (341–270 BCE)

SELECTED READINGS

- *Enchiridion*—Epictetus
- *Letter to Menoeceus*—Epicurus
- *Principle Doctrines*—Epicurus

Enchiridion

Epictetus

(Translated by Elizabeth Carter)

1.

Some things are in our control and others not. Things in our control are opinion, pursuit, desire, aversion, and, in a word, whatever are our own actions. Things not in our control are body, property, reputation, station, and, in one word, whatever are not our own actions.

The things in our control are by nature free, unrestrained, unhindered; but those not in our control are weak, slavish, restrained, belonging to others. Remember, then, that if you suppose that things which are slavish by nature are also free, and that what belongs to others is your own, then you will be hindered. You will lament, you will be disturbed, and you will blame both gods and men. But if you suppose that only to be your own which is your own, and what belongs to others such as it really is, then no one will ever compel you or restrain you. Further, you will find fault with no one or accuse no one. You will do nothing against your will. No one will hurt you, you will have no enemies, and you will not be harmed.

Aiming therefore at such great things, remember that you must not allow yourself to be carried, even with a slight tendency, towards the attainment of lesser things. Instead, you must entirely quit some things and for the present postpone the rest. But if you would both have these great things, along with power and riches, then you will not gain even the latter, because you aim at the former too: but you will absolutely fail of the former, by which alone happiness and freedom are achieved.

Work, therefore to be able to say to every harsh appearance, "You are but an appearance, and not absolutely the thing you appear to be." And then examine it by those rules which you have, and first, and chiefly, by this: whether it concerns the things which are in our own control, or those which are not; and, if it concerns anything not in our control, be prepared to say that it is nothing to you.

2.

Remember that following desire promises the attainment of that of which you are desirous; and aversion promises the avoiding that to which you are averse. However, he who fails to obtain the object of his desire is disappointed, and he who incurs the object of his aversion, miserable. If, then, you confine your aversion to those objects only which are contrary to the natural use of your faculties, which you have in your own control, you will never incur anything to which you are averse. But if you are averse to sickness, or death, or poverty, you will be miserable. Remove aversion, then, from all things that are not in our control, and transfer it to things contrary to the nature of what is in our control. But, for the present, totally suppress desire: for, if you desire any of the things which are not in your own control, you must necessarily be disappointed; and of those which are, and which it would be laudable to desire, nothing is yet in your possession. Use only the appropriate actions of pursuit and avoidance; and even these lightly, and with gentleness and reservation.

3.

With regard to whatever objects give you delight, are useful, or are deeply loved, remember to tell yourself of what general nature they are, beginning from the most insignificant things. If, for example, you are fond of a specific ceramic cup, remind yourself that it is only ceramic cups in general of which you are fond. Then, if it breaks, you will not be disturbed. If you kiss your child, or your wife, say that you only kiss things which are human, and thus you will not be disturbed if either of them dies.

4.

When you are going about any action, remind yourself what nature the action is. If you are going to bathe, picture to yourself the things which usually happen in the bath: some people splash the water, some push, some use abusive language, and others steal. Thus you will more safely go about this action if you say to yourself, "I will now go bathe, and keep my own mind in a state conformable to nature." And in the same manner with regard to every other action. For thus, if any hindrance arises in bathing, you will have it ready to say, "It was not only to bathe that I desired, but to keep my mind in a state conformable to nature; and I will not keep it if I am bothered at things that happen."

5.

Men are disturbed, not by things, but by the principles and notions which they form concerning things. Death, for instance, is not terrible, else it would have appeared so to Socrates. But the terror consists in our notion of death that it is terrible. When therefore we are hindered, or disturbed, or grieved, let us never attribute it to others, but to ourselves; that is, to our own principles. An uninstructed person will lay the fault of his own bad condition upon others. Someone just starting instruction will lay the fault on himself. Some who is perfectly instructed will place blame neither on others nor on himself.

6.

Don't be prideful with any excellence that is not your own. If a horse should be prideful and say, "I am handsome," it would be supportable. But when you are prideful, and say, "I have a handsome horse," know that you are proud of what is, in fact, only the good of the horse. What, then, is your own? Only your reaction to the appearances of things. Thus, when you behave conformably to nature in reaction to how things appear, you will be proud with reason; for you will take pride in some good of your own.

7.

Consider when, on a voyage, your ship is anchored; if you go on shore to get water you may along the way amuse yourself with picking up a shell, or an onion. However, your thoughts and continual attention ought to be bent towards the ship, waiting for the captain to call on board; you must then immediately leave all these things, otherwise you will be thrown into the ship, bound neck and feet like a sheep.

So it is with life. If, instead of an onion or a shellfish, you are given a wife or child, that is fine. But if the captain calls, you must run to the ship, leaving them, and regarding none of them. But if you are old, never go far from the ship: lest, when you are called, you should be unable to come in time.

8.

Don't demand that things happen as you wish, but wish that they happen as they do happen, and you will live well.

9.

Sickness is a hindrance to the body, but not to your ability to choose, unless that is your choice. Lameness is a hindrance to the leg, but not to your ability to choose. Say this to yourself with regard to everything that happens, then you will see such obstacles as hindrances to something else, but not to yourself.

10.

With every accident, ask yourself what abilities you have for making a proper use of it. If you see an attractive person, you will find that self-restraint is the ability you have against your desire.

If you are in pain, you will find fortitude. If you hear unpleasant language, you will find patience. And thus habituated, the appearances of things will not hurry you away along with them.

11.

Never say of anything, "I have lost it"; but, "I have returned it." Is your child dead? It is returned. Is your wife dead? She is returned. Is your estate taken away? Well, and is not that likewise returned? "But he who took it away is a bad man." What difference is it to you who the giver assigns to take it back? While he gives it to you to possess, take care of it; but don't view it as your own, just as travelers view a hotel.

12.

If you want to improve, reject such reasonings as these: "If I neglect my affairs, I'll have no income; if I don't correct my servant, he will be bad." For it is better to die with hunger, free from grief and fear, than to live in affluence with anxiety; and it is better your servant should be bad, than you unhappy.

Begin therefore from little things. Is a little oil spilt? A little wine stolen? Say to yourself, "This is the price paid for apathy, for tranquility, and nothing is to be had for nothing." When you call your servant, it is possible that he may not come; or, if he does, he may not do what you want. But he is by no means of such importance that it should be in his power to give you any disturbance.

13.

If you want to improve, be content to be thought foolish and stupid with regard to external things. Don't wish to be thought to know anything; and even if you appear to be somebody important to others, distrust yourself. For, it is difficult to both keep your faculty of choice in a state conformable to nature, and at the same time acquire external things. But while you are careful about the one, you must of necessity neglect the other.

14.

If you wish your children, and your wife, and your friends to live forever, you are stupid; for you wish to be in control of things which you cannot, you wish for things that belong to others to be your own. So likewise, if you wish your servant to be without fault, you are a fool; for you wish vice not to be vice," but something else. But, if you wish to have your desires undisappointed, this is in your own control. Exercise, therefore, what is in your control. He is the master of every other person who is able to confer or remove whatever that person wishes either to have or to avoid. Whoever, then, would be free, let him wish nothing, let him decline nothing, which depends on others else he must necessarily be a slave.

15.

Remember that you must behave in life as at a dinner party. Is anything brought around to you? Put out your hand and take your share with moderation. Does it pass by you? Don't stop it. Is it not yet come? Don't stretch your desire towards it, but wait till it reaches you. Do this with regard to children, to a wife, to public posts, to riches, and you will eventually be a worthy partner of the feasts of the gods. And if you don't even take the things which are set before you, but are able even to reject them, then you will not only be a partner at the feasts of the gods, but also of their empire. For, by doing this, Diogenes, Heraclitus and others like them, deservedly became, and were called, divine.

16.

When you see anyone weeping in grief because his son has gone abroad, or is dead, or because he has suffered in his affairs, be careful that the appearance may not misdirect you. Instead, distinguish within your own mind, and be prepared to say, "It's not the accident that distresses this person, because it doesn't distress another person; it is the judgment which he makes about it." As far as words go, however, don't reduce yourself to his level, and certainly do not moan with him. Do not moan inwardly either.

17.

Remember that you are an actor in a drama, of such a kind as the author pleases to make it. If short, of a short one; if long, of a long one. If it is his pleasure you should act a poor man, a cripple, a governor, or a private citizen, see that you act it naturally. For this is your business, to act well the character assigned you; to choose it is another's.

18.

When a raven happens to croak unluckily, don't allow the appearance hurry you away with it, but immediately make the distinction to yourself, and say, "None of these things are foretold to me; but either to my paltry body, or property, or reputation, or children, or wife. But to me all omens are lucky, if I will. For whichever of these things happens, it is in my control to derive advantage from it."

19.

You will be unconquerable, if you enter into no combat in which it is not in your own control to conquer. When, therefore, you see anyone eminent in honors, or power, or in high esteem on any other account, take heed not to be hurried away with the appearance, and to pronounce him happy; for, if the essence of good consists in things in our own control, there will be no room for envy or emulation. But, for your part, don't wish to be a general, or a senator, or a consul, but to be free; and the only way to this is a contempt of things not in our own control.

20.

Remember, that not he who gives ill language or a blow insults, but the principle which represents these things as insulting. When, therefore, anyone provokes you, be assured that it is your own opinion which provokes you. Try, therefore, in the first place, not to be hurried away with the appearance. For if you once gain time and respite, you will more easily command yourself.

21.

Let death and exile, and all other things which appear terrible be daily before your eyes, but chiefly death, and you win never entertain any abject thought, nor too eagerly covet anything.

22.

If you have an earnest desire of attaining to philosophy, prepare yourself from the very first to be laughed at, to be sneered by the multitude, to hear them say, "He is returned to us a philosopher all of a sudden," and "Whence this arrogant look?" Now, for your part, don't have an arrogant look, indeed; but keep steadily to those things which appear best to you as one appointed by God to this station. For remember that, if you adhere to the same point, those very persons who at first ridiculed will afterwards admire you. But if you are conquered by them, you will incur a double ridicule.

23.

If you ever happen to turn your attention to externals, so as to wish to please anyone, be assured that you have ruined your scheme of life. Be contented, then, in everything with being a philosopher; and, if you wish to be thought so likewise by anyone, appear so to yourself, and it will suffice.

24.

Don't allow such considerations as these distress you. "I will live in dishonor, and be nobody anywhere." For, if dishonor is an evil, you can no more be involved in any evil by the means of another, than be engaged in anything base. Is it any business of yours, then, to get power, or to be admitted to an entertainment? By no means.

How, then, after all, is this a dishonor? And how is it true that you will be nobody anywhere, when you ought to be somebody in those things only which are in your own control, in which you may be of the greatest consequence? "But my friends will be unassisted." – What do you mean by unassisted? They will not have money from you, nor will you make them Roman citizens. Who told you, then, that these are among the things in our own control, and not the affair of others?

And who can give to another the things which he has not himself? "Well, but get them, then, that we too may have a share." If I can get them with the preservation of my own honor and fidelity and greatness of mind, show me the way and I will get them; but if you require me to lose my own proper good that you may gain what is not good, consider how inequitable and foolish you are.

Besides, which would you rather have, a sum of money, or a friend of fidelity and honor? Rather assist me, then, to gain this character than require me to do those things by which I may lose it. Well, but my country, say you, as far as depends on me, will be unassisted. Here again, what assistance is this you mean? "It will not have porticoes nor baths of your providing." And what signifies that? Why, neither does a smith provide it with shoes, or a shoemaker with arms. It is enough if everyone fully performs his own proper business. And were you to supply it with another citizen of honor and fidelity, would not he be of use to it? Yes. Therefore neither are you yourself useless to it. "What place, then, say you, will I hold in the state?" Whatever you can hold with the preservation of your fidelity and honor. But if, by desiring to be useful to that, you lose these, of what use can you be to your country when you are become faithless and void of shame.

25.

Is anyone preferred before you at an entertainment, or in a compliment, or in being admitted to a consultation? If these things are good, you ought to be glad that he has gotten them; and if they are evil, don't be grieved that you have not gotten them. And remember that you cannot, without using the same means which others do to acquire things not in our own control, expect to be thought worthy of an equal share of them. For how can he who does not frequent the door of any great man, does not attend him, does not praise him, have an equal share with him who does? You are unjust, then, and insatiable, if you are unwilling to pay the price for which these things are sold, and would have them for nothing. For how much is lettuce sold? Fifty cents, for instance. If another, then, paying fifty cents, takes the lettuce, and you, not paying it, go without them, and don't imagine that he has gained any advantage over you. For as he has the lettuce, so you have the fifty cents which you did not give. So, in the present case, you have not been invited to such a person's entertainment, because you have not paid him the price for which a supper is sold. It is sold for praise; it is sold for attendance. Give him then the value, if it is for your advantage. But if you would, at the same time, not pay the one and yet receive the other, you are insatiable, and a blockhead. Have you nothing, then, instead of the supper? Yes, indeed, you have: the not praising him, whom you don't like to praise; the not bearing with his behavior at coming in.

26.

The will of nature may be learned from those things in which we don't distinguish from each other. For example, when our neighbor's boy breaks a cup, or the like, we are presently ready to say, "These things will happen." Be assured, then, that when your own cup likewise is broken, you ought to be affected just as when another's cup was broken. Apply this in like manner to greater things. Is the child or wife of another dead? There is no one who would not say, "This is a human accident." but if anyone's own child happens to die, it is presently, "Alas I how miserable am I!" But it should be remembered how we are affected in hearing the same thing concerning others.

27.

As a mark is not set up for the sake of missing the aim, so neither does the nature of evil exist in the world.

28.

If a person gave your body to any stranger he met on his way, you would certainly be angry. And do you feel no shame in handing over your own mind to be confused and mystified by anyone who happens to verbally attack you?

29.

In every affair consider what precedes and follows, and then undertake it. Otherwise you will begin with spirit; but not having thought of the consequences, when some of them appear you will shamefully desist. "I would conquer at the Olympic games." But consider what precedes and follows, and then, if it is for your advantage, engage in the affair. You must conform to rules, submit to a diet, refrain from dainties; exercise your body, whether you choose it or not, at a stated hour, in heat and cold; you must drink no cold water, nor sometimes even wine. In a word, you must give yourself up to your master, as to a physician. Then, in the combat, you may be thrown into a ditch, dislocate your arm, turn your ankle, swallow dust, be whipped, and, after all, lose the victory. When you have evaluated all this, if your inclination still holds, then go to war. Otherwise, take notice, you will behave like children who sometimes play like wrestlers, sometimes gladiators, sometimes blow a trumpet, and sometimes act a tragedy when they have seen and admired these shows. Thus you too will be at one time a wrestler, at another a gladiator, now a philosopher, then an orator; but with your whole soul, nothing at all. Like an ape, you mimic all you see, and one thing after another is sure to please you, but is out of favor as soon as it becomes familiar. For you have never entered upon anything considerately, nor after having viewed the whole matter on all sides, or made any scrutiny into it, but rashly, and with a cold inclination. Thus some, when they have seen a philosopher and heard a man speaking like Euphrates (though, indeed, who can speak like him?), have a mind to be philosophers too. Consider first, man, what the matter is, and what your own nature is able to bear. If you would be a wrestler, consider your shoulders, your back, = your thighs; for different persons are made for different things. Do you think that you can act as you do, and be a philosopher? That you can eat and drink, and be angry and discontented as you are now? You must watch, you must labor, you must get the better of certain appetites, must quit your acquaintance, be despised by your servant, be laughed at by those you meet; come off worse than others in everything, in magistracies, in honors, in courts of judicature. When you have considered all these things round, approach, if you please; if, by parting with them, you have a mind to purchase apathy, freedom, and tranquility. If not, don't come here; don't, like children, be one while a philosopher, then a publican, then an orator, and then one of Caesar's officers. These things are not consistent. You must be one man, either good or bad. You must cultivate either your own ruling faculty or externals, and apply yourself either to things within or without you; that is, be either a philosopher, or one of the vulgar.

30.

Duties are universally measured by relations. Is anyone a father? If so, it is implied that the children should take care of him, submit to him in everything, patiently listen to his reproaches, his correction. But he is a bad father. Is you naturally entitled, then, to a good father? No, only to a father. Is a brother unjust? Well, keep your own situation towards him. Consider not what he does, but what you are to do to keep your own faculty of choice in a state conformable to nature. For another will not hurt you unless you please. You will then be hurt when you think you are hurt. In this manner, therefore, you will find, from the idea of a neighbor, a citizen, a general, the corresponding duties if you accustom yourself to contemplate the several relations.

31.

Be assured that the essential property of piety towards the gods is to form right opinions concerning them, as existing "I and as governing the universe with goodness and justice. And fix yourself in this resolution, to obey them, and yield to them, and willingly follow them in all events, as produced by the most perfect understanding. For thus you will never find fault with the gods, nor accuse them as neglecting you. And it is not possible for this to be effected any other way than by withdrawing yourself from things not in our own control, and placing good or evil in those only which are. For if you suppose any of the things not in our own control to be either good or evil, when you are disappointed of what you wish, or incur what you would avoid, you must necessarily find fault with and blame the authors. For every animal is naturally formed to fly and abhor things that appear hurtful, and the causes of them; and to pursue and admire those which appear beneficial, and the causes of them. It is impractical, then, that one who supposes himself to be hurt should be happy about the person who, he thinks, hurts him, just as it is impossible to be happy about the hurt itself.

Hence, also, a father is reviled by a son, when he does not impart to him the things which he takes to be good; and the supposing empire to be a good made Polynices and Eteocles mutually enemies. On this account the husbandman, the sailor, the merchant, on this account those who lose wives and children, revile the gods.

For where interest is, there too is piety placed. So that, whoever is careful to regulate his desires and aversions as he ought, is, by the very same means, careful of piety likewise. But it is also incumbent on everyone to offer libations and sacrifices and first fruits, conformably to the customs of his country, with purity, and not in a slovenly manner, nor negligently, nor sparingly, nor beyond his ability.

32.

When you have recourse to divination, remember that you know not what the event will be, and you come to learn it of the diviner; but of what nature it is you know before you come, at least if you are a philosopher. For if it is among the things not in our own control, it can by no means be either good or evil. Don't, therefore, bring either desire or aversion with you to the diviner (else you will approach him trembling), but first acquire a distinct knowledge that every event is indifferent and nothing to you, of whatever sort it may be, for it will be in your power to make a right use of it, and this no one can hinder; then come with confidence to the gods, as your counselors, and afterwards, when any counsel is given you, remember what counselors you have assumed, and whose advice you will neglect if you disobey. Come to divination, as Socrates prescribed, in cases of which the whole consideration relates to the event, and in which no opportunities are afforded by reason, or any other art, to discover the thing proposed to be learned. When, therefore, it is our duty to share the danger of a friend or of our country, we ought not to consult the oracle whether we will share it with them or not. For, though the diviner should forewarn you that the victims are unfavorable, this means no more than that either death or mutilation or exile is portended. But we have reason within us, and it directs, even with these hazards, to the greater diviner, the Pythian god, who cast out of the temple the person who gave no assistance to his friend while another was murdering him.

33.

Immediately prescribe some character and form of conduct to yourself, which you may keep both alone and in company.

Be for the most part silent, or speak merely what is necessary, and in few words. We may, however, enter, though sparingly, into discourse sometimes when occasion calls for it, but not on any of the common subjects, of gladiators, or horse races, or athletic champions, or feasts, the vulgar topics of conversation; but principally not of men, so as either to blame, or praise, or make comparisons. If you are able, then, by your own conversation bring over that of your company to proper subjects; but, if you happen to be taken among strangers, be silent.

Don't allow your laughter be much, nor on many occasions, nor profuse.

Avoid swearing, if possible, altogether; if not, as far as you are able.

Avoid public and vulgar entertainments; but, if ever an occasion calls you to them, keep your attention upon the stretch, that you may not imperceptibly slide into vulgar manners. For be assured that if a person be ever so sound himself, yet, if his companion be infected, he who converses with him will be infected likewise.

Provide things relating to the body no further than mere use; as meat, drink, clothing, house, family. But strike off and reject everything relating to show and delicacy.

As far as possible, before marriage, keep yourself pure from familiarities with women, and, if you indulge them, let it be lawfully." But don't therefore be troublesome and full of reproofs to those who use these liberties, nor frequently boast that you yourself don't.

If anyone tells you that such a person speaks ill of you, don't make excuses about what is said of you, but answer: "He does not know my other faults, else he would not have mentioned only these."

It is not necessary for you to appear often at public spectacles; but if ever there is a proper occasion for you to be there, don't appear more solicitous for anyone than for yourself; that is, wish things to be only just as they are, and him only to conquer who is the conqueror, for thus you will meet with no hindrance. But abstain entirely from declamations and derision and violent emotions. And when you come away, don't discourse a great deal on what has passed, and what does not contribute to your own amendment. For it would appear by such discourse that you were immoderately struck with the show.

Go not of your own accord to the rehearsals of any authors, nor appear at them readily. But, if you do appear, keep your gravity and sedateness, and at the same time avoid being morose.

When you are going to confer with anyone, and particularly of those in a superior station, represent to yourself how Socrates or Zeno would behave in such a case, and you will not be at a loss to make a proper use of whatever may occur.

When you are going to any of the people in power, represent to yourself that you will not find him at home; that you will not be admitted; that the doors will not be opened to you; that he will take no notice of you. If, with all this, it is your duty to go, bear what happens, and never say to yourself, "It was not worth so much." For this is vulgar, and like a man dazed by external things.

In parties of conversation, avoid a frequent and excessive mention of your own actions and dangers. For, however agreeable it may be to yourself to mention the risks you have run, it is not equally agreeable to others to hear your adventures. Avoid, likewise, an endeavor to excite laughter. For this is a slippery point, which may throw you into vulgar manners, and, besides, may be apt to lessen you in the esteem of your acquaintance. Approaches to indecent discourse are likewise dangerous. Whenever, therefore, anything of this sort happens, if there be a proper opportunity, rebuke him who makes advances that way; or, at least, by silence and blushing and a forbidding look, show yourself to be displeased by such talk.

34.

If you are struck by the appearance of any promised pleasure, guard yourself against being hurried away by it; but let the affair wait your leisure, and procure yourself some delay. Then bring to your mind both points of time: that in which you will enjoy the pleasure, and that in which you will repent and reproach yourself after you have enjoyed it; and set before you, in opposition to these, how you will be glad and applaud yourself if you abstain. And even though it should appear to you a seasonable gratification, take heed that its enticing, and agreeable and attractive force may not subdue you; but set in opposition to this how much better it is to be conscious of having gained so great a victory.

35.

When you do anything from a clear judgment that it ought to be done, never shun the being seen to do it, even though the world should make a wrong supposition about it; for, if you don't act right, shun the action itself; but, if you do, why are you afraid of those who censure you wrongly?

36.

As the proposition, "Either it is day or it is night," is extremely proper for a disjunctive argument, but quite improper in a conjunctive one, so, at a feast, to choose the largest share is very suitable to the bodily appetite, but utterly inconsistent with the social spirit of an entertainment. When you eat with another, then, remember not only the value of those things which are set before you to the body, but the value of that behavior which ought to be observed towards the person who gives the entertainment.

37.

If you have assumed any character above your strength, you have both made an ill figure in that and quitted one which you might have supported.

38.

When walking, you are careful not to step on a nail or turn your foot; so likewise be careful not to hurt the ruling faculty of your mind. And, if we were to guard against this in every action, we should undertake the action with the greater safety.

39.

The body is to everyone the measure of the possessions proper for it, just as the foot is of the shoe. If, therefore, you stop at this, you will keep the measure; but if you move beyond it, you must necessarily be carried forward, as down a cliff; as in the case of a shoe, if you go beyond its fitness to the foot, it comes first to be gilded, then purple, and then studded with jewels. For to that which once exceeds a due measure, there is no bound.

40.

Women from the time they are teenagers are flattered with the title of "mistresses" by the men. Therefore, perceiving that they are regarded only as qualified to give the men pleasure, they begin to adorn themselves, and in that to place ill their hopes. We should, therefore, fix our attention on making them sensible that they are valued for the appearance of decent, modest and discreet behavior.

41.

It is a mark of want of genius to spend much time in things relating to the body, as to be long in our exercises, in eating and drinking, and in the discharge of other animal functions. These should be done incidentally and slightly, and our whole attention be engaged in the care of the understanding.

42.

When any person harms you, or speaks badly of you, remember that he acts or speaks from a supposition of its being his duty. Now, it is not possible that he should follow what appears right to you, but what appears so to himself. Therefore, if he judges from a wrong appearance, he is the person hurt, since he too is the person deceived.

For if anyone should suppose a true proposition to be false, the proposition is not hurt, but he who is deceived about it. Setting out, then, from these principles, you will meekly bear a person who reviles you, for you will say upon every occasion, "It seemed so to him."

43.

Everything has two handles, the one by which it may be carried, the other by which it cannot. If your brother acts unjustly, don't lay hold on the action by the handle of his injustice, for by that it cannot be carried; but by the opposite, that he is your brother, that he was brought up with you; and thus you will lay hold on it, as it is to be carried.

44.

These reasonings are unconnected: "I am richer than you, therefore I am better"; "I am more eloquent than you, therefore I am better."

The connection is rather this: "I am richer than you, therefore my property is greater than yours;" "I am more eloquent than you, therefore my style is better than yours." But you, after all, are neither your property nor your style.

45.

Does anyone bathe in a mighty little time? Don't say that he does it ill, but in a mighty little time. Does anyone drink a great quantity of wine? Don't say that he does ill, but that he drinks a great quantity. For, unless you perfectly understand the principle from which anyone acts, how should you know if he acts ill? Thus you will not run the hazard of assenting to any appearances but such as you fully comprehend.

46.

Never call yourself a philosopher, nor talk a great deal among the unlearned about theorems, but act conformably to them. Thus, at a feast, don't talk how persons ought to eat, but eat as you ought. For remember that in this manner Socrates also universally avoided all ostentation. And when persons came to him and desired to be recommended by him to philosophers, he took and recommended them, so well did he bear being overlooked. So that if ever any talk should happen among the unlearned concerning philosophic theorems, be you, for the most part, silent. For there is great danger in immediately throwing out what you have not digested. And, if anyone tells you that you know nothing, and you are not nettled at it, then you may be sure that you have begun your business. For sheep don't throw up the grass to show the shepherds how much they have eaten; but, inwardly digesting their food, they outwardly produce wool and milk. Thus, therefore, do you likewise not show theorems to the unlearned, but the actions produced by them after they have been digested.

47.

When you have brought yourself to supply the necessities of your body at a small price, don't pique yourself upon it; nor, if you drink water, be saying upon every occasion, "I drink water." But first consider how much more sparing and patient of hardship the poor are than we. But if at any time you would inure yourself by exercise to labor, and bearing hard trials, do it for your own sake, and not for the world; don't grasp statues, but, when you are violently thirsty, take a little cold water in your mouth, and spurt it out and tell nobody.

48.

The condition and characteristic of a vulgar person, is, that he never expects either benefit or hurt from himself, but from externals. The condition and characteristic of a philosopher is, that he expects all hurt and benefit from himself. The marks of a proficient person are, that he censures no one, praises no one, blames no one, accuses no one, says nothing concerning himself as being anybody, or knowing anything: when he is, in any instance, hindered or restrained, he accuses himself; and, if he is praised, he secretly laughs at the person who praises him; and, if he is censured, he makes no defense.

But he goes about with the caution of sick or injured people, dreading to move anything that is set right, before it is perfectly fixed. He suppresses all desire in himself; he transfers his aversion to those things only which thwart the proper use of our own faculty of choice; the exertion of his active powers towards anything is very gentle; if he appears stupid or ignorant, he does not care, and, in a word, he watches himself as an enemy, and one in ambush.

49.

When anyone shows himself overly confident in ability to understand and interpret the works of Chrysippus, say to yourself, "Unless Chrysippus had written obscurely, this person would have had no subject for his vanity. But what do I desire? To understand nature and follow her. I ask, then, who interprets her, and, finding Chrysippus does, I have recourse to him. I don't understand his writings. I seek, therefore, one to interpret them." So far there is nothing to value myself upon.

And when I find an interpreter, what remains is to make use of his instructions. This alone is the valuable thing. But, if I admire nothing but merely the interpretation, what do I become more than a grammarian instead of a philosopher? Except, indeed, that instead of Homer I interpret Chrysippus. When anyone, therefore, desires me to read Chrysippus to him, I rather blush when I cannot show my actions agreeable and consonant to his discourse.

50.

Whatever moral rules you have deliberately proposed to yourself, abide by them as if they were laws, and as if you would be guilty of impiety by violating any of them. Don't regard what anyone says of you, for this, after all, is no concern of yours. How long, then, will you put off thinking yourself worthy of the highest improvements and follow the distinctions of reason? You have received the philosophical theorems, with which you ought to be familiar, and you have been familiar with them. What other master, then, do you wait for, to throw upon that the delay of reforming yourself? You are no longer a child, but a grown person. If, therefore, you will be negligent and slothful, and always add procrastination to procrastination, purpose to purpose, and fix day after day in which you will attend to yourself, you will insensibly continue without proficiency, and, living and dying, persevere in being one of the vulgar. This instant, then, think yourself worthy of living as a man grown up, and proficient. Let whatever appears to be the best be to you an inviolable law. And if any instance of pain or pleasure, or glory or disgrace, is set before you, remember that now is the combat, now the Olympiad comes on, nor can it be put off. By once being defeated and giving way, proficiency is lost, or by the contrary preserved. Thus was Socrates perfected, improving himself by everything, attending to nothing but reason. And though you are not yet a Socrates, you should live as one who desires to become a Socrates.

51.

The first and most necessary topic in philosophy is that of the use of moral theorems, such as, "We ought not to lie;" the second is that of demonstrations, such as, "What is the origin of our obligation not to lie;" the third gives strength and articulation to the other two, such as, "What is the origin of this is a demonstration." For what is demonstration? What is consequence? What contradiction? What truth? What falsehood? The third topic, then, is necessary on the account of the second, and the second on the account of the first.

But the most necessary, and that whereon we ought to rest, is the first. But we actually act on the contrary. For we spend all our time on the third topic, and employ all our diligence about that, and entirely neglect the first. Therefore, at the same time that we lie, we are immediately prepared to show how it is demonstrated that lying is not right.

52.

Upon all occasions we ought to have these maxims ready at hand:

"Conduct me, Jove, and you, O Destiny,
Wherever your decrees have fixed my station."
(Cleanthes)

"I follow cheerfully; and, did I not,
Wicked and miserable, I must follow still
Whoever yields properly to Fate, is deemed
Wise among men, and knows the laws of heaven."
(Euripides, Frag. 965)

And this third:

"O Crito, if it thus pleases the gods, thus let it be. Anytus and Meletus may kill me indeed, but hurt me they cannot."
(Plato's Crito and Apology)

[*Enchiridion*. Translated by Elizabeth Carter, 1759.]

Letter to Menoeceus

Epicurus

EPICURUS TO MENOECEUS, GREETINGS:

Let no one be slow to seek wisdom when he is young nor weary in the search of it when he has grown old. For no age is too early or too late for the health of the soul. And to say that the season for studying philosophy has not yet come, or that it is past and gone, is like saying that the season for happiness is not yet or that it is now no more. Therefore, both old and young alike ought to seek wisdom, the former in order that, as age comes over him, he may be young in good things because of the grace of what has been, and the latter in order that, while he is young, he may at the same time be old, because he has no fear of the things which are to come. So we must exercise ourselves in the things which bring happiness, since, if that be present, we have everything, and, if that be absent, all our actions are directed towards attaining it.

Those things which without ceasing I have declared unto you, do them, and exercise yourself in them, holding them to be the elements of right life. First believe that God is a living being immortal and blessed, according to the notion of a god indicated by the common sense of mankind; and so believing, you shall not affirm of him anything that is foreign to his immortality or that is repugnant to his blessedness. Believe about him whatever may uphold both his blessedness and his immortality. For there are gods, and the knowledge of them is manifest; but they are not such as the multitude believe, seeing that men do not steadfastly maintain the notions they form respecting them. Not the man who denies the gods worshipped by the multitude, but he who affirms of the gods what the multitude believes about them is truly impious. For the utterances of the multitude about the gods are not true preconceptions but false assumptions; hence it is that the greatest evils happen to the wicked and the greatest blessings happen to the good from the hand of the gods, seeing that they are always favorable to their own good qualities and take pleasure in men like themselves, but reject as alien whatever is not of their kind.

Accustom yourself to believing that death is nothing to us, for good and evil imply the capacity for sensation, and death is the privation of all sentience; therefore a correct understanding that death is nothing to us makes the mortality of life enjoyable, not by adding to life a limitless time, but by taking away the yearning after immortality. For life has no terrors for him who has thoroughly understood that there are no terrors for him in ceasing to live. Foolish, therefore, is the man who says that he fears death, not because it will pain when it comes, but because it pains in the prospect. Whatever causes no annoyance when it is present, causes only a groundless pain in the expectation. Death, therefore, the most awful of evils, is nothing to us, seeing that, when we are, death is not come, and, when death is come, we are not. It is nothing, then, either to the living or to the dead, for with the living it is not and the dead exist no longer.

But in the world, at one time men shun death as the greatest of all evils, and at another time choose it as a respite from the evils in life. The wise man does not deprecate life nor does he fear the cessation of life. The thought of life is no offense to him, nor is the cessation of life regarded as an evil. And even as men choose of food not merely and simply the larger portion, but the more pleasant, so the wise seek to enjoy the time which is most pleasant and not merely that which is longest. And he who admonishes the young to live well and the old to make a good end speaks foolishly, not merely because of the desirability of life, but because the same exercise at once teaches to live well and to die well. Much worse is he who says that it were good not to be born, but when once one is born to pass quickly through the gates of Hades. For if he truly believes this, why does he not depart from life? It would be easy for him to do so once he were firmly convinced. If he speaks only in jest, his words are foolishness as those who hear him do not believe.

We must remember that the future is neither wholly ours nor wholly not ours, so that neither must we count upon it as quite certain to come nor despair of it as quite certain not to come.

We must also reflect that of desires some are natural, others are groundless; and that of the natural some are necessary as well as natural, and some natural only. And of the necessary desires some are necessary if we are to be happy, some if the body is to be rid of uneasiness, some if we are even to live. He who has a clear and certain understanding of these things will direct every preference and aversion toward securing health of body and tranquility of mind, seeing that this is the sum and end of a blessed life. For the end of all our actions is to be free from pain and fear, and, when once we have attained all this, the tempest of the soul is laid; seeing that the living creature has no need to go in search of something that is lacking, nor to look for anything else by which the good of the soul and of the body will be fulfilled. When we are pained because of the absence of pleasure, then, and then only, do we feel the need of pleasure. Wherefore we call pleasure the alpha and omega of a blessed life. Pleasure is our first and kindred good. It is the starting-point of every choice and of every aversion, and to it we come back, inasmuch as we make feeling the rule by which to judge of every good thing.

And since pleasure is our first and native good, for that reason we do not choose every pleasure whatsoever, but will often pass over many pleasures when a greater annoyance ensues from them. And often we consider pains superior to pleasures when submission to the pains for a long time brings us as a consequence a greater pleasure. While therefore all pleasure because it is naturally akin to us is good, not all pleasure is should be chosen, just as all pain is an evil and yet not all pain is to be shunned. It is, however, by measuring one against another, and by looking at the conveniences and inconveniences, that all these matters must be judged. Sometimes we treat the good as an evil, and the evil, on the contrary, as a good.

Again, we regard independence of outward things as a great good, not so as in all cases to use little, but so as to be contented with little if we have not much, being honestly persuaded that they have the sweetest enjoyment of luxury who stand least in need of it, and that whatever is natural is easily procured and only the vain and worthless hard to win. Plain fare gives as much pleasure as a costly diet, when once the pain of want has been removed, while bread and water confer the highest possible pleasure when they are brought to hungry lips. To habituate one's self, therefore, to simple and inexpensive diet supplies all that is needful for health, and enables a man to meet the necessary requirements of life without shrinking, and it places us in a better condition when we approach at intervals a costly fare and renders us fearless of fortune.

When we say, then, that pleasure is the end and aim, we do not mean the pleasures of the prodigal or the pleasures of sensuality, as we are understood to do by some through ignorance, prejudice, or willful misrepresentation. By pleasure we mean the absence of pain in the body and of trouble in the soul. It is not an unbroken succession of drinking-bouts and of revelry, not sexual lust, not the enjoyment of the fish and other delicacies of a luxurious table, which produce a pleasant life; it is sober reasoning, searching out the grounds of every choice and avoidance, and banishing those beliefs through which the greatest tumults take possession of the soul. Of all this the beginning and the greatest good is wisdom. Therefore wisdom is a more precious thing even than philosophy; from it spring all the other virtues, for it teaches that we cannot live pleasantly without living wisely, honorably, and justly; nor live wisely, honorably, and justly without living pleasantly. For the virtues have grown into one with a pleasant life, and a pleasant life is inseparable from them.

Who, then, is superior in your judgment to such a man? He holds a holy belief concerning the gods, and is altogether free from the fear of death. He has diligently considered the end fixed by nature, and understands how easily the limit of good things can be reached and attained, and how either the duration or the intensity of evils is but slight. Fate, which some introduce as sovereign over all things, he scorns, affirming rather that some things happen of necessity, others by chance, others through our own agency. For he sees that necessity destroys responsibility and that chance is inconstant; whereas our own actions are autonomous, and it is to them that praise and blame naturally attach. It were better, indeed, to accept the legends of the gods than to bow beneath that yoke of destiny which the natural philosophers have imposed. The one holds out some faint hope that we may escape if we honor the gods, while the necessity of the naturalists is deaf to all entreaties. Nor does he hold chance to be a god, as the world in general does, for in the acts of a god there is no disorder; nor to be a cause, though an uncertain one, for he believes that no good or evil is dispensed by chance to men so as to make life blessed, though it supplies the starting-point of great good and great evil. He believes that the misfortune of the wise is better than the prosperity of the fool. It is better, in short, that what is well judged in action should not owe its successful issue to the aid of chance.

Exercise yourself in these and related precepts day and night, both by yourself and with one who is like-minded; then never, either in waking or in dream, will you be disturbed, but will live as a god among men. For man loses all semblance of mortality by living in the midst of immortal blessings.

Letter to Menoeceus. Translated by R. D. Hicks. (Charles Scribner's Sons, New York: 1910).

Principle Doctrines

Epicurus

1.

A blessed and indestructible being has no trouble himself and brings no trouble upon any other being; so he is free from anger and partiality, for all such things imply weakness.

2.

Death is nothing to us; for that which has been dissolved into its elements experiences no sensations, and that which has no sensation is nothing to us.

3.

The magnitude of pleasure reaches its limit in the removal of all pain. When such pleasure is present, so long as it is uninterrupted, there is no pain either of body or of mind or of both together.

4.

Continuous bodily pain does not last long; instead, pain, if extreme, is present a very short time, and even that degree of pain which slightly exceeds bodily pleasure does not last for many days at once. Diseases of long duration allow an excess of bodily pleasure over pain.

5.

It is impossible to live a pleasant life without living wisely and honorably and justly, and it is impossible to live wisely and honorably and justly without living pleasantly. Whenever any one of these is lacking, when, for instance, the man is not able to live wisely, though he lives honorably and justly, it is impossible for him to live a pleasant life.

6.

In order to obtain protection from other men, any means for attaining this end is a natural good.

7.

Some men want fame and status, thinking that they would thus make themselves secure against other men. If the life of such men really were secure, they have attained a natural good; if, however, it is insecure, they have not attained the end which by nature's own prompting they originally sought.

8.

No pleasure is a bad thing in itself, but the things which produce certain pleasures entail disturbances many times greater than the pleasures themselves.

9.

If every pleasure had been capable of accumulation, not only over time but also over the entire body or at least over the principal parts of our nature, then pleasures would never differ from one another.

10.

If the things that produce the pleasures of profligate men really freed them from fears of the mind concerning celestial and atmospheric phenomena, the fear of death, and the fear of pain; if, further, they taught them to limit their desires, we should never have any fault to find with such persons, for they would then be filled with pleasures from every source and would never have pain of body or mind, which is what is bad.

11.

If we had never been troubled by celestial and atmospheric phenomena, nor by fears about death, nor by our ignorance of the limits of pains and desires, we should have had no need of natural science.

12.

It is impossible for someone to dispel his fears about the most important matters if he doesn't know the nature of the universe but still gives some credence to myths. So without the study of nature there is no enjoyment of pure pleasure.

13.

There is no advantage to obtaining protection from other men so long as we are alarmed by events above or below the earth or in general by whatever happens in the boundless universe.

14.

Protection from other men, secured to some extent by the power to expel and by material prosperity, in its purest form comes from a quiet life withdrawn from the multitude.

15.

The wealth required by nature is limited and is easy to procure; but the wealth required by vain ideals extends to infinity.

16.

Chance seldom interferes with the wise man; his greatest and highest interests have been, are, and will be, directed by reason throughout his whole life.

17.

The just man is most free from disturbance, while the unjust is full of the utmost disturbance.

18.

Bodily pleasure does not increase when the pain of want has been removed; after that it only admits of variation. The limit of mental pleasure, however, is reached when we reflect on these bodily pleasures and their related emotions, which used to cause the mind the greatest alarms.

19.

Unlimited time and limited time afford an equal amount of pleasure, if we measure the limits of that pleasure by reason.

20.

The flesh receives as unlimited the limits of pleasure; and to provide it requires unlimited time. But the mind, intellectually grasping what the end and limit of the flesh is, and banishing the terrors of the future, procures a complete and perfect life, and we have no longer any need of unlimited time. Nevertheless the mind does not shun pleasure, and even when circumstances make death imminent, the mind does not lack enjoyment of the best life.

21.

He who understands the limits of life knows that it is easy to obtain that which removes the pain of want and makes the whole of life complete and perfect. Thus he has no longer any need of things which involve struggle.

22.

We must consider both the ultimate end and all clear sensory evidence, to which we refer our opinions; for otherwise everything will be full of uncertainty and confusion.

23.

If you fight against all your sensations, you will have no standard to which to refer, and thus no means of judging even those sensations which you claim are false.

24.

If you reject absolutely any single sensation without stopping to distinguish between opinion about things awaiting confirmation and that which is already confirmed to be present, whether in sensation or in feelings or in any application of intellect to the presentations, you will confuse the rest of your sensations by your groundless opinion and so you will reject every standard of truth. If in your ideas based upon opinion you hastily affirm as true all that awaits confirmation as well as that which does not, you will not avoid error, as you will be maintaining the entire basis for doubt in every judgment between correct and incorrect opinion.

25.

If you do not on every occasion refer each of your actions to the ultimate end prescribed by nature, but instead of this in the act of choice or avoidance turn to some other end, your actions will not be consistent with your theories.

26.

All desires that do not lead to pain when they remain unsatisfied are unnecessary, but the desire is easily got rid of, when the thing desired is difficult to obtain or the desires seem likely to produce harm.

27.

Of all the means which wisdom acquires to ensure happiness throughout the whole of life, by far the most important is friendship.

28.

The same conviction which inspires confidence that nothing we have to fear is eternal or even of long duration, also enables us to see that in the limited evils of this life nothing enhances our security so much as friendship.

29.

Of our desires some are natural and necessary, others are natural but not necessary; and others are neither natural nor necessary, but are due to groundless opinion.

30.

Those natural desires which entail no pain when unsatisfied, though pursued with an intense effort, are also due to groundless opinion; and it is not because of their own nature they are not got rid of but because of man's groundless opinions.

31.

Natural justice is a pledge of reciprocal benefit, to prevent one man from harming or being harmed by another.

32.
Those animals which are incapable of making binding agreements with one another not to inflict nor suffer harm are without either justice or injustice; and likewise for those peoples who either could not or would not form binding agreements not to inflict nor suffer harm.

33.
There never was such a thing as absolute justice, but only agreements made in mutual dealings among men in whatever places at various times providing against the infliction or suffering of harm.

34.
Injustice is not an evil in itself, but only in consequence of the fear which is associated with the apprehension of being discovered by those appointed to punish such actions.

35.
It is impossible for a man who secretly violates the terms of the agreement not to harm or be harmed to feel confident that he will remain undiscovered, even if he has already escaped ten thousand times; for until his death he is never sure that he will not be detected.

36.
In general justice is the same for all, for it is something found mutually beneficial in men's dealings, but in its application to particular places or other circumstances the same thing is not necessarily just for everyone.

37.
Among the things held to be just by law, whatever is proved to be of advantage in men's dealings has the stamp of justice, whether or not it be the same for all; but if a man makes a law and it does not prove to be mutually advantageous, then this is no longer just. And if what is mutually advantageous varies and only for a time corresponds to our concept of justice, nevertheless for that time it is just for those who do not trouble themselves about empty words, but look simply at the facts.

38.
Where without any change in circumstances the things held to be just by law are seen not to correspond with the concept of justice in actual practice, such laws are not really just; but wherever the laws have ceased to be advantageous because of a change in circumstances, in that case the laws were for that time just when they were advantageous for the mutual dealings of the citizens, and subsequently ceased to be just when they were no longer advantageous.

39.
The man who best knows how to meet external threats makes into one family all the creatures he can; and those he can not, he at any rate does not treat as aliens; and where he finds even this impossible, he avoids all dealings, and, so far as is advantageous, excludes them from his life.

40.
Those who possess the power to defend themselves against threats by their neighbors, being thus in possession of the surest guarantee of security, live the most pleasant life with one another; and their enjoyment of the fullest intimacy is such that if one of them dies prematurely, the others do not lament his death as though it called for pity.

Translated by R. D. Hicks. (Charles Scribner's Sons, New York: 1910).

Key Terms and Concepts

Stoicism
logos
nomos
pathos
ataraxia
apatheia
eupatheia
fate
Stoic control
"externals"
Epicureanism
Hedonism
natural and necessary desires
natural but unnecessary desires
unnatural and unnecessary desires
aponia
the *Tetrapharmakos*
atoms and the void

Questions for Further Reflection

1. How and why does Epictetus distinguish between the things we can control and the things that we cannot?
2. What do Stoics means by the term "externals" and how is this related to Stoic practice more generally?
3. In what sense is Epicureanism a form of philosophical hedonism? In what way does it differ from popular or "vulgar" conceptions of hedonism as mindless self-indulgence?
4. What are the four elements of the *Tetrapharmakos* in Epicureanism?
5. In what way is Epicurus's materialism (i.e., his atomism) consistent with his ethical teachings?
6. Compare and contrast Stoicism and Epicureanism on the topics of death and pleasure. Where do they agree? Where do they disagree? With whom do you tend to agree and why?

Homework Assignment #5b

Name: ______________________________ Section: ______________________________

Evaluate Epictetus's claim: "Don't demand that things happen as you wish, but wish that they happen as they do happen, and you will live well." Do you agree with this claim? Why or why not?

Homework Assignment #5c

Name: ______________________________ Section: ______________________________

Evaluate Epictetus's claim: "Let death and exile, and all other things which appear terrible, be daily before your eyes, but chiefly death, and you win never entertain any abject thought, nor too eagerly covet anything." Do you agree with this claim? Why or why not?

Homework Assignment #5d

Name: ________________________________ Section: ________________________________

Compare and *contrast* Stoicism and Epicureanism on the topics of pleasure and death.

CHAPTER SIX

Bentham and Mill on Utility, Happiness, and Morality

© Georgios Kollidas/Shutterstock.com

Jeremy Bentham (1748–1832)

Courtesy of Library of Congress

John Stuart Mill (1806–1873)

SELECTED READINGS

- *An Introduction to the Principles of Morality and Legislation*—Jeremy Bentham
- *Utilitarianism*—John Stuart Mill

An Introduction to the Principles of Morality and Legislation

Jeremy Bentham

CHAPTER I: OF THE PRINCIPLE OF UTILITY

I.1

I. Nature has placed mankind under the governance of two sovereign masters, pain and pleasure. It is for them alone to point out what we ought to do, as well as to determine what we shall do. On the one hand the standard of right and wrong, on the other the chain of causes and effects, are fastened to their throne. They govern us in all we do, in all we say, in all we think: every effort we can make to throw off our subjection, will serve but to demonstrate and confirm it. In words a man may pretend to abjure their empire: but in reality he will remain subject to it all the while. The principle of utility recognizes this subjection, and assumes it for the foundation of that system, the object of which is to rear the fabric of felicity by the hands of reason and of law. Systems which attempt to question it, deal in sounds instead of sense, in caprice instead of reason, in darkness instead of light.

I.2

But enough of metaphor and declamation: it is not by such means that moral science is to be improved.

I.3

II. The principle of utility is the foundation of the present work: it will be proper therefore at the outset to give an explicit and determinate account of what is meant by it. By the principle of utility is meant that principle which approves or disapproves of every action whatsoever, according to the tendency it appears to have to augment or diminish the happiness of the party whose interest is in question: or, what is the same thing in other words, to promote or to oppose that happiness. I say of every action whatsoever, and therefore not only of every action of a private individual, but of every measure of government.

I.4

III. By utility is meant that property in any object, whereby it tends to produce benefit, advantage, pleasure, good, or happiness, (all this in the present case comes to the same thing) or (what comes again to the same thing) to prevent the happening of mischief, pain, evil, or unhappiness to the party whose interest is considered: if that party be the community in general, then the happiness of the community: if a particular individual, then the happiness of that individual.

I.5

IV. The interest of the community is one of the most general expressions that can occur in the phraseology of morals: no wonder that the meaning of it is often lost. When it has a meaning, it is this. The community is a fictitious body, composed of the individual persons who are considered as constituting as it were its members. The interest of the community then is, what?—the sum of the interests of the several members who compose it.

I.6

V. It is in vain to talk of the interest of the community, without understanding what is the interest of the individual. A thing is said to promote the interest, or to be for the interest, of an individual, when it tends to add to the sum total of his pleasures: or, what comes to the same thing, to diminish the sum total of his pains.

I.7

VI. An action then may be said to be conformable to the principle of utility, or, for shortness sake, to utility, (meaning with respect to the community at large) when the tendency it has to augment the happiness of the community is greater than any it has to diminish it.

I.8

VII. A measure of government (which is but a particular kind of action, performed by a particular person or persons) may be said to be conformable to or dictated by the principle of utility, when in like manner the tendency which it has to augment the happiness of the community is greater than any which it has to diminish it.

I.9

VIII. When an action, or in particular a measure of government, is supposed by a man to be conformable to the principle of utility, it may be convenient, for the purposes of discourse, to imagine a kind of law or dictate, called a law or dictate of utility: and to speak of the action in question, as being conformable to such law or dictate.

I.10

IX. A man may be said to be a partisan of the principle of utility, when the approbation or disapprobation he annexes to any action, or to any measure, is determined by and proportioned to the tendency which he conceives it to have to augment or to diminish the happiness of the community: or in other words, to its conformity or unconformity to the laws or dictates of utility.

I.11

X. Of an action that is conformable to the principle of utility one may always say either that it is one that ought to be done, or at least that it is not one that ought not to be done. One may say also, that it is right it should be done; at least that it is not wrong it should be done: that it is a right action; at least that it is not a wrong action. When thus interpreted, the words ought, and right and wrong and others of that stamp, have a meaning: when otherwise, they have none.

I.12

XI. Has the rectitude of this principle been ever formally contested? It should seem that it had, by those who have not known what they have been meaning. Is it susceptible of any direct proof? It should seem not: for that which is used to prove everything else, cannot itself be proved: a chain of proofs must have their commencement somewhere. To give such proof is as impossible as it is needless.

I.13

XII. Not that there is or ever has been that human creature at breathing, however stupid or perverse, who has not on many, perhaps on most occasions of his life, deferred to it. By the natural constitution of the human frame, on most occasions of their lives men in general embrace this principle, without thinking of it: if not for the ordering of their own actions, yet for the trying of their own actions, as well as of those of other men. There have been, at the same time, not many perhaps, even of the most intelligent, who have been disposed to embrace it purely and without reserve. There are even few who have not taken some occasion or other to quarrel with it, either on account of their not understanding always how to apply it, or on account of some prejudice or other which they were afraid to examine into, or could not bear to part with. For such is the stuff that man is made of: in principle and in practice, in a right track and in a wrong one, the rarest of all human qualities is consistency.

I.14

XIII. When a man attempts to combat the principle of utility, it is with reasons drawn, without his being aware of it, from that very principle itself. His arguments, if they prove anything, prove not that the principle is wrong, but that, according to the applications he supposes to be made of it, it is misapplied. Is it possible for a man to move the earth? Yes; but he must first find out another earth to stand upon.

CHAPTER II: OF PRINCIPLES ADVERSE TO THAT OF UTILITY

II.1

I. If the principle of utility be a right principle to be governed by, and that in all cases, it follows from what has been just observed, that whatever principle differs from it in any case must necessarily be a wrong one. To prove any other principle, therefore, to be a wrong one, there needs no more than just to show it to be what it is, a principle of which the dictates are in some point or other different from those of the principle of utility: to state it is to confute it.

II.2

II. A principle may be different from that of utility in two ways: 1. By being constantly opposed to it: this is the case with a principle which may be termed the principle of asceticism. 2. By being sometimes opposed to it, and sometimes not, as it may happen: this is the case with another, which may be termed the principle of sympathy and antipathy.

II.3

III. By the principle of asceticism I mean that principle, which, like the principle of utility, approves or disapproves of any action, according to the tendency which it appears to have to augment or diminish the happiness of the party whose interest is in question; but in an inverse manner: approving of actions in as far as they tend to diminish his happiness; disapproving of them in as far as they tend to augment it.

II.4

IV. It is evident that anyone who reprobates any the least particle of pleasure, as such, from whatever source derived, is *pro tanto* a partisan of the principle of asceticism. It is only upon that principle, and not from the principle of utility, that the most abominable pleasure which the vilest of malefactors ever reaped from his crime would be to be reprobated, if it stood alone. The case is, that it never does stand alone; but is necessarily followed by such a quantity of pain (or, what comes to the same thing, such a chance for a certain quantity of pain) that the pleasure in comparison of it, is as nothing: and this is the true and sole, but perfectly sufficient, reason for making it a ground for punishment.

II.5

V. There are two classes of men of very different complexions, by whom the principle of asceticism appears to have been embraced; the one a set of moralists, the other a set of religionists. Different accordingly have been the motives which appear to have recommended it to the notice of these different parties. Hope, that is the prospect of pleasure, seems to have animated the former: hope, the aliment of philosophic pride: the hope of honor and reputation at the hands of men. Fear, that is, the prospect of pain, the latter: fear, the offspring of superstitious fancy: the fear of future punishment at the hands of a splenetic and revengeful Deity. I say in this case fear: for of the invisible future, fear is more powerful than hope. These circumstances characterize the two different parties among the partisans of the principle of asceticism; the parties and their motives different, the principle the same.

II.6

VI. The religious party, however, appear to have carried it farther than the philosophical: they have acted more consistently and less wisely. The philosophical party have scarcely gone farther than to reprobate pleasure: the religious party have frequently gone so far as to make it a matter of merit and of duty to court pain. The philosophical party have hardly gone farther than the making pain a matter of indifference. It is no evil, they have said: they have not said, it is a good. They have not so much as reprobated all pleasure in the lump. They have discarded only what they have called the gross; that is, such as are organical, or of which the origin is easily traced up to such as are organical: they have even cherished and magnified the refined. Yet this, however, not under the name of pleasure: to cleanse itself from the sordidness of its impure original, it was necessary it should change its name: the honorable, the glorious, the reputable, the becoming, the virtuous, the decorum it was to be called: in short, anything but pleasure.

II.7

VII. From these two sources have flowed the doctrines from which the sentiments of the bulk of mankind have all along received a tincture of this principle; some from the philosophical, some from the religious, some from both. Men of education more frequently from the philosophical, as more suited to the elevation of their sentiments: the vulgar more frequently from the superstitious, as more suited to the narrowness of their intellect, undilated by knowledge: and to the abjectness of their condition, continually open to the attacks of fear. The tinctures, however, derived from the two sources, would naturally intermingle, insomuch that a man would not always know by which of them he was most influenced: and they would often serve to corroborate and enliven one another. It was this conformity that made a kind of alliance between parties of a complexion otherwise so dissimilar: and disposed them to unite upon various occasions against the common enemy, the partisan of the principle of utility, whom they joined in branding with the odious name of Epicurean.

II.8

VIII. The principle of asceticism, however, with whatever warmth it may have been embraced by its partisans as a rule of private conduct, seems not to have been carried to any considerable length, when applied to the business of government. In a few instances it has been carried a little way by the philosophical party: witness the Spartan regimen. Though then, perhaps, it may be considered as having been a measure of security: and an application, though a precipitate and perverse application, of the principle of utility. Scarcely in any instances, to any considerable length, by the religious: for the various monastic orders, and the societies of the Quakers, Dumplers, Moravians, and other religionists, have been free societies, whose regimen no man has been restricted to without the intervention of his own consent. Whatever merit a man may have thought there would be in making himself miserable, no such notion seems ever to have occurred to any of them, that it may be a merit, much less a duty, to make others miserable: although it should seem, that if a certain quantity of misery were a thing so desirable, it would not matter much whether it were brought by each man upon himself, or by one man upon another. It is true, that from the same source from whence, among the religionists, the attachment to the principle of asceticism took its rise, flowed other doctrines and practices, from which misery in abundance was produced in one man by the instrumentality of another: witness the holy wars, and the persecutions for religion. But the passion for producing misery in these cases proceeded upon some special ground: the exercise of it was confined to persons of particular descriptions: they were tormented, not as men, but as heretics and infidels. To have inflicted the same miseries on their fellow believers and fellow-sectaries, would have been as blamable in the eyes even of these religionists, as in those of a partisan of the principle of utility. For a man to give himself a certain number of stripes was indeed meritorious: but to give the same number of stripes to another man, not consenting, would have been a sin. We read of saints, who for the good of their souls, and the mortification of their bodies, have voluntarily yielded themselves a prey to vermin: but though many persons of this class have wielded the reins of empire, we read of none who have set themselves to work, and made laws on purpose, with a view of stocking the body politic with the breed of highwaymen, housebreakers, or incendiaries. If at any time they have suffered the nation to be preyed upon by swarms of idle pensioners, or useless placemen, it has rather been from negligence and imbecility, than from any settled plan for oppressing and plundering of the people. If at any time they have sapped the sources of national wealth, by cramping commerce, and driving the inhabitants into emigration, it has been with other views, and in pursuit of other ends. If they have declaimed against the pursuit of pleasure, and the use of wealth, they have commonly stopped at declamation: they have not, like Lycurgus, made express ordinances for the purpose of banishing the precious metals. If they have established idleness by a law, it has been not because idleness, the mother of vice and misery, is itself a virtue, but because idleness (say they) is the road to holiness. If under the notion of fasting, they have joined in the plan of confining their subjects to a diet, thought by some to be of the most nourishing and prolific nature, it has been not for the sake of making them tributaries to the nations by whom that diet was to be supplied, but for the sake of manifesting their own power, and exercising the obedience of the people. If they have established, or suffered to be established, punishments for the breach of celibacy, they have done no more than comply with the petitions of those deluded rigorists, who, dupes to the ambitious and deep-laid policy of their rulers, first laid themselves under that idle obligation by a vow.

II.9

IX. The principle of asceticism seems originally to have been the reverie of certain hasty speculators, who having perceived, or fancied, that certain pleasures, when reaped in certain circumstances, have, at the long run, been attended with pains more than equivalent to them, took occasion to quarrel with every thing that offered itself under the name of pleasure. Having then got thus far, and having forgot the point which they set out from, they pushed on, and went so much further as to think it meritorious to fall in love with pain. Even this, we see, is at bottom but the principle of utility misapplied.

II.10

X. The principle of utility is capable of being consistently pursued; and it is but tautology to say, that the more consistently it is pursued, the better it must ever be for human-kind. The principle of asceticism never was, nor ever can be, consistently pursued by any living creature. Let but one tenth part of the inhabitants of this earth pursue it consistently, and in a day's time they will have turned it into a hell.

CHAPTER IV: VALUE OF A LOT OF PLEASURE OR PAIN, HOW TO BE MEASURED

IV.1

I. Pleasures then, and the avoidance of pains, are the ends that the legislator has in view; it behooves him therefore to understand their value. Pleasures and pains are the instruments he has to work with: it behooves him therefore to understand their force, which is again, in other words, their value.

IV.2

II. To a person considered by himself, the value of a pleasure or pain considered by itself, will be greater or less, according to the four following circumstances:

1. Its *intensity*.

2. Its *duration*.

3. Its *certainty* or *uncertainty*.

4. Its *propinquity* or *remoteness*.

IV.3

III. These are the circumstances which are to be considered in estimating a pleasure or a pain considered each of them by itself. But when the value of any pleasure or pain is considered for the purpose of estimating the tendency of any act by which it is produced, there are two other circumstances to be taken into the account; these are,

IV.4

5. Its *fecundity*, or the chance it has of being followed by sensations of the same kind: that is, pleasures, if it be a pleasure: pains, if it be a pain.

IV.5

6. Its *purity*, or the chance it has of not being followed by sensations of the opposite kind: that is, pains, if it be a pleasure: pleasures, if it be a pain.

IV.6

These two last, however, are in strictness scarcely to be deemed properties of the pleasure or the pain itself; they are not, therefore, in strictness to be taken into the account of the value of that pleasure or that pain. They are in strictness to be deemed properties only of the act, or other event, by which such pleasure or pain has been produced; and accordingly are only to be taken into the account of the tendency of such act or such event.

IV.7

IV. To a number of persons, with reference to each of whom to the value of a pleasure or a pain is considered, it will be greater or less, according to seven circumstances: to wit, the six preceding ones; viz.

1. Its *intensity*.
2. Its *duration*.
3. Its *certainty* or *uncertainty*.
4. Its *propinquity* or *remoteness*.
5. Its *fecundity*.
6. Its *purity*.

And one other; to wit:

7. Its *extent*; that is, the number of persons to whom it extends; or (in other words) who are affected by it.

IV.8

V. To take an exact account then of the general tendency of any act, by which the interests of a community are affected, proceed as follows. Begin with any one person of those whose interests seem most immediately to be affected by it: and take an account,

IV.9

1. Of the value of each distinguishable pleasure which appears to be produced by it in the first instance.

IV.10

2. Of the value of each pain which appears to be produced by it in the first instance.

IV.11

3. Of the value of each pleasure which appears to be produced by it after the first. This constitutes the fecundity of the first pleasure and the impurity of the first pain.

IV.12

4. Of the value of each pain which appears to be produced by it after the first. This constitutes the fecundity of the first pain, and the impurity of the first pleasure.

IV.13

5. Sum up all the values of all the pleasures on the one side, and those of all the pains on the other. The balance, if it be on the side of pleasure, will give the good tendency of the act upon the whole, with respect to the interests of that individual person; if on the side of pain, the bad tendency of it upon the whole.

IV.14

6. Take an account of the number of persons whose interests appear to be concerned; and repeat the above process with respect to each. Sum up the numbers expressive of the degrees of good tendency, which the act has, with respect to each individual, in regard to whom the tendency of it is good upon the whole: do this again with respect to each individual, in regard to whom the tendency of it is good upon the whole: do this again with respect to each individual, in regard to whom the tendency of it is bad upon the whole. Take the balance which if on the side of pleasure, will give the general good tendency of the act, with respect to the total number or community of individuals concerned; if on the side of pain, the general evil tendency, with respect to the same community.

IV.15

VI. It is not to be expected that this process should be strictly pursued previously to every moral judgment, or to every legislative or judicial operation. It may, however, be always kept in view: and as near as the process actually pursued on these occasions approaches to it, so near will such process approach to the character of an exact one.

IV.16

VII. The same process is alike applicable to pleasure and pain, in whatever shape they appear: and by whatever denomination they are distinguished: to pleasure, whether it be called good (which is properly the cause or instrument of pleasure) or profit (which is distant pleasure, or the cause or instrument of distant pleasure,) or convenience, or advantage, benefit, emolument, happiness, and so forth: to pain, whether it be called evil, (which corresponds to good) or mischief, or inconvenience, or disadvantage, or loss, or unhappiness, and so forth.

IV.17

VIII. Nor is this a novel and unwarranted, any more than it is a useless theory. In all this there is nothing but what the practice of mankind, wheresoever they have a clear view of their own interest, is perfectly conformable to. An article of property, an estate in land, for instance, is valuable, on what account? On account of the pleasures of all kinds which it enables a man to produce, and what comes to the same thing the pains of all kinds which it enables him to avert. But the value of such an article of property is universally understood to rise or fall according to the length or shortness of the time which a man has in it: the certainty or uncertainty of its coming into possession: and the nearness or remoteness of the time at which, if at all, it is to come into possession. As to the intensity of the pleasures which a man may derive from it, this is never thought of, because it depends upon the use which each particular person may come to make of it; which cannot be estimated till the particular pleasures he may come to derive from it, or the particular pains he may come to exclude by means of it, are brought to view. For the same reason, neither does he think of the fecundity or purity of those pleasures.

[*An Introduction to the Principles of Morals and Legislation.* (London: W. Pickering, 1823)]

Utilitarianism

John Stuart Mill

CHAPTER I: GENERAL REMARKS

There are few circumstances among those which make up the present condition of human knowledge, more unlike what might have been expected, or more significant of the backward state in which speculation on the most important subjects still lingers, than the little progress which has been made in the decision of the controversy respecting the criterion of right and wrong. From the dawn of philosophy, the question concerning the *summum bonum*, or, what is the same thing, concerning the foundation of morality, has been accounted the main problem in speculative thought, has occupied the most gifted intellects, and divided them into sects and schools, carrying on a vigorous warfare against one another. And after more than two thousand years the same discussions continue, philosophers are still ranged under the same contending banners, and neither thinkers nor mankind at large seem nearer to being unanimous on the subject, than when the youth Socrates listened to the old Protagoras, and asserted (if Plato's dialogue be grounded on a real conversation) the theory of utilitarianism against the popular morality of the so-called sophist.

It is true that similar confusion and uncertainty, and in some cases similar discordance, exist respecting the first principles of all the sciences, not excepting that which is deemed the most certain of them, mathematics; without much impairing, generally indeed without impairing at all, the trustworthiness of the conclusions of those sciences. An apparent anomaly, the explanation of which is, that the detailed doctrines of a science are not usually deduced from, nor depend for their evidence upon, what are called its first principles. Were it not so, there would be no science more precarious, or whose conclusions were more insufficiently made out, than algebra; which derives none of its certainty from what are commonly taught to learners as its elements, since these, as laid down by some of its most eminent teachers, are as full of fictions as English law, and of mysteries as theology. The truths which are ultimately accepted as the first principles of a science, are really the last results of metaphysical analysis, practiced on the elementary notions with which the science is conversant; and their relation to the science is not that of foundations to an edifice, but of roots to a tree, which may perform their office equally well though they be never dug down to and exposed to light. But though in science the particular truths precede the general theory, the contrary might be expected to be the case with a practical art, such as morals or legislation. All action is for the sake of some end, and rules of action, it seems natural to suppose, must take their whole character and color from the end to which they are subservient. When we engage in a pursuit, a clear and precise conception of what we are pursuing would seem to be the first thing we need, instead of the last we are to look forward to. A test of right and wrong must be the means, one would think, of ascertaining what is right or wrong, and not a consequence of having already ascertained it.

The difficulty is not avoided by having recourse to the popular theory of a natural faculty, a sense or instinct, informing us of right and wrong. For—besides that the existence of such a moral instinct is itself one of the matters in dispute—those believers in it who have any pretensions to philosophy, have been obliged to abandon the idea that it discerns what is right or wrong in the particular case in hand, as our other senses discern the sight or sound actually present. Our moral faculty, according to all those of its interpreters who are entitled to the name of thinkers, supplies us only with the general principles of moral judgments; it is a branch of our reason, not of our sensitive faculty; and must be looked to for the abstract doctrines of morality, not for perception of it in the concrete. The intuitive, no less than what may be termed the inductive, school of ethics, insists on the necessity of general laws. They both agree that the morality of an individual action is not a question of direct perception, but of the application of a law to an individual case. They recognize also, to a great extent, the same moral laws; but differ as to their evidence, and the source from which they derive their authority. According to the one opinion, the principles of morals are evident à priori, requiring nothing to command assent, except that the meaning of the terms be understood. According to the other doctrine, right and wrong, as well as truth and falsehood, are questions of observation and experience. But both hold equally that morality must be deduced from principles; and the intuitive school affirm as strongly as the inductive, that there is a science of morals. Yet they seldom attempt to make out a list of the à priori principles which are to serve as the premises of the science; still more rarely do they make any effort to reduce those various principles to one first principle, or common ground of obligation. They either assume the ordinary precepts of morals as of *a priori* authority, or they lay down as the common groundwork of those maxims, some generality much less obviously authoritative than the maxims themselves, and which has never succeeded in gaining popular acceptance. Yet to support their pretensions there ought either to be some one fundamental principle or law, at the root of all morality, or if there be several, there should be a determinate order of precedence among them; and the one principle, or the rule for deciding between the various principles when they conflict, ought to be self-evident.

To inquire how far the bad effects of this deficiency have been mitigated in practice, or to what extent the moral beliefs of mankind have been vitiated or made uncertain by the absence of any distinct recognition of an ultimate standard, would imply a complete survey and criticism of past and present ethical doctrine. It would, however, be easy to show that whatever steadiness or consistency these moral beliefs have attained, has been mainly due to the tacit influence of a standard not recognized. Although the non-existence of an acknowledged first principle has made ethics not so much a guide as a consecration of men's actual sentiments, still, as men's sentiments, both of favor and of aversion, are greatly influenced by what they suppose to be the effects of things upon their happiness, the principle of utility, or as Bentham latterly called it, the greatest happiness principle, has had a large share in forming the moral doctrines even of those who most scornfully reject its authority. Nor is there any school of thought which refuses to admit that the influence of actions on happiness is a most material and even predominant consideration in many of the details of morals, however unwilling to acknowledge it as the fundamental principle of morality, and the source of moral obligation. I might go much further, and say that to all those *a priori* moralists who deem it necessary to argue at all, utilitarian arguments are indispensable. It is not my present purpose to criticize these thinkers; but I cannot help referring, for illustration, to a systematic treatise by one of the most illustrious of them, the Metaphysics of Ethics, by Kant. This remarkable man, whose system of thought will long remain one of the landmarks in the history of philosophical speculation, does, in the treatise in question, lay down an universal first principle as the origin and ground of moral obligation; it is this:—'So act, that the rule on which thou actest would admit of being adopted as a law by all rational beings.' But when he begins to deduce from this precept any of the actual duties of morality, he fails, almost grotesquely, to show that there would be any contradiction, any logical (not to say physical) impossibility, in the adoption by all rational beings of the most outrageously immoral rules of conduct. All he shows is that the consequences of their universal adoption would be such as no one would choose to incur.

On the present occasion, I shall, without further discussion of the other theories, attempt to contribute something towards the understanding and appreciation of the Utilitarian or Happiness theory, and towards such proof as it is susceptible of. It is evident that this cannot be proof in the ordinary and popular meaning of the term. Questions of ultimate ends are not amenable to direct proof. Whatever can be proved to be good, must be so by being shown to be a means to something admitted to be good without proof. The medical art is proved to be good, by its conducing to health; but how is it possible to prove that health is good? The art of music is good, for the reason, among others, that it produces pleasure; but what proof is it possible to give that pleasure is good? If, then, it is asserted that there is a comprehensive formula, including all things which are in themselves good, and that whatever else is good, is not so as an end, but as a mean, the formula may be accepted or rejected, but is not a subject of what is commonly understood by proof. We are not, however, to infer that its acceptance or rejection must depend on blind impulse, or arbitrary choice. There is a larger meaning of the word proof, in which this question is as amenable to it as any other of the disputed questions of philosophy. The subject is within the cognizance of the rational faculty; and neither does that faculty deal with it solely in the way of intuition. Considerations may be presented capable of determining the intellect either to give or withhold its assent to the doctrine; and this is equivalent to proof.

We shall examine presently of what nature are these considerations; in what manner they apply to the case, and what rational grounds, therefore, can be given for accepting or rejecting the utilitarian formula. But it is a preliminary condition of rational acceptance or rejection, that the formula should be correctly understood. I believe that the very imperfect notion ordinarily formed of its meaning, is the chief obstacle which impedes its reception; and that could it be cleared, even from only the grosser misconceptions, the question would be greatly simplified, and a large proportion of its difficulties removed. Before, therefore, I attempt to enter into the philosophical grounds which can be given for assenting to the utilitarian standard, I shall offer some illustrations of the doctrine itself; with the view of showing more clearly what it is, distinguishing it from what it is not, and disposing of such of the practical objections to it as either originate in, or are closely connected with, mistaken interpretations of its meaning. Having thus prepared the ground, I shall afterwards endeavor to throw such light as I can upon the question, considered as one of philosophical theory.

CHAPTER II: WHAT UTILITARIANISM IS

A passing remark is all that needs be given to the ignorant blunder of supposing that those who stand up for utility as the test of right and wrong, use the term in that restricted and merely colloquial sense in which utility is opposed to pleasure. An apology is due to the philosophical opponents of utilitarianism, for even the momentary appearance of confounding them with any one capable of so absurd a misconception; which is the more extraordinary, inasmuch as the contrary accusation, of referring everything to pleasure, and that too in its grossest form, is another of the common charges against utilitarianism: and, as has been pointedly remarked by an able writer, the same sort of persons, and often the very same persons, denounce the theory "as impracticably dry when the word utility precedes the word pleasure, and as too practicably voluptuous when the word pleasure precedes the word utility." Those who know anything about the matter are aware that every writer, from Epicurus to Bentham, who maintained the theory of utility, meant by it, not something to be contradistinguished from pleasure, but pleasure itself, together with exemption from pain; and instead of opposing the useful to the agreeable or the ornamental, have always declared that the useful means these, among other things. Yet the common herd, including the herd of writers, not only in newspapers and periodicals, but in books of weight and pretension, are perpetually falling into this shallow mistake. Having caught up the word utilitarian, while knowing nothing whatever about it but its sound, they habitually express by it the rejection, or the neglect, of pleasure in some of its forms; of beauty, of ornament, or of amusement. Nor is the term thus ignorantly misapplied solely in disparagement, but occasionally in compliment; as though it implied superiority to frivolity and the mere pleasures of the moment. And this perverted use is the only one in which the word is popularly known, and the one from which the new generation are acquiring their sole notion of its meaning. Those who introduced the word, but who had for many years discontinued it as a distinctive appellation, may well feel themselves called upon to resume it, if by doing so they can hope to contribute anything towards rescuing it from this utter degradation.

The creed which accepts as the foundation of morals, Utility, or the Greatest Happiness Principle, holds that actions are right in proportion as they tend to promote happiness, wrong as they tend to produce the reverse of happiness. By happiness is intended pleasure, and the absence of pain; by unhappiness, pain, and the privation of pleasure. To give a clear view of the moral standard set up by the theory, much more requires to be said; in particular, what things it includes in the ideas of pain and pleasure; and to what extent this is left an open question. But these supplementary explanations do not affect the theory of life on which this theory of morality is grounded—namely, that pleasure, and freedom from pain, are the only things desirable as ends; and that all desirable things (which are as numerous in the utilitarian as in any other scheme) are desirable either for the pleasure inherent in themselves, or as means to the promotion of pleasure and the prevention of pain.

Now, such a theory of life excites in many minds, and among them in some of the most estimable in feeling and purpose, inveterate dislike. To suppose that life has (as they express it) no higher end than pleasure—no better and nobler object of desire and pursuit—they designate as utterly mean and groveling; as a doctrine worthy only of swine, to whom the followers of Epicurus were, at a very early period, contemptuously likened; and modern holders of the doctrine are occasionally made the subject of equally polite comparisons by its German, French, and English assailants.

When thus attacked, the Epicureans have always answered, that it is not they, but their accusers, who represent human nature in a degrading light; since the accusation supposes human beings to be capable of no pleasures except those of which swine are capable. If this supposition were true, the charge could not be gainsaid, but would then be no longer an imputation; for if the sources of pleasure were precisely the same to human beings and to swine, the rule of life which is good enough for the one would be good enough for the other. The comparison of the Epicurean life to that of beasts is felt as degrading, precisely because a beast's pleasures do not satisfy a human being's conceptions of happiness. Human beings have faculties more elevated than the animal appetites, and when once made conscious of them, do not regard anything as happiness which does not include their gratification. I do not, indeed, consider the Epicureans to have been by any means faultless in drawing out their scheme of consequences from the utilitarian principle. To do this in any sufficient manner, many Stoic, as well as Christian elements require to be included. But there is no known Epicurean theory of life which does not assign to the pleasures of the intellect; of the feelings and imagination, and of the moral sentiments, a much higher value as pleasures than to those of mere sensation. It must be admitted, however, that utilitarian writers in general have placed the superiority of mental over bodily pleasures chiefly in the greater permanency, safety, uncostliness, etc., of the former—that is, in their circumstantial advantages rather than in their intrinsic nature. And on all these points utilitarians have fully proved their case; but they might have taken the other, and, as it may be called, higher ground, with entire consistency. It is quite compatible with the principle of utility to recognize the fact, that some kinds of pleasure are more desirable and more valuable than others. It would be absurd that while, in estimating all other things, quality is considered as well as quantity, the estimation of pleasures should be supposed to depend on quantity alone.

If I am asked, what I mean by difference of quality in pleasures, or what makes one pleasure more valuable than another, merely as a pleasure, except its being greater in amount, there is but one possible answer. Of two pleasures, if there be one to which all or almost all who have experience of both give a decided preference, irrespective of any feeling of moral obligation to prefer it, that is the more desirable pleasure. If one of the two is, by those who are competently acquainted with both, placed so far above the other that they prefer it, even though knowing it to be attended with a greater amount of discontent, and would not resign it for any quantity of the other pleasure which their nature is capable of, we are justified in ascribing to the preferred enjoyment a superiority in quality, so far outweighing quantity as to render it, in comparison, of small account.

Now it is an unquestionable fact that those who are equally acquainted with, and equally capable of appreciating and enjoying, both, do give a most marked preference to the manner of existence which employs their higher faculties. Few human creatures would consent to be changed into any of the lower animals, for a promise of the fullest allowance of a beast's pleasures; no intelligent human being would consent to be a fool, no instructed person would be an ignoramus, no person of feeling and conscience would be selfish and base, even though they should be persuaded that the fool, the dunce, or the rascal is better satisfied with his lot than they are with theirs. They would not resign what they possess more than he, for the most complete satisfaction of all the desires which they have in common with him. If they ever fancy they would, it is only in cases of unhappiness so extreme, that to escape from it they would exchange their lot for almost any other, however undesirable in their own eyes. A being of higher faculties requires more to make him happy, is capable probably of more acute suffering, and is certainly accessible to it at more points, than one of an inferior type; but in spite of these liabilities, he can never really wish to sink into what he feels to be a lower grade of existence. We may give what explanation we please of this unwillingness; we may attribute it to pride, a name which is given indiscriminately to some of the most and to some of the least estimable feelings of which mankind are capable; we may refer it to the love of liberty and personal independence, an appeal to which was with the Stoics one of the most effective means for the inculcation of it; to the love of power, or to the love of excitement, both of which do really enter into and contribute to it: but its most appropriate appellation is a sense of dignity, which all human beings possess in one form or other, and in some, though by no means in exact, proportion to their higher faculties, and which is so essential a part of the happiness of those in whom it is strong, that nothing which conflicts with it could be, otherwise than momentarily, an object of desire to them. Whoever supposes that this preference takes place at a sacrifice of happiness-that the superior being, in anything like equal circumstances, is not happier than the inferior-confounds the two very different ideas, of happiness, and content. It is indisputable that the being whose capacities of enjoyment are low, has the greatest chance of having them fully satisfied; and a highly-endowed being will always feel that any happiness which he can look for, as the world is constituted, is imperfect. But he can learn to bear its imperfections, if they are at all bearable; and they will not make him envy the being who is indeed unconscious of the imperfections, but only because he feels not at all the good which those imperfections qualify. It is better to be a human being dissatisfied than a pig satisfied; better to be Socrates dissatisfied than a fool satisfied. And if the fool, or the pig, is of a different opinion, it is because they only know their own side of the question. The other party to the comparison knows both sides.

It may be objected, that many who are capable of the higher pleasures, occasionally, under the influence of temptation, postpone them to the lower. But this is quite compatible with a full appreciation of the intrinsic superiority of the higher. Men often, from infirmity of character, make their election for the nearer good, though they know it to be the less valuable; and this no less when the choice is between two bodily pleasures, than when it is between bodily and mental. They pursue sensual indulgences to the injury of health, though perfectly aware that health is the greater good. It may be further objected, that many who begin with youthful enthusiasm for everything noble, as they advance in years sink into indolence and selfishness. But I do not believe that those who undergo this very common change, voluntarily choose the lower description of pleasures in preference to the higher. I believe that before they devote themselves exclusively to the one, they have already become incapable of the other. Capacity for the nobler feelings is in most natures a very tender plant, easily killed, not only by hostile influences, but by mere want of sustenance; and in the majority of young persons it speedily dies away if the occupations to which their position in life has devoted them, and the society into which it has thrown them, are not favorable to keeping that higher capacity in exercise. Men lose their high aspirations as they lose their intellectual tastes, because they have not time or opportunity for indulging them; and they addict themselves to inferior pleasures, not because they deliberately prefer them, but because they are either the only ones to which they have access, or the only ones which they are any longer capable of enjoying. It may be questioned whether anyone who has remained equally susceptible to both classes of pleasures, ever knowingly and calmly preferred the lower; though many, in all ages, have broken down in an ineffectual attempt to combine both.

From this verdict of the only competent judges, I apprehend there can be no appeal. On a question which is the best worth having of two pleasures, or which of two modes of existence is the most grateful to the feelings, apart from its moral attributes and from its consequences, the judgment of those who are qualified by knowledge of both, or, if they differ, that of the majority among them, must be admitted as final. And there needs be the less hesitation to accept this judgment respecting the quality of pleasures, since there is no other tribunal to be referred to even on the question of quantity. What means are there of determining which is the acutest of two pains, or the most intense of two pleasurable sensations, except the general suffrage of those who are familiar with both? Neither pains nor pleasures are homogeneous, and pain is always heterogeneous with pleasure. What is there to decide whether a particular pleasure is worth purchasing at the cost of a particular pain, except the feelings and judgment of the experienced? When, therefore, those feelings and judgment declare the pleasures derived from the higher faculties to be preferable in kind, apart from the question of intensity, to those of which the animal nature, disjoined from the higher faculties, is susceptible, they are entitled on this subject to the same regard.

I have dwelt on this point, as being a necessary part of a perfectly just conception of Utility or Happiness, considered as the directive rule of human conduct. But it is by no means an indispensable condition to the acceptance of the utilitarian standard; for that standard is not the agent's own greatest happiness, but the greatest amount of happiness altogether; and if it may possibly be doubted whether a noble character is always the happier for its nobleness, there can be no doubt that it makes other people happier, and that the world in general is immensely a gainer by it. Utilitarianism, therefore, could only attain its end by the general cultivation of nobleness of character, even if each individual were only benefited by the nobleness of others, and his own, so far as happiness is concerned, were a sheer deduction from the benefit. But the bare enunciation of such an absurdity as this last, renders refutation superfluous.

According to the Greatest Happiness Principle, as above explained, the ultimate end, with reference to and for the sake of which all other things are desirable (whether we are considering our own good or that of other people), is an existence exempt as far as possible from pain, and as rich as possible in enjoyments, both in point of quantity and quality; the test of quality, and the rule for measuring it against quantity, being the preference felt by those who, in their opportunities of experience, to which must be added their habits of self-consciousness and self-observation, are best furnished with the means of comparison. This, being, according to the utilitarian opinion, the end of human action, is necessarily also the standard of morality; which may accordingly be defined, the rules and precepts for human conduct, by the observance of which an existence such as has been described might be, to the greatest extent possible, secured to all mankind; and not to them only, but, so far as the nature of things admits, to the whole sentient creation.

Against this doctrine, however, arises another class of objectors, who say that happiness, in any form, cannot be the rational purpose of human life and action; because, in the first place, it is unattainable: and they contemptuously ask, "What right hast thou to be happy?"—a question which Mr. Carlyle clenches by the addition, "What right, a short time ago, hadst thou even to be?" Next, they say, that men can do without happiness; that all noble human beings have felt this, and could not have become noble but by learning the lesson of Entsagen, or renunciation; which lesson, thoroughly learnt and submitted to, they affirm to be the beginning and necessary condition of all virtue.

The first of these objections would go to the root of the matter were it well founded; for if no happiness is to be had at all by human beings, the attainment of it cannot be the end of morality, or of any rational conduct. Though, even in that case, something might still be said for the utilitarian theory; since utility includes not solely the pursuit of happiness, but the prevention or mitigation of unhappiness; and if the former aim be chimerical, there will be all the greater scope and more imperative need for the latter, so long at least as mankind think fit to live, and do not take refuge in the simultaneous act of suicide recommended under certain conditions by Novalis. When, however, it is thus positively asserted to be impossible that human life should be happy, the assertion, if not something like a verbal quibble, is at least an exaggeration. If by happiness be meant a continuity of highly pleasurable excitement, it is evident enough that this is impossible. A state of exalted pleasure lasts only moments, or in some cases, and with some intermissions, hours or days, and is the occasional brilliant flash of enjoyment, not its permanent and steady flame. Of this the philosophers who have taught that happiness is the end of life were as fully aware as those who taunt them. The happiness which they meant was not a life of rapture, but moments of such, in an existence made up of few and transitory pains, many and various pleasures, with a decided predominance of the active over the passive, and having as the foundation of the whole, not to expect more from life than it is capable of bestowing. A life thus composed, to those who have been fortunate enough to obtain it, has always appeared worthy of the name of happiness. And such an existence is even now the lot of many, during some considerable portion of their lives. The present wretched education, and wretched social arrangements, are the only real hindrance to its being attainable by almost all.

The objectors perhaps may doubt whether human beings, if taught to consider happiness as the end of life, would be satisfied with such a moderate share of it. But great numbers of mankind have been satisfied with much less. The main constituents of a satisfied life appear to be two, either of which by itself is often found sufficient for the purpose: tranquility, and excitement. With much tranquility, many find that they can be content with very little pleasure: with much excitement, many can reconcile themselves to a considerable quantity of pain. There is assuredly no inherent impossibility in enabling even the mass of mankind to unite both; since the two are so far from being incompatible that they are in natural alliance, the prolongation of either being a preparation for, and exciting a wish for, the other. It is only those in whom indolence amounts to a vice, that do not desire excitement after an interval of repose; it is only those in whom the need of excitement is a disease, that feel the tranquility which follows excitement dull and insipid, instead of pleasurable in direct proportion to the excitement which preceded it. When people who are tolerably fortunate in their outward lot do not find in life sufficient enjoyment to make it valuable to them, the cause generally is, caring for nobody but themselves. To those who have neither public nor private affections, the excitements of life are much curtailed, and in any case dwindle in value as the time approaches when all selfish interests must be terminated by death: while those who leave after them objects of personal affection, and especially those who have also cultivated a fellow-feeling with the collective interests of mankind, retain as lively an interest in life on the eve of death as in the vigor of youth and health. Next to selfishness, the principal cause which makes life unsatisfactory, is want of mental cultivation. A cultivated mind—I do not mean that of a philosopher, but any mind to which the fountains of knowledge have been opened, and which has been taught, in any tolerable degree, to exercise its faculties—finds sources of inexhaustible interest in all that surrounds it; in the objects of nature, the achievements of art, the imaginations of poetry, the incidents of history, the ways of mankind past and present, and their prospects in the future. It is possible, indeed, to become indifferent to all this, and that too without having exhausted a thousandth part of it; but only when one has had from the beginning no moral or human interest in these things, and has sought in them only the gratification of curiosity.

Now there is absolutely no reason in the nature of things why an amount of mental culture sufficient to give an intelligent interest in these objects of contemplation, should not be the inheritance of every one born in a civilized country. As little is there an inherent necessity that any human being should be a selfish egotist, devoid of every feeling or care but those which center in his own miserable individuality. Something far superior to this is sufficiently common even now, to give ample earnest of what the human species may be made. Genuine private affections, and a sincere interest in the public good, are possible, though in unequal degrees, to every rightly brought-up human being. In a world in which there is so much to interest, so much to enjoy, and so much also to correct and improve, everyone who has this moderate amount of moral and intellectual requisites is capable of an existence which may be called enviable; and unless such a person, through bad laws, or subjection to the will of others, is denied the liberty to use the sources of happiness within his reach, he will not fail to find this enviable existence, if he escape the positive evils of life, the great sources of physical and mental suffering—such as indigence, disease, and the unkindness, worthlessness, or premature loss of objects of affection. The main stress of the problem lies, therefore, in the contest with these calamities, from which it is a rare good fortune entirely to escape; which, as things now are, cannot be obviated, and often cannot be in any material degree mitigated. Yet no one whose opinion deserves a moment's consideration can doubt that most of the great positive evils of the world are in themselves removable, and will, if human affairs continue to improve, be in the end reduced within narrow limits. Poverty, in any sense implying suffering, may be completely extinguished by the wisdom of society, combined with the good sense and providence of individuals. Even that most intractable of enemies, disease, may be indefinitely reduced in dimensions by good physical and moral education, and proper control of noxious influences; while the progress of science holds out a promise for the future of still more direct conquests over this detestable foe. And every advance in that direction relieves us from some, not only of the chances which cut short our own lives, but, what concerns us still more, which deprive us of those in whom our happiness is wrapped up. As for vicissitudes of fortune, and other disappointments connected with worldly circumstances, these are principally the effect either of gross imprudence, of ill-regulated desires, or of bad or imperfect social institutions. All the grand sources, in short, of human suffering are in a great degree, many of them almost entirely, conquerable by human care and effort; and though their removal is grievously slow—though a long succession of generations will perish in the breach before the conquest is completed, and this world becomes all that, if will and knowledge were not wanting, it might easily be made—yet every mind sufficiently intelligent and generous to bear a part, however small and inconspicuous, in the endeavor, will draw a noble enjoyment from the contest itself, which he would not for any bribe in the form of selfish indulgence consent to be without.

And this leads to the true estimation of what is said by the objectors concerning the possibility, and the obligation, of learning to do without happiness. Unquestionably it is possible to do without happiness; it is done involuntarily by nineteen-twentieths of mankind, even in those parts of our present world which are least deep in barbarism; and it often has to be done voluntarily by the hero or the martyr, for the sake of something which he prizes more than his individual happiness. But this something, what is it, unless the happiness of others, or some of the requisites of happiness? It is noble to be capable of resigning entirely one's own portion of happiness, or chances of it: but, after all, this self-sacrifice must be for some end; it is not its own end; and if we are told that its end is not happiness, but virtue, which is better than happiness, I ask, would the sacrifice be made if the hero or martyr did not believe that it would earn for others immunity from similar sacrifices? Would it be made, if he thought that his renunciation of happiness for himself would produce no fruit for any of his fellow creatures, but to make their lot like his, and place them also in the condition of persons who have renounced happiness? All honor to those who can abnegate for themselves the personal enjoyment of life, when by such renunciation they contribute worthily to increase the amount of happiness in the world; but he who does it, or professes to do it, for any other purpose, is no more deserving of admiration than the ascetic mounted on his pillar. He may be an inspiriting proof of what men can do, but assuredly not an example of what they should.

Though it is only in a very imperfect state of the world's arrangements that anyone can best serve the happiness of others by the absolute sacrifice of his own, yet so long as the world is in that imperfect state, I fully acknowledge that the readiness to make such a sacrifice is the highest virtue which can be found in man. I will add, that in this condition of the world, paradoxical as the assertion may be, the conscious ability to do without happiness gives the best prospect of realizing such happiness as is attainable. For nothing except that consciousness can raise a person above the chances of life, by making him feel that, let fate and fortune do their worst, they have not power to subdue him: which, once felt, frees him from excess of anxiety concerning the evils of life, and enables him, like many a Stoic in the worst times of the Roman Empire, to cultivate in tranquility the sources of satisfaction accessible to him, without concerning himself about the uncertainty of their duration, any more than about their inevitable end.

Meanwhile, let utilitarians never cease to claim the morality of self-devotion as a possession which belongs by as good a right to them, as either to the Stoic or to the Transcendentalist. The utilitarian morality does recognize in human beings the power of sacrificing their own greatest good for the good of others. It only refuses to admit that the sacrifice is itself a good. A sacrifice which does not increase, or tend to increase, the sum total of happiness, it considers as wasted. The only self-renunciation which it applauds, is devotion to the happiness, or to some of the means of happiness, of others; either of mankind collectively, or of individuals within the limits imposed by the collective interests of mankind.

I must again repeat, what the assailants of utilitarianism seldom have the justice to acknowledge, that the happiness which forms the utilitarian standard of what is right in conduct, is not the agent's own happiness, but that of all concerned. As between his own happiness and that of others, utilitarianism requires him to be as strictly impartial as a disinterested and benevolent spectator. In the golden rule of Jesus of Nazareth, we read the complete spirit of the ethics of utility. To do as one would be done by, and to love one's neighbor as oneself, constitute the ideal perfection of utilitarian morality. As the means of making the nearest approach to this ideal, utility would enjoin, first, that laws and social arrangements should place the happiness, or (as speaking practically it may be called) the interest, of every individual, as nearly as possible in harmony with the interest of the whole; and secondly, that education and opinion, which have so vast a power over human character, should so use that power as to establish in the mind of every individual an indissoluble association between his own happiness and the good of the whole; especially between his own happiness and the practice of such modes of conduct, negative and positive, as regard for the universal happiness prescribes: so that not only he may be unable to conceive the possibility of happiness to himself, consistently with conduct opposed to the general good, but also that a direct impulse to promote the general good may be in every individual one of the habitual motives of action, and the sentiments connected therewith may fill a large and prominent place in every human being's sentient existence. If the impugners of the utilitarian morality represented it to their own minds in this its true character, I know not what recommendation possessed by any other morality they could possibly affirm to be wanting to it: what more beautiful or more exalted developments of human nature any other ethical system can be supposed to foster, or what springs of action, not accessible to the utilitarian, such systems rely on for giving effect to their mandates.

The objectors to utilitarianism cannot always be charged with representing it in a discreditable light. On the contrary, those among them who entertain anything like a just idea of its disinterested character, sometimes find fault with its standard as being too high for humanity. They say it is exacting too much to require that people shall always act from the inducement of promoting the general interests of society. But this is to mistake the very meaning of a standard of morals, and to confound the rule of action with the motive of it. It is the business of ethics to tell us what are our duties, or by what test we may know them; but no system of ethics requires that the sole motive of all we do shall be a feeling of duty; on the contrary, ninety-nine hundredths of all our actions are done from other motives, and rightly so done, if the rule of duty does not condemn them. It is the more unjust to utilitarianism that this particular misapprehension should be made a ground of objection to it, inasmuch as utilitarian moralists have gone beyond almost all others in affirming that the motive has nothing to do with the morality of the action, though much with the worth of the agent. He who saves a fellow creature from drowning does what is morally right, whether his motive be duty, or the hope of being paid for his trouble: he who betrays the friend that trusts him, is guilty of a crime, even if his object be to serve another friend to whom he is under greater obligations.[B] But to speak only of actions done from the motive of duty, and in direct obedience to principle: it is a misapprehension of the utilitarian mode of thought, to conceive it as implying that people should fix their minds upon so wide a generality as the world, or society at large. The great majority of good actions are intended, not for the benefit of the world, but for that of individuals, of which the good of the world is made up; and the thoughts of the most virtuous man need not on these occasions travel beyond the particular persons concerned, except so far as is necessary to assure himself that in benefiting them he is not violating the rights—that is, the legitimate and authorized expectations—of anyone else. The multiplication of happiness is, according to the utilitarian ethics, the object of virtue: the occasions on which any person (except one in a thousand) has it in his power to do this on an extended scale, in other words, to be a public benefactor, are but exceptional; and on these occasions alone is he called on to consider public utility; in every other case, private utility, the interest or happiness of some few persons, is all he has to attend to. Those alone the influence of whose actions extends to society in general, need concern themselves habitually about so large an object. In the case of abstinences indeed—of things which people forbear to do, from moral considerations, though the consequences in the particular case might be beneficial—it would be unworthy of an intelligent agent not to be consciously aware that the action is of a class which, if practiced generally, would be generally injurious, and that this is the ground of the obligation to abstain from it. The amount of regard for the public interest implied in this recognition, is no greater than is demanded by every system of morals; for they all enjoin to abstain from whatever is manifestly pernicious to society.

The same considerations dispose of another reproach against the doctrine of utility, founded on a still grosser misconception of the purpose of a standard of morality, and of the very meaning of the words right and wrong. It is often affirmed that utilitarianism renders men cold and unsympathizing; that it chills their moral feelings towards individuals; that it makes them regard only the dry and hard consideration of the consequences of actions, not taking into their moral estimate the qualities from which those actions emanate. If the assertion means that they do not allow their judgment respecting the rightness or wrongness of an action to be influenced by their opinion of the qualities of the person who does it, this is a complaint not against utilitarianism, but against having any standard of morality at all; for certainly no known ethical standard decides an action to be good or bad because it is done by a good or a bad man, still less because done by an amiable, a brave, or a benevolent man or the contrary. These considerations are relevant, not to the estimation of actions, but of persons; and there is nothing in the utilitarian theory inconsistent with the fact that there are other things which interest us in persons besides the rightness and wrongness of their actions. The Stoics, indeed, with the paradoxical misuse of language which was part of their system, and by which they strove to raise themselves above all concern about anything but virtue, were fond of saying that he who has that has everything; that he, and only he, is rich, is beautiful, is a king. But no claim of this description is made for the virtuous man by the utilitarian doctrine. Utilitarians are quite aware that there are other desirable possessions and qualities besides virtue, and are perfectly willing to allow to all of them their full worth. They are also aware that a right action does not necessarily indicate a virtuous character, and that actions which are blamable often proceed from qualities entitled to praise. When this is apparent in any particular case, it modifies their estimation, not certainly of the act, but of the agent. I grant that they are, notwithstanding, of opinion, that in the long run the best proof of a good character is good actions; and resolutely refuse to consider any mental disposition as good, of which the predominant tendency is to produce bad conduct. This makes them unpopular with many people; but it is an unpopularity which they must share with everyone who regards the distinction between right and wrong in a serious light; and the reproach is not one which a conscientious utilitarian need be anxious to repel.

If no more be meant by the objection than that many utilitarians look on the morality of actions, as measured by the utilitarian standard, with too exclusive a regard, and do not lay sufficient stress upon the other beauties of character which go towards making a human being loveable or admirable, this may be admitted. Utilitarians who have cultivated their moral feelings, but not their sympathies nor their artistic perceptions, do fall into this mistake; and so do all other moralists under the same conditions. What can be said in excuse for other moralists is equally available for them, namely, that if there is to be any error, it is better that it should be on that side. As a matter of fact, we may affirm that among utilitarians as among adherents of other systems, there is every imaginable degree of rigidity and of laxity in the application of their standard: some are even puritanically rigorous, while others are as indulgent as can possibly be desired by sinner or by sentimentalist. But on the whole, a doctrine which brings prominently forward the interest that mankind have in the repression and prevention of conduct which violates the moral law, is likely to be inferior to no other in turning the sanctions of opinion against such violations. It is true, the question: "What does violate the moral law?" is one on which those who recognize different standards of morality are likely now and then to differ. But difference of opinion on moral questions was not first introduced into the world by utilitarianism, while that doctrine does supply, if not always an easy, at all events a tangible and intelligible mode of deciding such differences.

It may not be superfluous to notice a few more of the common misapprehensions of utilitarian ethics, even those which are so obvious and gross that it might appear impossible for any person of candor and intelligence to fall into them: since persons, even of considerable mental endowments, often give themselves so little trouble to understand the bearings of any opinion against which they entertain a prejudice, and men are in general so little conscious of this voluntary ignorance as a defect, that the most vulgar misunderstandings of ethical doctrines are continually met with in the deliberate writings of persons of the greatest pretensions both to high principle and to philosophy. We not uncommonly hear the doctrine of utility inveighed against as a godless doctrine. If it be necessary to say anything at all against so mere an assumption, we may say that the question depends upon what idea we have formed of the moral character of the Deity. If it be a true belief that God desires, above all things, the happiness of his creatures, and that this was his purpose in their creation, utility is not only not a godless doctrine, but more profoundly religious than any other. If it be meant that utilitarianism does not recognize the revealed will of God as the supreme law of morals, I answer, that a utilitarian who believes in the perfect goodness and wisdom of God, necessarily believes that whatever God has thought fit to reveal on the subject of morals, must fulfil the requirements of utility in a supreme degree. But others besides utilitarians have been of opinion that the Christian revelation was intended, and is fitted, to inform the hearts and minds of mankind with a spirit which should enable them to find for themselves what is right, and incline them to do it when found, rather than to tell them, except in a very general way, what it is: and that we need a doctrine of ethics, carefully followed out, to interpret to us the will of God. Whether this opinion is correct or not, it is superfluous here to discuss; since whatever aid religion, either natural or revealed, can afford to ethical investigation, is as open to the utilitarian moralist as to any other. He can use it as the testimony of God to the usefulness or hurtfulness of any given course of action, by as good a right as others can use it for the indication of a transcendental law, having no connection with usefulness or with happiness.

Again, Utility is often summarily stigmatized as an immoral doctrine by giving it the name of Expediency, and taking advantage of the popular use of that term to contrast it with Principle. But the Expedient, in the sense in which it is opposed to the Right, generally means that which is expedient for the particular interest of the agent himself: as when a minister sacrifices the interest of his country to keep himself in place. When it means anything better than this, it means that which is expedient for some immediate object, some temporary purpose, but which violates a rule whose observance is expedient in a much higher degree. The Expedient, in this sense, instead of being the same thing with the useful, is a branch of the hurtful. Thus, it would often be expedient, for the purpose of getting over some momentary embarrassment, or attaining some object immediately useful to ourselves or others, to tell a lie. But inasmuch as the cultivation in ourselves of a sensitive feeling on the subject of veracity, is one of the most useful, and the enfeeblement of that feeling one of the most hurtful, things to which our conduct can be instrumental; and inasmuch as any, even unintentional, deviation from truth, does that much towards weakening the trustworthiness of human assertion, which is not only the principal support of all present social well-being, but the insufficiency of which does more than any one thing that can be named to keep back civilization, virtue, everything on which human happiness on the largest scale depends; we feel that the violation, for a present advantage, of a rule of such transcendent expediency, is not expedient, and that he who, for the sake of a convenience to himself or to some other individual, does what depends on him to deprive mankind of the good, and inflict upon them the evil, involved in the greater or less reliance which they can place in each other's word, acts the part of one of their worst enemies. Yet that even this rule, sacred as it is, admits of possible exceptions, is acknowledged by all moralists; the chief of which is when the withholding of some fact (as of information from a male-factor, or of bad news from a person dangerously ill) would preserve some one (especially a person other than oneself) from great and unmerited evil, and when the withholding can only be effected by denial. But in order that the exception may not extend itself beyond the need, and may have the least possible effect in weakening reliance on veracity, it ought to be recognized, and, if possible, its limits defined; and if the principle of utility is good for anything, it must be good for weighing these conflicting utilities against one another, and marking out the region within which one or the other preponderates.

What if there was?

Again, defenders of utility often find themselves called upon to reply to such objections as this—that there is not time, previous to action, for calculating and weighing the effects of any line of conduct on the general happiness. This is exactly as if any one were to say that it is impossible to guide our conduct by Christianity, because there is not time, on every occasion on which anything has to be done, to read through the Old and New Testaments. The answer to the objection is, that there has been ample time, namely, the whole past duration of the human species. During all that time mankind have been learning by experience the tendencies of actions; on which experience all the prudence, as well as all the morality of life, is dependent. People talk as if the commencement of this course of experience had hitherto been put off, and as if, at the moment when some man feels tempted to meddle with the property or life of another, he had to begin considering for the first time whether murder and theft are injurious to human happiness. Even then I do not think that he would find the question very puzzling; but, at all events, the matter is now done to his hand. It is truly a whimsical supposition, that if mankind were agreed in considering utility to be the test of morality, they would remain without any agreement as to what is useful, and would take no measures for having their notions on the subject taught to the young, and enforced by law and opinion. There is no difficulty in proving any ethical standard whatever to work ill, if we suppose universal idiocy to be conjoined with it, but on any hypothesis short of that, mankind must by this time have acquired positive beliefs as to the effects of some actions on their happiness; and the beliefs which have thus come down are the rules of morality for the multitude, and for the philosopher until he has succeeded in finding better. That philosophers might easily do this, even now, on many subjects; that the received code of ethics is by no means of divine right; and that mankind have still much to learn as to the effects of actions on the general happiness, I admit, or rather, earnestly maintain. The corollaries from the principle of utility, like the precepts of every practical art, admit of indefinite improvement, and, in a progressive state of the human mind, their improvement is perpetually going on. But to consider the rules of morality as improvable, is one thing; to pass over the intermediate generalizations entirely, and endeavor to test each individual action directly by the first principle, is another. It is a strange notion that the acknowledgment of a first principle is inconsistent with the admission of secondary ones. To inform a traveler respecting the place of his ultimate destination, is not to forbid the use of landmarks and direction-posts on the way. The proposition that happiness is the end and aim of morality, does not mean that no road ought to be laid down to that goal, or that persons going thither should not be advised to take one direction rather than another. Men really ought to leave off talking a kind of nonsense on this subject, which they would neither talk nor listen to on other matters of practical concernment. Nobody argues that the art of navigation is not founded on astronomy, because sailors cannot wait to calculate the Nautical Almanac. Being rational creatures, they go to sea with it ready calculated; and all rational creatures go out upon the sea of life with their minds made up on the common questions of right and wrong, as well as on many of the far more difficult questions of wise and foolish. And this, as long as foresight is a human quality, it is to be presumed they will continue to do. Whatever we adopt as the fundamental principle of morality, we require subordinate principles to apply it by: the impossibility of doing without them, being common to all systems, can afford no argument against any one in particular: but gravely to argue as if no such secondary principles could be had, and as if mankind had remained till now, and always must remain, without drawing any general conclusions from the experience of human life, is as high a pitch, I think, as absurdity has ever reached in philosophical controversy.

The remainder of the stock arguments against utilitarianism mostly consist in laying to its charge the common infirmities of human nature, and the general difficulties which embarrass conscientious persons in shaping their course through life. We are told that a utilitarian will be apt to make his own particular case an exception to moral rules, and, when under temptation, will see an utility in the breach of a rule, greater than he will see in its observance. But is utility the only creed which is able to furnish us with excuses for evil doing, and means of cheating our own conscience? They are afforded in abundance by all doctrines which recognize as a fact in morals the existence of conflicting considerations; which all doctrines do, that have been believed by sane persons. It is not the fault of any creed, but of the complicated nature of human affairs, that rules of conduct cannot be so framed as to require no exceptions, and that hardly any kind of action can safely be laid down as either always obligatory or always condemnable. There is no ethical creed which does not temper the rigidity of its laws, by giving a certain latitude, under the moral responsibility of the agent, for accommodation to peculiarities of circumstances; and under every creed, at the opening thus made, self-deception and dishonest casuistry get in. There exists no moral system under which there do not arise unequivocal cases of conflicting obligation. These are the real difficulties, the knotty points both in the theory of ethics, and in the conscientious guidance of personal conduct. They are overcome practically with greater or with less success according to the intellect and virtue of the individual; but it can hardly be pretended that any one will be the less qualified for dealing with them, from possessing an ultimate standard to which conflicting rights and duties can be referred. If utility is the ultimate source of moral obligations, utility may be invoked to decide between them when their demands are incompatible. Though the application of the standard may be difficult, it is better than none at all: while in other systems, the moral laws all claiming independent authority, there is no common umpire entitled to interfere between them; their claims to precedence one over another rest on little better than sophistry, and unless determined, as they generally are, by the unacknowledged influence of considerations of utility, afford a free scope for the action of personal desires and partialities. We must remember that only in these cases of conflict between secondary principles is it requisite that first principles should be appealed to. There is no case of moral obligation in which some secondary principle is not involved; and if only one, there can seldom be any real doubt which one it is, in the mind of any person by whom the principle itself is recognized.

Footnote:

An opponent, whose intellectual and moral fairness it is a pleasure to acknowledge (the Rev. J. Llewellyn Davis), has objected to this passage, saying, "Surely the rightness or wrongness of saving a man from drowning does depend very much upon the motive with which it is done. Suppose that a tyrant, when his enemy jumped into the sea to escape from him, saved him from drowning simply in order that he might inflict upon him more exquisite tortures, would it tend to clearness to speak of that rescue as 'a morally right action?' Or suppose again, according to one of the stock illustrations of ethical inquiries, that a man betrayed a trust received from a friend, because the discharge of it would fatally injure that friend himself or someone belonging to him, would utilitarianism compel one to call the betrayal 'a crime' as much as if it had been done from the meanest motive?"

I submit, that he who saves another from drowning in order to kill him by torture afterwards, does not differ only in motive from him who does the same thing from duty or benevolence; the act itself is different. The rescue of the man is, in the case supposed, only the necessary first step of an act far more atrocious than leaving him to drown would have been. Had Mr. Davis said, "The rightness or wrongness of saving a man from drowning does depend very much"—not upon the motive, but—"upon the intention" no utilitarian would have differed from him. Mr. Davis, by an oversight too common not to be quite venial, has in this case confounded the very different ideas of Motive and Intention. There is no point which utilitarian thinkers (and Bentham pre-eminently) have taken more pains to illustrate than this. The morality of the action depends entirely upon the intention—that is, upon what the agent wills to do. But the motive, that is, the feeling which makes him will so to do, when it makes no difference in the act, makes none in the morality: though it makes a great difference in our moral estimation of the agent, especially if it indicates a good or a bad habitual disposition—a bent of character from which useful, or from which hurtful actions are likely to arise.

CHAPTER III: OF THE ULTIMATE SANCTION OF THE PRINCIPLE OF UTILITY

The question is often asked, and properly so, in regard to any supposed moral standard: "What is its sanction? What are the motives to obey it?" or, more specifically, "What is the source of its obligation? Whence does it derive its binding force?" It is a necessary part of moral philosophy to provide the answer to this question; which, though frequently assuming the shape of an objection to the utilitarian morality, as if it had some special applicability to that above others, really arises in regard to all standards. It arises, in fact, whenever a person is called on to adopt a standard or refer morality to any basis on which he has not been accustomed to rest it. For the customary morality, that which education and opinion have consecrated, is the only one which presents itself to the mind with the feeling of being in itself obligatory; and when a person is asked to believe that this morality derives its obligation from some general principle round which custom has not thrown the same halo, the assertion is to him a paradox; the supposed corollaries seem to have a more binding force than the original theorem; the superstructure seems to stand better without, than with, what is represented as its foundation. He says to himself, I feel that I am bound not to rob or murder, betray or deceive; but why am I bound to promote the general happiness? If my own happiness lies in something else, why may I not give that the preference?

If the view adopted by the utilitarian philosophy of the nature of the moral sense be correct, this difficulty will always present itself, until the influences which form moral character have taken the same hold of the principle which they have taken of some of the consequences—until, by the improvement of education, the feeling of unity with our fellow creatures shall be (what it cannot be doubted that Christ intended it to be) as deeply rooted in our character, and to our own consciousness as completely a part of our nature, as the horror of crime is in an ordinarily well-brought-up young person. In the meantime, however, the difficulty has no peculiar application to the doctrine of utility, but is inherent in every attempt to analyze morality and reduce it to principles; which, unless the principle is already in men's minds invested with as much sacredness as any of its applications, always seems to divest them of a part of their sanctity.

The principle of utility either has, or there is no reason why it might not have, all the sanctions which belong to any other system of morals. Those sanctions are either external or internal. Of the external sanctions it is not necessary to speak at any length. They are, the hope of favor and the fear of displeasure from our fellow creatures or from the Ruler of the Universe, along with whatever we may have of sympathy or affection for them or of love and awe of Him, inclining us to do His will independently of selfish consequences. There is evidently no reason why all these motives for observance should not attach themselves to the utilitarian morality, as completely and as powerfully as to any other. Indeed, those of them which refer to our fellow creatures are sure to do so, in proportion to the amount of general intelligence; for whether there be any other ground of moral obligation than the general happiness or not, men do desire happiness; and however imperfect may be their own practice, they desire and commend all conduct in others towards themselves, by which they think their happiness is promoted. With regard to the religious motive, if men believe, as most profess to do, in the goodness of God, those who think that conduciveness to the general happiness is the essence, or even only the criterion, of good, must necessarily believe that it is also that which God approves. The whole force therefore of external reward and punishment, whether physical or moral, and whether proceeding from God or from our fellow men, together with all that the capacities of human nature admit, of disinterested devotion to either, become available to enforce the utilitarian morality, in proportion as that morality is recognized; and the more powerfully, the more the appliances of education and general cultivation are bent to the purpose.

So far as to external sanctions. The internal sanction of duty, whatever our standard of duty may be, is one and the same—a feeling in our own mind; a pain, more or less intense, attendant on violation of duty, which in properly cultivated moral natures rises, in the more serious cases, into shrinking from it as an impossibility. This feeling, when disinterested, and connecting itself with the pure idea of duty, and not with some particular form of it, or with any of the merely accessory circumstances, is the essence of Conscience; though in that complex phenomenon as it actually exists, the simple fact is in general all encrusted over with collateral associations, derived from sympathy, from love, and still more from fear; from all the forms of religious feeling; from the recollections of childhood and of all our past life; from self-esteem, desire of the esteem of others, and occasionally even self-abasement. This extreme complication is, I apprehend, the origin of the sort of mystical character which, by a tendency of the human mind of which there are many other examples, is apt to be attributed to the idea of moral obligation, and which leads people to believe that the idea cannot possibly attach itself to any other objects than those which, by a supposed mysterious law, are found in our present experience to excite it. Its binding force, however, consists in the existence of a mass of feeling which must be broken through in order to do what violates our standard of right, and which, if we do nevertheless violate that standard, will probably have to be encountered afterwards in the form of remorse. Whatever theory we have of the nature or origin of conscience, this is what essentially constitutes it.

The ultimate sanction, therefore, of all morality (external motives apart) being a subjective feeling in our own minds, I see nothing embarrassing to those whose standard is utility, in the question, what is the sanction of that particular standard? We may answer, the same as of all other moral standards—the conscientious feelings of mankind. Undoubtedly this sanction has no binding efficacy on those who do not possess the feelings it appeals to; but neither will these persons be more obedient to any other moral principle than to the utilitarian one. On them morality of any kind has no hold but through the external sanctions. Meanwhile the feelings exist, a feat in human nature, the reality of which, and the great power with which they are capable of acting on those in whom they have been duly cultivated, are proved by experience. No reason has ever been shown why they may not be cultivated to as great intensity in connection with the utilitarian, as with any other rule of morals.

There is, I am aware, a disposition to believe that a person who sees in moral obligation a transcendental fact, an objective reality belonging to the province of "Things in themselves," is likely to be more obedient to it than one who believes it to be entirely subjective, having its seat in human consciousness only. But whatever a person's opinion may be on this point of Ontology, the force he is really urged by is his own subjective feeling, and is exactly measured by its strength. No one's belief that Duty is an objective reality is stronger than the belief that God is so; yet the belief in God, apart from the expectation of actual reward and punishment, only operates on conduct through, and in proportion to, the subjective religious feeling. The sanction, so far as it is disinterested, is always in the mind itself; and the notion, therefore, of the transcendental moralists must be, that this sanction will not exist in the mind unless it is believed to have its root out of the mind; and that if a person is able to say to himself, That which is restraining me, and which is called my conscience, is only a feeling in my own mind, he may possibly draw the conclusion that when the feeling ceases the obligation ceases, and that if he find the feeling inconvenient, he may disregard it, and endeavor to get rid of it. But is this danger confined to the utilitarian morality? Does the belief that moral obligation has its seat outside the mind make the feeling of it too strong to be got rid of? The fact is so far otherwise, that all moralists admit and lament the ease with which, in the generality of minds, conscience can be silenced or stifled. The question: "Need I obey my conscience?" is quite as often put to themselves by persons who never heard of the principle of utility, as by its adherents. Those whose conscientious feelings are so weak as to allow of their asking this question, if they answer it affirmatively, will not do so because they believe in the transcendental theory, but because of the external sanctions.

It is not necessary, for the present purpose, to decide whether the feeling of duty is innate or implanted. Assuming it to be innate, it is an open question to what objects it naturally attaches itself; for the philosophic supporters of that theory are now agreed that the intuitive perception is of principles of morality, and not of the details. If there be anything innate in the matter, I see no reason why the feeling which is innate should not be that of regard to the pleasures and pains of others. If there is any principle of morals which is intuitively obligatory, I should say it must be that. If so, the intuitive ethics would coincide with the utilitarian, and there would be no further quarrel between them. Even as it is, the intuitive moralists, though they believe that there are other intuitive moral obligations, do already believe this to be one; for they unanimously hold that a large portion of morality turns upon the consideration due to the interests of our fellow creatures. Therefore, if the belief in the transcendental origin of moral obligation gives any additional efficacy to the internal sanction, it appears to me that the utilitarian principle has already the benefit of it.

On the other hand, if, as is my own belief, the moral feelings are not innate, but acquired, they are not for that reason the less natural. It is natural to man to speak, to reason, to build cities, to cultivate the ground, though these are acquired faculties. The moral feelings are not indeed a part of our nature, in the sense of being in any perceptible degree present in all of us; but this, unhappily, is a fact admitted by those who believe the most strenuously in their transcendental origin. Like the other acquired capacities above referred to, the moral faculty, if not a part of our nature, is a natural outgrowth from it; capable, like them, in a certain small degree, of springing up spontaneously; and susceptible of being brought by cultivation to a high degree of development. Unhappily it is also susceptible, by a sufficient use of the external sanctions and of the force of early impressions, of being cultivated in almost any direction: so that there is hardly anything so absurd or so mischievous that it may not, by means of these influences, be made to act on the human mind with all the authority of conscience. To doubt that the same potency might be given by the same means to the principle of utility, even if it had no foundation in human nature, would be flying in the face of all experience.

But moral associations which are wholly of artificial creation, when intellectual culture goes on, yield by degrees to the dissolving force of analysis: and if the feeling of duty, when associated with utility, would appear equally arbitrary; if there were no leading department of our nature, no powerful class of sentiments, with which that association would harmonize, which would make us feel it congenial, and incline us not only to foster it in others (for which we have abundant interested motives), but also to cherish it in ourselves; if there were not, in short, a natural basis of sentiment for utilitarian morality, it might well happen that this association also, even after it had been implanted by education, might be analyzed away.

But there is this basis of powerful natural sentiment; and this it is which, when once the general happiness is recognized as the ethical standard, will constitute the strength of the utilitarian morality. This firm foundation is that of the social feelings of mankind; the desire to be in unity with our fellow creatures, which is already a powerful principle in human nature, and happily one of those which tend to become stronger, even without express inculcation, from the influences of advancing civilization. The social state is at once so natural, so necessary, and so habitual to man, that, except in some unusual circumstances or by an effort of voluntary abstraction, he never conceives himself otherwise than as a member of a body; and this association is riveted more and more, as mankind are further removed from the state of savage independence. Any condition, therefore, which is essential to a state of society, becomes more and more an inseparable part of every person's conception of the state of things which he is born into, and which is the destiny of a human being. Now, society between human beings, except in the relation of master and slave, is manifestly impossible on any other footing than that the interests of all are to be consulted. Society between equals can only exist on the understanding that the interests of all are to be regarded equally. And since in all states of civilization, every person, except an absolute monarch, has equals, everyone is obliged to live on these terms with somebody; and in every age some advance is made towards a state in which it will be impossible to live permanently on other terms with anybody. In this way people grow up unable to conceive as possible to them a state of total disregard of other people's interests. They are under a necessity of conceiving themselves as at least abstaining from all the grosser injuries, and (if only for their own protection.) living in a state of constant protest against them. They are also familiar with the fact of co-operating with others, and proposing to themselves a collective, not an individual, interest, as the aim (at least for the time being) of their actions. So long as they are co-operating, their ends are identified with those of others; there is at least a temporary feeling that the interests of others are their own interests. Not only does all strengthening of social ties, and all healthy growth of society, give to each individual a stronger personal interest in practically consulting the welfare of others; it also leads him to identify his feelings more and more with their good, or at least with an ever greater degree of practical consideration for it. He comes, as though instinctively, to be conscious of himself as a being who of course pays regard to others. The good of others becomes to him a thing naturally and necessarily to be attended to, like any of the physical conditions of our existence. Now, whatever amount of this feeling a person has, he is urged by the strongest motives both of interest and of sympathy to demonstrate it, and to the utmost of his power encourage it in others; and even if he has none of it himself, he is as greatly interested as anyone else that others should have it. Consequently, the smallest germs of the feeling are laid hold of and nourished by the contagion of sympathy and the influences of education; and a complete web of corroborative association is woven round it, by the powerful agency of the external sanctions. This mode of conceiving ourselves and human life, as civilization goes on, is felt to be more and more natural. Every step in political improvement renders it more so, by removing the sources of opposition of interest, and levelling those inequalities of legal privilege between individuals or classes, owing to which there are large portions of mankind whose happiness it is still practicable to disregard. In an improving state of the human mind, the influences are constantly on the increase, which tend to generate in each individual a feeling of unity with all the rest; which feeling, if perfect, would make him never think of, or desire, any beneficial condition for himself, in the benefits of which they are not included. If we now suppose this feeling of unity to be taught as a religion, and the whole force of education, of institutions, and of opinion, directed, as it once was in the case of religion, to make every person grow up from infancy surrounded on all sides both by the profession and by the practice of it, I think that no one, who can realize this conception, will feel any misgiving about the sufficiency of the ultimate sanction for the Happiness morality. To any ethical student who finds the realization difficult, I recommend, as a means of facilitating it, the second of M. Comte's two principal works, the *Système de Politique Positive*. I entertain the strongest objections to the system of politics and morals set forth in that treatise; but I think it has superabundantly shown the possibility of giving to the service of humanity, even without the aid of belief in a Providence, both the physical power and the social efficacy of a religion; making it take hold of human life, and color all thought, feeling, and action, in a manner of which the greatest ascendency ever exercised by any religion may be but a type and foretaste; and of which the danger is, not that it should be insufficient, but that it should be so excessive as to interfere unduly with human freedom and individuality.

Neither is it necessary to the feeling which constitutes the binding force of the utilitarian morality on those who recognize it, to wait for those social influences which would make its obligation felt by mankind at large. In the comparatively early state of human advancement in which we now live, a person cannot indeed feel that entireness of sympathy with all others, which would make any real discordance in the general direction of their conduct in life impossible; but already a person in whom the social feeling is at all developed, cannot bring himself to think of the rest of his fellow creatures as struggling rivals with him for the means of happiness, whom he must desire to see defeated in their object in order that he may succeed in his. The deeply-rooted conception which every individual even now has of himself as a social being, tends to make him feel it one of his natural wants that there should be harmony between his feelings and aims and those of his fellow creatures. If differences of opinion and of mental culture make it impossible for him to share many of their actual feelings-perhaps make him denounce and defy those feelings-he still needs to be conscious that his real aim and theirs do not conflict; that he is not opposing himself to what they really wish for, namely, their own good, but is, on the contrary, promoting it. This feeling in most individuals is much inferior in strength to their selfish feelings, and is often wanting altogether. But to those who have it, it possesses all the characters of a natural feeling. It does not present itself to their minds as a superstition of education, or a law despotically imposed by the power of society, but as an attribute which it would not be well for them to be without. This conviction is the ultimate sanction of the greatest-happiness morality. This it is which makes any mind, of well-developed feelings, work with, and not against, the outward motives to care for others, afforded by what I have called the external sanctions; and when those sanctions are wanting, or act in an opposite direction, constitutes in itself a powerful internal binding force, in proportion to the sensitiveness and thoughtfulness of the character; since few but those whose mind is a moral blank, could bear to lay out their course of life on the plan of paying no regard to others except so far as their own private interest compels.

CHAPTER IV: OF WHAT SORT OF PROOF THE PRINCIPLE OF UTILITY IS SUSCEPTIBLE

It has already been remarked, that questions of ultimate ends do not admit of proof, in the ordinary acceptation of the term. To be incapable of proof by reasoning is common to all first principles; to the first premises of our knowledge, as well as to those of our conduct. But the former, being matters of fact, may be the subject of a direct appeal to the faculties which judge of fact—namely, our senses, and our internal consciousness. Can an appeal be made to the same faculties on questions of practical ends? Or by what other faculty is cognizance taken of them?

Questions about ends are, in other words, questions what things are desirable. The utilitarian doctrine is, that happiness is desirable, and the only thing desirable, as an end; all other things being only desirable as means to that end. What ought to be required of this doctrine—what conditions is it requisite that the doctrine should fulfil—to make good its claim to be believed?

The only proof capable of being given that an object is visible, is that people actually see it. The only proof that a sound is audible, is that people hear it: and so of the other sources of our experience. In like manner, I apprehend, the sole evidence it is possible to produce that anything is desirable, is that people do actually desire it. If the end which the utilitarian doctrine proposes to itself were not, in theory and in practice, acknowledged to be an end, nothing could ever convince any person that it was so. No reason can be given why the general happiness is desirable, except that each person, so far as he believes it to be attainable, desires his own happiness. This, however, being a fact, we have not only all the proof which the case admits of, but all which it is possible to require, that happiness is a good: that each person's happiness is a good to that person, and the general happiness, therefore, a good to the aggregate of all persons. Happiness has made out its title as one of the ends of conduct, and consequently one of the criteria of morality.

But it has not, by this alone, proved itself to be the sole criterion. To do that, it would seem, by the same rule, necessary to show, not only that people desire happiness, but that they never desire anything else. Now it is palpable that they do desire things which, in common language, are decidedly distinguished from happiness. They desire, for example, virtue, and the absence of vice, no less really than pleasure and the absence of pain. The desire of virtue is not as universal, but it is as authentic a fact, as the desire of happiness. And hence the opponents of the utilitarian standard deem that they have a right to infer that there are other ends of human action besides happiness, and that happiness is not the standard of approbation and disapprobation.

But does the utilitarian doctrine deny that people desire virtue, or maintain that virtue is not a thing to be desired? The very reverse. It maintains not only that virtue is to be desired, but that it is to be desired disinterestedly, for itself. Whatever may be the opinion of utilitarian moralists as to the original conditions by which virtue is made virtue; however they may believe (as they do) that actions and dispositions are only virtuous because they promote another end than virtue; yet this being granted, and it having been decided, from considerations of this description, what is virtuous, they not only place virtue at the very head of the things which are good as means to the ultimate end, but they also recognize as a psychological fact the possibility of its being, to the individual, a good in itself, without looking to any end beyond it; and hold, that the mind is not in a right state, not in a state conformable to Utility, not in the state most conducive to the general happiness, unless it does love virtue in this manner—as a thing desirable in itself, even although, in the individual instance, it should not produce those other desirable consequences which it tends to produce, and on account of which it is held to be virtue. This opinion is not, in the smallest degree, a departure from the Happiness principle. The ingredients of happiness are very various, and each of them is desirable in itself, and not merely when considered as swelling an aggregate. The principle of utility does not mean that any given pleasure, as music, for instance, or any given exemption from pain, as for example health, are to be looked upon as means to a collective something termed happiness, and to be desired on that account. They are desired and desirable in and for themselves; besides being means, they are a part of the end. Virtue, according to the utilitarian doctrine, is not naturally and originally part of the end, but it is capable of becoming so; and in those who love it disinterestedly it has become so, and is desired and cherished, not as a means to happiness, but as a part of their happiness.

To illustrate this farther, we may remember that virtue is not the only thing, originally a means, and which if it were not a means to anything else, would be and remain indifferent, but which by association with what it is a means to, comes to be desired for itself, and that too with the utmost intensity. What, for example, shall we say of the love of money? There is nothing originally more desirable about money than about any heap of glittering pebbles. Its worth is solely that of the things which it will buy; the desires for other things than itself, which it is a means of gratifying. Yet the love of money is not only one of the strongest moving forces of human life, but money is, in many cases, desired in and for itself; the desire to possess it is often stronger than the desire to use it, and goes on increasing when all the desires which point to ends beyond it, to be compassed by it, are falling off. It may be then said truly, that money is desired not for the sake of an end, but as part of the end. From being a means to happiness, it has come to be itself a principal ingredient of the individual's conception of happiness. The same may be said of the majority of the great objects of human life—power, for example, or fame; except that to each of these there is a certain amount of immediate pleasure annexed, which has at least the semblance of being naturally inherent in them; a thing which cannot be said of money. Still, however, the strongest natural attraction, both of power and of fame, is the immense aid they give to the attainment of our other wishes; and it is the strong association thus generated between them and all our objects of desire, which gives to the direct desire of them the intensity it often assumes, so as in some characters to surpass in strength all other desires. In these cases the means have become a part of the end, and a more important part of it than any of the things which they are means to. What was once desired as an instrument for the attainment of happiness, has come to be desired for its own sake. In being desired for its own sake it is, however, desired as part of happiness. The person is made, or thinks he would be made, happy by its mere possession; and is made unhappy by failure to obtain it. The desire of it is not a different thing from the desire of happiness, any more than the love of music, or the desire of health. They are included in happiness. They are some of the elements of which the desire of happiness is made up. Happiness is not an abstract idea, but a concrete whole; and these are some of its parts. And the utilitarian standard sanctions and approves their being so. Life would be a poor thing, very ill provided with sources of happiness, if there were not this provision of nature, by which things originally indifferent, but conducive to, or otherwise associated with, the satisfaction of our primitive desires, become in themselves sources of pleasure more valuable than the primitive pleasures, both in permanency, in the space of human existence that they are capable of covering, and even in intensity. Virtue, according to the utilitarian conception, is a good of this description. There was no original desire of it, or motive to it, save its conduciveness to pleasure, and especially to protection from pain. But through the association thus formed, it may be felt a good in itself, and desired as such with as great intensity as any other good; and with this difference between it and the love of money, of power, or of fame, that all of these may, and often do, render the individual noxious to the other members of the society to which he belongs, whereas there is nothing which makes him so much a blessing to them as the cultivation of the disinterested, love of virtue. And consequently, the utilitarian standard, while it tolerates and approves those other acquired desires, up to the point beyond which they would be more injurious to the general happiness than promotive of it, enjoins and requires the cultivation of the love of virtue up to the greatest strength possible, as being above all things important to the general happiness.

It results from the preceding considerations, that there is in reality nothing desired except happiness. Whatever is desired otherwise than as a means to some end beyond itself, and ultimately to happiness, is desired as itself a part of happiness, and is not desired for itself until it has become so. Those who desire virtue for its own sake, desire it either because the consciousness of it is a pleasure, or because the consciousness of being without it is a pain, or for both reasons united; as in truth the pleasure and pain seldom exist separately, but almost always together, the same person feeling pleasure in the degree of virtue attained, and pain in not having attained more. If one of these gave him no pleasure, and the other no pain, he would not love or desire virtue, or would desire it only for the other benefits which it might produce to himself or to persons whom he cared for.

We have now, then, an answer to the question, of what sort of proof the principle of utility is susceptible. If the opinion which I have now stated is psychologically true—if human nature is so constituted as to desire nothing which is not either a part of happiness or a means of happiness, we can have no other proof, and we require no other, that these are the only things desirable. If so, happiness is the sole end of human action, and the promotion of it the test by which to judge of all human conduct; from whence it necessarily follows that it must be the criterion of morality, since a part is included in the whole.

And now to decide whether this is really so; whether mankind do desire nothing for itself but that which is a pleasure to them, or of which the absence is a pain; we have evidently arrived at a question of fact and experience, dependent, like all similar questions, upon evidence. It can only be determined by practiced self-consciousness and self-observation, assisted by observation of others. I believe that these sources of evidence, impartially consulted, will declare that desiring a thing and finding it pleasant, aversion to it and thinking of it as painful, are phenomena entirely inseparable, or rather two parts of the same phenomenon; in strictness of language, two different modes of naming the same psychological fact: that to think of an object as desirable (unless for the sake of its consequences), and to think of it as pleasant, are one and the same thing; and that to desire anything, except in proportion as the idea of it is pleasant, is a physical and metaphysical impossibility.

So obvious does this appear to me, that I expect it will hardly be disputed: and the objection made will be, not that desire can possibly be directed to anything ultimately except pleasure and exemption from pain, but that the will is a different thing from desire; that a person of confirmed virtue, or any other person whose purposes are fixed, carries out his purposes without any thought of the pleasure he has in contemplating them, or expects to derive from their fulfilment; and persists in acting on them, even though these pleasures are much diminished, by changes in his character or decay of his passive sensibilities, or are outweighed by the pains which the pursuit of the purposes may bring upon him. All this I fully admit, and have stated it elsewhere, as positively and emphatically as any one. Will, the active phenomenon, is a different thing from desire, the state of passive sensibility, and though originally an offshoot from it, may in time take root and detach itself from the parent stock; so much so, that in the case of an habitual purpose, instead of willing the thing because we desire it, we often desire it only because we will it. This, however, is but an instance of that familiar fact, the power of habit, and is nowise confined to the case of virtuous actions. Many indifferent things, which men originally did from a motive of some sort, they continue to do from habit. Sometimes this is done unconsciously, the consciousness coming only after the action: at other times with conscious volition, but volition which has become habitual, and is put into operation by the force of habit, in opposition perhaps to the deliberate preference, as often happens with those who have contracted habits of vicious or hurtful indulgence. Third and last comes the case in which the habitual act of will in the individual instance is not in contradiction to the general intention prevailing at other times, but in fulfilment of it; as in the case of the person of confirmed virtue, and of all who pursue deliberately and consistently any determinate end. The distinction between will and desire thus understood, is an authentic and highly important psychological fact; but the fact consists solely in this—that will, like all other parts of our constitution, is amenable to habit, and that we may will from habit what we no longer desire for itself, or desire only because we will it. It is not the less true that will, in the beginning, is entirely produced by desire; including in that term the repelling influence of pain as well as the attractive one of pleasure. Let us take into consideration, no longer the person who has a confirmed will to do right, but him in whom that virtuous will is still feeble, conquerable by temptation, and not to be fully relied on; by what means can it be strengthened? How can the will to be virtuous, where it does not exist in sufficient force, be implanted or awakened? Only by making the person desire virtue—by making him think of it in a pleasurable light, or of its absence in a painful one. It is by associating the doing right with pleasure, or the doing wrong with pain, or by eliciting and impressing and bringing home to the person's experience the pleasure naturally involved in the one or the pain in the other, that it is possible to call forth that will to be virtuous, which, when confirmed, acts without any thought of either pleasure or pain. Will is the child of desire, and passes out of the dominion of its parent only to come under that of habit. That which is the result of habit affords no presumption of being intrinsically good; and there would be no reason for wishing that the purpose of virtue should become independent of pleasure and pain, were it not that the influence of the pleasurable and painful associations which prompt to virtue is not sufficiently to be depended on for unerring constancy of action until it has acquired the support of habit. Both in feeling and in conduct, habit is the only thing which imparts certainty; and it is because of the importance to others of being able to rely absolutely on one's feelings and conduct, and to oneself of being able to rely on one's own, that the will to do right ought to be cultivated into this habitual independence. In other words, this state of the will is a means to good, not intrinsically a good; and does not contradict the doctrine that nothing is a good to human beings but in so far as it is either itself pleasurable, or a means of attaining pleasure or averting pain.

But if this doctrine be true, the principle of utility is proved. Whether it is so or not, must now be left to the consideration of the thoughtful reader. . . .

[*Utilitarianism.* (7th ed. London: Longmans, Green, Reader, and Dyer, 1879).]

Key Terms and Concepts

- consequentialism
- hedonism
- universalism
- utility
- Principle of Utility
- Principle of Asceticism
- Bentham's Hedonic Calculus
- Mill's Greatest Happiness Principle
- higher vs. lower pleasures
- Act Utilitarianism
- Rule Utilitarianism
- objections to Utilitarianism

Questions for Further Reflection

1. In what sense is Utilitarianism a consequentialist ethical theory? How does this differ from a deontological approach to ethics? Which approach—if any—do you most agree with? Why?

2. Compare and contrast Bentham and Mill on the concepts of pleasure and pain.

3. How does Mill distinguish between higher (i.e., superior) and lower (i.e., inferior) pleasures? Do you agree with his criterion? Why or why not?

4. What is the main difference between Act Utilitarianism and Rule Utilitarianism? Which objection to Utilitarian ethics is the shift to Rule Utilitarianism intended to address?

5. Apply Bentham's hedonic calculus to an ethical topic of your own choosing. What conclusion does his formula produce? Do you agree or disagree with the outcome? Why or why not?

6. Identify three criticisms of Utilitarianism addressed by Mill and his responses to them. Do you find his defenses of the theory persuasive? Why or why not?

7. How does Mill account for the fact that many people seem to prefer the lower pleasures at the expense of the so-called higher pleasures? Do you agree with his assessment? Why or why not?

Homework Assignment #6a

Name: ________________________________ Section: ________________________________

Explain Bentham's claim: "Nature has placed mankind under the governance of two sovereign masters, pain and pleasure." What, exactly, does Bentham mean by this? Do you agree? Why or why not?

Homework Assignment #6b

Name: ________________________________ Section: ________________________________

Explain the difference between what Bentham calls the Principle of Utility and the Principle of Asceticism. Which principle does Bentham endorse? Why? Do you agree with him? Why or why not?

Homework Assignment #6d

Name: ______________________________ Section: ______________________________

Explain John Stuart Mill's qualitative distinction between higher pleasures and lower pleasures. What criterion (i.e., standard) does Mill employ to determine the quality of a given pleasure?

Homework Assignment #6e

Name: ______________________________ Section: ______________________________

Explain how Mill tries to account for the fact that many people seem to prefer the lower pleasures at the expense of the higher pleasures. Do you agree with his assessment? Why or why not?

CHAPTER SEVEN

Kant on Duty and the Categorical Imperative

© Nicku/Shutterstock.com

Immanuel Kant (1724–1804)

SELECTED READINGS

- *Groundwork of the Metaphysics of Morals*—Immanuel Kant

Groundwork of the Metaphysics of Morals

Immanuel Kant
(Translated by Mary Gregor)

FIRST SECTION: TRANSITION FROM COMMON TO PHILOSOPHICAL MORAL RATIONAL COGNITION

It is impossible to think of anything at all in the world, or indeed even beyond it, that could be taken to be good without limitation, except a good will. Understanding, wit, judgment, and whatever else the *talents* of the mind may be called, or confidence, resolve, and persistency of intent, as qualities of *temperament*, are no doubt in many respects good and desirable; but they can also be extremely evil and harmful if the will that is to make use of these gifts of nature, and whose distinctive constitution is therefore called *character*, is not good. It is just the same with *gifts of fortune*. Power, riches, honor, even health, and the entire well-being and contentment with one's condition, under the name of *happiness*, inspire confidence and thereby quite often overconfidence as well, unless a good will is present to correct and make generally purposive[i] their influence on the mind, and with it also the whole principle for acting; not to mention that a rational impartial spectator can nevermore take any delight in the sight of the uninterrupted prosperity of a being adorned with no feature of a pure and good will, and that a good will thus appears to constitute the indispensable condition even of the worthiness to be happy.

Some qualities are even conducive to this good will itself and can make its work much easier; but regardless of this they have no inner unconditional worth, but always presuppose a good will, which limits the high esteem in which they are otherwise rightly held, and makes it impermissible to take them for good per se. Moderation in affects and passions, self-control and sober deliberation are not only good in many respects, they even appear to constitute part of the *inner* worth of a person; but they are far from deserving to be declared good without limitation (however unconditionally they were praised by the ancients). For without principles of a good will they can become most evil, and the cold blood of a scoundrel makes him not only far more dangerous, but also immediately more loathsome in our eyes than he would have been taken to be without it.

A good will is good not because of what it effects, or accomplishes, not because of its fitness to attain some intended end, but good just by its willing, i.e. in itself; and, considered by itself, it is to be esteemed beyond compare much higher than anything that could ever be brought about by it in favor of some inclination, and indeed, if you will, the sum of all inclinations. Even if by some particular disfavor of fate, or by the scanty endowment of a stepmotherly nature, this will should entirely lack the capacity to carry through its purpose; if despite its greatest striving it should still accomplish nothing, and only the good will were to remain (not, of course, as a mere wish, but as the summoning of all means that are within our control); then, like a jewel, it would still shine by itself, as something that has its full worth in itself. Usefulness or fruitlessness can neither add anything to this worth, nor take anything away from it. It would, as it were, be only the setting to enable us to handle it better in ordinary commerce, or to attract the attention of those who are not yet expert enough; but not to recommend it to experts, or to determine its worth.

Even so, in this idea of the absolute worth of a mere will, not taking into account any utility in its estimation, there is something so strange that, regardless of all the agreement with it even of common reason, a suspicion must yet arise that it might perhaps covertly be founded merely on some high-flown fantastication, and that we may have misunderstood Nature's[j] purpose in assigning Reason to our will as its ruler. We shall therefore submit this idea to examination from this point of view.

In the natural predispositions of an organized being, i.e. one arranged purposively[k] for life, we assume as a principle that no organ will be found in it for any end that is not also the most fitting for it and the most suitable. Now in a being that has reason and a will, if the actual end of Nature were its *preservation,* its *prosperity*, in a word its *happiness*, then she would have made very bad arrangements for this in appointing the creature's Reason as the accomplisher of this purpose. For all the actions that it has to perform with a view to this purpose, and the whole rule of its conduct, would be marked out for it far more accurately by instinct, and that end would thereby have been obtained much more reliably than can ever be done by reason; and if in addition reason should have been bestowed on the favored creature, it would have had to serve it only to contemplate the fortunate predisposition of its nature, to admire it, to rejoice in it, and to be grateful for it to the beneficent cause; but not to subject its desiderative faculty[l] to that weak and deceptive guidance and meddle with Nature's purpose; in a word, Nature would have prevented Reason from striking out into *practical use*, and from having the impudence, with its feeble insights, to devise its own plan for happiness and for the means of achieving it. Nature herself would have taken over the choice not only of ends, but also of means, and as a wise precaution would have entrusted them both solely to instinct.

In actual fact, we do find that the more a cultivated reason engages with the purpose of enjoying life and with happiness, so much the further does a human being stray from true contentment; and from this there arises in many, and indeed in those who are most experienced in its use, if only they are sincere enough to admit it, a certain degree of *misology*, i.e. hatred of reason, since after calculating all the advantages they derive—I do not say from the invention of all the arts of common luxury, but even from the sciences (which in the end also appear to them to be a luxury of the understanding)—they still find that they have in fact just brought more hardship upon their shoulders than they have gained in happiness, and that because of this they eventually envy, rather than disdain, the more common run of people, who are closer to the guidance of mere natural instinct, and who do not allow their reason much influence on their behavior. And to that extent one must admit that the judgment of those who greatly moderate and even reduce below zero the vainglorious eulogies extolling the advantages that reason was supposed to obtain for us with regard to the happiness and contentment of life, is by no means sullen, or ungrateful to the kindliness of the government of the world; but that these judgments are covertly founded on the idea of another and far worthier purpose of their existence, to which, and not to happiness, reason is quite properly destined, and to which, as its supreme condition, the private purpose of a human being must therefore largely take second place.

For since reason is not sufficiently fit to guide the will reliably with regard to its objects and the satisfaction of all our needs (which in part it does itself multiply)—an end to which an implanted natural instinct would have led much more reliably—but reason as a practical faculty, i.e. as one that is meant to influence the *will*, has yet been imparted to us, its true function[m] must be to produce a *will that is good*, not for other purposes *as a means*, but good *in itself*—for which reason was absolutely necessary—since nature has everywhere else gone to work purposively in distributing its predispositions. Therefore this will need not, indeed, be the only and the entire good, but it must yet be the highest good, and the condition of everything else, even of all longing for happiness; in which case it is quite consistent with the wisdom of nature when one perceives that the cultivation of reason, which is required for the first and unconditional purpose, in many ways limits—at least in this life—the attainment of the second, namely of happiness, which is always conditional, indeed that it may reduce it to less than nothing without nature's proceeding unpurposively in this; because reason, which recognizes as its highest practical function the grounding of a good will, in attaining this purpose, is capable only of a contentment after its own kind, namely from fulfilling an end that again is determined only by reason, even if this should involve much infringement on the ends of inclination.

In order, then, to unravel[n] the concept of a will to be highly esteemed in itself and good apart from any further purpose, as it already dwells in natural sound understanding and needs not so much to be taught as rather just to be brought to light,[o] this concept that always comes first in estimating the entire worth of our actions and constitutes the condition of everything else: we shall inspect the concept of duty, which contains that of a good will, though under certain subjective limitations and hindrances, which, however, far from concealing it and making it unrecognizable, rather bring it out by contrast and make it shine forth all the more brightly.

I here pass over all actions already recognized as contrary to duty, even though they may be useful in this or that respect; for in their case there is no question whether they might have been done *from duty*, since they even conflict with it. I also set aside actions that actually conform with duty but to which human beings immediately have *no inclination*, but which they still perform, because they are impelled to do so by another inclination. For there it is easy to distinguish whether the action that conforms with duty was done *from duty* or from a self-serving purpose. It is much more difficult to notice this difference when an action conforms with duty and the subject has in addition an *immediate* inclination towards it. E.g. it certainly conforms with duty that a shopkeeper not overcharge his inexperienced customer, and where there is much commerce, a prudent merchant actually does not do this, but keeps a fixed general price for everyone, so that a child may buy from him just as well as everyone else. Thus one is served *honestly*; but this is not nearly enough for us to believe that the merchant proceeded in this way from duty and principles of honesty; his advantage required it; it cannot be assumed here that he had, besides, an immediate inclination towards his customers, so as from love, as it were, to give no one preference over another in the matter of price. Thus the action was done neither from duty, nor from immediate inclination, but merely for a self-interested purpose.

By contrast, to preserve one's life is one's duty,[p] and besides everyone has an immediate inclination to do so. But on account of this the often anxious care with which the greatest part of humanity attends to it has yet no inner worth, and their maxim no moral content. They preserve their lives *in conformity with duty*, but not *from duty*. By contrast, if adversities and hopeless grief have entirely taken away the taste for life; if the unfortunate man, strong of soul, more indignant about his fate than despondent or dejected, wishes for death, and yet preserves his life, without loving it, not from inclination, or fear, but from duty; then his maxim has a moral content.

To be beneficent where one can is one's duty, and besides there are many souls so attuned to compassion that, even without another motivating ground of vanity, or self-interest, they find an inner gratification in spreading joy around them, and can relish the contentment of others, in so far as it is their work. But I assert that in such a case an action of this kind—however much it conforms with duty, however amiable it may be—still has no true moral worth, but stands on the same footing as other inclinations, e.g. the inclination to honor, which if it fortunately lights upon what is in fact in the general interest and in conformity with duty, and hence honorable, deserves praise and encouragement, but not high esteem; for the maxim lacks moral content, namely to do such actions not from inclination, but *from duty*. Suppose, then, that the mind of that friend of humanity were beclouded by his own grief, which extinguishes all compassion for the fate of others; that he still had the means to benefit others in need, but the need of others did not touch him because he is sufficiently occupied with his own; and that now, as inclination no longer stimulates him to it, he were yet to tear himself out of this deadly insensibility, and to do the action without any inclination, solely from duty; not until then does it have its genuine moral worth. Still further: if nature had as such placed little sympathy in the heart of this or that man; if (otherwise honest) he were by temperament cold and indifferent to the sufferings of others, perhaps because he himself is equipped with the peculiar gift of patience and enduring strength towards his own, and presupposes, or even requires, the same in every other; if nature had not actually formed such a man (who would truly not be its worst product) to be a friend of humanity, would he not still find within himself a source from which to give himself a far higher worth than that of a good-natured temperament may be? Certainly! It is just there that the worth of character commences, which is moral and beyond all comparison the highest, namely that he be beneficent, not from inclination, but from duty.

To secure one's own happiness is one's duty (at least indirectly); for lack of contentment with one's condition, in the trouble of many worries and amidst unsatisfied needs, could easily become a great *temptation to transgress one's duties*. But, even without taking note of duty, all human beings have already of their own the most powerful and intimate inclination to happiness, as it is just in this idea that all inclinations unite in one sum. However, the prescription of happiness is predominantly such, that it greatly infringes on some inclinations and yet human beings can form no determinate and reliable concept of the sum of the satisfaction of all under the name of happiness; which is why it is not surprising that a single inclination—if determinate with regard to what it promises, and to the time its satisfaction can be obtained[q]—can outweigh a wavering idea, and that a human being, e.g. someone suffering from gout of the foot, can choose to enjoy what he fancies and to suffer what he can since, according to his calculation, at least then he has not denied himself the enjoyment of the present moment because of perhaps groundless expectations of some good fortune that is meant to lie in health. But also in this case, if the universal inclination to happiness did not determine his will, if health, at least for him, did not enter into this calculation so necessarily, then here, as in all other cases, there still remains a law, namely to advance one's happiness,[r] not from inclination, but from duty; and it is not until then that his conduct has its actual moral worth.

It is in this way, no doubt, that we are to understand the passages from Scripture that contain the command to love one's neighbor, even our enemy. For love as inclination cannot be commanded, but beneficence from duty itself—even if no inclination whatsoever impels us to it, indeed if natural and unconquerable aversion resists—is *practical* and not *pathological*[s] love, which lies in the will and not in the propensity of sensation, in principles of action and not in melting compassion; and only the former can be commanded.

The second proposition is: an action from duty has its moral worth *not in the purpose* that is to be attained by it, but in the maxim according to which it is resolved upon,[t] and thus it does not depend on the actuality of the object of the action, but merely on the *principle* of *willing* according to which—regardless of any object of the desiderative faculty—the action is done. That the purposes that we may have when we act, and their effects, as ends and incentives[u] of the will, can bestow on actions no unconditional and moral worth, is clear from what was previously said. In what, then, can this worth lie, if it is not to consist in the will with reference to their hoped-for effect? It can lie nowhere else *than in the principle of the will*, regardless of the ends that can be effected by such action; for the will stands halfway between its a priori principle, which is formal, and its a posteriori incentive, which is material, as it were at a crossroads, and since it must after all be determined by something, it will have to be determined by the formal principle of willing as such when an action is done from duty, as every material principle has been taken away from it.

The third proposition, as the conclusion from both previous ones, I would express as follows: *duty is the necessity of an action from respect*[v] *for the law.* For the object as the effect of the action I have in mind I can indeed have *inclination,* but *never respect,* precisely because it is merely an effect and not activity of a will.[w] Likewise, I cannot have respect for inclination as such, whether it is mine or that of another; I can at most in the first case approve of it, in the second at times love it myself, i.e. view it as favorable to my own advantage. Only what is connected with my will merely as ground, never as effect, what does not serve my inclination, but outweighs it, or at least excludes it entirely from calculations when we make a choice, hence the mere law by itself, can be an object of respect and thus a command. Now, an action from duty is to separate off entirely the influence of inclination, and with it every object of the will; thus nothing remains for the will that could determine it except, objectively, the *law* and, subjectively, *pure respect* for this practical law, and hence the maxim[*] of complying with such a law, even if it infringes on all my inclinations.

Thus the moral worth of the action does not lie in the effect that is expected from it, nor therefore in any principle of action that needs to borrow its motivating ground from this expected effect. For all these effects (agreeableness of one's condition, indeed even advancement of the happiness of others) could also have been brought about by other causes, and thus there was, for this, no need of the will of a rational being; even so, in it alone can the highest and unconditional good be found. Nothing other than the *representation of the law* in itself—*which of course can take place only in a rational being*—in so far as it, not the hoped-for effect, is the determining ground of the will, can therefore constitute the pre-eminent good that we call moral, which is already present in the person himself who acts according to it, and is not first to be expected from the effect.[*]

But what kind of law can that possibly be, the representation of which—even without regard for the effect expected from it—must determine the will for it to be called good absolutely and without limitation? Since I have robbed the will of all impulses that could arise for it from following some particular law, nothing remains but as such the universal conformity of actions with law, which alone is to serve the will as its principle, i.e. I ought never to proceed except in such a way *that I could also will that my maxim should become a universal law.* Here, then, mere conformity with law as

---

*A *maxim* is the subjective principle of willing; the objective principle (i.e. the one that would also subjectively serve all rational beings as the practical principle if reason had complete control over the desiderative faculty) is the practical *law.*

*I might be accused of using the word *respect* just to seek refuge in an obscure feeling, instead of giving distinct information about the matter in question by means of a concept of reason. But even though respect is a feeling, it is not one *received* by influence, but one *self-wrought* by a rational concept and therefore specifically different from all feelings of the former kind, which come down to inclination or fear. What I recognize immediately as a law for myself I recognize with respect, which signifies merely the consciousness of the *subordination* of my will to a law, without mediation of other influences on my sense. The immediate determination of the will by the law and the consciousness of this is called *respect,* so that it is viewed as the *effect* of the law on the subject and not as its *cause.* Respect is actually the representation of a worth that infringes on my self-love. Thus it is something that is considered an object neither of inclination, nor of fear, even though it is at the same time somewhat analogous to both. The *object* of respect is therefore solely the *law,* the one that we impose upon *ourselves* and yet as in itself necessary. As a law we are subject to it, without consulting self-love; as imposed upon us by ourselves, it is yet a consequence of our will, and in the first regard it has an analogy with fear, in the second with inclination. All respect for a person is actually only respect for the law (of righteousness etc.) of which he gives us the example. Because we also view expanding our talents as our duty, we represent a person of talents also, as it were, as the *example of a law* (to become like him in this by practice)[x] and this is what constitutes our respect. All moral *interest,* so called, consists solely in *respect* for the law.

such (not founded on any law determined with a view to certain actions) is what serves the will as its principle, and must so serve it if duty is not to be as such an empty delusion and a chimerical concept; common human reason in its practical judging is actually in perfect agreement with this, and always has the envisaged principle before its eyes.

Let the question be, e.g., may I not, when I am in trouble, make a promise with the intention not to keep it? Here I easily discern the different meanings the question can have: whether it is prudent, or whether it conforms with duty to make a false promise. The former can no doubt quite often take place. I do see very well that it is not enough to extricate myself from the present predicament by means of this subterfuge, but that it requires careful deliberation whether this lie may not later give rise to much greater inconvenience for me than those from which I am now liberating myself; and—since with all my supposed *cunning* the consequences cannot be so easily foreseen that trust once lost might not be far more disadvantageous to me than any ill that I now mean to avoid—whether one might not act *more prudently* in this matter by proceeding according to a universal[y] maxim, and by making it one's habit to promise nothing except with the intention of keeping it. But here it soon becomes clear to me that such a maxim will still only be founded on the dreaded consequences. Now, to be truthful from duty is something quite different from being truthful from dread of adverse consequences; as in the first case, the concept of the action in itself already contains a law for me, whereas in the second I must first look around elsewhere to see what effects on me this might involve. For if I deviate from the principle of duty, this is quite certainly evil; but if I defect from my maxim of prudence, that can sometimes be very advantageous to me, though it is of course safer to adhere to it. However, to instruct myself in the very quickest and yet undeceptive[z] way with regard to responding to this problem—whether a lying promise conforms with duty—I ask myself: would I actually be content that my maxim (to extricate myself from a predicament by means of an untruthful promise) should hold as a universal law (for myself as well as for others), and would I be able to say to myself: everyone may make an untruthful promise when he finds himself in a predicament from which he can extricate himself in no other way? Then I soon become aware that I could indeed will the lie, but by no means a universal law to lie; for according to such a law there would actually be no promise at all, since it would be futile to pretend my will to others with regard to my future actions, who would not believe this pretense; or, if they rashly did so, would pay me back in like coin, and hence my maxim, as soon as it were made a universal law, would have to destroy itself.

I do not, therefore, need any wide-ranging acuteness to see what I have to do for my willing to be morally good. Inexperienced with regard to the course of the world, incapable of bracing myself for whatever might come to pass in it, I just ask myself: can you also will that your maxim become a universal law? If not, then it must be rejected, and that not because of some disadvantage to you, or to others, that might result, but because it cannot fit as a principle into a possible universal legislation, for which reason extracts from me immediate respect; and although I do not yet *see* on what it is founded (which the philosopher may investigate), at least I do understand this much: that it is an estimation of a worth that far outweighs any worth of what is extolled by inclination, and that the necessity of my actions from *pure* respect for the practical law is that which constitutes duty, to which every other motivating ground must give way, because it is the condition of a will good *in itself,* whose worth surpasses everything.

Thus, then, we have progressed in the moral cognition of common human reason to reach its principle, which admittedly it does not think of as separated in this way in a universal form, but yet always actually has before its eyes and uses as the standard of its judging. Here it would be easy to show how, with this compass in hand, it is very well informed in all cases that occur, to distinguish what is good, what is evil, what conforms with duty or is contrary to it, if—without in the least teaching it anything new—one only, as Socrates did, makes it aware of its own principle; and than there is thus no need of science and philosophy to know what one has to do in order to be honest and good, indeed even to be wise and virtuous.[a] It should actually have been possible to presume all along that acquaintance with what it is incumbent upon everyone to do, and hence also to know, would be the affair of every human being, even the commonest. Here one cannot without admiration observe the great advantage the practical capacity to judge has over the theoretical in common human understanding. In the latter, when common reason dares to depart from the laws of experience and the perceptions of the senses, it falls into nothing but sundry incomprehensibilities and internal contradictions, or at least into a chaos of uncertainty, obscurity, and instability. But in practical matters the power of judging first begins to show itself to advantage just when common understanding excludes all sensuous incentives from practical laws. Then it even becomes subtle, whether it seeks to engage in legalistic quibbles[a] with its conscience, or with other claims referring to what is to be called right, or seeks sincerely to determine the worth of actions for its own instruction; and, what is most important, in the latter case it stands just as good a chance of hitting the mark as a philosopher can ever expect; indeed it is almost more sure in this than even the latter, because he can have no other principle, but can easily confuse his judgment with a host of alien and irrelevant considerations and deflect it from the straight course. Accordingly, would it not be more advisable, in moral things, to leave it with the judgment of common reason, and at most to bring on philosophy to present the system of morals more completely and accessibly, and likewise its rules in a form more convenient for use (and still more for disputation), but not to let it lead common human understanding away from its fortunate simplicity for practical purposes, and by means of philosophy to put it on a new route of investigation and instruction?

Innocence is a glorious thing, but then again it is very sad that it is so hard to preserve and so easily seduced. Because of this even wisdom—which probably consists more in behavior than in knowledge elsewhere—yet needs science too, not in order to learn from it, but to obtain access and durability for its prescription. The human being feels within himself a powerful counterweight to all the commands of duty—which reason represents to him as so worthy of the highest respect—in his needs and inclinations, the entire satisfaction of which he sums up under the name of happiness. Now reason issues its prescriptions unrelentingly, yet without promising anything to the inclinations, and hence, as it were, with reproach and disrespect for those claims, which are so vehement and yet seem so reasonable[b] (and will not be eliminated by any command). But from this there arises a *natural dialectic*, i.e. a propensity to rationalize against those strict laws of duty, and to cast doubt on their validity, or at least their purity and strictness and, where possible, to make them better suited to our wishes and inclinations, i.e. fundamentally to corrupt them and deprive them of their entire dignity, something that in the end even common practical reason cannot endorse.

Thus *common human reason* is impelled to leave its sphere not by some need of speculation (which never comes over it as long as it is content to be mere sound reason), but rather on practical grounds, and to take a step into the field of a *practical philosophy*, in order to receive there intelligence and distinct instruction regarding the source of this principle and its correct determination in contrast with maxims based on need and inclination, so that it may escape from the predicament caused by mutual claims, and not run the risk of being deprived of all genuine moral principles because of the ambiguity into which it easily falls. Thus also in practical common reason, when it cultivates itself, a *dialectic* inadvertently unfolds that necessitates it to seek help in philosophy, just as happens to it in its theoretical use, and the one is therefore just as unlikely as the other to find rest anywhere but in a complete critique of our reason.

SECOND SECTION: TRANSITION FROM POPULAR MORAL PHILOSOPHY TO THE METAPHYSICS OF MORALS

If so far we have drawn our concept of duty from the common use of our practical reason, it is by no means to be inferred from this that we have treated it as an experiential concept. Rather, if we attend to our experience of the behavior of human beings we meet frequent and, as we ourselves concede, just complaints that no reliable example can be cited of the disposition[c] to act from pure duty; that, though much may be done that *conforms* with what *duty* commands, still it is always doubtful whether it is actually done *from duty* and thus has a moral worth. That is why there have been philosophers in every age who have absolutely denied the actuality of this disposition in human actions, and attributed everything to a more or less refined self-love, without however calling into doubt the correctness of the concept of morality because of this; rather, with intimate regret they made mention of the frailty and impurity of a human nature that is indeed noble enough to take an idea so worthy of respect as its prescription, but at the same time too weak to follow it, and that uses reason, which should serve it for legislation, only to take care of the interest of inclinations, whether singly or, at most, in their greatest compatibility with one another.

In fact, it is absolutely impossible by means of experience to make out with complete certainty a single case in which the maxim of an action that otherwise conforms with duty did rest solely on moral grounds and on the all, i.e. present actions objectively as practically *necessary*; that they are to be taken rather as counsels (consilia) than as commands (praecepta) of reason; that the problem of determining reliably and universally which action would advance the happiness of a rational being is completely insoluble, and hence that there can be no imperative with regard to it that would in the strict sense command to do what makes us happy because happiness is not an ideal of reason, but of the imagination, which rests merely on empirical grounds, of which it is futile to expect that they should determine an action by which the totality of an in fact infinite series of consequences would be attained. This imperative of prudence would, however, be an analytic practical proposition if one assumes that the means to happiness could be reliably stated; for it differs from the imperative of skill only in this, that in the case of the latter the end is merely possible, whereas in the former it is given: but since both merely command the means to that which one presupposes one wills as an end, the imperative that commands willing the means for someone who wills the end is in both cases analytic. There is thus no difficulty with regard to the possibility of such an imperative either.

By contrast, the question of how the imperative of *morality* is possible is no doubt the only one in need of a solution, since it is not hypothetical at all, and thus the objectively represented necessity cannot rely on any presupposition, as in the case of the hypothetical imperatives. However, it is never to slip our attention in this matter that it cannot be made out *by any example*, and hence empirically, whether there is any such imperative at all; but to be dreaded that all imperatives that appear categorical may yet in some hidden way be hypothetical. E.g. when it is said that you ought not to make deceitful promises; and one assumes that the necessity of this omission is not merely giving counsel for avoiding some other ill, so that what is said would be: you ought not to make lying promises lest, if it comes to light, you are deprived of your credit; but that an action° of this kind must be considered as by itself evil, thus that the imperative of the prohibition is categorical; one still cannot establish in any example with certainty that the will is here determined, without another incentive, merely by the law, even if it appears so; for it is always possible that fear of embarrassment, perhaps also an obscure dread of other dangers, may covertly influence the will. Who can prove the non-existence of a cause by experience when all that it teaches is that we do not perceive one? In that case, however, the so-called moral imperative, which as such appears categorical and unconditional, would in fact just be a pragmatic prescription that alerts us to our advantage, and merely teaches us to attend to it.

We shall thus have to investigate the possibility of a *categorical* imperative entirely a priori, since we do not here enjoy the advantage that its actuality is being given in experience, in which case its possibility would be necessary not for corroboration, but merely for explanation. For the time being, however, this much can be seen: that the categorical imperative alone expresses a practical law, and that the others can indeed one and all be called *principles* of the will, but not laws; since what it is necessary to do merely for attaining a discretionary purpose can be regarded as in itself contingent, and we can always be rid of the prescription if we give up the purpose, whereas the unconditional command leaves the will no free discretion with regard to the opposite, and hence alone carries with it that necessity which we demand for a law.

Secondly, in the case of this categorical imperative or law of morality the ground of the difficulty (of insight into its possibility) is actually very great. It is an a priori synthetic practical proposition,* and since gaining insight into the possibility of propositions of this kind causes so much difficulty in theoretical cognition, it can easily be inferred that in practical cognition there will be no less.

With this problem, we shall first try to see whether the mere concept of a categorical imperative may perhaps also furnish its formula, which contains the proposition that alone can be a categorical imperative; for how such an absolute command is possible, even if we know how to express it, will still require particular and arduous effort, which we suspend, however, until the final section.

When I think of a *hypothetical* imperative as such I do not know in advance what it will contain, until I am given the condition. But when I think of a *categorical* imperative I know at once what it contains. For since besides the law the imperative contains only

*Without a presupposed condition from any inclination, I connect the deed with the will a priori, and hence necessarily (though only objectively, i.e. under the idea of a reason that has complete control over all subjective motives). This is therefore a practical proposition that does not derive the willing of an action analytically from willing another that is already presupposed (for we have no such perfect will), but connects it immediately with the concept of the will of a rational being, as something that is not contained in it.

the necessity of the maxim† to conform with this law, whereas the law contains no condition to which it was limited, nothing is left but the universality of a law as such, with which the maxim of the action ought to conform, and it is this conformity alone that the imperative actually represents as necessary.

There is therefore only a single categorical imperative, and it is this: *act only according to that maxim through which you can at the same time will that it become a universal law.*

Now, if from this one imperative all imperatives of duty can be derived as from their principle, then, even though we leave it unsettled whether what is called duty is not as such an empty concept, we shall at least be able to indicate what we think by it and what the concept means.

Since the universality of the law according to which effects happen constitutes that which is actually called *nature* in the most general sense (according to its form), i.e. the existence of things in so far as it is determined according to universal laws, the universal imperative of duty could also be expressed as follows: *so act as if the maxim of your action were to become by your will a* **universal law of nature**.

We shall now enumerate some duties, according to their usual division, into duties to ourselves and to other human beings, into perfect and imperfect duties.*

1. Someone who feels weary of life because of a series of ills that has grown to the point of hopelessness is still so far in possession of his reason that he can ask himself whether it is not perhaps contrary to a duty to oneself to take one's own life. Now he tries out: whether the maxim of his action could possibly become a universal law of nature. But his maxim is: from self-love I make it my principle to shorten my life if, when protracted any longer, it threatens more ill than it promises agreeableness. The only further question is whether this principle of self-love could become a universal law of nature. But then one soon sees that a nature whose law it were to destroy life itself by means of the same sensation the function of which it is to impel towards the advancement of life, would contradict itself and would thus not subsist as a nature, hence that that maxim could not possibly take the place of a universal law of nature, and consequently conflicts entirely with the supreme principle of all duty.

2. Another sees himself pressured by need to borrow money. He knows full well that he will not be able to repay, but also sees that nothing will be lent to him unless he solemnly promises to repay it at a determinate time. He feels like making such a promise; but he still has enough conscience to ask himself: is it not impermissible and contrary to duty to help oneself out of need in such a way? Suppose that he still resolved to do so, his maxim of the action would go as follows: when I believe myself to be in need of money I shall borrow money, and promise to repay it, even though I know that it will never happen. Now this principle of self-love, or of one's own benefit, is perhaps quite consistent with my whole future well-being, but the question now is: whether it is right? I therefore transform the imposition of self-love into a universal law, and arrange the question as follows: how things would stand if my maxim became a universal law. Now, I then see at once that it could never hold as a universal law of nature and harmonize with itself, but must necessarily contradict itself. For the universality of a law that everyone, once he believes himself to be in need, could promise whatever he fancies with the intention not to keep it, would make the promise and the end one may pursue with it itself impossible, as no one would believe he was being promised anything, but would laugh about any such utterance, as a vain pretense.

3. A third finds in himself a talent that by means of some cultivation could make him a useful human being in all sorts of respects. However, he sees himself in comfortable circumstances and prefers to give himself up to gratification rather than to make the effort to expand and improve his fortunate natural predispositions. Yet he still asks himself: whether his maxim of neglecting his natural gifts, besides

---

†A *maxim* is the subjective principle for acting, and must be distinguished from the *objective principle*, namely the practical law. The former contains the practical rule that reason determines in conformity with the conditions of the subject (quite often his ignorance, or his inclinations), and is thus the principle according to which the subject *acts*, but the law is the objective principle, valid for every rational being, and the principle according to which it *ought to act*, i.e. an imperative.

*Here one must duly note that I reserve the division of duties entirely for my future *Metaphysics of Morals*, and that this one here is put forward only as discretionary (to order my examples).[14] Further, I here understand by a perfect duty the one that allows of no exception to the advantage of inclination, and then I have not merely external but also internal *perfect duties*, which runs counter to the use of the word adopted in the schools; but I do not mean to answer for it here, since for my purpose it is all one whether or not one concedes it to me.

its agreement with his propensity to amusement, also agrees with what one calls duty. Now he sees that a nature could indeed still subsist according to such a universal law, even if human beings (like the South Sea Islanders) should let their talents rust and be intent on devoting their lives merely to idleness, amusement, procreation, in a word, to enjoyment; but he cannot possibly will that this become a universal law of nature, or as such be placed in us by natural instinct. For as a rational being he necessarily wills that all capacities in him be developed, because they serve him and are given to him[p] for all sorts of possible purposes.

4. Yet a *fourth*, who is prospering while he sees that others have to struggle with great hardships (whom he could just as well help), thinks: what's it to me? May everyone be as happy as heaven wills, or as he can make himself, I shall take nothing away from him, not even envy him; I just do not feel like contributing anything to his well-being, or his assistance in need! Now, certainly, if such a way of thinking were to become a universal law of nature, the human race could very well subsist, and no doubt still better than when everyone chatters about compassion and benevolence, even develops the zeal to perform such actions occasionally, but also cheats wherever he can, sells out the right of human beings, or infringes it in some other way. But even though it is possible that a universal law of nature could very well subsist according to that maxim, it is still impossible to will that such a principle hold everywhere as a law of nature. For a will that resolved upon this would conflict with itself, as many cases can yet come to pass in which one needs the love and compassion of others, and in which, by such a law of nature sprung from his own will, he would rob himself of all hope of the assistance he wishes for himself.

These, then, are some of the many actual duties, or at least of what we take to be such, whose division[q] can clearly be seen from the one principle stated above. One must *be able to will* that a maxim of our action become a universal law: this is as such the canon of judging it morally. Some actions are such that their maxim cannot even be *thought* without contradiction as a universal law of nature; let alone that one could *will* that it *should* become such. In the case of others that inner impossibility is indeed not to be found, but it is still impossible to *will* that their maxim be elevated to the universality of a law of nature, because such a will would contradict itself. It is easy to see that the first conflicts with strict or narrower (unrelenting) duty, the second only with wider (meritorious) duty, and thus that all duties, as far as the kind of obligation (not the object of their action) is concerned, have by these examples been set out completely in their dependence on the one principle.

If we now attend to ourselves in every transgression of a duty, we find that we actually do not will that our maxim should become a universal law, since that is impossible for us, but that its opposite should rather generally remain a law; we just take the liberty of making an *exception* to it for ourselves, or[r] (just for this once) to the advantage of our inclination. Consequently, if we considered everything from one and the same point of view, namely that of reason, we would find a contradiction in our own will, namely that a certain principle be objectively necessary as a universal law and yet subjectively should not hold universally, but allow of exceptions. But since we consider our action at one time from the point of view of a will that entirely conforms with reason, but then just the same action also from the point of view of a will affected by inclination, there is actually no contradiction here, but rather a resistance of inclination to the prescription of reason (antagonismus), by which the universality of the principle (universalitas) is transformed into a mere general validity (generalitas), and by this the practical rational principle is meant to meet the maxim halfway. Now, even though this cannot be justified in our own impartially employed judgment, it still proves that we actually acknowledge the validity of the categorical imperative, and permit ourselves (with all respect for it) just a few exceptions that, as it seems to us, are immaterial and wrenched from us.

We have thus established at least this much, that if duty is a concept that is to contain significance and actual legislation for our actions it can be expressed only in categorical imperatives, but by no means in hypothetical ones; likewise we have—and this is already a lot—presented distinctly and determined for every use the content of the categorical imperative, which would have to contain the principle of all duty (if there were such a thing at all). But we are not yet ready to prove a priori that such an imperative is actually in place, that there is a practical law, which commands of itself, absolutely and without any incentives, and that following this law is one's duty.

For the purpose of achieving this, it is of the utmost importance to let this serve as a warning, that one must put the thought right out of one's mind that the reality of this principle can be derived from some *particular property of human nature.* For duty is to be practical unconditional necessity of action; it must thus hold for all rational beings (to which an imperative can at all apply), and *only in virtue of this* be a law also for every human will. By contrast, whatever is derived from the special natural predisposition of humanity, from certain feelings and propensity, and even, if possible, from a special tendency that would be peculiar to human reason and would not have to hold necessarily for the will of every rational being—that can indeed yield a maxim for us but not a law; it can yield a subjective principle on which we might act if we have the propensity and inclination, but not an objective principle on which we would be *directed* to act even though every propensity, inclination, and natural tendency of ours were against it—so much so that the sublimity and inner dignity of the command in a duty is all the more manifest the fewer are the subjective causes in favor of it and the more there are against it, without thereby weakening in the least the necessitation by the law or taking anything away from its validity.

Here, then, we see philosophy put in fact in a precarious position, which is to be firm even though there is nothing in heaven or on earth from which it depends or on which it is based. Here philosophy is to manifest its purity as sustainer of its own laws, not as herald of laws that an implanted sense or who knows what tutelary nature whispers to it, all of which—though they may always be better than nothing at all—can still never yield basic principles that reason dictates and that must have their source entirely and completely *a priori* and, at the same time, must have their commanding authority from this: that they expect nothing from the inclination of human beings but everything from the supremacy of the law and the respect owed it or, failing this, condemn the human being to contempt for himself and inner abhorrence.

Hence everything empirical, as an addition to the principle of morality, is not only quite inept for this; it is also highly prejudicial to the purity of morals, where the proper worth of an absolutely good will—a worth raised above all price—consists just in the principle of action being free from all influences of contingent grounds, which only experience can furnish. One cannot give too many or too frequent warnings against this laxity, or even mean cast of mind, which seeks its principle among empirical motives and laws; for, human reason in its weariness gladly rests on this pillow and in a dream of sweet illusions (which allow it to embrace a cloud instead of Juno) it substitutes for morality a bastard patched up from limbs of quite diverse ancestry, which looks like whatever one wants to see in it but not like virtue for him who has once seen virtue in her true form.

The question is therefore this: is it a necessary law *for all rational beings* always to appraise their actions in accordance with such maxims as they themselves could will to serve as universal laws? If there is such a law, then it must already be connected (completely a priori) with the concept of the will of a rational being as such. But in order to discover this connection we must, however reluctantly, step forth, namely into metaphysics, although into a domain of it that is distinct from speculative philosophy, namely into metaphysics of morals. In a practical philosophy, where we have to do not with assuming grounds for what happens but rather laws for what ought to happen even if it never does, that is, objective practical laws, we do not need to undertake an investigation into the grounds on account of which something pleases or displeases; how the satisfaction of mere sensation differs from taste, and whether the latter differs from a general satisfaction of reason; upon what the feeling of pleasure or displeasure rests, and how from it desires and inclinations arise, and from them, with the cooperation of reason, maxims; for all that belongs to an empirical doctrine of the soul, which would constitute the second part of the doctrine of nature when this is regarded as philosophy of nature insofar as it is based on empirical laws. Here, however, it is a question of objective practical laws and hence of the relation of a will to itself insofar as it determines itself only by reason; for then everything that has reference to the empirical falls away of itself, since if reason entirely by itself determines conduct (and the possibility of this is just what we want now to investigate), it must necessarily do so *a priori.*

The will is thought as a capacity to determine itself to acting in conformity with the *representation of certain laws.* And such a capacity can be found only in rational beings. Now, what serves the will as the objective ground of its self-determination is an end, and this, if it is given by reason alone, must hold equally for all rational beings. What, on the other hand, contains merely the ground of the possibility of an action the effect of which is an end is called a *means.* The subjective ground of desire is an *incentive*; the objective ground of volition is a *motive*; hence the distinction between subjective ends, which rest on incentives, and objective ends, which depend on motives, which hold for every rational being. Practical principles are *formal* if they abstract from all subjective ends, whereas they are *material* if they have put these, and consequently certain incentives, at their basis. The ends that a rational being proposes at his discretion as *effects* of his actions (material ends) are all only relative; for only their mere relation to a specially constituted faculty of desire on the part of the subject gives them their worth, which can therefore furnish no universal principles, no principles valid and necessary for all rational beings and also for every volition, that is, no practical laws. Hence all these relative ends are only the ground of hypothetical imperatives.

But suppose there were something *the existence of which in itself* has an absolute worth, something which as *an end in itself* could be a ground of determinate laws; then in it, and in it alone, would lie the ground of a possible categorical imperative, that is, of a practical law.

Now I say that the human being and in general every rational being exists as an end in itself, *not merely as a means* to be used by this or that will at its discretion; instead he must in all his actions, whether directed to himself or also to other rational beings, always be regarded at the same time as an end. All objects of the inclinations have only a conditional worth; for, if there were not inclinations and the needs based on them, their object would be without worth. But the inclinations themselves, as sources of needs, are so far from having an absolute worth, so as to make one wish to have them, that it must instead be the universal wish of every rational being to be altogether free from them. Thus the worth of any object *to be acquired* by our action is always conditional. Beings the existence of which rests not on our will but on nature, if they are beings without reason, still have only a relative worth, as means, and are therefore called *things*, whereas rational beings are called *persons* because their nature already marks them out as an end in itself, that is, as something that may not be used merely as a means, and hence so far limits all choice (and is an object of respect). These, therefore, are not merely subjective ends, the existence of which as an effect of our action has a worth *for us*, but rather *objective ends*, that is, beings the existence of which is in itself an end, and indeed one such that no other end, to which they would serve *merely* as means, can be put in its place, since without it nothing of *absolute worth* would be found anywhere; but if all worth were conditional and therefore contingent, then no supreme practical principle for reason could be found anywhere.

If, then, there is to be a supreme practical principle and, with respect to the human will, a categorical imperative, it must be one such that, from the representation of what is necessarily an end for everyone because it is an *end in itself*, it constitutes an *objective* principle of the will and thus can serve as a universal practical law. The ground of this principle is: *rational nature exists as an end in itself.* The human being necessarily represents his own existence in this way; so far it is thus a *subjective* principle of human actions. But every other rational being also represents his existence in this way consequent on just the same rational ground that also holds for me; thus it is at the same time an *objective* principle from which, as a supreme practical ground, it must be possible to derive all laws of the will. The practical imperative will therefore be the following: *So act that you use humanity, whether in your own person or in the person of any other, always at the same time as an end, never merely as a means.* We shall see whether this can be carried out.

To keep to the preceding examples:

First, as regards the concept of necessary duty to oneself, someone who has suicide in mind will ask himself whether his action can be consistent with the idea of humanity *as an end in itself.* If he destroys himself in order to escape from a trying condition he makes use of a person *merely as a means* to maintain a tolerable condition up to the end of life. A human being, however, is not a thing and hence not something that can be used *merely* as a means, but must in all his actions always be regarded as an end in itself. I cannot, therefore, dispose of a human being in my own person by maiming, damaging or killing him. (I must here pass over a closer determination of this principle that would prevent any misinterpretation, e.g., as to having limbs amputated in order to preserve myself, or putting my life in danger in order to preserve my life, and so forth; that belongs to morals proper.)

Second, as regards necessary duty to others or duty owed them, he who has it in mind to make a false promise to others sees at once that he wants to make use of another human being *merely as a means*, without the other at the same time containing in himself the end. For, he whom I want to use for my purposes by such a promise cannot possibly agree to my way of behaving toward him, and so himself contain the end of this action. This conflict with the principle of other human beings is seen more distinctly if examples of assaults on the freedom and property of others are brought forward. For then it is obvious that he who transgresses the rights of human beings intends to make use of the person of others merely as means, without taking into consideration that, as rational beings, they are always to be valued at the same time as ends, that is, only as beings who must also be able to contain in themselves the end of the very same action.

Third, with respect to contingent (meritorious) duty to oneself, it is not enough that the action does not conflict with humanity in our person as an end in itself; it must also *harmonize* with it. Now there are in humanity predispositions to greater perfection, which belong to the end of nature with respect to humanity in our subject; to neglect these might admittedly be consistent with the *preservation* of humanity as an end in itself but not with the *furtherance* of this end.

Fourth, concerning meritorious duty to others, the natural end that all human beings have is their own happiness. Now, humanity might indeed subsist if no one contributed to the happiness of others but yet did not intentionally withdraw anything from it; but there is still only a negative and not a positive agreement with *humanity as an end in itself* unless everyone also tries, as far as he can, to further the ends of others. For, the ends of a subject who is an end in itself must as far as possible be also *my* ends, if that representation is to have its *full* effect in me.

This principle of humanity, and in general of every rational nature, *as an end in itself* (which is the supreme limiting condition of the freedom of action of every human being) is not borrowed from experience; first because of its universality, since it applies to all rational beings as such and no experience is sufficient to determine anything about them; second because in it humanity is represented not as an end of human beings (subjectively), that is, not as an object that we of ourselves actually make our end, but as an objective end that, whatever ends we may have, ought as law to constitute the supreme limiting condition of all subjective ends, so that the principle must arise from pure reason. That is to say, the ground of all practical lawgiving lies (in accordance with the first principle) *objectively in the rule* and the form of universality which makes it fit to be a law (possibly a law of nature); *subjectively*, however, it lies in the end; but the subject of all ends is every rational being as an end in itself (in accordance with the second principle); from this there follows now the third practical principle of the will, as supreme condition of its harmony with universal practical reason, the idea *of the will of every rational being as a will giving universal law.*

In accordance with this principle all maxims are repudiated that are inconsistent with the will's own giving of universal law. Hence the will is not merely subject to the law but subject to it in such a way that it must be viewed as also giving the law to itself" and just because of this as first subject to the law (of which it can regard itself as the author).

Imperatives as they were represented above—namely in terms of the conformity of actions with universal law similar to a *natural order* or of the universal *supremacy as ends* of rational beings in themselves—did exclude from their commanding authority any admixture of interest as incentive, just by their having been represented as categorical; but they were only assumed to be categorical because we had to make such an assumption if we wanted to explain the concept of duty. But that there are practical propositions which command categorically could not itself be proved, any more than it could be proved either here or anywhere else in this section; one thing, however, could still have been done: namely, to indicate in the imperative itself the renunciation of all interest, in volition from duty, by means of some determination the imperative contains, as the specific mark distinguishing categorical from hypothetical imperatives; and this is done in the present third formula of the principle, namely the idea of the will of every rational being as *a will giving universal law.*

For when we think of a will of this kind, then although a will that stands under law may be bound to this law by means of some interest, a will that is itself the supreme lawgiver cannot possibly, as such, depend upon some interest; for, a will that is dependent in this way would itself need yet another law that would limit the interest of its self-love to the condition of a validity for universal law.

Thus the *principle* of every human will as *a will giving universal law through all its maxims,* provided it is otherwise correct, would be very *well suited* to be the categorical imperative by this: that just because of the idea of giving universal law *it is based on no interest* and therefore, among all possible imperatives, can alone be *unconditional*; or still better, by converting the proposition, if there is a categorical imperative (i.e., a law for every will of a rational being) it can only command that everything be done from the maxim of one's will as a will that could at the same time have as its object itself as giving universal law; for only then is the practical principle, and the imperative that the will obeys, unconditional, since it can have no interest as its basis.

If we look back upon all previous efforts that have ever been made to discover the principle of morality, we need not wonder now why all of them had to fail. It was seen that the human being is bound to laws by his duty, but it never occurred to them that he is subject *only to laws given by himself but still universal* and that he is bound only to act in conformity with his own will, which, however, in accordance with nature's end is a will giving universal law. For, if one thought of him only as subject to a law (whatever it may be), this law had to carry with it some interest by way of attraction or constraint, since it did not as a law arise from his will; in order to conform with the law, his will had instead to be constrained by *something else* to act in a certain way. By this quite necessary consequence, however, all the labor to find a supreme ground of duty was irretrievably lost. For, one never arrived at duty but instead at the necessity of an action from a certain interest. This might be one's own or another's interest. But then the imperative had to turn out always conditional and could not be fit for a moral command. I will therefore call this basic principle the principle of the **autonomy** of the will in contrast with every other, which I accordingly count as **heteronomy**.

The concept of every rational being as one who must regard himself as giving universal law through all the maxims of his will, so as to appraise himself and his actions from this point of view, leads to a very fruitful concept dependent upon it namely that of *a kingdom of ends.*

By a *kingdom* I understand a systematic union of various rational beings through common laws. Now since laws determine ends in terms of their universal validity, if we abstract from the personal differences of rational beings as well as from all the content of their private ends we shall be able to think of a whole of all ends in systematic connection (a whole both of rational beings as ends in themselves and of the ends of his own that each may set himself), that is, a kingdom of ends, which is possible in accordance with the above principles.

For, all rational beings stand under the *law* that each of them is to treat himself and all others *never merely as means* but always *at the same time as ends in themselves.* But from this there arises a systematic union of rational beings through common objective laws, that is, a kingdom, which can be called a kingdom of ends (admittedly only an ideal) because what these laws have as their purpose is just the relation of these beings to one another as ends and means.

A rational being belongs as a *member* to the kingdom of ends when he gives universal laws in it but is also himself subject to these laws. He belongs to it as *sovereign* when, as lawgiving, he is not subject to the will of any other.

A rational being must always regard himself as lawgiving in a kingdom of ends possible through freedom of the will, whether as a member or as sovereign. He cannot, however, hold the position of sovereign merely by the maxims of his will but only in case he is a completely independent being, without needs and with unlimited resources adequate to his will.

Morality consists, then, in the reference of all action to the lawgiving by which alone a kingdom of ends is possible. This lawgiving must, however, be found in every rational being himself and be able to arise from his will, the principle of which is, accordingly: to do no action on any other maxim than one such that it would be consistent with it to be a universal law, and hence to act only *so that the will could regard itself as at the same time giving universal law through its maxim.* Now, if maxims are not already of their nature in agreement with this objective principle of rational beings as givers of universal law, the necessity of an action in accordance with this principle is called practical necessitation, that is, *duty.* Duty does not apply to the sovereign in the kingdom of ends, but it does apply to every member of it and indeed to all in equal measure.

The practical necessity of acting in accordance with this principle, that is, duty, does not rest at all on feelings, impulses, and inclinations but merely on the relation of rational beings to one another, in which the will of a rational being must always be regarded as at the same time lawgiving, since otherwise it could not be thought as an *end in itself.* Reason accordingly refers every maxim of the will as giving universal law to every other will and also to every action toward oneself, and does so not for the sake of any other practical motive or any future advantage but from the idea of the *dignity* of a rational being, who obeys no law other than that which he himself at the same time gives.

In the kingdom of ends everything has either a *price* or a *dignity.* What has a price can be replaced by something else as its *equivalent*; what on the other hand is raised above all price and therefore admits of no equivalent has a dignity.

What is related to general human inclinations and needs has a *market price*; that which, even without presupposing a need, conforms with a certain taste, that is, with a delight in the mere purposeless play of our mental powers, has *a fancy price*; but that which constitutes the condition under which alone something can be an end in itself has not merely a relative worth, that is, a price, but an inner worth, that is, *dignity*.

Now, morality is the condition under which alone a rational being can be an end in itself, since only through this is it possible to be a lawgiving member in the kingdom of ends. Hence morality, and humanity insofar as it is capable of morality, is that which alone has dignity. Skill and diligence in work have a market price; wit, lively imagination and humor have a fancy price; on the other hand, fidelity in promises and benevolence from basic principles (not from instinct) have an inner worth. Nature, as well as art, contains nothing that, lacking these, it could put in their place; for their worth does not consist in the effects arising from them, in the advantage and use they provide, but in dispositions, that is, in maxims of the will that in this way are ready to manifest themselves through actions, even if success does not favor them. Such actions also need no recommendation from any subjective disposition or taste, so as to be looked upon with immediate favor and delight, nor do they need any immediate propensity or feeling for them; they present the will that practices them as the object of an immediate respect, and nothing but reason is required to *impose* them upon the will, not to *coax* them from it, which latter would in any case be a contradiction in the case of duties. This estimation therefore lets the worth of such a cast of mind be cognized as dignity and puts it infinitely above all price, with which it cannot be brought into comparison or competition at all without, as it were, assaulting its holiness.

And what is it, then, that justifies a morally good disposition, or virtue, in making such high claims? It is nothing less than the share it affords a rational being *in the giving of universal laws,* by which it makes him fit to be a member of a possible kingdom of ends, which he was already destined to be by his own nature as an end in itself and, for that very reason, as lawgiving in the kingdom of ends—as free with respect to all laws of nature, obeying only those which he himself gives and in accordance with which his maxims can belong to a giving of universal law (to which at the same time he subjects himself). For, nothing can have a worth other than that which the law determines for it. But the law-giving itself, which determines all worth, must for that very reason have a dignity, that is, an unconditional, incomparable worth; and the word *respect* alone provides a becoming expression for the estimate of it that a rational being must give. *Autonomy* is therefore the ground of the dignity of human nature and of every rational nature.

The above three ways of representing the principle of morality are at bottom only so many formulae of the very same law, and any one of them of itself unites the other two in it. There is nevertheless a difference among them, which is indeed subjectively rather than objectively practical, intended namely to bring an idea of reason closer to intuition (by a certain analogy) and thereby to feeling. All maxims have, namely,

1. a form, which consists in universality; and in this respect the formula of the moral imperative is expressed thus: that maxims must be chosen' as if they were to hold as universal laws of nature;
2. a *matter*, namely an end, and in this respect the formula says that a rational being, as an end by its nature and hence as an end in itself, must in every maxim serve as the limiting condition of all merely relative and arbitrary ends;
3. a *complete determination* of all maxims by means of that formula, namely that all maxims from one's own lawgiving are to harmonize with a possible kingdom of ends as with a kingdom of nature. A progression takes place here, as through the categories of the *unity* of the form of the will (its universality), the *plurality* of the matter (of objects, i.e., of ends), and the *all-ness* or totality of the system of these. But one does better always to proceed in moral *appraisal* by the strict method and put at its basis the universal formula of the categorical imperative: *act in accordance with a maxim that can at the same time make itself a universal law.* If, however, one wants also to provide *access* for the moral law, it is very useful to bring one and the same action under the three concepts mentioned above and thereby, as far as possible, bring it closer to intuition.

We can now end where we set out from at the beginning, namely with the concept of a will unconditionally good. *That will is absolutely good* which cannot be evil, hence whose maxim, if made a universal law, can never conflict with itself. This principle is, accordingly, also its supreme law: act always on that maxim whose universality as a law you can at the same time will; this is the sole condition under which a will can never be in conflict with itself, and such an imperative is categorical. Since the validity of the will as a universal law for possible actions has an analogy with the universal connection of the existence of things in accordance with universal laws, which is the formal aspect of nature in general, the categorical imperative can also be expressed thus: *act in accordance with maxims that can at the same time have as their object themselves as universal laws of nature.* In this way, then, the formula of an absolutely good will is provided.

Rational nature is distinguished from the rest of nature by this, that it sets itself an end. This end would be the matter of every good will. But since, in the idea of a will absolutely good without any limiting condition (attainment of this or that end) abstraction must be made altogether from every end to be *effected* (this would make every will only relatively good), the end must here be thought not as an end to be effected but as an *independently existing* end, and hence thought only negatively, that is, as that which must never be acted against and which must therefore in every volition be estimated never merely as a means but always at the same time as an end. Now, this end can be nothing other than the subject of all possible ends itself, because this subject is also the subject of a possible absolutely good will; for, such a will cannot without contradiction be subordinated to any other object. The principle, so act with reference to every rational being (yourself and others) that in your maxim it holds at the same time as an end in itself, is thus at bottom the same as the basic principle, act on a maxim that at the same time contains in itself its own universal validity for every rational being. For, to say that in the use of means to any end I am to limit my maxim to the condition of its universal validity as a law for every subject is tantamount to saying that the subject of ends, that is, the rational being itself, must be made the basis of all maxims of actions, never merely as a means but as the supreme limiting condition in the use of all means, that is, always at the same time as an end.

Now, from this it follows incontestably that every rational being, as an end in itself, must be able to regard himself as also giving universal laws with respect to any law whatsoever to which he may be subject; for, it is just this fitness of his maxims for giving universal law that marks him out as an end in itself; it also follows that this dignity (prerogative) he has over all merely natural beings brings with it that he must always take his maxims from the point of view of himself, and likewise every other rational being, as lawgiving beings (who for this reason are also called persons). Now in this way a world of rational beings (*mundus intelligibilis*) as a kingdom of ends is possible, through the giving of their own laws by all persons as members. Consequently, every rational being must act as if he were by his maxims at all times a lawgiving member of the universal kingdom of ends. The formal principle of these maxims is, act as if your maxims were to serve at the same time as a universal law (for all rational beings). A kingdom of ends is thus possible only by analogy with a kingdom of nature; the former, however, is possible only through maxims, that is, rules imposed upon oneself, the latter only through laws of externally necessitated efficient causes. Despite this, nature as a whole, even though it is regarded as a machine, is still given the name "a kingdom of nature" insofar as and because it has reference to rational beings as its ends. Now, such a kingdom of ends would actually come into existence through maxims whose rule the categorical imperative prescribes to all rational beings *if they were universally followed.* It is true that, even though a rational being scrupulously follows this maxim himself, he cannot for that reason count upon every other to be faithful to the same maxim nor can he count upon the kingdom of nature and its purposive order to harmonize with him, as a fitting member, toward a kingdom of ends possible through himself, that is, upon its favoring his expectation of happiness; nevertheless that law, act in accordance with the maxims of a member giving universal laws for a merely possible kingdom of ends, remains in its full force because it commands categorically. And just in this lies the paradox that the mere dignity of humanity as rational nature, without any other end or advantage to be attained by it—hence respect for a mere idea—is yet to serve as an inflexible precept of the will, and that it is just in this independence of maxims from all such incentives that their sublimity consists, and the worthiness of every rational subject to be a lawgiving member in the kingdom of ends; for otherwise he would have to be represented only as subject to the natural law of his needs. Even if the kingdom of nature as well as the kingdom of ends were thought as united under one sovereign, so that the latter would no longer remain a mere idea but would obtain true reality, it would no doubt gain the increment of a strong incentive but never any increase of its inner worth; for, even this sole absolute lawgiver would, despite this, still have to be represented as appraising the worth of rational beings only by their disinterested conduct, prescribed to themselves merely from that idea. The essence of things is not changed by their external relations; and that which, without taking account of such relations, alone constitutes the worth of a human being is that in terms of which he must also be appraised by whoever does it, even by the supreme being. *Morality* is thus the relation of actions to the autonomy of the will, that is, to a possible giving of universal law through its maxims. An action that can coexist with the autonomy of the will is *permitted*; one that does not accord with it is *forbidden*. A will whose maxims necessarily harmonize with the laws of autonomy is a holy, absolutely good will. The dependence upon the principle of autonomy of a will that is not absolutely good (moral necessitation) is obligation. This, accordingly, cannot be attributed to a holy being. The objective necessity of an action from obligation is called *duty*.

From what has just been said it is now easy to explain how it happens that, although in thinking the concept of duty we think of subjection to the law, yet at the same time we thereby represent a certain sublimity and *dignity* in the person who fulfills all his duties. For there is indeed no sublimity in him insofar as he is *subject* to the moral law, but there certainly is insofar as he is at the same time *lawgiving* with respect to it and only for that reason subordinated to it. We have also shown above how neither fear nor inclination but simply respect for the law is that incentive which can give actions a moral worth. Our own will insofar as it would act only under the condition of a possible giving of universal law through its maxims—this will possible for us in idea—is the proper object of respect; and the dignity of humanity consists just in this capacity to give universal law, though with the condition of also being itself subject to this very lawgiving.

NOTES

i *allgemein-zweckmäßig*; alternatively "universally purposive," a tricky expression not used elsewhere in the *Groundwork*.

j Nature, Reason, Philosophy, and Virtue are occasionally capitalized, and referred to with the feminine pronoun, to indicate that Kant is using these words allegorically. Allegorical and literal passages are not always easy to distinguish.

k *Zweck* is translated as "end" except when it occurs as part of *zweckmäßig* ("purposive") or *zwecklos* ("purposeless").

l *Begehrungsvermögen*. For Kant's definition of this term cf. the *Critique of Practical Reason* (5:8 n.) and the *Metaphysics of Morals* (6:211). In human beings, the desiderative faculty is the will.

m or "vocation" (Gregor), in the context of teleology; *Bestimmung* has been rendered "determination" elsewhere

n *entmickeln*; or perhaps "explicate" (Gregor)

o *aufgeklärt;* the usual English translation "clarified" obscures the connection with the project of the Enlightenment (*Aufklärung*)

p The standard translation is "is a duty," but when Kant uses the expression *ist Pflicht* he does not mean to say that there is, as such, a specific duty to do something, but simply that a certain action is obligatory (that one has to do it).

q alternatively "sustained," but Kant's usage elsewhere appears to imply the translation adopted here

r or possibly "his happiness" (Gregor), but the command should probably be formulated impersonally, as at the beginning of this paragraph

s love belonging to the passive, sensuous side of human nature, as opposed to reason; not used by Kant in the sense of morbid or obsessive

t "but in . . . resolved upon" is an addition of the second edition

u Gregor's term, now widely accepted, has been retained although it may seem to suggest some external thing that initiates motivation, rather than the internal "spring" or "drive" that Kant had in mind. Kantian "incentives" are motivating desires that propel the agent forward if he or she so decides. A *Triebfeder* is the mainspring of motion, as in a clock or an old-fashioned tin toy.

v H.J. Paton's "reverence" is in some ways a more natural word for a positive motivating moral force like Kantian *Achtung*; but "respect" is now generally used in discussions of Kantian ethics, and it has the additional advantage of resonating with readers beyond the world of Kant scholarship.

w Second edition; the first edition has "effect of my will"
x This parenthetical remark is an addition of the second edition.
y As so often, it is not entirely clear whether *allgemein* means "general" or "universal."
z *untrügliche Art*; the principle is reliable and trustworthy
a *sehikanieren,* to obstruct the claims of conscience, like a pettifogger in a law court
b or "fair"; "equitable" in a juridical context
c The standard translation has been retained, but it is problematic. *Gesinnung* is not just a disposition to behave in a certain way, but one's moral attitude, state of mind, conviction, or character.
o second edition; the first has "but when one asserts that an action"
p "and are given to him" is an addition of the second edition
q Both the first and the second original edition have *Ableilung* (division). Editors and translators since the nineteenth century, including Mary Gregor, tend to substitute *Ableitung* ("derivation"), but note that Kant has presented a division of duties that is meant to be evident *from the above principle,* i.e. the fourfold application of the law-of-nature formulation, further explained in the present paragraph.
r It makes good sense to move the bracket to include "or," as Mary Gregor does, to distinguish two kinds of exception: "for oneself" and "for this once," but the change is probably unnecessary.

Key Terms and Concepts

deontology
the good will
means vs. ends
duty / obligation
"acting from duty"
"acting in conformity with duty"
inclination
autonomy
imperatives
hypothetical imperatives
categorical imperatives
The Categorical Imperative
The Universal Law Formulation of the Categorical Imperative
The Respect for Persons Formulation of the Categorical Imperative
dignity
end-in-itself

Questions for Further Reflection

1. What does Kant mean by "a good will," and why does he consider it "good without limitation"?

2. How does Kant's conception of happiness differ from that of Aristotle? Of Mill?

3. How does Kant distinguish between acting "in conformity with duty" and acting "from duty"? Why is this distinction central to Kant's ethical theory?

4. Why does Kant insist that the moral law "must hold not only for human beings but for all *rational beings as such*"?

5. Explain the main difference between hypothetical imperatives and categorical imperatives. Provide examples of each. Why does Kant turn to an analysis of imperatives at all?

6. Explain in your own words the following: "If we now attend to ourselves in any transgression of a duty, we find that we do not really will that our maxim should become a universal law, since that is impossible for us, but that the opposite of our maxim should instead remain a universal law, only we take the liberty of making an *exception* to it for ourselves (or just for this once) to the advantage of our inclination."

7. For Kant, what does treating others *merely as a means* represent? What does treating *oneself* merely as a means represent? Provide examples of each.

8. Provide an example of a maxim that fails the Universal Law Formulation of Kant's Categorical Imperative. Is there any way to rehabilitate that maxim while remaining faithful to the spirit of Kant's ethical theory?

Homework Assignment #7a

Name: ______________________________ Section: ______________________________

Explain what Immanuel Kant means by "a good will" and why he considers it "good without limitation." Do you agree with his claim? Why or why not?

Homework Assignment #7b

Name: ______________________________ Section: ______________________________

Explain Kant's distinction between acting "in conformity with duty" and acting "from duty." Provide your own example of each kind of action.

Homework Assignment #7d

Name: ______________________________ Section: ______________________________

Explain in your own words Kant's claim: "If we not attend to ourselves in any transgression of a duty, we find that we do not really will that our maxim (i.e., principle) should become a universal law, since that is impossible for us, but that the *opposite* of our maxim (i.e., principle) should instead remain a universal law, only we take the liberty of making an *exception* to it for ourselves (or just for this once) to the advantage of our inclination."

Homework Assignment #7e

Name: ______________________________ Section: ______________________________

For Kant, what does treating others *merely as a means* represent? What might treating oneself merely as a means represent? Provide examples of each.

CHAPTER EIGHT

Hume, Smith, and Darwin on Sympathy and the Moral Sentiments

David Hume (1711–1776)

Adam Smith (1723–1790)

Charles Darwin (1809–1882)

SELECTED READINGS

- *A Treatise of Human Nature*—David Hume
- "Concerning Moral Sentiment" from *an Enquiry Concerning The Principles of Morals*—David Hume
- "Of Justice and Beneficence" from *The Theory of Moral Sentiments*—Adam Smith
- "The Origin of the Moral Sense" from *The Descent of Man*—Charles Darwin

A Treatise of Human Nature

David Hume

BOOK III – OF MORALS

PART I: OF VIRTUE AND VICE IN GENERAL

SECT. I Moral Distinctions Not Derived from Reason

There is an inconvenience which attends all abstruse reasoning that it may silence, without convincing an antagonist, and requires the same intense study to make us sensible of its force, that was at first requisite for its invention. When we leave our closet, and engage in the common affairs of life, its conclusions seem to vanish, like the phantoms of the night on the appearance of the morning; and it is difficult for us to retain even that conviction, which we had attained with difficulty. This is still more conspicuous in a long chain of reasoning, where we must preserve to the end the evidence of the first propositions, and where we often lose sight of all the most received maxims, either of philosophy or common life. I am not, however, without hopes, that the present system of philosophy will acquire new force as it advances; and that our reasonings concerning morals will corroborate whatever has been said concerning the *understanding* and the *passions*. Morality is a subject that interests us above all others: We fancy the peace of society to be at stake in every decision concerning it; and it is evident, that this concern must make our speculations appear more real and solid, than where the subject is, in a great measure, indifferent to us. What affects us, we conclude can never be a chimera; and as our passion is engaged on the one side or the other, we naturally think that the question lies within human comprehension; which, in other cases of this nature, we are apt to entertain some doubt of. Without this advantage I never should have ventured upon a third volume of such abstruse philosophy, in an age, wherein the greatest part of men seem agreed to convert reading into an amusement, and to reject everything that requires any considerable degree of attention to be comprehended.

It has been observed, that nothing is ever present to the mind but its perceptions; and that all the actions of seeing, hearing, judging, loving, hating, and thinking, fall under this denomination. The mind can never exert itself in any action, which we may not comprehend under the term of perception; and consequently that term is no less applicable to those judgments, by which we distinguish moral good and evil, than to every other operation of the mind. To approve of one character, to condemn another, are only so many different perceptions.

Now as perceptions resolve themselves into two kinds, *viz.* impressions and ideas, this distinction gives rise to a question, with which we shall open up our present enquiry concerning morals. *Whether it is by means of our ideas or impressions we distinguish betwixt vice and virtue, and pronounce an action blameable or praiseworthy*? This will immediately cut off all loose discourses and declamations, and reduce us to something precise and exact on the present subject.

Those who affirm that virtue is nothing but a conformity to reason; that there are eternal fitnesses and unfitnesses of things, which are the same to every rational being that considers them; that the immutable measures of right and wrong impose an obligation, not only on human creatures, but also on the Deity himself: All these systems concur in the opinion, that morality, like truth, is discerned merely by ideas, and by their juxtaposition and comparison. In order, therefore, to judge of these systems, we need only consider, whether it be possible, from reason alone, to distinguish betwixt moral good and evil, or whether there must concur some other principles to enable us to make that distinction.

If morality had naturally no influence on human passions and actions, it were in vain to take such pains to inculcate it; and nothing would be more fruitless than that multitude of rules and precepts, with which all moralists abound. Philosophy is commonly divided into speculative and practical; and as morality is always comprehended under the latter division, it is supposed to influence our passions and actions, and to go beyond the calm and indolent judgments of the understanding. And this is confirmed by common experience, which informs us, that men are often governed by their duties, and are deterred from some actions by the opinion of injustice, and impelled to others by that of obligation.

Since morals, therefore, have an influence on the actions and affections, it follows, that they cannot be derived from reason; and that because reason alone, as we have already proved, can never have any such influence. Morals excite passions, and produce or prevent actions. Reason of itself is utterly impotent in this particular. The rules of morality therefore, are not conclusions of our reason.

No one, I believe, will deny the justness of this inference; nor is there any other means of evading it, than by denying that principle, on which it is founded. As long as it is allowed, that reason has no influence on our passions and action, it is in vain to pretend, that morality is discovered only by a deduction of reason. An active principle can never be founded on an inactive; and if reason be inactive in itself, it must remain so in all its shapes and appearances, whether it exerts itself in natural or moral subjects, whether it considers the powers of external bodies, or the actions of rational beings.

It would be tedious to repeat all the arguments by which I have proved that reason is perfectly inert, and can never either prevent or produce any action or affection, it will be easy to recollect what has been said upon that subject. I shall only recall on this occasion one of these arguments, which I shall endeavor to render still more conclusive, and more applicable to the present subject.

Reason is the discovery of truth or falsehood. Truth or falsehood consists in an agreement or disagreement either to the real relations of ideas, or to real existence and matter of fact. Whatever, therefore, is not susceptible of this agreement or disagreement, is incapable of being true or false, and can never be an object of our reason. Now it is evident our passions, volitions, and actions, are not susceptible of any such agreement or disagreement; being original facts and realities, complete in themselves, and implying no reference to other passions, volitions, and actions. It is impossible, therefore, they can be pronounced either true or false, and be either contrary or conformable to reason.

This argument is of double advantage to our present purpose. For it proves *directly*, that actions do not derive their merit from a conformity to reason, nor their blame from a contrariety to it; and it proves the same truth more *indirectly*, by showing us, that as reason can never immediately prevent or produce any action by contradicting or approving of it, it cannot be the source of moral good and evil, which are found to have that influence. Actions may be laudable or blameable; but they cannot be reasonable: Laudable or blameable, therefore, are not the same with reasonable or unreasonable. The merit and demerit of actions frequently contradict, and sometimes control our natural propensities. But reason has no such influence. Moral distinctions, therefore, are not the offspring of reason. Reason is wholly inactive, and can never be the source of so active a principle as conscience, or a sense of morals.

But perhaps it may be said, that though no will or action can be immediately contradictory to reason, yet we may find such a contradiction in some of the attendants of the action, that is, in its causes or effects. The action may cause a judgment, or may be obliquely caused by one, when the judgment concurs with a passion; and by an abusive way of speaking, which philosophy will scarce allow of, the same contrariety may, upon that account, be ascribed to the action. How far this truth or falsehood may be the source of morals, it will now be proper to consider.

It has been observed, that reason, in a strict and philosophical sense, can have influence on our conduct only after two ways: Either when it excites a passion by informing us of the existence of something which is a proper object of it; or when it discovers the connection of causes and effects, so as to afford us means of exerting any passion. These are the only kinds of judgment, which can accompany our actions, or can be said to produce them in any manner; and it must be allowed, that these judgments may often be false and erroneous. A person may be affected with passion, by supposing a pain or pleasure to lie in an object, which has no tendency to produce either of these sensations, or which produces the contrary to what is imagined. A person may also take false measures for the attaining his end, and may retard, by his foolish conduct, instead of forwarding the execution of any project. These false judgments may be thought to affect the passions and actions, which are connected with them, and may be said to render them unreasonable, in a figurative and improper way of speaking. But though this be acknowledged, it is easy to observe, that these errors are so far from being the source of all immorality, that they are commonly very innocent, and draw no manner of guilt upon the person who is so unfortunate as to fail into them. They extend not beyond a mistake of fact, which moralists have not generally supposed criminal, as being perfectly involuntary. I am more to be lamented than blamed, if I am mistaken with regard to the influence of objects in producing pain or pleasure, or if I know not the proper means of satisfying my desires. No one can ever regard such errors as a defect in my moral character. A fruit, for instance, that is really disagreeable, appears to me at a distance, and through mistake I fancy it to be pleasant and delicious. Here is one error. I choose certain means of reaching this fruit, which are not proper for my end. Here is a second error; nor is there any third one, which can ever possibly enter into our reasonings concerning actions. I ask, therefore, if a man, in this situation, and guilty of these two errors, is to be regarded as vicious and criminal, however unavoidable they might have been? Or if it be possible to imagine, that such errors are the sources of all immorality?

And here it may be proper to observe, that if moral distinctions be derived from the truth or falsehood of those judgments, they must take place wherever we form the judgments; nor will there be any difference, whether the question be concerning an apple or a kingdom, or whether the error be avoidable or unavoidable. For as the very essence of morality is supposed to consist in an agreement or disagreement to reason, the other circumstances are entirely arbitrary, and can never either bestow on any action the character of virtuous or vicious, or deprive it of that character. To which we may add, that this agreement or disagreement, not admitting of degrees, all virtues and vices would of course be equal.

Should it be pretended, that though a mistake of fact be not criminal, yet a mistake of right often is; and that this may be the source of immorality: I would answer, that it is impossible such a mistake can ever be the original source of immorality, since it supposes a real right and wrong; that is, a real distinction in morals, independent of these judgments. A mistake, therefore, of right may become a species of immorality; but it is only a secondary one, and is founded on some other, antecedent to it.

As to those judgments which are the effects of our actions, and which, when false, give occasion to pronounce the actions contrary to truth and reason; we may observe, that our actions never cause any judgment, either true or false, in ourselves, and that it is only on others they have such an influence. It is certain, that an action, on many occasions, may give rise to false conclusions in others; and that a person, who through a window sees any lewd behavior of mine with my neighbor's wife, may be so simple as to imagine she is certainly my own. In this respect my action resembles somewhat a lie or falsehood; only with this difference, which is material, that I perform not the action with any intention of giving rise to a false judgment in another, but merely to satisfy my lust and passion. It causes, however, a mistake and false judgment by accident; and the falsehood of its effects may be ascribed, by some odd figurative way of speaking, to the action itself. But still I can see no pretext of reason for asserting, that the tendency to cause such an error is the first spring or original source of all immorality.

Thus upon the whole, it is impossible, that the distinction betwixt moral good and evil, can be made to reason; since that distinction has an influence upon our actions, of which reason alone is incapable. Reason and judgment may, indeed, be the mediate cause of an action, by prompting, or by directing a passion: But it is not pretended, that a judgment of this kind, either in its truth or falsehood, is attended with virtue or vice. And as to the judgments, which are caused by our judgments, they can still less bestow those moral qualities on the actions, which are their causes.

But to be more particular, and to show, that those eternal immutable fitnesses and unfitnesses of things cannot be defended by sound philosophy, we may weigh the following considerations.

If the thought and understanding were alone capable of fixing the boundaries of right and wrong, the character of virtuous and vicious either must lie in some relations of objects, or must be a matter of fact, which is discovered by our reasoning. This consequence is evident. As the operations of human understanding divide themselves into two kinds, the comparing of ideas, and the inferring of matter of fact; were virtue discovered by the understanding; it must be an object of one of these operations, nor is there any third operation of the understanding. which can discover it. There has been an opinion very industriously propagated by certain philosophers, that morality is susceptible of demonstration; and though no one has ever been able to advance a single step in those demonstrations; yet it is taken for granted, that this science may be brought to an equal certainty with geometry or algebra. Upon this supposition vice and virtue must consist in some relations; since it is allowed on all hands, that no matter of fact is capable of being demonstrated. Let us, therefore, begin with examining this hypothesis, and endeavor, if possible, to fix those moral qualities, which have been so long the objects of our fruitless researches. Point out distinctly the relations, which constitute morality or obligation, that we may know wherein they consist, and after what manner we must judge of them.

If you assert, that vice and virtue consist in relations susceptible of certainty and demonstration, you must confine yourself to those four relations, which alone admit of that degree of evidence; and in that case you run into absurdities, from which you will never be able to extricate yourself. For as you make the very essence of morality to lie in the relations, and as there is no one of these relations but what is applicable, not only to an irrational, but also to an inanimate object; it follows, that even such objects must be susceptible of merit or demerit. Resemblance, contrariety, degrees in quality, and *proportions in quantity and number*; all these relations belong as properly to matter, as to our actions, passions, and volitions. It is unquestionable, therefore, that morality lies not in any of these relations, nor the sense of it in their discovery.

Should it be asserted, that the sense of morality consists in the discovery of some relation, distinct from these, and that our enumeration was not complete, when we comprehended all demonstrable relations under four general heads: To this I know not what to reply, until someone be so good as to point out to me this new relation. It is impossible to refute a system, which has never yet been explained. In such a manner of fighting in the dark, a man loses his blows in the air, and often places them where the enemy is not present.

I must, therefore, on this occasion, rest contented with requiring the two following conditions of any one that would undertake to clear up this system. First, As moral good and evil belong only to the actions of the mind, and are derived from our situation with regard to external objects, the relations, from which these moral distinctions arise, must lie only betwixt internal actions, and external objects, and must not be applicable either to internal actions, compared among themselves, or to external objects, when placed in opposition to other external objects. For as morality is supposed to attend certain relations, if these relations could belong to internal actions considered singly, it would follow, that we might be guilty of crimes in ourselves, and independent of our situation, with respect to the universe: And in like manner, if these moral relations could be applied to external objects, it would follow, that even inanimate beings would be susceptible of moral beauty and deformity. Now it seems difficult to imagine, that any relation can be discovered betwixt our passions, volitions and actions, compared to external objects, which relation might not belong either to these passions and volitions, or to these external objects, compared among themselves. But it will be still more difficult to fulfil the second condition, requisite to justify this system. According to the principles of those who maintain an abstract rational difference betwixt moral good and evil, and a natural fitness and unfitness of things, it is not only supposed, that these relations, being eternal and immutable, are the same, when considered by every rational creature, but their effects are also supposed to be necessarily the same; and it is concluded they have no less, or rather a greater, influence in directing the will of the deity, than in governing the rational and virtuous of our own species. These two particulars are evidently distinct. It is one thing to know virtue, and another to conform the will to it. In order, therefore, to prove, that the measures of right and wrong are eternal laws, obligatory on every rational mind, it is not sufficient to show the relations upon which they are founded: We must also point out the connection betwixt the relation and the will; and must prove that this connection is so necessary, that in every well-disposed mind, it must take place and have its influence; though the difference betwixt these minds be in other respects immense and infinite. Now besides what I have already proved, that even in human nature no relation can ever alone produce any action: besides this, I say, it has been shown, in treating of the understanding, that there is no connection of cause and effect, such as this is supposed to be, which is discoverable otherwise than by experience, and of which we can pretend to have any security by the simple consideration of the objects. All beings in the universe, considered in themselves, appear entirely loose and independent of each other. It is only by experience we learn their influence and connection; and this influence we ought never to extend beyond experience.

Thus it will be impossible to fulfil the first condition required to the system of eternal measures of right and wrong; because it is impossible to show those relations, upon which such a distinction may be founded: And it is as impossible to fulfil the second condition; because we cannot prove *a priori*, that these relations, if they really existed and were perceived, would be universally forcible and obligatory.

But to make these general reflections more dear and convincing, we may illustrate them by some particular instances, wherein this character of moral good or evil is the most universally acknowledged. Of all crimes that human creatures are capable of committing, the most horrid and unnatural is ingratitude, especially when it is committed against parents, and appears in the more flagrant instances of wounds and death. This is acknowledged by all mankind, philosophers as well as the people; the question only arises among philosophers, whether the guilt or moral deformity of this action be discovered by demonstrative reasoning, or be felt by an internal sense, and by means of some sentiment, which the reflecting on such an action naturally occasions. This question will soon be decided against the former opinion, if we can show the same relations in other objects, without the notion of any guilt or iniquity attending them. Reason or science is nothing but the comparing of ideas, and the discovery of their relations; and if the same relations have different characters, it must evidently follow, that those characters are not discovered merely by reason. To put the affair, therefore, to this trial, let us choose any inanimate object, such as an oak or elm; and let us suppose, that by the dropping of its seed, it produces a sapling below it, which springing up by degrees, at last overtops and destroys the parent tree: I ask, if in this instance there be wanting any relation, which is discoverable in parricide or ingratitude? Is not the one tree the cause of the other's existence; and the latter the cause of the destruction of the former, in the same manner as when a child murders his parent? It is not sufficient to reply, that a choice or will is wanting. For in the case of parricide, a will does not give rise to any *different* relations, but is only the cause from which the action is derived; and consequently produces the same relations, that in the oak or elm arise from some other principles. It is a will or choice, that determines a man to kill his parent; and they are the laws of matter and motion, that determine a sapling to destroy the oak, from which it sprung. Here then the same relations have different causes; but still the relations are the same: And as their discovery is not in both cases attended with a notion of immorality, it follows, that that notion does not arise from such a discovery.

But to choose an instance, still more resembling; I would fain ask any one, why incest in the human species is criminal, and why the very same action, and the same relations in animals have not the smallest moral turpitude and deformity? If it be answered, that this action is innocent in animals, because they have not reason sufficient to discover its turpitude; but that man, being endowed with that faculty which ought to restrain him to his duty, the same action instantly becomes criminal to him; should this be said, I would reply, that this is evidently arguing in a circle. For before reason can perceive this turpitude, the turpitude must exist; and consequently is independent of the decisions of our reason, and is their object more properly than their effect. According to this system, then, every animal, that has sense, and appetite, and will; that is, every animal must be susceptible of all the same virtues and vices, for which we ascribe praise and blame to human creatures. All the difference is, that our superior reason may serve to discover the vice or virtue, and by that means may augment the blame or praise: But still this discovery supposes a separate being in these moral distinctions, and a being, which depends only on the will and appetite, and which, both in thought and reality, may be distinguished from the reason. Animals are susceptible of the same relations, with respect to each other, as the human species, and therefore would also be susceptible of the same morality, if the essence of morality consisted in these relations. Their want of a sufficient degree of reason may hinder them from perceiving the duties and obligations of morality, but can never hinder these duties from existing; since they must antecedently exist, in order to their being perceived. Reason must find them, and can never produce them. This argument deserves to be weighed, as being, in my opinion, entirely decisive.

Nor does this reasoning only prove, that morality consists not in any relations, that are the objects of science; but if examined, will prove with equal certainty, that it consists not in any matter of fact, which can be discovered by the understanding. This is the second part of our argument; and if it can be made evident, we may conclude, that morality is not an object of reason. But can there be any difficulty in proving, that vice and virtue are not matters of fact, whose existence we can infer by reason? Take any action allowed to be vicious: Wilful murder, for instance. Examine it in all lights, and see if you can find that matter of fact, or real existence, which you call vice. In which-ever way you take it, you find only certain passions, motives, volitions and thoughts. There is no other matter of fact in the case. The vice entirely escapes you, as long as you consider the object. You never can find it, till you turn your reflection into your own breast, and find a sentiment of disapprobation, which arises in you, towards this action. Here is a matter of fact; but it is the object of feeling, not of reason. It lies in yourself, not in the object. So that when you pronounce any action or character to be vicious, you mean nothing, but that from the constitution of your nature you have a feeling or sentiment of blame from the contemplation of it. Vice and virtue, therefore, may be compared to sounds, colors, heat and cold, which, according to modern philosophy, are not qualities in objects, but perceptions in the mind: And this discovery in morals, like that other in physics, is to be regarded as a considerable advancement of the speculative sciences; though, like that too, it has little or no influence on practice. Nothing can be more real, or concern us more, than our own sentiments of pleasure and uneasiness; and if these be favorable to virtue, and unfavorable to vice, no more can be requisite to the regulation of our conduct and behavior.

I cannot forbear adding to these reasonings an observation, which may, perhaps, be found of some importance. In every system of morality, which I have hitherto met with, I have always remarked, that the author proceeds for some time in the ordinary way of reasoning, and establishes the being of a God, or makes observations concerning human affairs; when of a sudden I am surprised to find, that instead of the usual copulations of propositions, is, and is not, I meet with no proposition that is not connected with an ought, or an ought not. This change is imperceptible; but is, however, of the last consequence. For as this ought, or ought not, expresses some new relation or affirmation, it is necessary that it should be observed and explained; and at the same time that a reason should be given, for what seems altogether inconceivable, how this new relation can be a deduction from others, which are entirely different from it. But as authors do not commonly use this precaution, I shall presume to recommend it to the readers; and am persuaded, that this small attention would subvert all the vulgar systems of morality, and let us see, that the distinction of vice and virtue is not founded merely on the relations of objects, nor is perceived by reason.

SECT. II: Moral Distinctions Derived from a Moral Sense Thus the course of the argument leads us to conclude, that since vice and virtue are not discoverable merely by reason, or the comparison of ideas, it must be by means of some impression or sentiment they occasion, that we are able to mark the difference betwixt them. Our decisions concerning moral rectitude and depravity are evidently perceptions; and as all perceptions are either impressions or ideas, the exclusion of the one is a convincing argument for the other. Morality, therefore, is more properly felt than judged of; though this feeling or sentiment is commonly so soft and gentle, that we are apt to confound it with an idea, according to our common custom of taking all things for the same, which have any near resemblance to each other.

The next question is, Of what nature are these impressions, and after what manner do they operate upon us? Here we cannot remain long in suspense, but must pronounce the impression arising from virtue, to be agreeable, and that proceeding from vice to be uneasy. Every moments experience must convince us of this. There is no spectacle so fair and beautiful as a noble and generous action; nor any which gives us more abhorrence than one that is cruel and treacherous. No enjoyment equals the satisfaction we receive from the company of those we love and esteem; as the greatest of all punishments is to be obliged to pass our lives with those we hate or contemn. A very play or romance may afford us instances of this pleasure, which virtue conveys to us; and pain, which arises from vice.

Now since the distinguishing impressions, by which moral good or evil is known, are nothing but particular pains or pleasures; it follows, that in all enquiries concerning these moral distinctions, it will be sufficient to show the principles, which make us feel a satisfaction or uneasiness from the survey of any character, in order to satisfy us why the character is laudable or blameable. An action, or sentiment, or character is virtuous or vicious; why? Because its view causes a pleasure or uneasiness of a particular kind. In giving a reason, therefore, for the pleasure or uneasiness, we sufficiently explain the vice or virtue. To have the sense of virtue, is nothing but to feel a satisfaction of a particular kind from the contemplation of a character. The very feeling constitutes our praise or admiration. We go no farther; nor do we enquire into the cause of the satisfaction. We do not infer a character to be virtuous, because it pleases: But in feeling that it pleases after such a particular manner, we in effect feel that it is virtuous. The case is the same as in our judgments concerning all kinds of beauty, and tastes, and sensations. Our approbation is implied in the immediate pleasure they convey to us.

I have objected to the system, which establishes eternal rational measures of right and wrong, that it is impossible to show, in the actions of reasonable creatures, any relations, which are not found in external objects; and therefore, if morality always attended these relations, it were possible for inanimate matter to become virtuous or vicious. Now it may, in like manner, be objected to the present system, that if virtue and vice be determined by pleasure and pain, these qualities must, in every case, arise from the sensations; and consequently any object, whether animate or inanimate, rational or irrational, might become morally good or evil, provided it can excite a satisfaction or uneasiness. But though this objection seems to be the very same, it has by no means the same force, in the one case as in the other. For, first, tis evident, that under the term pleasure, we comprehend sensations, which are very different from each other, and which have only such a distant resemblance, as is requisite to make them be expressed by the same abstract term. A good composition of music and a bottle of good wine equally produce pleasure; and what is more, their goodness is determined merely by the pleasure. But shall we say upon that account, that the wine is harmonious, or the music of a good flavor? In like manner an inanimate object, and the character or sentiments of any person may, both of them, give satisfaction; but as the satisfaction is different, this keeps our sentiments concerning them from being confounded, and makes us ascribe virtue to the one, and not to the other. Nor is every sentiment of pleasure or pain, which arises from characters and actions, of that peculiar kind, which makes us praise or condemn. The good qualities of an enemy are hurtful to us; but may still command our esteem and respect. It is only when a character is considered in general, without reference to our particular interest, that it causes such a feeling or sentiment, as denominates it morally good or evil. It is true, those sentiments, from interest and morals, are apt to be confounded, and naturally run into one another. It seldom happens, that we do not think an enemy vicious, and can distinguish betwixt his opposition to our interest and real villainy or baseness. But this hinders not, but that the sentiments are, in themselves, distinct; and a man of temper and judgment may preserve himself from these illusions. In like manner, though it is certain a musical voice is nothing but one that naturally gives a particular kind of pleasure; yet it is difficult for a man to be sensible, that the voice of an enemy is agreeable, or to allow it to be musical. But a person of a fine ear, who has the command of himself, can separate these feelings, and give praise to what deserves it.

Secondly, we may call to remembrance the preceding system of the passions, in order to remark a still more considerable difference among our pains and pleasures. Pride and humility, love and hatred are excited, when there is anything presented to us, that both bears a relation to the object of the passion, and produces a separate sensation related to the sensation of the passion. Now virtue and vice are attended with these circumstances. They must necessarily be placed either in ourselves or others, and excite either pleasure or uneasiness; and therefore must give rise to one of these four passions; which clearly distinguishes them from the pleasure and pain arising from inanimate objects, that often bear no relation to us: And this is, perhaps, the most considerable effect that virtue and vice have upon the human mind.

It may now be asked in general, concerning this pain or pleasure, that distinguishes moral good and evil, *from what principles is it derived, and whence does it arise in the human mind*? To this I reply, first, that it is absurd to imagine, that in every particular instance, these sentiments are produced by an original quality and primary constitution. For as the number of our duties is, in a manner, infinite, it is impossible that our original instincts should extend to each of them, and from our very first infancy impress on the human mind all that multitude of precepts, which are contained in the most complete system of ethics. Such a method of proceeding is not conformable to the usual maxims, by which nature is conducted, where a few principles produce all that variety we observe in the universe, and everything is carried on in the easiest and most simple manner. It is necessary, therefore, to abridge these primary impulses, and find some more general principles, upon which all our notions of morals are founded.

But in the second place, should it be asked, whether we ought to search for these principles in nature, or whether we must look for them in some other origin? I would reply, that our answer to this question depends upon the definition of the word, Nature, than which there is none more ambiguous and equivocal. If nature be opposed to miracles, not only the distinction betwixt vice and virtue is natural, but also every event, which has ever happened in the world . . . In saying, then, that the sentiments of vice and virtue are natural in this sense, we make no very extraordinary discovery.

But nature may also be opposed to rare and unusual; and in this sense of the word, which is the common one, there may often arise disputes concerning what is natural or unnatural; and one may in general affirm, that we are not possessed of any very precise standard, by which these disputes can be decided. Frequent and rare depend upon the number of examples we have observed; and as this number may gradually increase or diminish, it will be impossible to fix any exact boundaries betwixt them. We may only affirm on this head, that if ever there was anything, which could be called natural in this sense, the sentiments of morality certainly may; since there never was any nation of the world, nor any single person in any nation, who was utterly deprived of them, and who never, in any instance, showed the least approbation or dislike of manners. These sentiments are so rooted in our constitution and temper, that without entirely confounding the human mind by disease or madness, it is impossible to extirpate and destroy them.

But nature may also be opposed to artifice, as well as to what is rare and unusual; and in this sense it may be disputed, whether the notions of virtue be natural or not. We readily forget, that the designs, and projects, and views of men are principles as necessary in their operation as heat and cold, moist and dry: But taking them to be free and entirely our own, it is usual for us to set them in opposition to the other principles of nature should it, therefore, be demanded, whether the sense of virtue be natural or artificial, I am of opinion, that it is impossible for me at present to give any precise answer to this question. Perhaps it will appear afterwards, that our sense of some virtues is artificial, and that of others natural. The discussion of this question will be more proper, when we enter upon an exact detail of each particular vice and

Meanwhile it may not be amiss to observe from these definitions of natural and unnatural, that nothing can be more unphilosophical than those systems, which assert, that virtue is the same with what is natural, and vice with what is unnatural. For in the first sense of the word, Nature, as opposed to miracles, both vice and virtue are equally natural; and in the second sense, as opposed to what is unusual, perhaps virtue will be found to be the most unnatural. At least it must be owned, that heroic virtue, being as unusual, is as little natural as the most brutal barbarity. As to the third sense of the word, it is certain, that both vice and virtue are equally artificial, and out of nature. For however it may be disputed, whether the notion of a merit or demerit in certain actions be natural or artificial, it is evident, that the actions themselves are artificial, and are performed with a certain design and intention; otherwise they could never be ranked under any of these denominations. It is impossible, therefore, that the character of natural and unnatural can ever, in any sense, mark the boundaries of vice and virtue.

Thus we are still brought back to our first position, that virtue is distinguished by the pleasure, and vice by the pain, that any action, sentiment or character gives us by the mere view and contemplation. This decision is very commodious; because it reduces us to this simple question, Why any action or sentiment upon the general view or survey, gives a certain satisfaction or uneasiness, in order to show the origin of its moral rectitude or depravity, without looking for any incomprehensible relations and qualities, which never did exist in nature, nor even in our imagination, by any clear and distinct conception. I flatter myself I have executed a great part of my present design by a state of the question, which appears to me so free from ambiguity and obscurity. . . .

PART III: OF THE OTHER VIRTUES AND VICES

SECT. I Of the Origin of the Natural Virtues and Vices

We come now to the examination of such virtues and vices as are entirely natural, and have no dependence on the artifice and contrivance of men. The examination of these will conclude this system of morals.

The chief spring or actuating principle of the human mind is pleasure or pain; and when these sensations are removed, both from our thought and feeling, we are, in a great measure, incapable of passion or action, of desire or volition. The most immediate effects of pleasure and pain are the propense and averse motions of the mind; which are diversified into volition, into desire and aversion, grief and joy, hope and fear, according as the pleasure or pain changes its situation, and becomes probable or improbable, certain or uncertain, or is considered as out of our power for the present moment. But when along with this, the objects, that cause pleasure or pain, acquire a relation to ourselves or others; they still continue to excite desire and aversion, grief and joy: But cause, at the same time, the indirect passions of pride or humility, love or hatred, which in this case have a double relation of impressions and ideas to the pain or pleasure.

We have already observed, that moral distinctions depend entirely on certain peculiar sentiments of pain and pleasure, and that whatever mental quality in ourselves or others gives us a satisfaction, by the survey or reflection, is of course virtuous; as everything of this nature, that gives uneasiness, is vicious. Now since every quality in ourselves or others, which gives pleasure, always causes pride or love; as everyone, that produces uneasiness, excites humility or hatred: It follows, that these two particulars are to be considered as equivalent, with regard to our mental qualities, virtue and the power of producing love or pride, vice and the power of producing humility or hatred. In every case, therefore, we must judge of the one by the other; and may pronounce any quality of the mind virtuous, which causes love or pride; and any one vicious, which causes hatred or humility.

If any action be either virtuous or vicious, it is only as a sign of some quality or character. It must depend upon durable principles of the mind, which extend over the whole conduct, and enter into the personal character. Actions themselves, not proceeding from any constant principle, have no influence on love or hatred, pride or humility; and consequently are never considered in morality.

This reflection is self-evident, and deserves to be attended to, as being of the utmost importance in the present subject. We are never to consider any single action in our enquiries concerning the origin of morals; but only the quality or character from which the action proceeded. These alone are durable enough to affect our sentiments concerning the person. Actions are, indeed, better indications of a character than words, or even wishes and sentiments; but it is only so far as they are such indications, that they are attended with love or hatred, praise or blame.

To discover the true origin of morals, and of that love or hatred, which arises from mental qualities, we must take the matter pretty deep, and compare some principles, which have been already examined and explained.

We may begin with considering a-new the nature and force of sympathy. The minds of all men are similar in their feelings and operations; nor can anyone be actuated by any affection, of which all others are not, in some degree, susceptible. As in strings equally wound up, the motion of one communicates itself to the rest; so all the affections readily pass from one person to another, and beget correspondent movements in every human creature. When I see the effects of passion in the voice and gesture of any person, my mind immediately passes from these effects to their causes, and forms such a lively idea of the passion, as is presently converted into the passion itself. In like manner, when I perceive the causes of any emotion, my mind is conveyed to the effects, and is actuated with a like emotion. Were I present at any of the more terrible operations of surgery, it is certain, that even before it begun, the preparation of the instruments, the laying of the bandages in order, the heating of the irons, with all the signs of anxiety and concern in the patient and assistants, would have a great effect upon my mind, and excite the strongest sentiments of pity and terror. No passion of another discovers itself immediately to the mind. We are only sensible of its causes or effects. From these we infer the passion: And consequently these give rise to our sympathy.

Our sense of beauty depends very much on this principle; and where any object has a tendency to produce pleasure in its possessor, it is always regarded as beautiful; as every object, that has a tendency to produce pain, is disagreeable and deformed. Thus the convenience of a house, the fertility of a field, the strength of a horse, the capacity, security, and swift-sailing of a vessel, form the principal beauty of these several objects. Here the object, which is denominated beautiful, pleases only by its tendency to produce a certain effect. That effect is the pleasure or advantage of some other person. Now the pleasure of a stranger, for whom we have no friendship, pleases us only by sympathy. To this principle, therefore, is owing the beauty, which we find in everything that is useful. How considerable a part this is of beauty can easily appear upon reflection. Wherever an object has a tendency to produce pleasure in the possessor, or in other words, is the proper cause of pleasure, it is sure to please the spectator, by a delicate sympathy with the possessor. Most of the works of art are esteemed beautiful, in proportion to their fitness for the use of man, and even many of the productions of nature derive their beauty from that source. Handsome and beautiful, on most occasions, is nor an absolute but a relative quality, and pleases us by nothing but its tendency to produce an end that is agreeable.

The same principle produces, in many instances, our sentiments of morals, as well as those of beauty. No virtue is more esteemed than justice, and no vice more detested than injustice; nor are there any qualities, which go farther to the fixing the character, either as amiable or odious. Now justice is a moral virtue, merely because it has that tendency to the good of mankind; and, indeed, is nothing but an artificial invention to that purpose. The same may be said of allegiance, of the laws of nations, of modesty, and of good-manners. All these are mere human contrivances for the interest of society. And since there is a very strong sentiment of morals, which in all nations, and all ages, has attended them, we must allow, that the reflecting on the tendency of characters and mental qualities, is sufficient to give us the sentiments of approbation and blame. Now as the means to an end can only be agreeable, where the end is agreeable; and as the good of society, where our own interest is not concerned, or that of our friends, pleases only by sympathy: It follows, that sympathy is the source of the esteem, which we pay to all the artificial virtues.

Thus it appears, that sympathy is a very powerful principle in human nature, that it has a great influence on our taste of beauty, and that it produces our sentiment of morals in all the artificial virtues. From thence we may presume, that it also gives rise to many of the other virtues; and that qualities acquire our approbation, because of their tendency to the good of mankind. This presumption must become a certainty, when we find that most of those qualities, which we naturally approve of, have actually that tendency, and render a man a proper member of society: While the qualities, which we naturally disapprove of, have a contrary tendency, and render any intercourse with the person dangerous or disagreeable. For having found, that such tendencies have force enough to produce the strongest sentiment of morals, we can never reasonably, in these cases, look for any other cause of approbation or blame; it being an inviolable maxim in philosophy, that where any particular cause is sufficient for an effect, we ought to rest satisfied with it, and ought not to multiply causes without necessity. We have happily attained experiments in the artificial virtues, where the tendency of qualities to the good of society, is the sole cause of our approbation, without any suspicion of the concurrence of another principle. From thence we learn the force of that principle. And where that principle may take place, and the quality approved of is really beneficial to society, a true philosopher will never require any other principle to account for the strongest approbation and esteem.

That many of the natural virtues have this tendency to the good of society, no one can doubt of. Meekness, beneficence, charity, generosity, clemency, moderation, equity bear the greatest figure among the moral qualities, and are commonly denominated the social virtues, to mark their tendency to the good of society. This goes so far, that some philosophers have represented all moral distinctions as the effect of artifice and education, when skilful politicians endeavored to restrain the turbulent passions of men, and make them operate to the public good, by the notions of honor and shame. This system, however, is nor consistent with experience. For, first, there are other virtues and vices beside those which have this tendency to the public advantage and loss. Secondly, had not men a natural sentiment of approbation and blame, it could never be excited by politicians; nor would the words laudable and praise-worthy, blameable and odious be any more intelligible, than if they were a language perfectly known to us, as we have already observed. But though this system be erroneous, it may teach us, that moral distinctions arise, in a great measure, from the tendency of qualities and characters to the interests of society, and that it is our concern for that interest, which makes us approve or disapprove of them. Now we have no such extensive concern for society but from sympathy; and consequently it is that principle, which takes us so far out of ourselves, as to give us the same pleasure or uneasiness in the characters of others, as if they had a tendency to our own advantage or loss.

The only difference betwixt the natural virtues and justice lies in this, that the good, which results from the former, arises from every single act, and is the object of some natural passion: Whereas a single act of justice, considered in itself, may often be contrary to the public good; and it is only the concurrence of mankind, in a general scheme or system of action, which is advantageous. When I relieve persons in distress, my natural humanity is my motive; and so far as my succor extends, so far have I promoted the happiness of my fellow-creatures. But if we examine all the questions, that come before any tribunal of justice, we shall find, that, considering each case apart, it would as often be an instance of humanity to decide contrary to the laws of justice as conformable them. Judges take from a poor man to give to a rich; they bestow on the dissolute the labor of the industrious; and put into the hands of the vicious the means of harming both themselves and others. The whole scheme, however, of law and justice is advantageous to the society; and it was with a view to this advantage, that men, by their voluntary conventions, established it. After it is once established by these conventions, it is naturally attended with a strong sentiment of morals; which can proceed from nothing but our sympathy with the interests of society. We need no other explication of that esteem, which attends such of the natural virtues, as have a tendency to the public good. I must farther add, that there are several circumstances, which render this hypothesis much more probable with regard to the natural than the artificial virtues. It is certain that the imagination is more affected by what is particular, than by what is general; and that the sentiments are always moved with difficulty, where their objects are, in any degree, loose and undetermined: Now every particular act of justice is not beneficial to society, but the whole scheme or system: And it may not, perhaps, be any individual person for whom we are concerned, who receives benefit from justice, but the whole society alike. On the contrary, every particular act of generosity, or relief of the industrious and indigent, is beneficial; and is beneficial to a particular person, who is not undeserving of it. It is more natural, therefore, to think, that the tendencies of the latter virtue will affect our sentiments, and command our approbation, than those of the former; and therefore, since we find, that the approbation of the former arises from their tendencies, we may ascribe, with better reason, the same cause to the approbation of the latter. In any number of similar effects, if a cause can be discovered for one, we ought to extend that cause to all the other effects, which can be accounted for by it: But much more, if these other effects be attended with peculiar circumstances, which facilitate the operation of that cause.

Before I proceed farther, I must observe two remarkable circumstances in this affair, which may seem objections to the present system. The first may be thus explained. When any quality, or character, has a tendency to the good of mankind, we are pleased with it, and approve of it; because it presents the lively idea of pleasure; which idea affects us by sympathy, and is itself a kind of pleasure. But as this sympathy is very variable, it may be thought that our sentiments of morals must admit of all the same variations. We sympathize more with persons contiguous to us, than with persons remote from us: With our acquaintance, than with strangers: With our countrymen, than with foreigners. But notwithstanding this variation of our sympathy, we give the same approbation to the same moral qualities in China as in England. They appear equally virtuous, and recommend themselves equally to the esteem of a judicious spectator. The sympathy varies without a variation in our esteem. Our esteem, therefore, proceeds not from sympathy.

To this I answer: The approbation of moral qualities most certainly is not derived from reason, or any comparison of ideas; but proceeds entirely from a moral taste, and from certain sentiments of pleasure or disgust, which arise upon the contemplation and view of particular qualities or characters. Now it is evident, that those sentiments, whence-ever they are derived, must vary according to the distance or contiguity of the objects; nor can I feel the same lively pleasure from the virtues of a person, who lived in Greece two thousand years ago, that I feel from the virtues of a familiar friend and acquaintance. Yet I do not say, that I esteem the one more than the other: And therefore, if the variation of the sentiment, without a variation of the esteem, be an objection, it must have equal force against every other system, as against that of sympathy. But to consider the matter a-right, it has no force at all; and it is the easiest matter in the world to account for it. Our situation, with regard both to persons and things, is in continual fluctuation; and a man, that lies at a distance from us, may, in a little time, become a familiar acquaintance. Besides, every particular man has a peculiar position with regard to others; and it is impossible we could ever converse together on any reasonable terms, were each of us to consider characters and persons, only as they appear from his peculiar point of view. In order, therefore, to prevent those continual contradictions, and arrive at a more stable judgment of things, we fix on some steady and general points of view; and always, in our thoughts, place ourselves in them, whatever may be our present situation. In like manner, external beauty is determined merely by pleasure; and it is evident, a beautiful countenance cannot give so much pleasure, when seen at the distance of twenty paces, as when it is brought nearer us. We say not, however, that it appears to us less beautiful: Because we know what effect it will have in such a position, and by that reflection we correct its momentary appearance.

In general, all sentiments of blame or praise are variable, according to our situation of nearness or remoteness, with regard to the person blamed or praised, and according to the present disposition of our mind. But these variations we regard not in our general decision, but still apply the terms expressive of our liking or dislike, in the same manner, as if we remained in one point of view. Experience soon teaches us this method of correcting our sentiments, or at least, of correcting our language, where the sentiments are more stubborn and inalterable. Our servant, if diligent and faithful, may excite stronger sentiments of love and kindness than Marcus Brutus, as represented in history; but we say not upon that account, that the former character is more laudable than the latter. We know, that were we to approach equally near to that renowned patriot, he would command a much higher degree of affection and admiration. Such corrections are common with regard to all the senses; and indeed it were impossible we could ever make use of language, or communicate our sentiments to one another, did we not correct the momentary appearances of things, and overlook our present situation.

It is therefore from the influence of characters and qualities, upon those who have an intercourse with any person, that we blame or praise him. We consider not whether the persons, affected by the qualities, be our acquaintance or strangers, countrymen or foreigners. Nay, we over-look our own interest in those general judgments; and blame not a man for opposing us in any of our pretensions, when his own interest is particularly concerned. We make allowance for a certain degree of selfishness in men; because we know it to be inseparable from human nature, and inherent in our frame and constitution. By this reflection we correct those sentiments of blame, which so naturally arise upon any opposition.

But however the general principle of our blame or praise may be corrected by those other principles, it is certain, they are not altogether efficacious, nor do our passions often correspond entirely to the present theory. It is seldom men heartily love what lies at a distance from them, and what no way redounds to their particular benefit; as it is no less rare to meet with persons, who can pardon another any opposition he makes to their interest, however justifiable that opposition may be by the general rules of morality. Here we are contented with saying, that reason requires such an Impartial conduct, but that it is seldom we can bring ourselves to it, and that our passions do not readily follow the determination of our judgment. This language will be easily understood, if we consider what we formerly said concerning that reason, which is able to oppose our passion; and which we have found to be nothing but a general calm determination of the passions, founded on some distant view or reflection. When we form our judgments of persons, merely from the tendency of their characters to our own benefit, or to that of our friends, we find so many contradictions to our sentiments in society and conversation, and such an uncertainty from the incessant changes of our situation, that we seek some other standard of merit and demerit, which may not admit of so great variation. Being thus loosened from our first station, we cannot afterwards fix ourselves so commodiously by any means as by a sympathy with those, who have any commerce with the person we consider. This is far from being as lively as when our own interest is concerned, or that of our particular friends; nor has it such an influence on our love and hatred: But being equally conformable to our calm and general principles, it is said to have an equal authority over our reason, and to command our judgment and opinion. We blame equally a bad action, which we read of in history, with one performed in our neighborhood the other day: The meaning of which is, that we know from reflection, that the former action would excite as strong sentiments of disapprobation as the latter, were it placed in the same position.

I now proceed to the second remarkable circumstance, which I proposed to take notice of. Where a person is possessed of a character, that in its natural tendency is beneficial to society, we esteem him virtuous, and are delighted with the view of his character, even though particular accidents prevent its operation, and incapacitate him from being serviceable to his friends and country. Virtue in rags is still virtue; and the love, which it procures, attends a man into a dungeon or desert, where the virtue can no longer be exerted in action, and is lost to all the world. Now this may be esteemed an objection to the present system. Sympathy interests us in the good of mankind; and if sympathy were the source of our esteem for virtue, that sentiment of approbation could only take place, where the virtue actually attained its end, and was beneficial to mankind. Where it fails of its end, it is only an imperfect means; and therefore can never acquire any merit from that end. The goodness of an end can bestow a merit on such means alone as are complete, and actually produce the end.

To this we may reply, that where any object, in all its parts, is fitted to attain any agreeable end, it naturally gives us pleasure, and is esteemed beautiful, even though some external circumstances be wanting to render it altogether effectual. It is sufficient if everything be complete in the object itself. A house, that is contrived with great judgment for all the commodities of life, pleases us upon that account; though perhaps we are sensible, that no-one will ever dwell in it. A fertile soil, and a happy climate, delight us by a reflection on the happiness which they would afford the inhabitants, though at present the country be desert and uninhabited. A man, whose limbs and shape promise strength and activity, is esteemed handsome, though condemned to perpetual imprisonment. The imagination has a set of passions belonging to it, upon which our sentiments of beauty much depend. These passions are moved by degrees of liveliness and strength, which are inferior to belief, and independent of the real existence of their objects. Where a character is, in every respect, fitted to be beneficial to society, the imagination passes easily from the cause to the effect, without considering that there are some circumstances wanting to render the cause a complete one. General rules create a species of probability, which sometimes influences the judgment, and always the imagination.

It is true, when the cause is complete, and a good disposition is attended with good fortune, which renders it really beneficial to society, it gives a stronger pleasure to the spectator, and is attended with a more lively sympathy. We are more affected by it; and yet we do not say that it is more virtuous, or that we esteem it more. We know, that an alteration of fortune may render the benevolent disposition entirely impotent; and therefore we separate, as much as possible, the fortune from the disposition. The case is the same, as when we correct the different sentiments of virtue, which proceed from its different distances from ourselves. The passions do not always follow our corrections; but these corrections serve sufficiently to regulate our abstract notions, and are alone regarded, when we pronounce in general concerning the degrees of vice and virtue.

It is observed by critics, that all words or sentences, which are difficult to the pronunciation, are disagreeable to the ear. There is no difference, whether a man hear them pronounced, or read them silently to himself. When I run over a book with my eye, I Imagine I hear it all; and also, by the force of imagination, enter into the uneasiness, which the delivery of it would give the speaker. The uneasiness is not real; but as such a composition of words has a natural tendency to produce it, this is sufficient to affect the mind with a painful sentiment, and render the discourse harsh and disagreeable. It is a similar case, where any real quality is, by accidental circumstances, rendered impotent, and is deprived of its natural influence on society.

Upon these principles we may easily remove any contradiction, which may appear to be betwixt the extensive sympathy, on which our sentiments of virtue depend, and that limited generosity which I have frequently observed to be natural to men, and which justice and property suppose, according to the precedent reasoning. My sympathy with another may give me the sentiment of pain and disapprobation, when any object is presented, that has a tendency to give him uneasiness; though I may not be willing to sacrifice anything of my own interest, or cross any of my passions, for his satisfaction. A house may displease me by being ill-contrived for the convenience of the owner; and yet I may refuse to give a shilling towards the rebuilding of it. Sentiments must touch the heart, to make them control our passions: But they need not extend beyond the imagination, to make them influence our taste. When a building seems clumsy and tottering to the eye, it is ugly and disagreeable; though we be fully assured of the solidity of the workmanship. It is a kind of fear, which causes this sentiment of disapprobation; but the passion is not the same with that which we feel, when obliged to stand under a wall, that we really think tottering and insecure. The seeming tendencies of objects affect the mind: And the emotions they excite are of a like species with those, which proceed from the real consequences of objects, but their feeling is different. Nay, these emotions are so different in their feeling, that they may often be contrary, without destroying each other; as when the fortifications of a city belonging to an enemy are esteemed beautiful upon account of their strength, though we could wish that they were entirely destroyed. The imagination adheres to the general views of things, and distinguishes the feelings they produce, from those which arise from our particular and momentary situation.

If we examine the panegyrics that are commonly made of great men, we shall find, that most of the qualities, which are attributed to them, may be divided into two kinds, *viz.* such as make them perform their part in society; and such as render them serviceable to themselves, and enable them to promote their own interest. Their prudence, temperance, frugality, industry, assiduity, enterprise, dexterity, are celebrated, as well as their generosity and humanity. If we ever give an indulgence to any quality, that disables a man from making a figure in life, it is to that of indolence, which is not supposed to deprive one of his parts and capacity, but only suspends their exercise; and that without any inconvenience to the person himself, since it is, in some measure, from his own choice. Yet indolence is always allowed to be a fault, and a very great one, if extreme: Nor do a man's friends ever acknowledge him to be subject to it, but in order to save his character in more material articles. He could make a figure, say they, if he pleased to give application: His understanding is sound, his conception quick, and his memory tenacious; but he hates business, and is indifferent about his fortune. And this a man sometimes may make even a subject of vanity; though with the air of confessing a fault: Because he may think, that his incapacity for business implies much more noble qualities; such as a philosophical spirit, a fine taste, a delicate wit, or a relish for pleasure and society. But take any other case: Suppose a quality, that without being an indication of any other good qualities, incapacitates a man always for business, and is destructive to his interest; such as a blundering understanding, and a wrong judgment of everything in life; inconstancy and irresolution; or a want of address in the management of men and business: These are all allowed to be imperfections in a character; and many men would rather acknowledge the greatest crimes, than have it suspected, that they are, in any degree, subject to them.

It is very happy, in our philosophical researches, when we find the same phenomenon diversified by a variety of circumstances; and by discovering what is common among them, can the better assure ourselves of the truth of any hypothesis we may make use of to explain it. Were nothing esteemed virtue but what were beneficial to society, I am persuaded, that the foregoing explication of the moral sense ought still to be received, and that upon sufficient evidence: But this evidence must grow upon us, when we find other kinds of virtue, which will not admit of any explication except from that hypothesis. Here is a man, who is not remarkably defective in his social qualities; but what principally recommends him is his dexterity in business, by which he has extricated himself from the greatest difficulties, and conducted the most delicate affairs with a singular address and prudence. I find an esteem for him immediately to arise in me: His company is a satisfaction to me; and before I have any farther acquaintance with him, I would rather do him a service than another, whose character is in every other respect equal, but is deficient in that particular. In this case, the qualities that please me are all considered as useful to the person, and as having a tendency to promote his interest and satisfaction. They are only regarded as means to an end, and please me in proportion to their fitness for that end. The end, therefore, must be agreeable to me. But what makes the end agreeable? The person is a stranger: I am no way interested in him, nor lie under any obligation to him: His happiness concerns not me, farther than the happiness of every human, and indeed of every sensible creature: That is, it affects me only by sympathy. From that principle, whenever I discover his happiness and good, whether in its causes or effects, I enter so deeply into it, that it gives me a sensible emotion. The appearance of qualities, that have a tendency to promote it, have an agreeable effect upon my imagination, and command my love and esteem.

This theory may serve to explain, why the same qualities, in all cases, produce both pride and love, humility and hatred; and the same man is always virtuous or vicious, accomplished or despicable to others, who is so to himself. A person, in whom we discover any passion or habit, which originally is only incommodious to himself, becomes always disagreeable to us, merely on its account; as on the other hand, one whose character is only dangerous and disagreeable to others, can never be satisfied with himself, as long as he is sensible of that disadvantage. Nor is this observable only with regard to characters and manners, but may be remarked even in the most minute circumstances. A violent cough in another gives us uneasiness; though in itself it does not in the least affect us. A man will be mortified, if you tell him he has a stinking breath; though it is evidently no annoyance to himself. Our fancy easily changes its situation; and either surveying ourselves as we appear to others, or considering others as they feel themselves, we enter, by that means, into sentiments, which no way belong to us, and in which nothing but sympathy is able to interest us. And this sympathy we sometimes carry so far, as even to be displeased with a quality commodious to us, merely because it displeases others, and makes us disagreeable in their eyes; though perhaps we never can have any interest in rendering ourselves agreeable to them.

There have been many systems of morality advanced by philosophers in all ages; but if they are strictly examined, they may be reduced to two, which alone merit our attention. Moral good and evil are certainly distinguished by our sentiments, not by reason: But these sentiments may arise either from the mere species or appearance of characters and passions, or from reflections on their tendency to the happiness of mankind, and of particular persons. My opinion is, that both these causes are intermixed in our judgments of morals; after the same manner as they are in our decisions concerning most kinds of external beauty: Though I am also of opinion, that reflections on the tendencies of actions have by far the greatest influence, and determine all the great lines of our duty. There are, however, instances, in cases of less moment, wherein this immediate taste or sentiment produces our approbation. Wit, and a certain easy and disengaged behavior, are qualities immediately agreeable to others, and command their love and esteem. Some of these qualities produce satisfaction in others by particular original principles of human nature, which cannot be accounted for: Others may be resolved into principles, which are more general. This will best appear upon a particular enquiry.

As some qualities acquire their merit from their being immediately agreeable to others, without any tendency to public interest; so some are denominated virtuous from their being immediately agreeable to the person himself, who possesses them. Each of the passions and operations of the mind has a particular feeling, which must be either agreeable or disagreeable. The first is virtuous, the second vicious. This particular feeling constitutes the very nature of the passion; and therefore needs not be accounted for.

But however directly the distinction of vice and virtue may seem to flow from the immediate pleasure or uneasiness, which particular qualities cause to ourselves or others; it is easy to observe, that it has also a considerable dependence on the principle of sympathy so often insisted on. We approve of a person, who is possessed of qualities immediately agreeable to those, with whom he has any commerce; though perhaps we ourselves never reaped any pleasure from them. We also approve of one, who is possessed of qualities, that are immediately agreeable to himself; though they be of no service to any mortal. To account for this we must have recourse to the foregoing principles.

Thus, to take a general review of the present hypothesis: Every quality of the mind is denominated virtuous, which gives pleasure by the mere survey; as every quality, which produces pain, is called vicious. This pleasure and this pain may arise from four different sources. For we reap a pleasure from the view of a character, which is naturally fitted to be useful to others, or to the person himself, or which is agreeable to others, or to the person himself. One may, perhaps, be surprised that amidst all these interests and pleasures, we should forget our own, which touch us so nearly on every other occasion. But we shall easily satisfy ourselves on this head, when we consider, that every particular person s pleasure and interest being different, it is impossible men could ever agree in their sentiments and judgments, unless they chose some common point of view, from which they might survey their object, and which might cause it to appear the same to all of them. Now in judging of characters, the only interest or pleasure, which appears the same to every spectator, is that of the person himself, whose character is examined; or that of persons, who have a connection with him. And though such interests and pleasures touch us more faintly than our own, yet being more constant and universal, they counter-balance the latter even in practice, and are alone admitted in speculation as the standard of virtue and morality. They alone produce that particular feeling or sentiment, on which moral distinctions depend.

As to the good or ill desert of virtue or vice, it is an evident consequence of the sentiments of pleasure or uneasiness. These sentiments produce love or hatred; and love or hatred, by the original constitution of human passion, is attended with benevolence or anger; that is, with a desire of making happy the person we love, and miserable the person we hate. We have treated of this more fully on another occasion.

SECT. III: Of Goodness and Benevolence Having thus explained the origin of that praise and approbation, which attends everything we call great in human affections; we now proceed to give an account of their goodness, and show whence its merit is derived.

When experience has once given us a competent knowledge of human affairs, and has taught us the proportion they bear to human passion, we perceive, that the generosity of men is very limited, and that it seldom extends beyond their friends and family, or, at most, beyond their native country. Being thus acquainted with the nature of man, we expect not any impossibilities from him; but confine our view to that narrow circle, in which any person moves, in order to form a judgment of his moral character. When the natural tendency of his passions leads him to be serviceable and useful within his sphere, we approve of his character, and love his person, by a sympathy with the sentiments of those, who have a more particular connection with him. We are quickly obliged to forget our own interest in our judgments of this kind, by reason of the perpetual contradictions, we meet with in society and conversation, from persons that are not placed in the same situation, and have not the same interest with ourselves. The only point of view, in which our sentiments concur with those of others, is, when we consider the tendency of any passion to the advantage or harm of those, who have any immediate connection or intercourse with the person possessed of it. And though this advantage or harm be often very remote from ourselves, yet sometimes it is very near us, and interests us strongly by sympathy. This concern we readily extend to other cases, that are resembling; and when these are very remote, our sympathy is proportionally weaker, and our praise or blame fainter and more doubtful. The case is here the same as in our judgments concerning external bodies. All objects seem to diminish by their distance: But though the appearance of objects to our senses be the original standard, by which we judge of them, yet we do not say, that they actually diminish by the distance; but correcting the appearance by reflection, arrive at a more constant and established judgment concerning them. In like manner, though sympathy be much fainter than our concern for ourselves, and a sympathy with persons remote from us much fainter than that with persons near and contiguous; yet we neglect all these differences in our calm judgments concerning the characters of men. Besides, that we ourselves often change our situation in this particular, we every day meet with persons, who are in a different situation from ourselves, and who could never converse with us on any reasonable terms, were we to remain constantly in that situation and point of view, which is peculiar to us. The intercourse of sentiments, therefore, in society and conversation, makes us form some general inalterable standard, by which we may approve or disapprove of characters and manners. And though the heart does not always take part with those general notions, or regulate its love and hatred by them, yet are they sufficient for discourse, and serve all our purposes m company, in the pulpit, on the theatre, and in the schools.

From these principles we may easily account for that merit, which is commonly ascribed to generosity, humanity, compassion, gratitude, friendship, fidelity, zeal, disinterestedness, liberality, and all those other qualities, which form the character of good and benevolent. A propensity to the tender passions makes a man agreeable and useful in all the parts of life; and gives a just direction to all his other qualities, which otherwise may become prejudicial to society. Courage and ambition, when not regulated by benevolence, are fit only to make a tyrant and public robber. It is the same case with judgment and capacity, and all the qualities of that kind. They are indifferent in themselves to the interests of society, and have a tendency to the good or ill of mankind, according as they are directed by these other passions.

As love is immediately agreeable to the person, who is actuated by it, and hatred immediately disagreeable; this may also be a considerable reason, why we praise all the passions that partake of the former, and blame all those that have any considerable share of the latter. It is certain we are infinitely touched with a tender sentiment, as well as with a great one. The tears naturally start in our eyes at the conception of it; nor can we forbear giving a loose to the same tenderness towards the person who exerts it. All this seems to me a proof, that our approbation has, in those cases, an origin different from the prospect of utility and advantage, either to ourselves or others. To which we may add, that men naturally, without reflection, approve of that character, which is most like their own. The man of a mild disposition and tender affections, in forming a notion of the most perfect virtue, mixes in it more of benevolence and humanity, than the man of courage and enterprise, who naturally looks upon a certain elevation of mind as the most accomplished character. This must evidently proceed from an immediate sympathy, which men have with characters similar to their own. They enter with more warmth into such sentiments, and feel more sensibly the pleasure, which arises from them.

It is remarkable, that nothing touches a man of humanity more than any instance of extraordinary delicacy in love or friendship, where a person is attentive to the smallest concerns of his friend, and is willing to sacrifice to them the most considerable interest of his own. Such delicacies have little influence on society; because they make us regard the greatest trifles: But they are the more engaging, the more minute the concern is, and are a proof of the highest merit in any one, who is capable of them. The passions are so contagious, that they pass with the greatest facility from one person to another, and produce correspondent movements in all human breasts. Where friendship appears in very signal instances, my heart catches the same passion, and is warmed by those warm sentiments, that display themselves before me. Such agreeable movements must give me an affection to everyone that excites them. This is the case with everything that is agreeable in any person. The transition from pleasure to love is easy: But the transition must here be still more easy; since the agreeable sentiment, which is excited by sympathy, is love itself; and there is nothing required but to change the object.

Hence the peculiar merit of benevolence in all its shapes and appearances. Hence even its weaknesses are virtuous and amiable; and a person, whose grief upon the loss of a friend were excessive, would be esteemed upon that account. His tenderness bestows a merit, as it does a pleasure, on his melancholy.

We are not, however, to imagine, that all the angry passions are vicious, though they are disagreeable. There is a certain indulgence due to human nature in this respect. Anger and hatred are passions inherent in our very frame and constitutions. The want of them, on some occasions, may even be a proof of weakness and imbecility. And where they appear only in a low degree, we not only excuse them because they are natural; but even bestow our applauses on them, because they are inferior to what appears in the greatest part of mankind.

Where these angry passions rise up to cruelty, they form the most detested of all vices. All the pity and concern which we have for the miserable sufferers by this vice, turns against the person guilty of it, and produces a stronger hatred than we are sensible of on any other occasion. Even when the vice of inhumanity rises not to this extreme degree, our sentiments concerning it are very much influenced by reflections on the harm that results from it. And we may observe in general, that if we can find any quality in a person, which renders him incommodious to those, who live and converse with him, we always allow it to be a fault or blemish, without any farther examination. On the other hand, when we enumerate the good qualities of any person, we always mention those parts of his character, which render him a safe companion, an easy friend, a gentle master, an agreeable husband, or an indulgent father. We consider him with all his relations in society; and love or hate him, according as he affects those, who have any immediate intercourse with him. And it is a most certain rule, that if there be no relation of life, in which I could not wish to stand to a particular person, his character must so far be allowed to be perfect. If he be as little wanting to himself as to others, his character is entirely perfect. This is the ultimate test of merit and virtue.

SECT. VI: Conclusion Thus upon the whole I am hopeful, that nothing is wanting to an accurate proof of this system of ethics. We are certain, that sympathy is a very powerful principle in human nature. We are also certain, that it has a great influence on our sense of beauty, when we regard external objects, as well as when we judge of morals. We find, that it has force sufficient to give us the strongest sentiments of approbation, when it operates alone, without the concurrence of any other principle; as in the cases of justice, allegiance, chastity, and good-manners. We may observe, that all the circumstances requisite for its operation are found in most of the virtues; which have, for the most part, a tendency to the good of society, or to that of the person possessed of them. If we compare all these circumstances, we shall not doubt, that sympathy is the chief source of moral distinctions; especially when we reflect, that no objection can be raised against this hypothesis in one case, which will not extend to all cases. Justice is certainly approved of for no other reason, than because it has a tendency to the public good: And the public good is indifferent to us, except so far as sympathy interests us in it. We may presume the like with regard to all the other virtues, which have a like tendency to the public good. They must derive all their merit from our sympathy with those, who reap any advantage from them: As the virtues, which have a tendency to the good of the person possessed of them, derive their merit from our sympathy with him.

Most people will readily allow, that the useful qualities of the mind are virtuous, because of their utility. This way of thinking is so natural, and occurs on so many occasions, that few will make any scruple of admitting it. Now this being once admitted, the force of sympathy must necessarily be acknowledged. Virtue is considered as means to an end. Means to an end are only valued so far as the end is valued. But the happiness of strangers affects us by sympathy alone. To that principle, therefore, we are to ascribe the sentiment of approbation, which arises from the survey of all those virtues, that are useful to society, or to the person possessed of them. These form the most considerable part of morality.

Were it proper in such a subject to bribe the reader's assent, or employ anything but solid argument, we are here abundantly supplied with topics to engage the affections. All lovers of virtue (and such we all are in speculation, however we may degenerate in practice) must certainly be pleased to see moral distinctions derived from so noble a source, which gives us a just notion both of the generosity and capacity of human nature. It requires but very little knowledge of human affairs to perceive, that a sense of morals is a principle inherent in the soul, and one of the most powerful that enters into the composition. But this sense must certainly acquire new force, when reflecting on itself, it approves of those principles, from whence it is derived, and finds nothing but what is great and good in its rise and origin. Those who resolve the sense of morals into original instincts of the human mind, may defend the cause of virtue with sufficient authority; but want the advantage, which those possess, who account for that sense by an extensive sympathy with mankind. According to their system, not only virtue must be approved of, but also the sense of virtue: And not only that sense, but also the principles, from whence it is derived. So that nothing is presented on any side, but what is laudable and good.

This observation may be extended to justice, and the other virtues of that kind. Though justice be artificial, the sense of its morality is natural. It is the combination of men, in a system of conduct, which renders any act of justice beneficial to society. But when once it has that tendency, we naturally approve of it; and if we did not so, it is impossible any combination or convention could ever produce that sentiment.

Most of the inventions of men are subject to change. They depend upon humor and caprice. They have a vogue for a time, and then sink into oblivion. It may, perhaps, be apprehended, that if justice were allowed to be a human invention, it must be placed on the same footing. But the cases are widely different. The interest, on which justice is founded, is the greatest imaginable, and extends to all times and places. It cannot possibly be served by any other invention. It is obvious, and discovers itself on the very first formation of society. All these causes render the rules of justice steadfast and immutable; at least, as immutable as human nature. And if they were founded on original instincts, could they have any greater stability?

The same system may help us to form a just notion of the happiness, as well as of the dignity of virtue, and may interest every principle of our nature in the embracing and cherishing that noble quality. Who indeed does not feel an accession of alacrity in his pursuits of knowledge and ability of every kind, when he considers, that besides the advantage, which immediately result from these acquisitions, they also give him a new luster in the eyes of mankind, and are universally attended with esteem and approbation? And who can think any advantages of fortune a sufficient compensation for the least breach of the social virtues, when he considers, that not only his character with regard to others, but also his peace and inward satisfaction entirely depend upon his strict observance of them; and that a mind will never be able to bear its own survey, that has been wanting in its part to mankind and society? But I forbear insisting on this subject. Such reflections require a work a-part, very different from the genius of the present. The anatomist ought never to emulate the painter; nor in his accurate dissections and portraitures of the smaller parts of the human body, pretend to give his figures any graceful and engaging attitude or expression. There is even something hideous, or at least minute in the views of things, which he presents; and it is necessary the objects should be set more at a distance, and be more covered up from sight, to make them engaging to the eye and imagination. An anatomist, however, is admirably fitted to give advice to a painter; and it is even impracticable to excel in the latter art, without the assistance of the former. We must have an exact knowledge of the parts, their situation and connection, before we can design with any elegance or correctness. And thus the most abstract speculations concerning human nature, however cold and unentertaining, become subservient to practical morality; and may render this latter science more correct in its precepts, and more persuasive in its exhortations.

[from *A Treatise of Human Nature* (1790)]

"Concerning Moral Sentiment" from *An Enquiry Concerning the Principles of Morals*

David Hume

APPENDIX I. CONCERNING MORAL SENTIMENT

If the foregoing hypothesis be received, it will now be easy for us to determine the question first started, concerning the general principles of morals; and though we postponed the decision of that question, lest it should then involve us in intricate speculations, which are unfit for moral discourses, we may resume it at present, and examine how far either *Reason* or *Sentiment* enters into all decisions of praise or censure.

One principal foundation of moral praise being supposed to lie in the usefulness of any quality or action, it is evident that *reason* must enter for a considerable share in all decisions of this kind; since nothing but that faculty can instruct us in the tendency of qualities and actions, and point out their beneficial consequences to society and to their possessor. In many cases this is an affair liable to great controversy: doubts may arise; opposite interests may occur; and a preference must be given to one side, from very nice views, and a small overbalance of utility. This is particularly remarkable in questions with regard to justice; as is, indeed, natural to suppose, from that species of utility which attends this virtue. Were every single instance of justice, like that of benevolence, useful to society; this would be a more simple state of the case, and seldom liable to great controversy. But as single instances of justice are often pernicious in their first and immediate tendency, and as the advantage to society results only from the observance of the general rule, and from the concurrence and combination of several persons in the same equitable conduct; the case here becomes more intricate and involved. The various circumstances of society; the various consequences of any practice; the various interests which may be proposed; these, on many occasions, are doubtful, and subject to great discussion and inquiry. The object of municipal laws is to fix all the questions with regard to justice: the debates of civilians; the reflections of politicians; the precedents of history and public records, are all directed to the same purpose. And a very accurate *reason* or *judgment* is often requisite, to give the true determination, amidst such intricate doubts arising from obscure or opposite utilities.

But though reason, when fully assisted and improved, be sufficient to instruct us in the pernicious or useful tendency of qualities and actions; it is not alone sufficient to produce any moral blame or approbation. Utility is only a tendency to a certain end; and were the end totally indifferent to us, we should feel the same indifference towards the means. It is requisite a *sentiment* should here display itself, in order to give a preference to the useful above the pernicious tendencies. This *sentiment* can be no other than a feeling for the happiness of mankind, and a resentment of their misery; since these are the different ends which virtue and vice have a tendency to promote. Here therefore *reason* instructs us in the several tendencies of actions, and *humanity* makes a distinction in favor of those which are useful and beneficial.

This partition between the faculties of understanding and sentiment, in all moral decisions, seems clear from the preceding hypothesis. But I shall suppose that hypothesis false: it will then be requisite to look out for some other theory that may be satisfactory; and I dare venture to affirm that none such will ever be found, so long as we suppose reason to be the sole source of morals. To prove this, it will be proper to weigh the five following considerations.

I.

It is easy for a false hypothesis to maintain some appearance of truth, while it keeps wholly in generals, makes use of undefined terms, and employs comparisons, instead of instances. This is particularly remarkable in that philosophy, which ascribes the discernment of all moral distinctions to reason alone, without the concurrence of sentiment. It is impossible that, in any particular instance, this hypothesis can so much as be rendered intelligible, whatever specious figure it may make in general declamations and discourses. Examine the crime of *ingratitude*, for instance; which has place, wherever we observe good-will, expressed and known, together with good-offices performed, on the one side, and a return of ill-will or indifference, with ill-offices or neglect on the other: anatomize all these circumstances, and examine, by your reason alone, in what consists the demerit or blame. You never will come to any issue or conclusion.

Reason judges either of *matter of fact* or of *relations*. Enquire then, first, where is that matter of fact which we here call crime; point it out; determine the time of its existence; describe its essence or nature; explain the sense or faculty to which it discovers itself. It resides in the mind of the person who is ungrateful. He must, therefore, feel it, and be conscious of it. But nothing is there, except the passion of ill-will or absolute indifference. You cannot say that these, of themselves, always, and in all circumstances, are crimes. No, they are only crimes when directed towards persons who have before expressed and displayed good-will towards us. Consequently, we may infer, that the crime of ingratitude is not any particular individual *fact*; but arises from a complication of circumstances, which, being presented to the spectator, excites the *sentiment* of blame, by the particular structure and fabric of his mind.

This representation, you say, is false. Crime, indeed, consists not in a particular *fact*, of whose reality we are assured by reason; but it consists in certain *moral relations*, discovered by reason, in the same manner as we discover by reason the truths of geometry or algebra. But what are the relations, I ask, of which you here talk? In the case stated above, I see first good-will and good-offices in one person; then ill-will and ill-offices in the other. Between these, there is a relation of *contrariety*. Does the crime consist in that relation? But suppose a person bore me ill-will or did me ill-offices; and I, in return, were indifferent towards him, or did him good offices. Here is the same relation of *contrariety*; and yet my conduct is often highly laudable. Twist and turn this matter as much as you will, you can never rest the morality on relation; but must have recourse to the decisions of sentiment.

When it is affirmed that two and three are equal to the half of ten, this relation of equality I understand perfectly. I conceive, that if ten be divided into two parts, of which one has as many units as the other; and if any of these parts be compared to two added to three, it will contain as many units as that compound number. But when you draw thence a comparison to moral relations, I own that I am altogether at a loss to understand you. A moral action, a crime, such as ingratitude, is a complicated object. Does the morality consist in the relation of its parts to each other? How? After what manner? Specify the relation: be more particular and explicit in your propositions, and you will easily see their falsehood.

No, say you, the morality consists in the relation of actions to the rule of right; and they are denominated good or ill, according as they agree or disagree with it. What then is this rule of right? In what does it consist? How is it determined? By reason, you say, which examines the moral relations of actions. So that moral relations are determined by the comparison of action to a rule. And that rule is determined by considering the moral relations of objects. Is not this fine reasoning?

All this is metaphysics, you cry. That is enough; there needs nothing more to give a strong presumption of falsehood. Yes, reply I, here are metaphysics surely; but they are all on your side, who advance an abstruse hypothesis, which can never be made intelligible, nor quadrate with any particular instance or illustration. The hypothesis which we embrace is plain. It maintains that morality is determined by sentiment. It defines virtue to be *whatever mental action or quality gives to a spectator the pleasing sentiment of approbation*; and vice the contrary. We then proceed to examine a plain matter of fact, to wit, what actions have this influence. We consider all the circumstances in which these actions agree, and thence endeavor to extract some general observations with regard to these sentiments. If you call this metaphysics, and find anything abstruse here, you need only conclude that your turn of mind is not suited to the moral sciences.

II.

When a man, at any time, deliberates concerning his own conduct (as, whether he had better, in a particular emergence, assist a brother or a benefactor), he must consider these separate relations, with all the circumstances and situations of the persons, in order to determine the superior duty and obligation; and in order to determine the proportion of lines in any triangle, it is necessary to examine the nature of that figure, and the relation which its several parts bear to each other. But notwithstanding this appearing similarity in the two cases, there is, at bottom, an extreme difference between them. A speculative reasoner concerning triangles or circles considers the several known and given relations of the parts of these figures; and thence infers some unknown relation, which is dependent on the former. But in moral deliberations we must be acquainted beforehand with all the objects, and all their relations to each other; and from a comparison of the whole, fix our choice or approbation. No new fact to be ascertained; no new relation to be discovered. All the circumstances of the case are supposed to be laid before us, ere we can fix any sentence of blame or approbation. If any material circumstance be yet unknown or doubtful, we must first employ our inquiry or intellectual faculties to assure us of it; and must suspend for a time all moral decision or sentiment. While we are ignorant whether a man were aggressor or not, how can we determine whether the person who killed him be criminal or innocent? But after every circumstance, every relation is known, the understanding has no further room to operate, nor any object on which it could employ itself. The approbation or blame which then ensues, cannot be the work of the judgment, but of the heart; and is not a speculative proposition or affirmation, but an active feeling or sentiment. In the disquisitions of the understanding, from known circumstances and relations, we infer some new and unknown. In moral decisions, all the circumstances and relations must be previously known; and the mind, from the contemplation of the whole, feels some new impression of affection or disgust, esteem or contempt, approbation or blame.

Hence the great difference between a mistake of *fact* and one of *right*; and hence the reason why the one is commonly criminal and not the other. When Oedipus killed Laius, he was ignorant of the relation, and from circumstances, innocent and involuntary, formed erroneous opinions concerning the action which he committed. But when Nero killed Agrippina, all the relations between himself and the person, and all the circumstances of the fact, were previously known to him; but the motive of revenge, or fear, or interest, prevailed in his savage heart over the sentiments of duty and humanity. And when we express that detestation against him to which he himself, in a little time, became insensible, it is not that we see any relations, of which he was ignorant; but that, for the rectitude of our disposition, we feel sentiments against which he was hardened from flattery and a long perseverance in the most enormous crimes.

In these sentiments then, not in a discovery of relations of any kind, do all moral determinations consist. Before we can pretend to form any decision of this kind, everything must be known and ascertained on the side of the object or action. Nothing remains but to feel, on our part, some sentiment of blame or approbation; whence we pronounce the action criminal or virtuous.

III.

This doctrine will become still more evident, if we compare moral beauty with natural, to which in many particulars it bears so near a resemblance. It is on the proportion, relation, and position of parts, that all natural beauty depends; but it would be absurd thence to infer, that the perception of beauty, like that of truth in geometrical problems, consists wholly in the perception of relations, and was performed entirely by the understanding or intellectual faculties. In all the sciences, our mind from the known relations investigates the unknown. But in all decisions of taste or external beauty, all the relations are beforehand obvious to the eye; and we thence proceed to feel a sentiment of complacency or disgust, according to the nature of the object, and disposition of our organs.

Euclid has fully explained all the qualities of the circle; but has not in any proposition said a word of its beauty. The reason is evident. The beauty is not a quality of the circle. It lies not in any part of the line, whose parts are equally distant from a common center. It is only the effect which that figure produces upon the mind, whose peculiar fabric of structure renders it susceptible of such sentiments. In vain would you look for it in the circle, or seek it, either by your senses or by mathematical reasoning, in all the properties of that figure.

Attend to Palladio and Perrault, while they explain all the parts and proportions of a pillar. They talk of the cornice, and frieze, and base, and entablature, and shaft, and architrave; and give the description and position of each of these members. But should you ask the description and position of its beauty, they would readily reply, that the beauty is not in any of the parts or members of a pillar, but results from the whole, when that complicated figure is presented to an intelligent mind, susceptible to those finer sensations. Till such a spectator appear, there is nothing but a figure of such particular dimensions and proportions: from his sentiments alone arise its elegance and beauty.

Again; attend to Cicero, while he paints the crimes of a Verres or a Catiline. You must acknowledge that the moral turpitude results, in the same manner, from the contemplation of the whole, when presented to a being whose organs have such a particular structure and formation. The orator may paint rage, insolence, barbarity on the one side; meekness, suffering, sorrow, innocence on the other. But if you feel no indignation or compassion arise in you from this complication of circumstances, you would in vain ask him, in what consists the crime or villainy, which he so vehemently exclaims against? At what time, or on what subject it first began to exist? And what has a few months afterwards become of it, when every disposition and thought of all the actors is totally altered or annihilated? No satisfactory answer can be given to any of these questions, upon the abstract hypothesis of morals; and we must at last acknowledge, that the crime or immorality is no particular fact or relation, which can be the object of the understanding, but arises entirely from the sentiment of disapprobation, which, by the structure of human nature, we unavoidably feel on the apprehension of barbarity or treachery.

IV.

Inanimate objects may bear to each other all the same relations which we observe in moral agents; though the former can never be the object of love or hatred, nor are consequently susceptible of merit or iniquity. A young tree, which over-tops and destroys its parent, stands in all the same relations with Nero, when he murdered Agrippina; and if morality consisted merely in relations, would no doubt be equally criminal.

V.

It appears evident that—the ultimate ends of human actions can never, in any case, be accounted for by reason, but recommend themselves entirely to the sentiments and affections of mankind, without any dependence on the intellectual faculties. Ask a man *why he uses exercise*; he will answer, *because he desires to keep his health*. If you then enquire, *why he desires health*, he will readily reply, *because sickness is painful*. If you push your enquiries farther, and desire a reason *why he hates pain*, it is impossible he can ever give any. This is an ultimate end, and is never referred to any other object.

Perhaps to your second question, *why he desires health*, he may also reply, that *it is necessary for the exercise of his calling*. If you ask, *why he is anxious on that head*, he will answer, *because he desires to get money*. If you demand *why*? *it is the instrument of pleasure*, says he. And beyond this it is an absurdity to ask for a reason. It is impossible there can be a progress *in infinitum*; and that one thing can always be a reason why another is desired. Something must be desirable on its own account, and because of its immediate accord or agreement with human sentiment and affection.

Now as virtue is an end, and is desirable on its own account, without fee and reward, merely for the immediate satisfaction which it conveys; it is requisite that there should be some sentiment which it touches, some internal taste or feeling, or whatever you may please to call it, which distinguishes moral good and evil, and which embraces the one and rejects the other.

Thus the distinct boundaries and offices of *reason* and of *taste* are easily ascertained. The former conveys the knowledge of truth and falsehood: the latter gives the sentiment of beauty and deformity, vice and virtue. The one discovers objects as they really stand in nature, without addition and diminution: the other has a productive faculty, and gilding or staining all natural objects with the colors, borrowed from internal sentiment, raises in a manner a new creation. Reason being cool and disengaged, is no motive to action, and directs only the impulse received from appetite or inclination, by showing us the means of attaining happiness or avoiding misery: Taste, as it gives pleasure or pain, and thereby constitutes happiness or misery, becomes a motive to action, and is the first spring or impulse to desire and volition. From circumstances and relations, known or supposed, the former leads us to the discovery of the concealed and unknown: after all circumstances and relations are laid before us, the latter makes us feel from the whole a new sentiment of blame or approbation. The standard of the one, being founded on the nature of things, is eternal and inflexible, even by the will of the Supreme Being: the standard of the other arising from the eternal frame and constitution of animals, is ultimately derived from that Supreme Will, which bestowed on each being its peculiar nature, and arranged the several classes and orders of existence.

[from *An Enquiry Concerning the Principles of Morals. (1777).*]

"Of Justice and Beneficence" from *The Theory of Moral Sentiments*

Adam Smith

SECTION II: OF JUSTICE AND BENEFICENCE

Chapter I: Comparison of those two virtues

1. Actions of a beneficent tendency, which proceed from proper motives, seem alone to require reward; because such alone are the approved objects of gratitude, or excite the sympathetic gratitude of the spectator.

2. Actions of a hurtful tendency, which proceed from improper motives, seem alone to deserve punishment; because such alone are the approved objects of resentment, or excite the sympathetic resentment of the spectator.

3. Beneficence is always free, it cannot be extorted by force, the mere want of it exposes to no punishment; because the mere want of beneficence tends to do no real positive evil. It may disappoint of the good which might reasonably have been expected, and upon that account it may justly excite dislike and disapprobation: it cannot, however, provoke any resentment which mankind will go along with. The man who does not recompense his benefactor when he has it in his power, and when his benefactor needs his assistance, is, no doubt, guilty of the blackest ingratitude. The heart of every impartial spectator rejects all fellow-feeling with the selfishness of his motives, and he is the proper object of the highest disapprobation. But still he does no positive hurt to anybody. He only does not do that good which in propriety he ought to have done. He is the object of hatred, a passion which is naturally excited by impropriety of sentiment and behavior; not of resentment . . .

5. There is, however, another virtue, of which the observance is not left to the freedom of our own wills, which may be extorted by force, and of which the violation exposes to resentment, and consequently to punishment. This virtue is justice: the violation of justice is injury: it does real and positive hurt to some particular persons, from motives which are naturally disapproved of. It is, therefore, the proper object of resentment, and of punishment, which is the natural consequence of resentment. As mankind go along with, and approve of the violence employed to avenge the hurt which is done by injustice, so they much more go along with, and approve of, that which is employed to prevent and beat off the injury, and to restrain the offender from hurting his neighbors. The person himself who meditates an injustice is sensible of this, and feels that force may, with the utmost propriety, be made use of, both by the person whom he is about to injure, and by others, either to obstruct the execution of his crime, or to punish him when he has executed it. And upon this is founded that remarkable distinction between justice and all the other social virtues, which has of late been particularly insisted upon by an author of very great and original genius, that we feel ourselves to be under a stricter obligation to act according to justice, than agreeably to friendship, charity, or generosity; that the practice of these last mentioned virtues seems to be left in some measure to our own choice, but that, somehow or other, we feel ourselves to be in a peculiar manner tied, bound, and obliged to the observation of justice. We feel, that is to say, that force may, with the utmost propriety, and with the approbation of all mankind, be made use of to constrain us to observe the rules of the one, but not to follow the precepts of the other.

6. We must always, however, carefully distinguish what is only blamable, or the proper object of disapprobation, from what force may be employed either to punish or to prevent. That seems blamable which falls short of that ordinary degree of proper beneficence which experience teaches us to expect of everybody; and on the contrary, that seems praiseworthy which goes beyond it. The ordinary degree itself seems neither blamable nor praise-worthy. A father, a son, a brother, who behaves to the correspondent relation neither better nor worse than the greater part of men commonly do, seems properly to deserve neither praise nor blame. He who surprises us by extraordinary and unexpected, though still proper and suitable kindness, or on the contrary by extraordinary and unexpected, as well as unsuitable unkindness, seems praise-worthy in the one case, and blamable in the other.

7. Even the most ordinary degree of kindness or beneficence, however, cannot, among equals, be extorted by force. Among equals each individual is naturally, and antecedent to the institution of civil government, regarded as having a right both to defend himself from injuries, and to exact a certain degree of punishment for those which have been done to him. Every generous spectator not only approves of his conduct when he does this, but enters so far into his sentiments as often to be willing to assist him. When one man attacks, or robs, or attempts to murder another, all the neighbors take the alarm, and think that they do right when they run, either to revenge the person who has been injured, or to defend him who is in danger of being so. But when a father fails in the ordinary degree of parental affection towards a son; when a son seems to want that filial reverence which might be expected to his father; when brothers are without the usual degree of brotherly affection; when a man shuts his breast against compassion, and refuses to relieve the misery of his fellow-creatures, when he can with the greatest ease; in all these cases, though everybody blames the conduct, nobody imagines that those who might have reason, perhaps, to expect more kindness, have any right to extort it by force. The sufferer can only complain, and the spectator can intermeddle no other way than by advice and persuasion. Upon all such occasions, for equals to use force against one another, would be thought the highest degree of insolence and presumption.

8. A superior may, indeed, sometimes, with universal approbation, oblige those under his jurisdiction to behave, in this respect, with a certain degree of propriety to one another. The laws of all civilized nations oblige parents to maintain their children, and children to maintain their parents, and impose upon men many other duties of beneficence. The civil magistrate is entrusted with the power not only of preserving the public peace by restraining injustice, but of promoting the prosperity of the commonwealth, by establishing good discipline, and by discouraging every sort of vice and impropriety; he may prescribe rules, therefore, which not only prohibit mutual injuries among fellow-citizens, but command mutual good offices to a certain degree. When the sovereign commands what is merely indifferent, and what, antecedent to his orders, might have been omitted without any blame, it becomes not only blamable but punishable to disobey him. When he commands, therefore, what, antecedent to any such order, could not have been omitted without the greatest blame, it surely becomes much more punishable to be wanting in obedience. Of all the duties of a law-giver, however, this, perhaps, is that which it requires the greatest delicacy and reserve to execute with propriety and judgment. To neglect it altogether exposes the commonwealth to many gross disorders and shocking enormities, and to push it too far is destructive of all liberty, security, and justice.

9. Though the mere want of beneficence seems to merit no punishment from equals, the greater exertions of that virtue appear to deserve the highest reward. By being productive of the greatest good, they are the natural and approved objects of the liveliest gratitude. Though the breach of justice, on the contrary, exposes to punishment, the observance of the rules of that virtue seems scarce to deserve any reward. There is, no doubt, a propriety in the practice of justice, and it merits, upon that account, all the approbation which is due to propriety. But as it does no real positive good, it is entitled to very little gratitude. Mere justice is, upon most occasions, but a negative virtue, and only hinders us from hurting our neighbor. The man who barely abstains from violating either the person, or the estate, or the reputation of his neighbors, has surely very little positive merit. He fulfils, however, all the rules of what is peculiarly called justice, and does everything which his equals can with propriety force him to do, or which they can punish him for not doing. We may often fulfil all the rules of justice by sitting still and doing nothing.

10. As every man doeth, so shall it be done to him, and retaliation seems to be the great law which is dictated to us by Nature. Beneficence and generosity we think due to the generous and beneficent. Those whose hearts never open to the feelings of humanity, should, we think, be shut out, in the same manner, from the affections of all their fellow-creatures, and be allowed to live in the midst of society, as in a great desert where there is nobody to care for them, or to inquire after them. The violator of the laws of justice ought to be made to feel himself that evil which he has done to another; and since no regard to the sufferings of his brethren is capable of restraining him, he ought to be over-awed by the fear of his own. The man who is barely innocent, who only observes the laws of justice with regard to others, and merely abstains from hurting his neighbors, can merit only that his neighbors in their turn should respect his innocence, and that the same laws should be religiously observed with regard to him.

Chapter II: Of the Sense of Justice, of Remorse, and of the Consciousness of Merit

1. There can be no proper motive for hurting our neighbor, there can be no incitement to do evil to another, which mankind will go along with, except just indignation for evil which that other has done to us. To disturb his happiness merely because it stands in the way of our own, to take from him what is of real use to him merely because it may be of equal or of more use to us, or to indulge, in this manner, at the expense of other people, the natural preference which every man has for his own happiness above that of other people, is what no impartial spectator can go along with. Every man is, no doubt, by nature, first and principally recommended to his own care; and as he is fitter to take care of himself than of any other person, it is fit and right that it should be so. Every man, therefore, is much more deeply interested in whatever immediately concerns himself, than in what concerns any other man: and to hear, perhaps, of the death of another person, with whom we have no particular connection, will give us less concern, will spoil our stomach, or break our rest much less than a very insignificant disaster which has befallen ourselves. But though the ruin of our neighbor may affect us much less than a very small misfortune of our own, we must not ruin him to prevent that small misfortune, nor even to prevent our own ruin. We must, here, as in all other cases, view ourselves not so much according to that light in which we may naturally appear to ourselves, as according to that in which we naturally appear to others. Though every man may, according to the proverb, be the whole world to himself, to the rest of mankind he is a most insignificant part of it. Though his own happiness may be of more importance to him than that of all the world besides, to every other person it is of no more consequence than that of any other man. Though it may be true, therefore, that every individual, in his own breast, naturally prefers himself to all mankind, yet he dares not look mankind in the face, and avow that he acts according to this principle. He feels that in this preference they can never go along with him, and that how natural whatsoever it may be to him, it must always appear excessive and extravagant to them. When he views himself in the light in which he is conscious that others will view him, he sees that to them he is but one of the multitude in no respect better than any other in it. If he would act so as that the impartial spectator may enter into the principles of his conduct, which is what of all things he has the greatest desire to do, he must, upon this, as upon all other occasions, humble the arrogance of his self-love, and bring it down to something which other men can go along with. They will indulge it so far as to allow him to be more anxious about, and to pursue with more earnest assiduity, his own happiness than that of any other person. Thus far, whenever they place themselves in his situation, they will readily go along with him. In the race for wealth, and honors, and preferments, he may run as hard as he can, and strain every nerve and every muscle, in order to outstrip all his competitors. But if he should jostle, or throw down any of them, the indulgence of the spectators is entirely at an end. It is a violation of fair play, which they cannot admit of. This man is to them, in every respect, as good as he: they do not enter into that self-love by which he prefers himself so much to this other, and cannot go along with the motive from which he hurt him. They readily, therefore, sympathize with the natural resentment of the injured, and the offender becomes the object of their hatred and indignation. He is sensible that he becomes so, and feels that those sentiments are ready to burst out from all sides against him.

2. As the greater and more irreparable the evil that is done, the resentment of the sufferer runs naturally the higher; so does likewise the sympathetic indignation of the spectator, as well as the sense of guilt in the agent. Death is the greatest evil which one man can inflict upon another, and excites the highest degree of resentment in those who are immediately connected with the slain. Murder, therefore, is the most atrocious of all crimes which affect individuals only, in the sight both of mankind, and of the person who has committed it. To be deprived of that which we are possessed of, is a greater evil than to be disappointed of what we have only the expectation. Breach of property, therefore, theft and robbery, which take from us what we are possessed of, are greater crimes than breach of contract, which

only disappoints us of what we expected. The most sacred laws of justice, therefore, those whose violation seems to call loudest for vengeance and punishment, are the laws which guard the life and person of our neighbor; the next are those which guard his property and possessions; and last of all come those which guard what are called his personal rights, or what is due to him from the promises of others.

3. The violator of the more sacred laws of justice can never reflect on the sentiments which mankind must entertain with regard to him, without feeling all the agonies of shame, and horror, and consternation. When his passion is gratified, and he begins coolly to reflect on his past conduct, he can enter into none of the motives which influenced it. They appear now as detestable to him as they did always to other people. By sympathizing with the hatred and abhorrence which other men must entertain for him, he becomes in some measure the object of his own hatred and abhorrence. The situation of the person, who suffered by his injustice, now calls upon his pity. He is grieved at the thought of it; regrets the unhappy effects of his own conduct, and feels at the same time that they have rendered him the proper object of the resentment and indignation of mankind, and of what is the natural consequence of resentment, vengeance and punishment. The thought of this perpetually haunts him, and fills him with terror and amazement. He dares no longer look society in the face, but imagines himself as it were rejected, and thrown out from the affections of all mankind. He cannot hope for the consolation of sympathy in this his greatest and most dreadful distress. The remembrance of his crimes has shut out all fellow-feeling with him from the hearts of his fellow-creatures. The sentiments which they entertain with regard to him, are the very thing which he is most afraid of. Everything seems hostile, and he would be glad to fly to some inhospitable desert, where he might never more behold the face of a human creature, nor read in the countenance of mankind the condemnation of his crimes. But solitude is still more dreadful than society. His own thoughts can present him with nothing but what is black, unfortunate, and disastrous, the melancholy forebodings of incomprehensible misery and ruin. The horror of solitude drives him back into society, and he comes again into the presence of mankind, astonished to appear before them, loaded with shame and distracted with fear, in order to supplicate some little protection from the countenance of those very judges, who he knows have already all unanimously condemned him. Such is the nature of that sentiment, which is properly called remorse; of all the sentiments which can enter the human breast the most dreadful. It is made up of shame from the sense of the impropriety of past conduct; of grief for the effects of it; of pity for those who suffer by it; and of the dread and terror of punishment from the consciousness of the justly provoked resentment of all rational creatures.

4. The opposite behavior naturally inspires the opposite sentiment. The man who, not from frivolous fancy, but from proper motives, has performed a generous action, when he looks forward to those whom he has served, feels himself to be the natural object of their love and gratitude, and, by sympathy with them, of the esteem and approbation of all mankind. And when he looks backward to the motive from which he acted, and surveys it in the light in which the indifferent spectator will survey it, he still continues to enter into it, and applauds himself by sympathy with the approbation of this supposed impartial judge. In both these points of view his own conduct appears to him every way agreeable. His mind, at the thought of it, is filled with cheerfulness, serenity, and composure. He is in friendship and harmony with all mankind, and looks upon his fellow-creatures with confidence and benevolent satisfaction, secure that he has rendered himself worthy of their most favorable regards. In the combination of all these sentiments consists the consciousness of merit, or of deserved reward.

["Of Justice and Beneficence" from *The Theory of Moral Sentiments* (1759).]

"The Origin of the Moral Sense" from *The Descent of Man*

Charles Darwin

I fully subscribe to the judgment of those writers who maintain that of all the differences between man and the lower animals, the moral sense or conscience is by far the most important. This sense, as Mackintosh remarks, "has a rightful supremacy over every other principle of human action"; it is summed up in that short but imperious word *ought*, so full of high significance. It is the most noble of all the attributes of man, leading him without a moment's hesitation to risk his life for that of a fellow-creature; or after due deliberation, impelled simply by the deep feeling of right or duty, to sacrifice it in some great cause. Immanuel Kant exclaims, "Duty! Wondrous thought, that workest neither by fond insinuation, flattery, nor by any threat, but merely by holding up thy naked law in the soul, and so extorting for thyself always reverence, if not always obedience; before whom all appetites are dumb, however secretly they rebel; whence thy original?"

This great question has been discussed by many writers of consummate ability; and my sole excuse for touching on it, is the impossibility of here passing it over; and because, as far as I know, no one has approached it exclusively from the side of natural history. The investigation possesses, also, some independent interest, as an attempt to see how far the study of the lower animals throws light on one of the highest psychical faculties of man.

The following proposition seems to me in a high degree probable – namely, that any animal whatever, endowed with well-marked social instincts, the parental and filial affections being here included, would inevitably acquire a moral sense or conscience, as soon as its intellectual powers had become as well, or nearly as well developed, as in man. For, *firstly*, the social instincts lead an animal to take pleasure in the society of its fellows, to feel a certain amount of sympathy with them, and to perform various services for them. The services may be of a definite and evidently instinctive nature; or there may be only a wish and readiness, as with most of the higher social animals, to aid their fellows in certain general ways. But these feelings and services are by no means extended to all the individuals of the same species, only to those of the same association. *Secondly*, as soon as the mental faculties had become highly developed, images of all past actions and motives would be incessantly passing through the brain of each individual: and that feeling of dissatisfaction, or even misery, which invariably results, as we shall hereafter see, from any unsatisfied instinct, would arise, as often as it was perceived that the enduring and always present social instinct had yielded to some other instinct, at the time stronger, but neither enduring in its nature, nor leaving behind it a very vivid impression. It is clear that many instinctive desires, such as that of hunger, are in their nature of short duration; and after being satisfied, are not readily or vividly recalled. *Thirdly*, after the power of language had been acquired, and the wishes of the community could be expressed, the common opinion how each member ought to act for the public good, would naturally become in a paramount degree the guide to action. But it should be borne in mind that however great weight we may attribute to public opinion, our regard for the approbation and disapprobation of our fellows depends on sympathy, which, as we shall see, forms an essential part of the social instinct, and is indeed its foundation-stone. *Lastly*, habit in the individual would ultimately play a very important part in guiding the conduct of each member; for the social instinct, together with sympathy, is, like any other instinct, greatly strengthened by habit, and so consequently would be obedience to the wishes and judgment of the community. These several subordinate propositions must now be discussed, and some of them at considerable length.

It may be well first to premise that I do not wish to maintain that any strictly social animal, if its intellectual faculties were to become as active and as highly developed as in man, would acquire exactly the same moral sense as ours. In the same manner as various animals have some sense of beauty, though they admire widely-different objects, so they might have a sense of right and wrong, though led by it to follow widely different lines of conduct. If, for instance, to take an extreme case, men were reared under precisely the same conditions as hive-bees, there can hardly be a doubt that our unmarried females would, like the worker-bees, think it a sacred duty to kill their brothers, and mothers would strive to kill their fertile daughters; and no one would think of interfering. Nevertheless, the bee, or any other social animal, would gain in our supposed case, as it appears to me, some feeling of right or wrong, or a conscience. For each individual would have an inward sense of possessing certain stronger or more enduring instincts, and others less strong or enduring; so that there would often be a struggle as to which impulse should be followed; and satisfaction, dissatisfaction, or even misery would be felt, as past impressions were compared during their incessant passage through the mind. In this case an inward monitor would tell the animal that it would have been better to have followed the one impulse rather than the other. The one course ought to have been followed, and the other ought not; the one would have been right and the other wrong; but to these terms I shall recur.

SOCIABILITY

Animals of many kinds are social; we find even distinct species living together; for example, some American monkeys; and united flocks of rooks, jackdaws, and starlings. Man shows the same feeling in his strong love for the dog, which the dog returns with interest. Everyone must have noticed how miserable horses, dogs, sheep, etc., are when separated from their companions, and what strong mutual affection the two former kinds, at least, show on their reunion. It is curious to speculate on the feelings of a dog, who will rest peacefully for hours in a room with his master or any of the family, without the least notice being taken of him; but if left for a short time by himself, barks or howls dismally. We will confine our attention to the higher social animals; and pass over insects, although some of these are social, and aid one another in many important ways. The most common mutual service in the higher animals is to warn one another of danger by means of the united senses of all. . . . Social animals perform many little services for each other: horses nibble, and cows lick each other, on any spot which itches: monkeys search each other for external parasites; and Brehm states that after a troop of the *Cercopithecus griseoviridis* has rushed through a thorny brake, each monkey stretches itself on a branch, and another monkey sitting by, "conscientiously" examines its fur, and extracts every thorn or burr.

Animals also render more important services to one another: thus wolves and some other beasts of prey hunt in packs, and aid one another in attacking their victims. Pelicans fish in concert. The

Hamadryas baboons turn over stones to find insects, etc.; and when they come to a large one, as many as can stand round, turn it over together and share the booty. Social animals mutually defend each other. Bull bisons in North America, when there is danger, drive the cows and calves into the middle of the herd, whilst they defend the outside. . . .

In Abyssinia, Brehm encountered a great troop of baboons who were crossing a valley; some had already ascended the opposite mountain, and some were still in the valley; the latter were attacked by the dogs, but the old males immediately hurried down from the rocks, and with mouths widely opened, roared so fearfully, that the dogs quickly drew back. They were again encouraged to the attack; but by this time all the baboons had re-ascended the heights, excepting a young one, about six months old, who, loudly calling for aid, climbed on a block of rock, and was surrounded. Now one of the largest males, a true hero, came down again from the mountain, slowly went to the young one, coaxed him, and triumphantly led him away –the dogs being too much astonished to make an attack.

I cannot resist giving another scene which was witnessed by this same naturalist; an eagle seized a young *Cercopithecus*, which, by clinging to a branch, was not at once carried off; it cried loudly for assistance, upon which the other members of the troop, with much uproar, rushed to the rescue, surrounded the eagle, and pulled out so many feathers, that he no longer thought of his prey, but only how to escape. This eagle, as Brehm remarks, assuredly would never again attack a single monkey of a troop.

. . . It is certain that associated animals have a feeling of love for each other, which is not felt by non-social adult animals. How far in most cases they actually sympathize in the pains and pleasures of others, is more doubtful, especially with respect to pleasures. Mr. Buxton, however, who had excellent means of observation, states that his macaws, which lived free in Norfolk, took "an extravagant interest" in a pair with a nest; and whenever the female left it, she was surrounded by a troop "screaming horrible acclamations in her honor." It is often difficult to judge whether animals have any feeling for the sufferings of others of their kind. Who can say what cows feel, when they surround and stare intently on a dying or dead companion; apparently, however, as Houzeau remarks, they feel no pity.

That animals sometimes are far from feeling any sympathy is too certain; for they will expel a wounded animal from the herd, or gore or worry it to death. This is almost the blackest fact in natural history, unless, indeed, the explanation which has been suggested is true, that their instinct or reason leads them to expel an injured companion, lest beasts of prey, including man, should be tempted to follow the troop.

. . . Many animals, however, certainly sympathize with each other's distress or danger. This is the case even with birds. Captain Stansbury found on a salt lake in Utah an old and completely blind pelican, which was very fat, and must have been well fed for a long time by his companions. Mr. Blyth, as he informs me, saw Indian crows feeding two or three of their companions which were blind; (I have myself seen a dog, who never passed a cat who lay sick in a basket, and was a great friend of his, without giving her a few licks with his tongue, the surest sign of kind feeling in a dog). . . .

We may, if we choose, call these actions instinctive; but such cases are much too rare for the development of any special instinct. It must be called sympathy that leads a courageous dog to fly at anyone who strikes his master, as he certainly will. I saw a person pretending to beat a lady, who had a very timid little dog on her lap, and the trial had never been made before; the little creature instantly jumped away, but after the pretended beating was over, it was really pathetic to see how perseveringly he tried to lick his mistress's face, and comfort her. Brehm states that when a baboon in confinement was pursued to be punished, the others tried to protect him. It must have been sympathy in the cases above given which led the baboons and *Cercopitheci* to defend their young comrades from the dogs and the eagle. I will give only one other instance of sympathetic and heroic conduct, in the case of a little American monkey. Several years ago a keeper at the Zoological Gardens showed me some deep and scarcely healed wounds on the nape of his own neck, inflicted on him, whilst kneeling on the floor, by a fierce baboon. The little American monkey, who was a warm friend of this keeper, lived in the same compartment, and was dreadfully afraid of the great baboon.

Nevertheless, as soon as he saw his friend in peril, he rushed to the rescue, and by screams and bites so distracted the baboon that the man was able to escape, after, as the surgeon thought, running great risk of his life.

Besides love and sympathy, animals exhibit other qualities connected with the social instincts, which in us would be called moral; and I agree with Agassiz that dogs possess something very like a conscience.

Dogs possess some power of self-command, and this does not appear to be wholly the result of fear. As Braubach remarks, they will refrain from stealing food in the absence of their master. They have long been accepted as the very type of fidelity and obedience. But the elephant is likewise very faithful to his driver or keeper, and probably considers him as the leader of the herd. Dr. Hooker informs me that an elephant, which he was riding in India, became so deeply bogged that he remained stuck fast until the next day, when he was extricated by men with ropes. Under such circumstances elephants will seize with their trunks any object, dead or alive, to place under their knees, to prevent their sinking deeper in the mud; and the driver was dreadfully afraid lest the animal should have seized Dr. Hooker and crushed him to death. But the driver himself, as Dr. Hooker was assured, ran no risk. This forbearance under an emergency so dreadful for a heavy animal, is a wonderful proof of noble fidelity.

All animals living in a body, which defend themselves or attack their enemies in concert, must indeed be in some degree faithful to one another; and those that follow a leader must be in some degree obedient. . . .

It has often been assumed that animals were in the first place rendered social, and that they feel as a consequence uncomfortable when separated from each other, and comfortable whilst together; but it is a more probable view that these sensations were first developed, in order that those animals which would profit by living in society, should be induced to live together, in the same manner as the sense of hunger and the pleasure of eating were, no doubt, first acquired in order to induce animals to eat. The feeling of pleasure from society is probably an extension of the parental or filial affections, since the social instinct seems to be developed by the young remaining for a long time with their parents; and this extension may be attributed in part to habit, but chiefly to natural selection. With those animals which were benefited by living in close association, the individuals which took the greatest pleasure in society would best escape various dangers, whilst those that cared least for their comrades, and lived solitary, would perish in greater numbers. With respect to the origin of the parental and filial affections, which apparently lie at the base of the social instincts, we know not the steps by which they have been gained; but we may infer that it has been to a large extent through natural selection.

MAN A SOCIAL ANIMAL

Everyone will admit that man is a social being. We see this in his dislike of solitude, and in his wish for society beyond that of his own family. Solitary confinement is one of the severest punishments which can be inflicted. . . . As man is a social animal, it is almost certain that he would inherit a tendency to be faithful to his comrades, and obedient to the leader of his tribe; for these qualities are common to most social animals. He would consequently possess some capacity for self-command. He would from an inherited tendency be willing to defend, in concert with others, his fellow-men; and would be ready to aid them in any way, which did not too greatly interfere with his own welfare or his own strong desires.

The social animals which stand at the bottom of the scale are guided almost exclusively, and those which stand higher in the scale are largely guided, by special instincts in the aid which they give to the members of the same community; but they are likewise in part impelled by mutual love and sympathy, assisted apparently by some amount of reason. Although man, as just remarked, has no special instincts to tell him how to aid his fellow-men, he still has the impulse, and with his improved intellectual faculties would naturally be much guided in this respect by reason and experience. Instinctive sympathy would also cause him to value highly the approbation of his fellows. . . . Consequently man would be influenced in the highest degree by the wishes, approbation, and blame of his fellow-men, as expressed by their gestures and language. Thus the social instincts, which must have been acquired by man in a very rude state, and probably even by his early ape-like progenitors, still give the impulse to some of his best actions; but his actions are in a higher degree determined by the expressed wishes and judgment of his fellow-men, and unfortunately very often by his own strong selfish desires. But as love, sympathy and self-command become strengthened by habit, and as the power of reasoning becomes clearer, so that man can value justly the judgments of his fellows, he will feel himself impelled, apart from any transitory pleasure or pain, to certain lines of conduct. He might then declare—not that any barbarian or uncultivated man could thus think—I am the supreme judge of my own conduct, and in the words of Kant, I will not in my own person violate the dignity of humanity.

["The Origin of the Moral Sense" from *The Descent of Man,* 3rd ed. (John Murray: London, 1875), pp. 97–111. First published in 1871.]

KEY TERMS AND CONCEPTS

- emotivism
- sentiment
- impressions
- ideas
- "the understanding"
- "the passions"
- approbation
- disapprobation
- sympathy
- virtue
- vice
- character
- natural virtues/vices
- artificial virtues/vices
- justice
- beneficence
- remorse
- sociability

Questions for Further Reflection

1. What roles do "the understanding" (i.e., reason) and "the passions" (i.e., our emotions) play in human action according to Hume?
2. How does Hume define virtue and vice? Compare and contrast his understanding of these terms with that of Aristotle.
3. In what sense is Hume's use of the term "sympathy" closer in spirit to the term "empathy"?
4. Why does Hume invoke the idea of beauty? How is it related to his ethical theory?
5. According to Smith, what is the central difference between justice and beneficence?
6. Summarize Darwin's account of the development of the moral sense (i.e., conscience). That is, where does he believe our conscience comes from and why? Do you agree with his assessment? Why or why not?

Homework Assignment #8a

Name: ______________________________ Section: ______________________________

Explain David Hume's account of the roles played by "the understanding" (i.e., reason) and "the passions" (i.e., our emotions) in human action. Do you agree with his assessment? Why or why not?

Homework Assignment #8b

Name: ______________________________ Section: ______________________________

Explain Hume's characterization of virtue and vice. Compare and contrast his understanding of these concepts with that of Aristotle.

Homework Assignment #8B

Name ______________________________ Section ______________________________

[illegible]

Homework Assignment #8c

Name: ______________________________ Section: ______________________________

Explain why Hume invokes the idea of beauty. How is the experience of beauty related to his moral theory? Do you agree with his assessment? Why or why not?

Homework Assignment #8d

Name: ______________________________ Section: ______________________________

Summarize Charles Darwin's account of the development of the moral sense (i.e., conscience). Where does he believe our conscience comes from and why? Do you agree with his assessment? Why or why not?

CHAPTER NINE

Locke and Hobbes on the Social Contract

John Locke (1632–1704)

Thomas Hobbes (1588–1679)

SELECTED READINGS

- "On the Social Contract" from *Leviathan*—Thomas Hobbes
- *A Second Treatise of Civil Government*—John Locke

"On the Social Contract" from *Leviathan*

Thomas Hobbes

CHAPTER XIII: OF THE NATURAL CONDITION OF MANKIND AS CONCERNING THEIR FELICITY AND MISERY

Nature has made men so equal in the faculties of body and mind as that, though there be found one man sometimes manifestly stronger in body or of quicker mind than another, yet when all is reckoned together the difference between man and man is not so considerable as that one man can thereupon claim to himself any benefit to which another may not pretend as well as he. For as to the strength of body, the weakest has strength enough to kill the strongest, either by secret machination or by confederacy with others that are in the same danger with himself.

And as to the faculties of the mind, setting aside the arts grounded upon words, and especially that skill of proceeding upon general and infallible rules, called science, which very few have and but in few things, as being not a native faculty born with us, nor attained, as prudence, while we look after somewhat else, I find yet a greater equality amongst men than that of strength. For prudence is but experience, which equal time equally bestows on all men in those things they equally apply themselves unto. That which may perhaps make such equality incredible is but a vain conceit of one's own wisdom, which almost all men think they have in a greater degree than the vulgar; that is, than all men but themselves, and a few others, whom by fame, or for concurring with themselves, they approve. For such is the nature of men that howsoever they may acknowledge many others to be more witty, or more eloquent or more learned, yet they will hardly believe there be many so wise as themselves; for they see their own wit at hand, and other men's at a distance. But this proves rather that men are in that point equal, than unequal. For there is not ordinarily a greater sign of the equal distribution of anything than that every man is contented with his share.

From this equality of ability arises equality of hope in the attaining of our ends. And therefore if any two men desire the same thing, which nevertheless they cannot both enjoy, they become enemies; and in the way to their end (which is principally their own conservation, and sometimes their delectation only) endeavor to destroy or subdue one another. And from hence it comes to pass that where an invader has no more to fear than another man's single power, if one plant, sow, build, or possess a convenient seat, others may probably be expected to come prepared with forces united to dispossess and deprive him, not only of the fruit of his labor, but also of his life or liberty. And the invader again is in the like danger of another.

And from this diffidence of one another, there is no way for any man to secure himself so reasonable as anticipation; that is, by force, or wiles, to master the persons of all men he can so long till he see no other power great enough to endanger him: and this is no more than his own conservation requires, and is generally allowed. Also, because there be some that, taking pleasure in contemplating their own power in the acts of conquest, which they pursue farther than their security requires, if others, that otherwise would be glad to be at ease within modest bounds, should not by invasion increase their power, they would not be able, long time, by standing only on their defense, to subsist. And by consequence, such augmentation of dominion over men being necessary to a man's conservation, it ought to be allowed him.

Again, men have no pleasure (but on the contrary a great deal of grief) in keeping company where there is no power able to overawe them all. For every man looketh that his companion should value him at the same rate he sets upon himself, and upon all signs of contempt or undervaluing naturally endeavors, as far as he dares (which amongst them that have no common power to keep them in quiet is far enough to make them destroy each other), to extort a greater value from his contemnors, by damage; and from others, by the example.

So that in the nature of man, we find three principal causes of quarrel. First, competition; secondly, diffidence; thirdly, glory.

The first makes men invade for gain; the second, for safety; and the third, for reputation. The first use violence, to make themselves masters of other men's persons, wives, children, and cattle; the second, to defend them; the third, for trifles, as a word, a smile, a different opinion, and any other sign of undervalue, either direct in their persons or by reflection in their kindred, their friends, their nation, their profession, or their name.

Hereby it is manifest that during the time men live without a common power to keep them all in awe, they are in that condition which is called war; and such a war as is of every man against every man. For war consists not in battle only, or the act of fighting, but in a tract of time, wherein the will to contend by battle is sufficiently known: and therefore the notion of time is to be considered in the nature of war, as it is in the nature of weather. For as the nature of foul weather lies not in a shower or two of rain, but in an inclination thereto of many days together: so the nature of war consists not in actual fighting, but in the known disposition thereto during all the time there is no assurance to the contrary. All other time is peace.

Whatsoever therefore is consequent to a time of war, where every man is enemy to every man, the same consequent to the time wherein men live without other security than what their own strength and their own invention shall furnish them withal. In such condition there is no place for industry, because the fruit thereof is uncertain: and consequently no culture of the earth; no navigation, nor use of the commodities that may be imported by sea; no commodious building; no instruments of moving and removing such things as require much force; no knowledge of the face of the earth; no account of time; no arts; no letters; no society; and which is worst of all, continual fear, and danger of violent death; and the life of man, solitary, poor, nasty, brutish, and short.

It may seem strange to some man that has not well weighed these things that Nature should thus dissociate and render men apt to invade and destroy one another: and he may therefore, not trusting to this inference, made from the passions, desire perhaps to have the same confirmed by experience. Let him therefore consider with himself: when taking a journey, he arms himself and seeks to go well accompanied; when going to sleep, he locks his doors; when even in his house he locks his chests; and this when he knows there be laws and public officers, armed, to revenge all injuries shall be done him; what opinion he has of his fellow subjects, when he rides armed; of his fellow citizens, when he locks his doors; and of his children, and servants, when he locks his chests. Does he not there as much accuse mankind by his actions as I do by my words? But neither of us accuse man's nature in it. The desires, and other passions of man, are in themselves no sin. No more are the actions that proceed from those passions till they know a law that forbids them; which till laws be made they cannot know, nor can any law be made till they have agreed upon the person that shall make it.

It may peradventure be thought there was never such a time nor condition of war as this; and I believe it was never generally so, over all the world: but there are many places where they live so now. . . . Howsoever, it may be perceived what manner of life there would be, where there were no common power to fear, by the manner of life which men that have formerly lived under a peaceful government use to degenerate into a civil war.

But though there had never been any time wherein particular men were in a condition of war one against another, yet in all times kings and persons of sovereign authority, because of their independency, are in continual jealousies, and in the state and posture of gladiators, having their weapons pointing, and their eyes fixed on one another; that is, their forts, garrisons, and guns upon the frontiers of their kingdoms, and continual spies upon their neighbors, which is a posture of war. But because they uphold thereby the industry of their subjects, there does not follow from it that misery which accompanies the liberty of particular men.

To this war of every man against every man, this also is consequent; that nothing can be unjust. The notions of right and wrong, justice and injustice, have there no place. Where there is no common power, there is no law; where no law, no injustice. Force and fraud are in war the two cardinal virtues. Justice and injustice are none of the faculties neither of the body nor mind. If they were, they might be in a man that were alone in the world, as well as his senses and passions. They are qualities that relate to men in society, not in solitude. It is consequent also to the same condition that there be no propriety, no dominion, no mine and thine distinct; but only that to be every man's that he can get, and for so long as he can keep it. And thus much for the ill condition which man by mere nature is actually placed in; though with a possibility to come out of it, consisting partly in the passions, partly in his reason.

The passions that incline men to peace are: fear of death; desire of such things as are necessary to commodious living; and a hope by their industry to obtain them. And reason suggests convenient articles of peace upon which men may be drawn to agreement. These articles are they which otherwise are called the laws of nature, whereof I shall speak more particularly in the two following chapters.

CHAPTER XIV: OF THE FIRST AND SECOND NATURAL LAWS, AND OF CONTRACTS

The right of nature, which writers commonly call *jus naturale*, is the liberty each man has to use his own power as he will himself for the preservation of his own nature; that is to say, of his own life; and consequently, of doing anything which, in his own judgment and reason, he shall conceive to be the most apt means thereunto.

By liberty is understood, according to the proper signification of the word, the absence of external impediments; which impediments may oft take away part of a man's power to do what he would, but cannot hinder him from using the power left him according as his judgment and reason shall dictate to him.

A law of nature, *lex naturalis*, is a precept, or general rule, found out by reason, by which a man is forbidden to do that which is destructive of his life, or takes away the means of preserving the same, and to omit that by which he thinks it may be best preserved. For though they that speak of this subject use to confound *jus* and *lex*, right and law, yet they ought to be distinguished, because right consists in liberty to do, or to forbear; whereas law determines and binds to one of them: so that law and right differ as much as obligation and liberty, which in one and the same matter are inconsistent.

And because the condition of man (as has been declared in the precedent chapter) is a condition of war of every one against every one, in which case everyone is governed by his own reason, and there is nothing he can make use of that may not be a help unto him in preserving his life against his enemies; it follows that in such a condition every man has a right to everything, even to one another's body. And therefore, as long as this natural right of every man to everything endures, there can be no security to any man, how strong or wise howsoever he be, of living out the time which nature ordinarily allows men to live. And consequently it is a precept, or general rule of reason: that every man ought to endeavor peace, as far as he has hope of obtaining it; and when he cannot obtain it, that he may seek and use all helps and advantages of war. The first branch of which rule contains the first and fundamental law of nature, which is: to seek peace and follow it. The second, the sum of the right of nature, which is: by all means we can to defend ourselves.

From this fundamental law of nature, by which men are commanded to endeavor peace, is derived this second law: that a man be willing, when others are so too, as far forth as for peace and defense of himself he shall think it necessary, to lay down this right to all things; and be contented with so much liberty against other men as he would allow other men against himself. For as long as every man holds this right, of doing anything he likes, so long are all men in the condition of war. But if other men will not lay down their right, as well as he, then there is no reason for anyone to divest himself of his: for that were to expose himself to prey, which no man is bound to, rather than to dispose himself to peace. This is that law of the gospel: "Whatsoever you require that others should do to you, that do ye to them." And that law of all men: *quod tibi fieri non vis, alteri ne feceris* [i.e., Do unto others as you would have done unto you"].

[*Leviathan, in The English Works of Thomas Hobbes.* Ed. Sir William Molesworth. London: John Bohn, 1839).]

Second Treatise of Civil Government

John Locke

CHAPTER II: OF THE STATE OF NATURE.

Sec. 4.

To understand political power right, and derive it from its original, we must consider, what state all men are naturally in, and that is, *a state of perfect freedom* to order their actions, and dispose of their possessions and persons, as they think fit, within the bounds of the law of nature, without asking leave, or depending upon the will of any other man.

A *state* also of *equality*, wherein all the power and jurisdiction is reciprocal, no one having more than another; there being nothing more evident, than that creatures of the same species and rank, promiscuously born to all the same advantages of nature, and the use of the same faculties, should also be equal one amongst another without subordination or subjection, unless the lord and master of them all should, by any manifest declaration of his will, set one above another, and confer on him, by an evident and clear appointment, an undoubted right to dominion and sovereignty.

Sec. 6.

But though this be *a state of liberty*, yet it is not *a state of license*: though man in that state have an uncontrollable liberty to dispose of his person or possessions, yet he has not liberty to destroy himself, or so much as any creature in his possession, but where some nobler use than its bare preservation calls for it. The *state of nature* has a law of nature to govern it, which obliges everyone: and reason, which is that law, teaches all mankind, who will but consult it, that being all *equal and independent*, no one ought to harm another in his life, health, liberty, or possessions: for men being all the workmanship of one omnipotent, and infinitely wise maker; all the servants of one sovereign master, sent into the world by his order, and about his business; they are his property, whose workmanship they are, made to last during his, not one another's pleasure: and being furnished with like faculties, sharing all in one community of nature, there cannot be supposed any such subordination among us, that may authorize us to destroy one another, as if we were made for one another's uses, as the inferior ranks of creatures are for ours. Every one, as he is *bound to preserve himself*, and not to quit his station wilfully, so by the like reason, when his own preservation comes not in competition, ought he, as much as he can, *to preserve the rest of mankind*, and may not, unless it be to do justice on an offender, take away, or impair the life, or what tends to the preservation of the life, the liberty, health, limb, or goods of another.

Sec. 7.

And that all men may be restrained from invading others rights, and from doing hurt to one another, and the law of nature be observed, which wills the peace and *preservation of all mankind*, the execution of the law of nature is, in that state, put into every man's hands, whereby everyone has a right to punish the transgressors of that law to such a degree, as may hinder its violation: for the law of nature would, as all other laws that concern men in this world 'be in vain, if there were no body that in the state of nature had a power to execute that law, and thereby preserve the innocent and restrain offenders. And if anyone in the state of nature may punish another for any evil he has done, every one may do so: for in that state of perfect equality, where naturally there is no superiority or jurisdiction of one over another, what any may do in prosecution of that law, everyone must needs have a right to do.

Sec. 8.

And thus, in the state of nature, *one man comes by a power over another*; but yet no absolute or arbitrary power, to use a criminal, when he has got him in his hands, according to the passionate heats, or boundless extravagancy of his own will; but only to retribute to him, so far as calm reason and conscience dictate, what is proportionate to his *transgression*, which is so much as may serve for *reparation* and *restraint*: for these two are the only reasons, why one man may lawfully do harm to another, which is that we call *punishment*. In transgressing the law of nature, the offender declares himself to live by another rule than that of reason and common equity, which is that measure God has set to the actions of men, for their mutual security; and so he becomes dangerous to mankind, the tie, which is to secure them from injury and violence, being slighted and broken by him. Which being a trespass against the whole species, and the peace and safety of it, provided for by the law of nature, every man upon this score, by the right he hath to preserve mankind in general, may restrain, or where it is necessary, destroy things noxious to them, and so may bring such evil on any one, who hath transgressed that law, as may make him repent the doing of it, and thereby deter him, and by his example others, from doing the like mischief. And in the case, and upon this ground, *every man has a right to punish the offender, and be executioner of the law of nature.*

Sec. 9.

I doubt not but this will seem a very strange doctrine to some men: but before they condemn it, I desire them to resolve me, by what right any prince or state can put to death, or punish an alien, for any crime he commits in their country. It is certain their laws, by virtue of any sanction they receive from the promulgated will of the legislative, reach not a stranger: they speak not to him, nor, if they did, is he bound to hearken to them. The legislative authority, by which they are in force over the subjects of that commonwealth, hath no power over him. Those who have the supreme power of making laws in England, France or Holland, are to an Indian, but like the rest of the world, men without authority: and therefore, if by the law of nature every man hath not a power to punish offences against it, as he soberly judges the case to require, I see not how the magistrates of any community can punish an alien of another country; since, in reference to him, they can have no more power than what every man naturally may have over another.

Sec. 11.

From these *two distinct rights*, the one of *punishing* the *crime for restraint*, and preventing the like offence, which right of punishing is in every body; the other of taking reparation, which belongs only to the injured party, comes it to pass that the magistrate, who by being magistrate hath the common right of punishing put into his hands, can often, where the public good demands not the execution of the law, remit the punishment of criminal offences by his own authority, but yet cannot remit the satisfaction due to any private man for the damage he has received. That, he who has suffered the damage has a right to demand in his own name, and he alone can remit: the damnified person has this power of appropriating to himself the goods or service of the offender, *by right of self-preservation*, as every man has a power to punish the crime, to prevent its being committed again, *by the right he has of preserving all mankind*, and doing all reasonable things he can in order to that end. . . .

Sec. 14.

It is often asked as a mighty objection, *where are*, or ever were there any *men in such a state of nature*? To which it may suffice as an answer at present, that since all princes and rulers of independent governments all through the world, are in a state of nature, it is plain the world never was, nor ever will be, without numbers of men in that state. I have named all governors of independent communities, whether they are, or are not, in league with others: for it is not every compact that puts an end to the state of nature between men, but only this one of agreeing together mutually to enter into one community, and make one body politic; other promises, and compacts, men may make one with another, and yet still be in the state of nature. . . .

CHAPTER III: OF THE STATE OF WAR

Sec. 16.

The *state of war* is a state of *enmity* and *destruction*: and therefore declaring by word or action, not a passionate and hasty, but a sedate settled design upon another man's life, *puts him in a state of war* with him against whom he has declared such an intention, and so has exposed his life to the other's power to be taken away by him, or any one that joins with him in his defense, and espouses his quarrel; it being reasonable and just, I should have a right to destroy that which threatens me with destruction: for, *by the fundamental law of nature, man being to be preserved* as much as possible, when all cannot be preserved, the safety of the innocent is to be preferred: and one may destroy a man who makes war upon him, or has discovered an enmity to his being, for the same reason that he may kill a *wolf* or a *lion*; because such men are not under the ties of the commonlaw of reason, have no other rule, but that of force and violence, and so may be treated as beasts of prey, those dangerous and noxious creatures, that will be sure to destroy him whenever he falls into their power.

Sec. 17.

And hence it is, that he who attempts to get another man into his absolute power, does thereby *put himself into a state of war* with him; it being to be understood as a declaration of a design upon his life: for I have reason to conclude, that he who would get me into his power without my consent, would use me as he pleased when he had got me there, and destroy me too when he had a fancy to it; for nobody can desire to *have me in his absolute power*, unless it be to compel me by force to that which is against the right of my freedom, i.e. make me a slave. To be free from such force is the only security of my preservation; and reason bids me look on him, as an enemy to my preservation, who would take away that freedom which is the fence to it; so that he who makes an *attempt to enslave* me, thereby puts himself into a state of war with me. He that, in the state of nature, *would take away the freedom* that belongs to any one in that state, must necessarily be supposed to design to take everything else, that *freedom* being the foundation of all the rest: As he that, in the state of society, would take away the freedom belonging to those of that society or commonwealth, must be supposed to design to take away from them everything else, and so be looked on as *in a state of war*. . . .

Sec. 19.

And here we have the plain *difference between the state of nature and the state of war*, which however some men have confounded, are as far distant, as a state of peace, good will, mutual assistance and preservation, and a state of enmity, malice, violence and mutual destruction, are one from another. Men living together according to reason, without a common superior on earth, with authority to judge between them, is *properly the state of nature*. But force, or a declared design of force, upon the person of another, where there is no common superior on earth to appeal to for relief, is *the state of war*: and it is the want of such an appeal gives a man the right of war even against an aggressor, though he be in society and a fellow subject. Thus a *thief*, whom I cannot harm, but by appeal to the law, for having stolen all that I am worth, I may kill, when he sets on me to rob me but of my horse or coat; because the law, which was made for my preservation, where it cannot interpose to secure my life from present force, which, if lost, is capable of no reparation, permits me my own defense, and the right of war, a liberty to kill the aggressor, because the aggressor allows not time to appeal to our common judge, nor the decision of the law, for remedy in a case where the mischief may be irreparable. *Want of a common judge with authority, puts all men in a state of nature: force without right, upon a man's person, makes a state of war*, both where there is, and is not, a common judge. . . .

Sec. 21.

To avoid this *state of war* (wherein there is no appeal but to heaven, and wherein every the least difference is apt to end, where there is no authority to decide between the contenders) is one great *reason of men's putting themselves into society*, and quitting the state of nature: for where there is an authority, a power on earth, from which relief can be had by *appeal*, there the continuance of the *state of war* is excluded, and the controversy is decided by that power

CHAPTER V: OF PROPERTY

Sec. 27.

Though the earth, and all inferior creatures, be common to all men, yet every man has a property in his own person: this nobody has any right to but himself. The labor of his body, and the work of his hands, we may say, are properly his. Whatsoever then he removes out of the state that nature hath provided, and left it in, he hath mixed his labor with, and joined to it something that is his own, and thereby makes it his property. It being by him removed from the common state nature hath placed it in, it hath by this labor something annexed to it, that excludes the common right of other men: for this labor being the unquestionable property of the laborer, no man but he can have a right to what that is once joined to, at least where there is enough, and as good, left in common for others.

Sec. 28.

He that is nourished by the acorns he picked up under an oak, or the apples he gathered from the trees in the wood, has certainly appropriated them to himself. Nobody can deny but the nourishment is his. I ask then, when did they begin to be his? When he digested? Or when he eat? Or when he boiled? Or when he brought them home? Or when he picked them up? And it is plain, if the first gathering made them not his, nothing else could. That labor put a distinction between them and common: that added something to them more than nature, the common mother of all, had done; and so they became his private right. And will anyone say, he had no right to those acorns or apples, he thus appropriated, because he had not the consent of all mankind to make them his? Was it a robbery thus to assume to himself what belonged to all in common? If such a consent as that was necessary, man had starved, notwithstanding the plenty God had given him. We see in commons, which remain so by compact, that it is the taking any part of what is common, and removing it out of the state nature leaves it in, which begins the property; without which the common is of no use. And the taking of this or that part, does not depend on the express consent of all the commoners. Thus the grass my horse has bit; the turfs my servant has cut; and the ore I have dug in any place, where I have a right to them in common with others, become my property, without the assignation or consent of any body. The labor that was mine, removing them out of that common state they were in, hath fixed my property in them. . . .

Sec. 34.

God gave the world to men in common; but since he gave it them for their benefit, and the greatest conveniences of life they were capable to draw from it, it cannot be supposed he meant it should always remain common and uncultivated. He gave it to the use of the industrious and rational, (and labor was to be his title to it;) not to the fancy or covetousness of the quarrelsome and contentious. He that had as good left for his improvement, as was already taken up, needed not complain, ought not to meddle with what was already improved by another's labor: if he did, it is plain he desired the benefit of another's pains, which he had no right to, and not the ground which God had given him in common with others to labor on, and whereof there was as good left, as that already possessed, and more than he knew what to do with, or his industry could reach to. . . .

Sec. 36.

The measure of property nature has well set by the extent of men's labor and the conveniences of life: no man's labor could subdue, or appropriate all; nor could his enjoyment consume more than a small part; so that it was impossible for any man, this way, to entrench upon the right of another, or acquire to himself a property, to the prejudice of his neighbor, who would still have room for as good, and as large a possession (after the other had taken out his) as before it was appropriated. This measure did confine every man's possession to a very moderate proportion, and such as he might appropriate to himself, without injury to anybody, in the first ages of the world, when men were more in danger to be lost, by wandering from their company, in the then vast wilderness of the earth, than to be straightened for want of room to plant in. And the same measure may be allowed still without prejudice to anybody, as full as the world seems. . . .

Sec. 51.

And thus, I think, it is very easy to conceive, without any difficulty, how labor could at first begin a title of property in the common things of nature, and how the spending it upon our uses bounded it. So that there could then be no reason of quarrelling about title, nor any doubt about the largeness of possession it gave. Right and convenience went together; for as a man had a right to all he could employ his labor upon, so he had no temptation to labor for more than he could make use of. This left no room for controversy about the title, nor for encroachment on the right of others; what portion a man carved to himself, was easily seen; and it was useless, as well as dishonest, to carve himself too much, or take more than he needed.

CHAPTER VII: OF POLITICAL OR CIVIL SOCIETY

Sec. 87.

Man being born, as has been proved, with a title to perfect freedom, and an uncontrolled enjoyment of all the rights and privileges of the law of nature, equally with any other man, or number of men in the world, hath by nature a power, not only to preserve his property, that is, his life, liberty and estate, against the injuries and attempts of other men; but to judge of, and punish the breaches of that law in others, as he is persuaded the offence deserves, even with death itself, in crimes where the heinousness of the fact, in his opinion, requires it. But because no political society can be, nor subsist, without having in itself the power to preserve the property, and in order thereunto, punish the offences of all those of that society; there, and there only is political society, where every one of the members hath quitted this natural power, resigned it up into the hands of the community in all cases that exclude him not from appealing for protection to the law established by it. And thus all private judgment of every particular member being excluded, the community comes to be umpire, by settled standing rules, indifferent, and the same to all parties; and by men having authority from the community, for the execution of those rules, decides all the differences that may happen between any members of that society concerning any matter of right; and punishes those offences which any member hath committed against the society, with such penalties as the law has established: whereby it is easy to discern, who are, and who are not, in political society together. Those who are united into one body, and have a common established law and judicature to appeal to, with authority to decide controversies between them, and punish offenders, are in civil society one with another: but those who have no such common appeal, I mean on earth, are still in the state of nature, each being, where there is no other, judge for himself, and executioner; which is, as I have before shown it, the perfect state of nature.

Sec. 88.

And thus the commonwealth comes by a power to set down what punishment shall belong to the several transgressions which they think worthy of it, committed amongst the members of that society, (which is the power of making laws) as well as it has the power to punish any injury done unto any of its members, by any one that is not of it, (which is the power of war and peace;) and all this for the preservation of the property of all the members of that society, as far as is possible. But though every man who has entered into civil society, and is become a member of any commonwealth, has thereby quitted his power to punish offences, against the law of nature, in prosecution of his own private judgment, yet with the judgment of offences, which he has given up to the legislative in all cases, where he can appeal to the magistrate, he has given a right to the commonwealth to employ his force, for the execution of the judgments of the commonwealth, whenever he shall be called to it; which indeed are his own judgments, they being made by himself, or his representative. And herein we have the original of the legislative and executive power of civil society, which is to judge by standing laws, how far offences are to be punished, when committed within the commonwealth; and also to determine, by occasional judgments founded on the present circumstances of the fact, how far injuries from without are to be vindicated; and in both these to employ all the force of all the members, when there shall be need.

Sec. 89.

Where-ever therefore any number of men are so united into one society, as to quit everyone his executive power of the law of nature, and to resign it to the public, there and there only is a political, or civil society. And this is done, where-ever any number of men, in the state of nature, enter into society to make one people, one body politic, under one supreme government; or else when any one joins himself to, and incorporates with any government already made: for hereby he authorizes the society, or which is all one, the legislative thereof, to make laws for him, as the public good of the society shall require; to the execution whereof, his own assistance (as to his own decrees) is due. And this puts men out of a state of nature into that of a commonwealth, by setting up a judge on earth, with authority to determine all the controversies, and redress the injuries that may happen to any member of the commonwealth; which judge is the legislative, or magistrates appointed by it. And where-ever there are any number of men, however associated, that have no such decisive power to appeal to, there they are still in the state of nature.

Sec. 90.

Hence it is evident, that absolute monarchy, which by some men is counted the only government in the world, is indeed inconsistent with civil society, and so can be no form of civil-government at all: for the end of civil society, being to avoid, and remedy those inconveniencies of the state of nature, which necessarily follow from every man's being judge in his own case, by setting up a known authority, to which every one of that society may appeal upon any injury received, or controversy that may arise, and which every one of the society ought to obey; where-ever any persons are, who have not such an authority to appeal to, for the decision of any difference between them, there those persons are still in the state of nature; and so is every absolute prince, in respect of those who are under his dominion.

Sec. 91.

For he being supposed to have all, both legislative and executive power in himself alone, there is no judge to be found, no appeal lies open to anyone, who may fairly, and indifferently, and with authority decide, and from whose decision relief and redress may be expected of any injury or inconvenience, that may be suffered from the prince, or by his order: so that such a man, however entitled, Czar, or Grand Seignior, or how you please, is as much in the state of nature, with all under his dominion, as he is with the rest of mankind: for where-ever any two men are, who have no standing rule, and common judge to appeal to on earth, for the determination of controversies of right betwixt them, there they are still in the state of* nature, and under all the inconveniencies of it, with only this woeful difference to the subject, or rather slave of an absolute prince: that whereas, in the ordinary state of nature, he has a liberty to judge of his right, and according to the best of his power, to maintain it; now, whenever his property is invaded by the will and order of his monarch, he has not only no appeal, as those in society ought to have, but as if he were degraded from the common state of rational creatures, is denied a liberty to judge of, or to defend his right; and so is exposed to all the misery and inconveniencies, that a man can fear from one, who being in the unrestrained state of nature, is yet corrupted with flattery, and armed with power.

CHAPTER VIII: OF THE BEGINNING OF POLITICAL SOCIETIES

Sec. 95.

Men being, as has been said, by nature, all free, equal, and independent, no one can be put out of this estate, and subjected to the political power of another, without his own consent. The only way whereby any one divests himself of his natural liberty, and puts on the bonds of civil society, is by agreeing with other men to join and unite into a community for their comfortable, safe, and peaceable living one amongst another, in a secure enjoyment of their properties, and a greater security against any, that are not of it. This any number of men may do, because it injures not the freedom of the rest; they are left as they were in the liberty of the state of nature. When any number of men have so consented to make one community or government, they are thereby presently incorporated, and make one body politic, wherein the majority have a right to act and conclude the rest.

Sec. 96.

For when any number of men have, by the consent of every individual, made a community, they have thereby made that community one body, with a power to act as one body, which is only by the will and determination of the majority: for that which acts any community, being only the consent of the individuals of it, and it being necessary to that which is one body to move one way; it is necessary the body should move that way whither the greater force carries it, which is the consent of the majority: or else it is impossible it should act or continue one body, one community, which the consent of every individual that united into it, agreed that it should; and so everyone is bound by that consent to be concluded by the majority. And therefore we see, that in assemblies, empowered to act by positive laws, where no number is set by that positive law which empowers them, the act of the majority passes for the act of the whole, and of course determines, as having, by the law of nature and reason, the power of the whole.

Sec. 97.

And thus every man, by consenting with others to make one body politic under one government, puts himself under an obligation, to every one of that society, to submit to the determination of the majority, and to be concluded by it; or else this original compact, whereby he with others incorporates into one society, would signify nothing, and be no compact, if he be left free, and under no other ties than he was in before in the state of nature. For what appearance would there be of any compact? What new engagement if he were no farther tied by any decrees of the society, than he himself thought fit, and did actually consent to? This would be still as great a liberty, as he himself had before his compact, or anyone else in the state of nature hath, who may submit himself, and consent to any acts of it if he thinks fit.

Sec. 98.

For if the consent of the majority shall not, in reason, be received as the act of the whole, and conclude every individual; nothing but the consent of every individual can make anything to be the act of the whole: but such a consent is next to impossible ever to be had, if we consider the infirmities of health, and avocations of business, which in a number, though much less than that of a commonwealth, will necessarily keep many away from the public assembly. To which if we add the variety of opinions, and contrariety of interests, which unavoidably happen in all collections of men, the coming into society upon such terms would be only like Cato's coming into the theatre, only to go out again. Such a constitution as this would make the mighty Leviathan of a shorter duration, than the feeblest creatures, and not let it outlast the day it was born in: which cannot be supposed, until we can think, that rational creatures should desire and constitute societies only to be dissolved: for where the majority cannot conclude the rest, there they cannot act as one body, and consequently will be immediately dissolved again.

Sec. 99.

Whosoever therefore out of a state of nature unite into a community, must be understood to give up all the power, necessary to the ends for which they unite into society, to the majority of the community, unless they expressly agreed in any number greater than the majority. And this is done by barely agreeing to unite into one political society, which is all the compact that is, or needs be, between the individuals, that enter into, or make up a commonwealth. And thus that, which begins and actually constitutes any political society, is nothing but the consent of any number of freemen capable of a majority to unite and incorporate into such a society. And this is that, and that only, which did, or could give beginning to any lawful government in the world.

CHAPTER IX: OF THE ENDS OF POLITICAL SOCIETY AND GOVERNMENT

Sec. 123.

If man in the state of nature be so free, as has been said; if he be absolute lord of his own person and possessions, equal to the greatest, and subject to no body, why will he part with his freedom? Why will he give up this empire, and subject himself to the dominion and controll of any other power? To which it is obvious to answer, that though in the state of nature he hath such a right, yet the enjoyment of it is very uncertain, and constantly exposed to the invasion of others: for all being kings as much as he, every man his equal, and the greater part no strict observers of equity and justice, the enjoyment of the property he has in this state is very unsafe, very unsecure. This makes him willing to quit a condition, which, however free, is full of fears and continual dangers: and it is not without reason, that he seeks out, and is willing to join in society with others, who are already united, or have a mind to unite, for the mutual preservation of their lives, liberties and estates, which I call by the general name, property.

Sec. 124.

The great and chief end, therefore, of men's uniting into commonwealths, and putting themselves under government, is the preservation of their property. To which in the state of nature there are many things wanting.

First, there wants an established, settled, known law, received and allowed by common consent to be the standard of right and wrong, and the common measure to decide all controversies between them: for though the law of nature be plain and intelligible to all rational creatures; yet men being biased by their interest, as well as ignorant for want of study of it, are not apt to allow of it as a law binding to them in the application of it to their particular cases.

Sec. 125.

Secondly, In the state of nature there wants a known and indifferent judge, with authority to determine all differences according to the established law: for everyone in that state being both judge and executioner of the law of nature, men being partial to themselves, passion and revenge is very apt to carry them too far, and with too much heat, in their own cases; as well as negligence, and unconcernedness, to make them too remiss in other men's.

Sec. 126.

Thirdly, In the state of nature there often wants power to back and support the sentence when right, and to give it due execution, They who by any injustice offended, will seldom fail, where they are able, by force to make good their injustice; such resistance many times makes the punishment dangerous, and frequently destructive, to those who attempt it.

Sec. 127.

Thus mankind, notwithstanding all the privileges of the state of nature, being but in an ill condition, while they remain in it, are quickly driven into society. Hence it comes to pass, that we seldom find any number of men live any time together in this state. The inconveniencies that they are therein exposed to, by the irregular and uncertain exercise of the power every man has of punishing the transgressions of others, make them take sanctuary under the established laws of government, and therein seek the preservation of their property. It is this makes them so willingly give up every one his single power of punishing, to be exercised by such alone, as shall be appointed to it amongst them; and by such rules as the community, or those authorized by them to that purpose, shall agree on. And in this we have the original right and rise of both the legislative and executive power, as well as of the governments and societies themselves.

[from *Second Treatise of Civil Government.* London: Routledge and Sons, 1887.]

CHAPTER TEN

Mill on Liberty and Society

Courtesy of Library of Congress

John Stuart Mill (1806–1873)

SELECTED READINGS

- *On Liberty*—John Stuart Mill

On Liberty

John Stuart Mill

CHAPTER I: INTRODUCTORY

The subject of this Essay is not the so-called Liberty of the Will, so unfortunately opposed to the misnamed doctrine of Philosophical Necessity; but Civil, or Social Liberty: the nature and limits of the power which can be legitimately exercised by society over the individual. A question seldom stated, and hardly ever discussed, in general terms, but which profoundly influences the practical controversies of the age by its latent presence, and is likely soon to make itself recognized as the vital question of the future. It is so far from being new, that, in a certain sense, it has divided mankind, almost from the remotest ages, but in the stage of progress into which the more civilized portions of the species have now entered, it presents itself under new conditions, and requires a different and more fundamental treatment.

The struggle between Liberty and Authority is the most conspicuous feature in the portions of history with which we are earliest familiar, particularly in that of Greece, Rome, and England. But in old times this contest was between subjects, or some classes of subjects, and the government. By liberty, was meant protection against the tyranny of the political rulers. The rulers were conceived (except in some of the popular governments of Greece) as in a necessarily antagonistic position to the people whom they ruled. They consisted of a governing One, or a governing tribe or caste, who derived their authority from inheritance or conquest; who, at all events, did not hold it at the pleasure of the governed, and whose supremacy men did not venture, perhaps did not desire, to contest, whatever precautions might be taken against its oppressive exercise. Their power was regarded as necessary, but also as highly dangerous; as a weapon which they would attempt to use against their subjects, no less than against external enemies. To prevent the weaker members of the community from being preyed upon by innumerable vultures, it was needful that there should be an animal of prey stronger than the rest, commissioned to keep them down. But as the king of the vultures would be no less bent upon preying upon the flock than any of the minor harpies, it was indispensable to be in a perpetual attitude of defense against his beak and claws. The aim, therefore, of patriots, was to set limits to the power which the ruler should be suffered to exercise over the community; and this limitation was what they meant by liberty. It was attempted in two ways. First, by obtaining a recognition of certain immunities, called political liberties or rights, which it was to be regarded as a breach of duty in the ruler to infringe, and which, if he did infringe, specific resistance, or general rebellion, was held to be justifiable. A second, and generally a later expedient, was the establishment of constitutional checks; by which the consent of the community, or of a body of some sort supposed to represent its interests, was made a necessary condition to some of the more important acts of the governing power. To the first of these modes of limitation, the ruling power, in most European countries, was compelled, more or less, to submit. It was not so with the second; and to attain this, or when already in some degree possessed, to attain it more completely, became everywhere the principal object of the lovers of liberty. And so long as mankind were content to combat one enemy by another, and to be ruled by a master, on condition of being guaranteed more or less efficaciously against his tyranny, they did not carry their aspirations beyond this point.

A time, however, came in the progress of human affairs, when men ceased to think it a necessity of nature that their governors should be an independent power, opposed in interest to themselves. It appeared to them much better that the various magistrates of the State should be their tenants or delegates, revocable at their pleasure. In that way alone, it seemed, could they have complete security that the powers of government would never be abused to their disadvantage. By degrees, this new demand for elective and temporary rulers became the prominent object of the exertions of the popular party, wherever any such party existed; and superseded, to a considerable extent, the previous efforts to limit the power of rulers. As the struggle proceeded for making the ruling power emanate from the periodical choice of the ruled, some persons began to think that too much importance had been attached to the limitation of the power itself. That (it might seem) was a resource against rulers whose interests were habitually opposed to those of the people. What was now wanted was, that the rulers should be identified with the people; that their interest and will should be the interest and will of the nation. The nation did not need to be protected against its own will. There was no fear of its tyrannizing over itself. Let the rulers be effectually responsible to it, promptly removable by it, and it could afford to trust them with power of which it could itself dictate the use to be made. Their power was but the nation's own power, concentrated, and in a form convenient for exercise. This mode of thought, or rather perhaps of feeling, was common among the last generation of European liberalism, in the Continental section of which, it still apparently predominates. Those who admit any limit to what a government may do, except in the case of such governments as they think ought not to exist, stand out as brilliant exceptions among the political thinkers of the Continent. A similar tone of sentiment might by this time have been prevalent in our own country, if the circumstances which for a time encouraged it had continued unaltered.

But, in political and philosophical theories, as well as in persons, success discloses faults and infirmities which failure might have concealed from observation. The notion, that the people have no need to limit their power over themselves, might seem axiomatic, when popular government was a thing only dreamed about, or read of as having existed at some distant period of the past. Neither was that notion necessarily disturbed by such temporary aberrations as those of the French Revolution, the worst of which were the work of an usurping few, and which, in any case, belonged, not to the permanent working of popular institutions, but to a sudden and convulsive outbreak against monarchical and aristocratic despotism. In time, however, a democratic republic came to occupy a large portion of the earth's surface, and made itself felt as one of the most powerful members of the community of nations; and elective and responsible government became subject to the observations and criticisms which wait upon a great existing fact. It was now perceived that such phrases as "self-government," and "the power of the people over themselves," do not express the true state of the case. The "people" who exercise the power, are not always the same people with those over whom it is exercised, and the "self-government" spoken of, is not the government of each by himself, but of each by all the rest. The will of the people, moreover, practically means, the will of the most numerous or the most active part of the people; the majority, or those who succeed in making themselves accepted as the majority; the people, consequently, may desire to oppress a part of their number; and precautions are as much needed against this, as against any other abuse of power. The limitation, therefore, of the power of government over individuals, loses none of its importance when the holders of power are regularly accountable to the community, that is, to the strongest party therein. This view of things, recommending itself equally to the intelligence of thinkers and to the inclination of those important classes in European society to whose real or supposed interests democracy is adverse, has had no difficulty in establishing itself; and in political speculations "the tyranny of the majority" is now generally included among the evils against which society requires to be on its guard.

Like other tyrannies, the tyranny of the majority was at first, and is still vulgarly, held in dread, chiefly as operating through the acts of the public authorities. But reflecting persons perceived that when society is itself the tyrant—society collectively, over the separate individuals who compose it—its means of tyrannizing are not restricted to the acts which it may do by the hands of its political functionaries. Society can and does execute its own mandates: and if it issues wrong mandates instead of right, or any mandates at all in things with which it ought not to meddle, it practices a social tyranny more formidable than many kinds of political oppression, since, though not usually upheld by such extreme penalties, it leaves fewer means of escape, penetrating much more deeply into the details of life, and enslaving the soul itself. Protection, therefore, against the tyranny of the magistrate is not enough; there needs protection also against the tyranny of the prevailing opinion and feeling; against the tendency of society to impose, by other means than civil penalties, its own ideas and practices as rules of conduct on those who dissent from them; to fetter the development, and, if possible, prevent the formation, of any individuality not in harmony with its ways, and compel all characters to fashion themselves upon the model of its own. There is a limit to the legitimate interference of collective opinion with individual independence; and to find that limit, and maintain it against encroachment, is as indispensable to a good condition of human affairs, as protection against political despotism.

But though this proposition is not likely to be contested in general terms, the practical question, where to place the limit—how to make the fitting adjustment between individual independence and social control—is a subject on which nearly everything remains to be done.

All that makes existence valuable to any one, depends on the enforcement of restraints upon the actions of other people. Some rules of conduct, therefore, must be imposed, by law in the first place, and by opinion on many things which are not fit subjects for the operation of law. What these rules should be, is the principal question in human affairs; but if we except a few of the most obvious cases, it is one of those which least progress has been made in resolving. No two ages, and scarcely any two countries, have decided it alike; and the decision of one age or country is a wonder to another. Yet the people of any given age and country no more suspect any difficulty in it, than if it were a subject on which mankind had always been agreed. The rules which obtain among themselves appear to them self-evident and self-justifying. This all but universal illusion is one of the examples of the magical influence of custom, which is not only, as the proverb says a second nature, but is continually mistaken for the first. The effect of custom, in preventing any misgiving respecting the rules of conduct which mankind impose on one another, is all the more complete because the subject is one on which it is not generally considered necessary that reasons should be given, either by one person to others, or by each to himself. People are accustomed to believe and have been encouraged in the belief by some who aspire to the character of philosophers, that their feelings, on subjects of this nature, are better than reasons, and render reasons unnecessary. The practical principle which guides them to their opinions on the regulation of human conduct, is the feeling in each person's mind that everybody should be required to act as he, and those with whom he sympathizes, would like them to act. No one, indeed, acknowledges to himself that his standard of judgment is his own liking; but an opinion on a point of conduct, not supported by reasons, can only count as one person's preference; and if the reasons, when given, are a mere appeal to a similar preference felt by other people, it is still only many people's liking instead of one. To an ordinary man, however, his own preference, thus supported, is not only a perfectly satisfactory reason, but the only one he generally has for any of his notions of morality, taste, or propriety, which are not expressly written in his religious creed; and his chief guide in the interpretation even of that. Men's opinions, accordingly, on what is laudable or blamable, are affected by all the multifarious causes which influence their wishes in regard to the conduct of others, and which are as numerous as those which determine their wishes on any other subject. Sometimes their reason—at other times their prejudices or superstitions: often their social affections, not seldom their anti-social ones, their envy or jealousy, their arrogance or contemptuousness: but most commonly, their desires or fears for themselves—their legitimate or illegitimate self-interest. Wherever there is an ascendant class, a large portion of the morality of the country emanates from its class interests, and its feelings of class superiority. The morality between . . . princes and subjects, between nobles and [persons of low birth], between men and women, has been for the most part the creation of these class interests and feelings: and the sentiments thus generated, react in turn upon the moral feelings of the members of the ascendant class, in their relations among themselves. Where, on the other hand, a class, formerly ascendant, has lost its ascendency, or where its ascendency is unpopular, the prevailing moral sentiments frequently bear the impress of an impatient dislike of superiority. Another grand determining principle of the rules of conduct, both in act and forbearance which have been enforced by law or opinion, has been the servility of mankind towards the supposed preferences or aversions of their temporal masters, or of their gods. This servility though essentially selfish, is not hypocrisy; it gives rise to perfectly genuine sentiments of abhorrence; it made men burn magicians and heretics. Among so many baser influences, the general and obvious interests of society have of course had a share, and a large one, in the direction of the moral sentiments: less, however, as a matter of reason, and on their own account, than as a consequence of the sympathies and antipathies which grew out of them: and sympathies and antipathies which had little or nothing to do with the interests of society, have made themselves felt in the establishment of moralities with quite as great force.

The likings and dislikings of society, or of some powerful portion of it, are thus the main thing which has practically determined the rules laid down for general observance, under the penalties of law or opinion. And in general, those who have been in advance of society in thought and feeling, have left this condition of things unassailed in principle, however they may have come into conflict with it in some of its details. They have occupied themselves rather in inquiring what things society ought to like or dislike, than in questioning whether its likings or dislikings should be a law to individuals. They preferred endeavoring to alter the feelings of mankind on the particular points on which they were themselves heretical, rather than make common cause in defense of freedom, with heretics generally.

The only case in which the higher ground has been taken on principle and maintained with consistency, by any but an individual here and there, is that of religious belief: a case instructive in many ways, and not least so as forming a most striking instance of the fallibility of what is called the moral sense: for the *odium theologicum* [i.e., theological hatred], in a sincere bigot, is one of the most unequivocal cases of moral feeling. Those who first broke the yoke of what called itself the Universal Church [i.e., the Roman Catholic Church], were in general as little willing to permit difference of religious opinion as that church itself. But when the heat of the conflict was over, without giving a complete victory to any party, and each church or sect was reduced to limit its hopes to retaining possession of the ground it already occupied; minorities, seeing that they had no chance of becoming majorities, were under the necessity of pleading to those whom they could not convert, for permission to differ. It is accordingly on this battlefield, almost solely, that the rights of the individual against society have been asserted on broad grounds of principle, and the claim of society to exercise authority over dissentients openly controverted. The great writers to whom the world owes what religious liberty it possesses, have mostly asserted freedom of conscience as an indefeasible right, and denied absolutely that a human being is accountable to others for his religious belief. Yet so natural to mankind is intolerance in whatever they really care about, that religious freedom has hardly anywhere been practically realized, except where religious indifference, which dislikes to have its peace disturbed by theological quarrels, has added its weight to the scale. In the minds of almost all religious persons, even in the most tolerant countries, the duty of toleration is admitted with tacit reserves. One person will bear with dissent in matters of church government, but not of dogma; another can tolerate everybody, short of a Papist [i.e., Catholic] or a Unitarian; another, everyone who believes in revealed religion; a few extend their charity a little further, but stop at the belief in a God and in a future state. Wherever the sentiment of the majority is still genuine and intense, it is found to have abated little of its claim to be obeyed.

In England, from the peculiar circumstances of our political history, though the yoke of opinion is perhaps heavier, that of law is lighter, than in most other countries of Europe; and there is considerable jealousy of direct interference, by the legislative or the executive power with private conduct; not so much from any just regard for the independence of the individual, as from the still subsisting habit of looking on the government as representing an opposite interest to the public. The majority have not yet learnt to feel the power of the government their power, or its opinions their opinions. When they do so, individual liberty will probably be as much exposed to invasion from the government, as it already is from public opinion. But, as yet, there is a considerable amount of feeling ready to be called forth against any attempt of the law to control individuals in things in which they have not hitherto been accustomed to be controlled by it; and this with very little discrimination as to whether the matter is, or is not, within the legitimate sphere of legal control; insomuch that the feeling, highly salutary on the whole, is perhaps quite as often misplaced as well grounded in the particular instances of its application.

There is, in fact, no recognized principle by which the propriety or impropriety of government interference is customarily tested. People decide according to their personal preferences. Some, whenever they see any good to be done, or evil to be remedied, would willingly instigate the government to undertake the business; while others prefer to bear almost any amount of social evil, rather than add one to the departments of human interests amenable to governmental control. And men range themselves on one or the other side in any particular case, according to this general direction of their sentiments; or according to the degree of interest which they feel in the particular thing which it is proposed that the government should do; or according to the belief they entertain that the government would, or would not, do it in the manner they prefer; but very rarely on account of any opinion to which they consistently adhere, as to what things are fit to be done by a government. And it seems to me that, in consequence of this absence of rule or principle, one side is at present as often wrong as the other; the interference of government is, with about equal frequency, improperly invoked and improperly condemned.

The object of this essay is to assert one very simple principle, as entitled to govern absolutely the dealings of society with the individual in the way of compulsion and control, whether the means used be physical force in the form of legal penalties, or the moral coercion of public opinion. That principle is, that *the sole end for which mankind are warranted, individually or collectively in interfering with the liberty of action of any of their number, is self-protection.* That the only purpose for which power can be rightfully exercised over any member of a civilized community, against his will, is to *prevent harm to others*. His own good, either physical or moral, is not a sufficient warrant. He cannot rightfully be compelled to do or forbear because it will be better for him to do so, because it will make him happier, because, in the opinions of others, to do so would be wise, or even right. These are good reasons for remonstrating with him, or reasoning with him, or persuading him, or entreating him, but not for compelling him, or visiting him with any evil, in case he do otherwise. To justify that, the conduct from which it is desired to deter him must be calculated to produce evil to someone else. *The only part of the conduct of any one, for which he is amenable to society, is that which concerns others*. In the part which merely concerns himself, his independence is, of right, absolute. Over himself, over his own body and mind, the individual is sovereign.

It is, perhaps, hardly necessary to say that this doctrine is meant to apply only to human beings in the maturity of their faculties. We are not speaking of children, or of young persons below the age which the law may fix as that of manhood or womanhood. Those who are still in a state to require being taken care of by others, must be protected against their own actions as well as against external injury. . . . The early difficulties in the way of spontaneous progress are so great, that there is seldom any choice of means for overcoming them; and a ruler full of the spirit of improvement is warranted in the use of any expedients that will attain an end, perhaps otherwise unattainable. . . . Liberty, as a principle, has no application to any state of things anterior to the time when mankind have become capable of being improved by free and equal discussion. . . . But as soon as mankind have attained the capacity of being guided to their own improvement by conviction or persuasion, compulsion, either in the direct form or in that of pains and penalties for non-compliance, is no longer admissible as a means to their own good, and justifiable only for the security of others.

It is proper to state that I forego any advantage which could be derived to my argument from the idea of abstract right as a thing independent of utility. I regard utility as the ultimate appeal on all ethical questions; but it must be utility in the largest sense, grounded on the permanent interests of man as a progressive being. Those interests, I contend, authorize the subjection of individual spontaneity to external control, only in respect to those actions of each, which concern the interest of other people. If any one does an act hurtful to others, there is a *prima facie* case for punishing him, by law, or, where legal penalties are not safely applicable, by general disapprobation. There are also many positive acts for the benefit of others, which he may rightfully be compelled to perform; such as, to give evidence in a court of justice; to bear his fair share in the common defense, or in any other joint work necessary to the interest of the society of which he enjoys the protection; and to perform certain acts of individual beneficence, such as saving a fellow-creature's life, or interposing to protect the defenseless against ill-usage, things which whenever it is obviously a man's duty to do, he may rightfully be made responsible to society for not doing. A person may cause evil to others not only by his actions but by his inaction, and in neither case he is justly accountable to them for the injury. The latter case, it is true, requires a much more cautious exercise of compulsion than the former. To make any one answerable for doing evil to others, is the rule; to make him answerable for not preventing evil, is, comparatively speaking, the exception. Yet there are many cases clear enough and grave enough to justify that exception. In all things which regard the external relations of the individual, he is *de jure* amenable to those whose interests are concerned, and if need be, to society as their protector. There are often good reasons for not holding him to the responsibility; but these reasons must arise from the special expediencies of the case: either because it is a kind of case in which he is on the whole likely to act better, when left to his own discretion, than when controlled in any way in which society have it in their power to control him; or because the attempt to exercise control would produce other evils, greater than those which it would prevent. When such reasons as these preclude the enforcement of responsibility, the conscience of the agent himself should step into the vacant judgment-seat, and protect those interests of others which have no external protection; judging himself all the more rigidly, because the case does not admit of his being made accountable to the judgment of his fellow-creatures.

But there is a sphere of action in which society, as distinguished from the individual, has, if any, only an indirect interest; comprehending all that portion of a person's life and conduct which affects only himself, or, if it also affects others, only with their free, voluntary, and undeceived consent and participation. When I say only himself, I mean directly, and in the first instance: for whatever affects himself, may affect others through himself; and the objection which may be grounded on this contingency, will receive consideration in the sequel. This, then, is the appropriate region of human liberty. It comprises, *first*, the **inward domain of consciousness**; demanding liberty of conscience, in the most comprehensive sense; liberty of thought and feeling; absolute freedom of opinion and sentiment on all subjects, practical or speculative, scientific, moral, or theological. The liberty of expressing and publishing opinions may seem to fall under a different principle, since it belongs to that part of the conduct of an individual which concerns other people; but, being almost of as much importance as the liberty of thought itself, and resting in great part on the same reasons, is practically inseparable from it. *Secondly*, the principle requires **liberty of tastes and pursuits**; of framing the plan of our life to suit our own character; of doing as we like, subject to such consequences as may follow; without impediment from our fellow-creatures, so long as what we do does not harm them even though they should think our conduct foolish, perverse, or wrong. *Thirdly*, from this liberty of each individual, follows the liberty, within the same limits, of **combination among individuals**; freedom to unite, for any purpose not involving harm to others: the persons combining being supposed to be of full age, and not forced or deceived.

No society in which these liberties are not, on the whole, respected, is free, whatever may be its form of government; and none is completely free in which they do not exist absolute and unqualified. The only freedom which deserves the name, is that of pursuing our own good in our own way, so long as we do not attempt to deprive others of theirs, or impede their efforts to obtain it. Each is the proper guardian of his own health, whether bodily, or mental or spiritual. Mankind are greater gainers by suffering each other to live as seems good to themselves, than by compelling each to live as seems good to the rest.

Though this doctrine is anything but new, and, to some persons, may have the air of a truism, there is no doctrine which stands more directly opposed to the general tendency of existing opinion and practice. Society has expended fully as much effort in the attempt (according to its lights) to compel people to conform to its notions of personal, as of social excellence. The ancient commonwealths thought themselves entitled to practice, and the ancient philosophers countenanced, the regulation of every part of private conduct by public authority, on the ground that the State had a deep interest in the whole bodily and mental discipline of every one of its citizens, a mode of thinking which may have been admissible in small republics surrounded by powerful enemies, in constant peril of being subverted by foreign attack or internal commotion, and to which even a short interval of relaxed energy and self-command might so easily be fatal, that they could not afford to wait for the salutary permanent effects of freedom. In the modern world, the greater size of political communities, and above all, the separation between the spiritual and temporal authority (which placed the direction of men's consciences in other hands than those which controlled their worldly affairs), prevented so great an interference by law in the details of private life; but the engines of moral repression have been wielded more strenuously against divergence from the reigning opinion in self-regarding, than even in social matters; religion, the most powerful of the elements which have entered into the formation of moral feeling, having almost always been governed either by the ambition of a hierarchy, seeking control over every department of human conduct, or by the spirit of Puritanism. And some of those modern reformers who have placed themselves in strongest opposition to the religions of the past, have been no way behind either churches or sects in their assertion of the right of spiritual domination: M. Comte, in particular, whose social system, as unfolded in his *Traite de Politique Positive*, aims at establishing (though by moral more than by legal appliances) a despotism of society over the individual, surpassing anything contemplated in the political ideal of the most rigid disciplinarian among the ancient philosophers.

Apart from the peculiar tenets of individual thinkers, there is also in the world at large an increasing inclination to stretch unduly the powers of society over the individual, both by the force of opinion and even by that of legislation: and as the tendency of all the changes taking place in the world is to strengthen society, and diminish the power of the individual, this encroachment is not one of the evils which tend spontaneously to disappear, but, on the contrary, to grow more and more formidable. The disposition of mankind, whether as rulers or as fellow-citizens, to impose their own opinions and inclinations as a rule of conduct on others, is so energetically supported by some of the best and by some of the worst feelings incident to human nature, that it is hardly ever kept under restraint by anything but want of power; and as the power is not declining, but growing, unless a strong barrier of moral conviction can be raised against the mischief, we must expect, in the present circumstances of the world, to see it increase.

It will be convenient for the argument, if, instead of at once entering upon the general thesis, we confine ourselves in the first instance to a single branch of it, on which the principle here stated is, if not fully, yet to a certain point, recognized by the current opinions. This one branch is the *Liberty of Thought*: from which it is impossible to separate the cognate liberty of speaking and of writing. Although these liberties, to some considerable amount, form part of the political morality of all countries which profess religious toleration and free institutions, the grounds, both philosophical and practical, on which they rest, are perhaps not so familiar to the general mind, nor so thoroughly appreciated by many even of the leaders of opinion, as might have been expected. Those grounds, when rightly understood, are of much wider application than to only one division of the subject, and a thorough consideration of this part of the question will be found the best introduction to the remainder. Those to whom nothing which I am about to say will be new, may therefore, I hope, excuse me, if on a subject which for now three centuries has been so often discussed, I venture on one discussion more.

CHAPTER II: OF THE LIBERTY OF THOUGHT AND DISCUSSION

The time, it is to be hoped, is gone by when any defense would be necessary of the "liberty of the press" as one of the securities against corrupt or tyrannical government. No argument, we may suppose, can now be needed, against permitting a legislature or an executive, not identified in interest with the people, to prescribe opinions to them, and determine what doctrines or what arguments they shall be allowed to hear. This aspect of the question, besides, has been so often and so triumphantly enforced by preceding writers, that it needs not be specially insisted on in this place. Though the law of England, on the subject of the press, is as servile to this day as it was in the time of the Tudors, there is little danger of its being actually put in force against political discussion, except during some temporary panic, when fear of insurrection drives ministers and judges from their propriety; and, speaking generally, it is not, in constitutional countries, to be apprehended that the government, whether completely responsible to the people or not, will often attempt to control the expression of opinion, except when in doing so it makes itself the organ of the general intolerance of the public. Let us suppose, therefore, that the government is entirely at one with the people, and never thinks of exerting any power of coercion unless in agreement with what it conceives to be their voice. But I deny the right of the people to exercise such coercion, either by themselves or by their government. The power itself is illegitimate. The best government has no more title to it than the worst. It is as noxious, or more noxious, when exerted in accordance with public opinion, than when in opposition to it. If all mankind minus one, were of one opinion, and only one person were of the contrary opinion, mankind would be no more justified in silencing that one person, than he, if he had the power, would be justified in silencing mankind. Were an opinion a personal possession of no value except to the owner; if to be obstructed in the enjoyment of it were simply a private injury, it would make some difference whether the injury was inflicted only on a few persons or on many. But the peculiar evil of silencing the expression of an opinion is, that it is robbing the human race; posterity as well as the existing generation; those who dissent from the opinion, still more than those who hold it. If the opinion is right, they are deprived of the opportunity of exchanging error for truth: if wrong, they lose, what is almost as great a benefit, the clearer perception and livelier impression of truth, produced by its collision with error.

It is necessary to consider separately these two hypotheses, each of which has a distinct branch of the argument corresponding to it. *We can never be sure that the opinion we are endeavoring to stifle is a false opinion; and if we were sure, stifling it would be an evil still.*

First, the opinion which it is attempted to suppress by authority may possibly be true. Those who desire to suppress it, of course deny its truth; but they are not infallible. They have no authority to decide the question for all mankind, and exclude every other person from the means of judging. To refuse a hearing to an opinion, because they are sure that it is false, is to assume that their certainty is the same thing as absolute certainty. All silencing of discussion is an assumption of infallibility. Its condemnation may be allowed to rest on this common argument, not the worse for being common.

Unfortunately for the good sense of mankind, the fact of their fallibility is far from carrying the weight in their practical judgment, which is always allowed to it in theory; for while everyone well knows himself to be fallible, few think it necessary to take any precautions against their own fallibility, or admit the supposition that any opinion of which they feel very certain, may be one of the examples of the error to which they acknowledge themselves to be liable. Absolute princes, or others who are accustomed to unlimited deference, usually feel this complete confidence in their own opinions on nearly all subjects. People more happily situated, who sometimes hear their opinions disputed, and are not wholly unused to be set right when they are wrong, place the same unbounded reliance only on such of their opinions as are shared by all who surround them, or to whom they habitually defer: for in proportion to a man's want of confidence in his own solitary judgment, does he usually repose, with implicit trust, on the infallibility of "the world" in general. And the world, to each individual, means the part of it with which he comes in contact; his party, his sect, his church, his class of society: the man may be called, by comparison, almost liberal and large-minded to whom it means anything so comprehensive as his own country or his own age. Nor is his faith in this collective authority at all shaken by his being aware that other ages, countries, sects, churches, classes, and parties have thought, and even now think, the exact reverse. He devolves upon his own world the responsibility of being in the right against the dissentient worlds of other people; and it never troubles him that mere accident has decided which of these numerous worlds is the object of his reliance, and that the same causes which make him a Churchman in London, would have made him a Buddhist or a Confucian in Peking. Yet it is as evident in itself as any amount of argument can make it, that ages are no more infallible than individuals; every age having held many opinions which subsequent ages have deemed not only false but absurd; and it is as certain that many opinions, now general, will be rejected by future ages, as it is that many, once general, are rejected by the present.

The objection likely to be made to this argument, would probably take some such form as the following. There is no greater assumption of infallibility in forbidding the propagation of error, than in any other thing which is done by public authority on its own judgment and responsibility. Judgment is given to men that they may use it. Because it may be used erroneously, are men to be told that they ought not to use it at all? To prohibit what they think pernicious, is not claiming exemption from error, but fulfilling the duty incumbent on them, although fallible, of acting on their conscientious conviction. If we were never to act on our opinions, because those opinions may be wrong, we should leave all our interests uncared for, and all our duties unperformed. An objection which applies to all conduct can be no valid objection to any conduct in particular. It is the duty of governments, and of individuals, to form the truest opinions they can; to form them carefully, and never impose them upon others unless they are quite sure of being right. But when they are sure (such reasoners may say), it is not conscientiousness but cowardice to shrink from acting on their opinions, and allow doctrines which they honestly think dangerous to the welfare of mankind, either in this life or in another, to be scattered abroad without restraint, because other people, in less enlightened times, have persecuted opinions now believed to be true. Let us take care, it may be said, not to make the same mistake: but governments and nations have made mistakes in other things, which are not denied to be fit subjects for the exercise of authority: they have laid on bad taxes, made unjust wars. Ought we therefore to lay on no taxes, and, under whatever provocation, make no wars? Men, and governments, must act to the best of their ability. There is no such thing as absolute certainty, but there is assurance sufficient for the purposes of human life. We may, and must, assume our opinion to be true for the guidance of our own conduct: and it is assuming no more when we forbid bad men to pervert society by the propagation of opinions which we regard as false and pernicious.

I answer, that it is assuming very much more. There is the greatest difference between presuming an opinion to be true, because, with every opportunity for contesting it, it has not been refuted, and assuming its truth for the purpose of not permitting its refutation. Complete liberty of contradicting and disproving our opinion, is the very condition which justifies us in assuming its truth for purposes of action; and on no other terms can a being with human faculties have any rational assurance of being right.

When we consider either the history of opinion, or the ordinary conduct of human life, to what is it to be ascribed that the one and the other are no worse than they are? Not certainly to the inherent force of the human understanding; for, on any matter not self-evident, there are ninety-nine persons totally incapable of judging of it, for one who is capable; and the capacity of the hundredth person is only comparative; for the majority of the eminent men of every past generation held many opinions now known to be erroneous, and did or approved numerous things which no one will now justify. Why is it, then, that there is on the whole a preponderance among mankind of rational opinions and rational conduct? If there really is this preponderance—which there must be, unless human affairs are, and have always been, in an almost desperate state—it is owing to a quality of the human mind, the source of everything respectable in man, either as an intellectual or as a moral being, namely, that his errors are corrigible. He is capable of rectifying his mistakes by discussion and experience. Not by experience alone. There must be discussion, to show how experience is to be interpreted. Wrong opinions and practices gradually yield to fact and argument: but facts and arguments, to produce any effect on the mind, must be brought before it. Very few facts are able to tell their own story, without comments to bring out their meaning. The whole strength and value, then, of human judgment, depending on the one property, that it can be set right when it is wrong, reliance can be placed on it only when the means of setting it right are kept constantly at hand. In the case of any person whose judgment is really deserving of confidence, how has it become so? Because he has kept his mind open to criticism of his opinions and conduct. Because it has been his practice to listen to all that could be said against him; to profit by as much of it as was just, and expound to himself, and upon occasion to others, the fallacy of what was fallacious. Because he has felt, that the only way in which a human being can make some approach to knowing the whole of a subject, is by hearing what can be said about it by persons of every variety of opinion, and studying all modes in which it can be looked at by every character of mind. No wise man ever acquired his wisdom in any mode but this; nor is it in the nature of human intellect to become wise in any other manner. The steady habit of correcting and completing his own opinion by collating it with those of others, so far from causing doubt and hesitation in carrying it into practice, is the only stable foundation for a just reliance on it: for, being cognizant of all that can, at least obviously, be said against him, and having taken up his position against all gainsayers knowing that he has sought for objections and difficulties, instead of avoiding them, and has shut out no light which can be thrown upon the subject from any quarter—he has a right to think his judgment better than that of any person, or any multitude, who have not gone through a similar process.

It is not too much to require that what the wisest of mankind, those who are best entitled to trust their own judgment, find necessary to warrant their relying on it, should be submitted to by that miscellaneous collection of a few wise and many foolish individuals, called the public. . . . The Roman Catholic Church, even at the canonization of a saint, admits, and listens patiently to, a "devil's advocate." The holiest of men, it appears, cannot be admitted to posthumous honors, until all that the devil could say against him is known and weighed. If even the Newtonian philosophy were not permitted to be questioned, mankind could not feel as complete assurance of its truth as they now do. The beliefs which we have most warrant for, have no safeguard to rest on, but a standing invitation to the whole world to prove them unfounded. If the challenge is not accepted, or is accepted and the attempt fails, we are far enough from certainty still; but we have done the best that the existing state of human reason admits of; we have neglected nothing that could give the truth a chance of reaching us: if the lists are kept open, we may hope that if there be a better truth, it will be found when the human mind is capable of receiving it; and in the meantime we may rely on having attained such approach to truth, as is possible in our own day. This is the amount of certainty attainable by a fallible being, and this the sole way of attaining it.

Strange it is, that men should admit the validity of the arguments for free discussion, but object to their being "pushed to an extreme;" not seeing that unless the reasons are good for an extreme case, they are not good for any case. Strange that they should imagine that they are not assuming infallibility when they acknowledge that there should be free discussion on all subjects which can possibly be doubtful, but think that some particular principle or doctrine should be forbidden to be questioned because it is so certain, that is, because they are certain that it is certain. To call any proposition certain, while there is anyone who would deny its certainty if permitted, but who is not permitted, is to assume that we ourselves, and those who agree with us, are the judges of certainty, and judges without hearing the other side.

In the present age—which has been described as "destitute of faith, but terrified at skepticism,"—in which people feel sure, not so much that their opinions are true, as that they should not know what to do without them—the claims of an opinion to be protected from public attack are rested not so much on its truth, as on its importance to society. There are, it is alleged, certain beliefs, so useful, not to say indispensable to well-being, that it is as much the duty of governments to uphold those beliefs, as to protect any other of the interests of society. In a case of such necessity, and so directly in the line of their duty, something less than infallibility may, it is maintained, warrant, and even bind, governments, to act on their own opinion, confirmed by the general opinion of mankind. It is also often argued, and still oftener thought, that none but bad men would desire to weaken these salutary beliefs; and there can be nothing wrong, it is thought, in restraining bad men, and prohibiting what only such men would wish to practice. This mode of thinking makes the justification of restraints on discussion not a question of the truth of doctrines, but of their usefulness; and flatters itself by that means to escape the responsibility of claiming to be an infallible judge of opinions. But those who thus satisfy themselves, do not perceive that the assumption of infallibility is merely shifted from one point to another. The usefulness of an opinion is itself matter of opinion: as disputable, as open to discussion and requiring discussion as much, as the opinion itself. There is the same need of an infallible judge of opinions to decide an opinion to be noxious, as to decide it to be false, unless the opinion condemned has full opportunity of defending itself. And it will not do to say that the heretic may be allowed to maintain the utility or harmlessness of his opinion, though forbidden to maintain its truth. The truth of an opinion is part of its utility. If we would know whether or not it is desirable that a proposition should be believed, is it possible to exclude the consideration of whether or not it is true? In the opinion, not of bad men, but of the best men, no belief which is contrary to truth can be really useful: and can you prevent such men from urging that plea, when they are charged with culpability for denying some doctrine which they are told is useful, but which they believe to be false? Those who are on the side of received opinions, never fail to take all possible advantage of this plea; you do not find them handling the question of utility as if it could be completely abstracted from that of truth: on the contrary, it is, above all, because their doctrine is "the truth," that the knowledge or the belief of it is held to be so indispensable. There can be no fair discussion of the question of usefulness, when an argument so vital may be employed on one side, but not on the other. And in point of fact, when law or public feeling do not permit the truth of an opinion to be disputed, they are just as little tolerant of a denial of its usefulness. The utmost they allow is an extenuation of its absolute necessity or of the positive guilt of rejecting it.

In order more fully to illustrate the mischief of denying a hearing to opinions because we, in our own judgment, have condemned them, it will be desirable to fix down the discussion to a concrete case; and I choose, by preference, the cases which are least favorable to me—in which the argument against freedom of opinion, both on the score of truth and on that of utility, is considered the strongest. Let the opinions impugned be the belief in a God and in a future state, or any of the commonly received doctrines of morality. To fight the battle on such ground, gives a great advantage to an unfair antagonist; since he will be sure to say (and many who have no desire to be unfair will say it internally), "Are these the doctrines which you do not deem sufficiently certain to be taken under the protection of law? Is the belief in a God one of the opinions, to feel sure of which, you hold to be assuming infallibility?" But I must be permitted to observe, that it is not the feeling sure of a doctrine (be it what it may) which I call an assumption of infallibility. It is the undertaking to decide that question for others, without allowing them to hear what can be said on the contrary side. And I denounce and reprobate this pretension not the less, if put forth on the side of my most solemn convictions. However positive any one's persuasion may be, not only of the falsity, but of the pernicious consequences—not only of the pernicious consequences, but (to adopt expressions which I altogether condemn) the immorality and impiety of an opinion; yet if, in pursuance of that private judgment, though backed by the public judgment of his country or his contemporaries, he prevents the opinion from being heard in its defense, he assumes infallibility. And so far from the assumption being less objectionable or less dangerous because the opinion is called immoral or impious, this is the case of all others in which it is most fatal. These are exactly the occasions on which the men of one generation commit those dreadful mistakes which excite the astonishment and horror of posterity. It is among such that we find the instances memorable in history, when the arm of the law has been employed to root out the best men and the noblest doctrines; with deplorable success as to the men, though some of the doctrines have survived to be (as if in mockery) invoked, in defense of similar conduct towards those who dissent from them, or from their received interpretation.

Mankind can hardly be too often reminded, that there was once a man named Socrates, between whom and the legal authorities and public opinion of his time, there took place a memorable collision. Born in an age and country abounding in individual greatness, this man has been handed down to us by those who best knew both him and the age, as the most virtuous man in it; while we know him as the head and prototype of all subsequent teachers of virtue, the source equally of the lofty inspiration of Plato and the judicious utilitarianism of Aristotle, "*i maestri di color che sanno*," the two headsprings of ethical as of all other philosophy. This acknowledged master of all the eminent thinkers who have since lived—whose fame, still growing after more than two thousand years, all but outweighs the whole remainder of the names which make his native city illustrious—was put to death by his countrymen, after a judicial conviction, for impiety and immorality. Impiety, in denying the gods recognized by the State; indeed his accuser asserted (see the *Apology*) that he believed in no gods at all. Immorality, in being, by his doctrines and instructions, a "corrupter of youth." Of these charges the tribunal, there is every ground for believing, honestly found him guilty, and condemned the man who probably of all then born had deserved best of mankind, to be put to death as a criminal.

To pass from this to the only other instance of judicial iniquity, the mention of which, after the condemnation of Socrates, would not be an anti-climax: the event which took place on Calvary rather more than eighteen hundred years ago. The man who left on the memory of those who witnessed his life and conversation, such an impression of his moral grandeur, that eighteen subsequent centuries have done homage to him as the Almighty in person, was ignominiously put to death, as what? As a blasphemer. Men did not merely mistake their benefactor; they mistook him for the exact contrary of what he was, and treated him as that prodigy of impiety, which they themselves are now held to be, for their treatment of him. The feelings with which mankind now regard these lamentable transactions, especially the latter of the two, render them extremely unjust in their judgment of the unhappy actors. These were, to all appearance, not bad men—not worse than men most commonly are, but rather the contrary; men who possessed in a full, or somewhat more than a full measure, the religious, moral, and patriotic feelings of their time and people: the very kind of men who, in all times, our own included, have every chance of passing through life blameless and respected. The high-priest who rent his garments when the words were pronounced, which, according to all the ideas of his country, constituted the blackest guilt, was in all probability quite as sincere in his horror and indignation, as the generality of respectable and pious men now are in the religious and moral sentiments they profess; and most of those who now shudder at his conduct, if they had lived in his time . . . would have acted precisely as he did. Orthodox Christians who are tempted to think that those who stoned to death the first martyrs must have been worse men than they themselves are, ought to remember that one of those persecutors was Saint Paul. . . .

But, indeed, the dictum that truth always triumphs over persecution, is one of those pleasant falsehoods which men repeat after one another till they pass into commonplaces, but which all experience refutes. History teems with instances of truth put down by persecution. If not suppressed forever, it may be thrown back for centuries. . . .

It is a piece of idle sentimentality that truth, merely as truth, has any inherent power denied to error, of prevailing against the dungeon and the stake. Men are not more zealous for truth than they often are for error, and a sufficient application of legal or even of social penalties will generally succeed in stopping the propagation of either. The real advantage which truth has, consists in this, that when an opinion is true, it may be extinguished once, twice, or many times, but in the course of ages there will generally be found persons to rediscover it, until some one of its reappearances falls on a time when from favorable circumstances it escapes persecution until it has made such head as to withstand all subsequent attempts to suppress it.

It will be said, that we do not now put to death the introducers of new opinions: we are not like our fathers who slew the prophets, we even build sepulchers to them. It is true we no longer put heretics to death; and the amount of penal infliction which modern feeling would probably tolerate, even against the most obnoxious opinions, is not sufficient to extirpate them. But let us not flatter ourselves that we are yet free from the stain even of legal persecution. Penalties for opinion, or at least for its expression, still exist by law; and their enforcement is not, even in these times, so unexampled as to make it at all incredible that they may someday be revived in full force. In the year 1857, at the summer assizes of the county of Cornwall, an unfortunate man, said to be of unexceptionable conduct in all relations of life, was sentenced to twenty-one months imprisonment, for uttering, and writing on a gate, some offensive words concerning Christianity. Within a month of the same time, at the Old Bailey, two persons, on two separate occasions, were rejected as jurymen, and one of them grossly insulted by the judge and one of the counsel, because they honestly declared that they had no theological belief; and a third, a foreigner, for the same reason, was denied justice against a thief. This refusal of redress took place in virtue of the legal doctrine, that no person can be allowed to give evidence in a court of justice, who does not profess belief in a God (any god is sufficient) and in a future state; which is equivalent to declaring such persons to be outlaws, excluded from the protection of the tribunals; who may not only be robbed or assaulted with impunity, if no one but themselves, or persons of similar opinions, be present, but anyone else may be robbed or assaulted with impunity, if the proof of the fact depends on their evidence. The assumption on which this is grounded, is that the oath is worthless, of a person who does not believe in a future state; a proposition which betokens much ignorance of history in those who assent to it (since it is historically true that a large proportion of infidels in all ages have been persons of distinguished integrity and honor); and would be maintained by no one who had the smallest conception how many of the persons in greatest repute with the world, both for virtues and for attainments, are well known, at least to their intimates, to be unbelievers. The rule, besides, is suicidal, and cuts away its own foundation. Under pretense that atheists must be liars, it admits the testimony of all atheists who are willing to lie, and rejects only those who brave the obloquy of publicly confessing a detested creed rather than affirm a falsehood. A rule thus self-convicted of absurdity so far as regards its professed purpose, can be kept in force only as a badge of hatred, a relic of persecution; a persecution, too, having the peculiarity that the qualification for undergoing it is the being clearly proved not to deserve it. The rule, and the theory it implies, are hardly less insulting to believers than to infidels. For if he who does not believe in a future state necessarily lies, it follows that they who do believe are only prevented from lying, if prevented they are, by the fear of hell. We will not do the authors and abettors of the rule the injury of supposing, that the conception which they have formed of Christian virtue is drawn from their own consciousness.

These, indeed, are but rags and remnants of persecution, and may be thought to be not so much an indication of the wish to persecute, as an example of that very frequent infirmity of English minds, which makes them take a preposterous pleasure in the assertion of a bad principle, when they are no longer bad enough to desire to carry it really into practice. But unhappily there is no security in the state of the public mind, that the suspension of worse forms of legal persecution, which has lasted for about the space of a generation, will continue. In this age the quiet surface of routine is as often ruffled by attempts to resuscitate past evils, as to introduce new benefits. What is boasted of at the present time as the revival of religion, is always, in narrow and uncultivated minds, at least as much the revival of bigotry; and where there is the strongest permanent leaven of intolerance in the feelings of a people, which at all times abides in the middle classes of this country, it needs but little to provoke them into actively persecuting those whom they have never ceased to think proper objects of persecution. For it is this—it is the opinions men entertain, and the feelings they cherish, respecting those who disown the beliefs they deem important, which makes this country not a place of mental freedom. For a long time past, the chief mischief of the legal penalties is that they strengthen the social stigma. It is that stigma which is really effective, and so effective is it, that the profession of opinions which are under the ban of society is much less common in England, than is, in many other countries, the avowal of those which incur risk of judicial punishment. In respect to all persons but those whose pecuniary circumstances make them independent of the good will of other people, opinion, on this subject, is as efficacious as law; men might as well be imprisoned, as excluded from the means of earning their bread. Those whose bread is already secured, and who desire no favors from men in power, or from bodies of men, or from the public, have nothing to fear from the open avowal of any opinions, but to be ill-thought of and ill-spoken of, and this it ought not to require a very heroic mold to enable them to bear. There is no room for any appeal *ad misericordiam* in behalf of such persons. But though we do not now inflict so much evil on those who think differently from us, as it was formerly our custom to do, it may be that we do ourselves as much evil as ever by our treatment of them. Socrates was put to death, but the Socratic philosophy rose like the sun in heaven, and spread its illumination over the whole intellectual firmament. Christians were cast to the lions, but the Christian Church grew up a stately and spreading tree, overtopping the older and less vigorous growths, and stifling them by its shade. Our merely social intolerance, kills no one, roots out no opinions, but induces men to disguise them, or to abstain from any active effort for their diffusion. With us, heretical opinions do not perceptibly gain or even lose, ground in each decade or generation; they never blaze out far and wide, but continue to smolder in the narrow circles of thinking and studious persons among whom they originate, without ever lighting up the general affairs of mankind with either a true or a deceptive light. And thus is kept up a state of things very satisfactory to some minds, because, without the unpleasant process of fining or imprisoning anybody, it maintains all prevailing opinions outwardly undisturbed, while it does not absolutely interdict the exercise of reason by dissentients afflicted with the malady of thought. A convenient plan for having peace in the intellectual world, and keeping all things going on therein very much as they do already. But the price paid for this sort of intellectual pacification, is the sacrifice of the entire moral courage of the human mind. A state of things in which a large portion of the most active and inquiring intellects find it advisable to keep the genuine principles and grounds of their convictions within their own breasts, and attempt, in what they address to the public, to fit as much as they can of their own conclusions to premises which they have internally renounced, cannot send forth the open, fearless characters, and logical, consistent intellects who once adorned the thinking world. The sort of men who can be looked for under it, are either mere conformers to commonplace, or time-servers for truth whose arguments on all great subjects are meant for their hearers, and are not those which have convinced themselves. Those who avoid this alternative, do so by narrowing their thoughts and interests to things which can be spoken of without venturing within the region of principles, that is, to small practical matters, which would come right of themselves, if but the minds of mankind were strengthened and enlarged, and which will never be made effectually right until then; while that which would strengthen and enlarge men's minds, free and daring speculation on the highest subjects, is abandoned.

Those in whose eyes this reticence on the part of heretics is no evil, should consider in the first place, that in consequence of it there is never any fair and thorough discussion of heretical opinions; and that such of them as could not stand such a discussion, though they may be prevented from spreading, do not disappear. But it is not the minds of heretics that are deteriorated most, by the ban placed on all inquiry which does not end in the orthodox conclusions. The greatest harm done is to those who are not heretics, and whose whole mental development is cramped, and their reason cowed, by the fear of heresy. Who can compute what the world loses in the multitude of promising intellects combined with timid characters, who dare not follow out any bold, vigorous, independent train of thought, lest it should land them in something which would admit of being considered irreligious or immoral? Among them we may occasionally see some man of deep conscientiousness, and subtle and refined understanding, who spends a life in sophisticating with an intellect which he cannot silence, and exhausts the resources of ingenuity in attempting to reconcile the promptings of his conscience and reason with orthodoxy, which yet he does not, perhaps, to the end succeed in doing. No one can be a great thinker who does not recognize, that as a thinker it is his first duty to follow his intellect to whatever conclusions it may lead. Truth gains more even by the errors of one who, with due study and preparation, thinks for himself, than by the true opinions of those who only hold them because they do not suffer themselves to think. Not that it is solely, or chiefly, to form great thinkers, that freedom of thinking is required. On the contrary, it is as much, and even more indispensable, to enable average human beings to attain the mental stature which they are capable of. There have been, and may again be, great individual thinkers, in a general atmosphere of mental slavery. But there never has been, nor ever will be, in that atmosphere, an intellectually active people. Where any people has made a temporary approach to such a character, it has been because the dread of heterodox speculation was for a time suspended. Where there is a tacit convention that principles are not to be disputed; where the discussion of the greatest questions which can occupy humanity is considered to be closed, we cannot hope to find that generally high scale of mental activity which has made some periods of history so remarkable. Never when controversy avoided the subjects which are large and important enough to kindle enthusiasm, was the mind of a people stirred up from its foundations, and the impulse given which raised even persons of the most ordinary intellect to something of the dignity of thinking beings. . . .

Let us now pass to the second division of the argument, and dismissing the supposition that any of the received opinions may be false, let us assume them to be true, and examine into the worth of the manner in which they are likely to be held, when their truth is not freely and openly canvassed. However unwillingly a person who has a strong opinion may admit the possibility that his opinion may be false, he ought to be moved by the consideration that however true it may be, if it is not fully, frequently, and fearlessly discussed, it will be held as a dead dogma, not a living truth.

There is a class of persons (happily not quite so numerous as formerly) who think it enough if a person assents undoubtingly to what they think true, though he has no knowledge whatever of the grounds of the opinion, and could not make a tenable defense of it against the most superficial objections. Such persons, if they can once get their creed taught from authority, naturally think that no good, and some harm, comes of its being allowed to be questioned. Where their influence prevails, they make it nearly impossible for the received opinion to be rejected wisely and considerately, though it may still be rejected rashly and ignorantly; for to shut out discussion entirely is seldom possible, and when it once gets in, beliefs not grounded on conviction are apt to give way before the slightest semblance of an argument. Waiving, however, this possibility—assuming that the true opinion abides in the mind, but abides as a prejudice, a belief independent of, and proof against, argument—this is not the way in which truth ought to be held by a rational being. This is not knowing the truth. Truth, thus held, is but one superstition the more, accidentally clinging to the words which enunciate a truth.

If the intellect and judgment of mankind ought to be cultivated . . . on what can these faculties be more appropriately exercised by any one, than on the things which concern him so much that it is considered necessary for him to hold opinions on them? If the cultivation of the understanding consists in one thing more than in another, it is surely in learning the grounds of one's own opinions. Whatever people believe, on subjects on which it is of the first importance to believe rightly, they ought to be able to defend against at least the common objections. But, someone may say, "Let them be taught the grounds of their opinions. It does not follow that opinions must be merely parroted because they are never heard controverted. Persons who learn geometry do not simply commit the theorems to memory, but understand and learn likewise the demonstrations; and it would be absurd to say that they remain ignorant of the grounds of geometrical truths, because they never hear any one deny, and attempt to disprove them." Undoubtedly: and such teaching suffices on a subject like mathematics, where there is nothing at all to be said on the wrong side of the question. The peculiarity of the evidence of mathematical truths is, that all the argument is on one side. There are no objections, and no answers to objections. But on every subject on which difference of opinion is possible, the truth depends on a balance to be struck between two sets of conflicting reasons. Even in natural philosophy, there is always some other explanation possible of the same facts; some geocentric theory instead of heliocentric, some phlogiston instead of oxygen; and it has to be shown why that other theory cannot be the true one: and until this is shown and until we know how it is shown, we do not understand the grounds of our opinion. But when we turn to subjects infinitely more complicated, to morals, religion, politics, social relations, and the business of life, three-fourths of the arguments for every disputed opinion consist in dispelling the appearances which favor some opinion different from it. The greatest orator, save one, of antiquity, has left it on record that he always studied his adversary's case with as great, if not with still greater, intensity than even his own. What Cicero practiced as the means of forensic success, requires to be imitated by all who study any subject in order to arrive at the truth. He who knows only his own side of the case, knows little of that. His reasons may be good, and no one may have been able to refute them. But if he is equally unable to refute the reasons on the opposite side; if he does not so much as know what they are, he has no ground for preferring either opinion. The rational position for him would be suspension of judgment, and unless he contents himself with that, he is either led by authority, or adopts, like the generality of the world, the side to which he feels most inclination. Nor is it enough that he should hear the arguments of adversaries from his own teachers, presented as they state them, and accompanied by what they offer as refutations. This is not the way to do justice to the arguments, or bring them into real contact with his own mind. He must be able to hear them from persons who actually believe them; who defend them in earnest, and do their very utmost for them. He must know them in their most plausible and persuasive form; he must feel the whole force of the difficulty which the true view of the subject has to encounter and dispose of, else he will never really possess himself of the portion of truth which meets and removes that difficulty. Ninety-nine in a hundred of what are called educated men are in this condition, even of those who can argue fluently for their opinions. Their conclusion may be true, but it might be false for anything they know: they have never thrown themselves into the mental position of those who think differently from them, and considered what such persons may have to say; and consequently they do not, in any proper sense of the word, know the doctrine which they themselves profess. They do not know those parts of it which explain and justify the remainder; the considerations which show that a fact which seemingly conflicts with another is reconcilable with it, or that, of two apparently strong reasons, one and not the other ought to be preferred. All that part of the truth which turns the scale, and decides the judgment of a completely informed mind, they are strangers to; nor is it ever really known, but to those who have attended equally and impartially to both sides, and endeavored to see the reasons of both in the strongest light. So essential is this discipline to a real understanding of moral and human subjects, that if opponents of all important truths do not exist, it is indispensable to imagine them and supply them with the strongest arguments which the most skilful devil's advocate can conjure up.

To abate the force of these considerations, an enemy of free discussion may be supposed to say, that there is no necessity for mankind in general to know and understand all that can be said against or for their opinions by philosophers and theologians. That it is not needful for common men to be able to expose all the misstatements or fallacies of an ingenious opponent. That it is enough if there is always somebody capable of answering them, so that nothing likely to mislead uninstructed persons remains unrefuted. That simple minds, having been taught the obvious grounds of the truths inculcated on them, may trust to authority for the rest, and being aware that they have neither knowledge nor talent to resolve every difficulty which can be raised, may repose in the assurance that all those which have been raised have been or can be answered, by those who are specially trained to the task.

Conceding to this view of the subject the utmost that can be claimed for it by those most easily satisfied with the amount of understanding of truth which ought to accompany the belief of it; even so, the argument for free discussion is no way weakened. For even this doctrine acknowledges that mankind ought to have a rational assurance that all objections have been satisfactorily answered; and how are they to be answered if that which requires to be answered is not spoken? Or how can the answer be known to be satisfactory, if the objectors have no opportunity of showing that it is unsatisfactory? If not the public, at least the philosophers and theologians who are to resolve the difficulties, must make themselves familiar with those difficulties in their most puzzling form; and this cannot be accomplished unless they are freely stated, and placed in the most advantageous light which they admit of. . . . Besides, in the present state of the world, it is practically impossible that writings which are read by the instructed can be kept from the uninstructed. If the teachers of mankind are to be cognizant of all that they ought to know, everything must be free to be written and published without restraint.

If, however, the mischievous operation of the absence of free discussion, when the received opinions are true, were confined to leaving men ignorant of the grounds of those opinions, it might be thought that this, if an intellectual, is no moral evil, and does not affect the worth of the opinions, regarded in their influence on the character. The fact, however, is, that not only the grounds of the opinion are forgotten in the absence of discussion, but too often the meaning of the opinion itself. The words which convey it, cease to suggest ideas, or suggest only a small portion of those they were originally employed to communicate. Instead of a vivid conception and a living belief, there remain only a few phrases retained by rote; or, if any part, the shell and husk only of the meaning is retained, the finer essence being lost. The great chapter in human history which this fact occupies and fills, cannot be too earnestly studied and meditated on.

It is illustrated in the experience of almost all ethical doctrines and religious creeds. They are all full of meaning and vitality to those who originate them, and to the direct disciples of the originators. Their meaning continues to be felt in undiminished strength, and is perhaps brought out into even fuller consciousness, so long as the struggle lasts to give the doctrine or creed an ascendency over other creeds. At last it either prevails, and becomes the general opinion, or its progress stops; it keeps possession of the ground it has gained, but ceases to spread further. When either of these results has become apparent, controversy on the subject flags, and gradually dies away. The doctrine has taken its place, if not as a received opinion, as one of the admitted sects or divisions of opinion: those who hold it have generally inherited, not adopted it; and conversion from one of these doctrines to another, being now an exceptional fact, occupies little place in the thoughts of their professors. Instead of being, as at first, constantly on the alert either to defend themselves against the world, or to bring the world over to them, they have subsided into acquiescence, and neither listen, when they can help it, to arguments against their creed, nor trouble dissentients (if there be such) with arguments in its favor. From this time may usually be dated the decline in the living power of the doctrine. We often hear the teachers of all creeds lamenting the difficulty of keeping up in the minds of believers a lively apprehension of the truth which they nominally recognize, so that it may penetrate the feelings, and acquire a real mastery over the conduct. No such difficulty is complained of while the creed is still fighting for its existence: even the weaker combatants then know and feel what they are fighting for, and the difference between it and other doctrines; and in that period of every creed's existence, not a few persons may be found, who have realized its fundamental principles in all the forms of thought, have weighed and considered them in all their important bearings, and have experienced the full effect on the character, which belief in that creed ought to produce in a mind thoroughly imbued with it. But when it has come to be an hereditary creed, and to be received passively, not actively—when the mind is no longer compelled, in the same degree as at first, to exercise its vital powers on the questions which its belief presents to it, there is a progressive tendency to forget all of the belief except the formularies, or to give it a dull and torpid assent, as if accepting it on trust dispensed with the necessity of realizing it in consciousness, or testing it by personal experience; until it almost ceases to connect itself at all with the inner life of the human being. Then are seen the cases, so frequent in this age of the world as almost to form the majority, in which the creed remains as it were outside the mind, encrusting and petrifying it against all other influences addressed to the higher parts of our nature; manifesting its power by not suffering any fresh and living conviction to get in, but itself doing nothing for the mind or heart, except standing sentinel over them to keep them vacant.

To what an extent doctrines intrinsically fitted to make the deepest impression upon the mind may remain in it as dead beliefs, without being ever realized in the imagination, the feelings, or the understanding, is exemplified by the manner in which the majority of believers hold the doctrines of Christianity. By Christianity I here mean what is accounted such by all churches and sects—the maxims and precepts contained in the New Testament. These are considered sacred, and accepted as laws, by all professing Christians. Yet it is scarcely too much to say that not one Christian in a thousand guides or tests his individual conduct by reference to those laws. The standard to which he does refer it, is the custom of his nation, his class, or his religious profession. He has thus, on the one hand, a collection of ethical maxims, which he believes to have been vouchsafed to him by infallible wisdom as rules for his government; and on the other, a set of everyday judgments and practices, which go a certain length with some of those maxims, not so great a length with others, stand in direct opposition to some, and are, on the whole, a compromise between the Christian creed and the interests and suggestions of worldly life. To the first of these standards he gives his homage; to the other his real allegiance. All Christians believe that the blessed are the poor and humble, and those who are ill-used by the world; that it is easier for a camel to pass through the eye of a needle than for a rich man to enter the kingdom of heaven; that they should judge not, lest they be judged; that they should swear not at all; that they should love their neighbor as themselves; that if one take their cloak, they should give him their coat also; that they should take no thought for the morrow; that if they would be perfect, they should sell all that they have and give it to the poor. They are not insincere when they say that they believe these things. They do believe them, as people believe what they have always heard lauded and never discussed. But in the sense of that living belief which regulates conduct, they believe these doctrines just up to the point to which it is usual to act upon them. The doctrines in their integrity are serviceable to pelt adversaries with; and it is understood that they are to be put forward (when possible) as the reasons for whatever people do that they think laudable. But anyone who reminded them that the maxims require an infinity of things which they never even think of doing would gain nothing but to be classed among those very unpopular characters who affect to be better than other people. The doctrines have no hold on ordinary believers—are not a power in their minds. They have a habitual respect for the sound of them, but no feeling which spreads from the words to the things signified, and forces the mind to take them in, and make them conform to the formula. Whenever conduct is concerned, they look round for Mr. A and B to direct them how far to go in obeying Christ. . . .

Even with the strictly religious, who are much in earnest about their doctrines, and attach a greater amount of meaning to many of them than people in general, it commonly happens that the part which is thus comparatively active in their minds is that which was made by Calvin, or Knox, or some such person much nearer in character to themselves. The sayings of Christ coexist passively in their minds, producing hardly any effect beyond what is caused by mere listening to words so amiable and bland. There are many reasons, doubtless, why doctrines which are the badge of a sect retain more of their vitality than those common to all recognized sects, and why more pains are taken by teachers to keep their meaning alive; but one reason certainly is, that the peculiar doctrines are more questioned, and have to be oftener defended against open gainsayers. Both teachers and learners go to sleep at their post, as soon as there is no enemy in the field.

The same thing holds true, generally speaking, of all traditional doctrines—those of prudence and knowledge of life, as well as of morals or religion. All languages and literatures are full of general observations on life, both as to what it is, and how to conduct oneself in it; observations which everybody knows, which everybody repeats, or hears with acquiescence, which are received as truisms, yet of which most people first truly learn the meaning, when experience, generally of a painful kind, has made it a reality to them. How often, when smarting under some unforeseen misfortune or disappointment, does a person call to mind some proverb or common saying familiar to him all his life, the meaning of which, if he had ever before felt it as he does now, would have saved him from the calamity. There are indeed reasons for this, other than the absence of discussion: there are many truths of which the full meaning cannot be realized, until personal experience has brought it home. But much more of the meaning even of these would have been understood, and what was understood would have been far more deeply impressed on the mind, if the man had been accustomed to hear it argued pro and con by people who did understand it. The fatal tendency of mankind to leave off thinking about a thing when it is no longer doubtful, is the cause of half their errors. A contemporary author has well spoken of "the deep slumber of a decided opinion."

But what! (it may be asked) Is the absence of unanimity an indispensable condition of true knowledge? Is it necessary that some part of mankind should persist in error, to enable any to realize the truth? Does a belief cease to be real and vital as soon as it is generally received—and is a proposition never thoroughly understood and felt unless some doubt of it remains? As soon as mankind have unanimously accepted a truth, does the truth perish within them? The highest aim and best result of improved intelligence, it has hitherto been thought, is to unite mankind more and more in the acknowledgment of all important truths: and does the intelligence only last as long as it has not achieved its object? Do the fruits of conquest perish by the very completeness of the victory?

I affirm no such thing. As mankind improve, the number of doctrines which are no longer disputed or doubted will be constantly on the increase: and the well-being of mankind may almost be measured by the number and gravity of the truths which have reached the point of being uncontested. The cessation, on one question after another, of serious controversy, is one of the necessary incidents of the consolidation of opinion; a consolidation as salutary in the case of true opinions, as it is dangerous and noxious when the opinions are erroneous. But though this gradual narrowing of the bounds of diversity of opinion is necessary in both senses of the term, being at once inevitable and indispensable, we are not therefore obliged to conclude that all its consequences must be beneficial. The loss of so important an aid to the intelligent and living apprehension of a truth, as is afforded by the necessity of explaining it to, or defending it against, opponents, though not sufficient to outweigh, is no trifling drawback from, the benefit of its universal recognition. Where this advantage can no longer be had, I confess I should like to see the teachers of mankind endeavoring to provide a substitute for it; some contrivance for making the difficulties of the question as present to the learner's consciousness, as if they were pressed upon him by a dissentient champion, eager for his conversion.

But instead of seeking contrivances for this purpose, they have lost those they formerly had. The Socratic dialectics, so magnificently exemplified in the dialogues of Plato, were a contrivance of this description. They were essentially a negative discussion of the great questions of philosophy and life, directed with consummate skill to the purpose of convincing anyone who had merely adopted the commonplaces of received opinion, that he did not understand the subject—that he as yet attached no definite meaning to the doctrines he professed; in order that, becoming aware of his ignorance, he might be put in the way to attain a stable belief, resting on a clear apprehension both of the meaning of doctrines and of their evidence. The school disputations of the Middle Ages had a somewhat similar object. They were intended to make sure that the pupil understood his own opinion, and (by necessary correlation) the opinion opposed to it, and could enforce the grounds of the one and confute those of the other. These last-mentioned contests had indeed the incurable defect, that the premises appealed to were taken from authority, not from reason; and, as a discipline to the mind, they were in every respect inferior to the powerful dialectics which formed the intellects of the "*Socratici viri*:" but the modern mind owes far more to both than it is generally willing to admit, and the present modes of education contain nothing which in the smallest degree supplies the place either of the one or of the other. A person who derives all his instruction from teachers or books, even if he escape the besetting temptation of contenting himself with cram, is under no compulsion to hear both sides; accordingly it is far from a frequent accomplishment, even among thinkers, to know both sides; and the weakest part of what everybody says in defense of his opinion, is what he intends as a reply to antagonists. It is the fashion of the present time to disparage negative logic—that which points out weaknesses in theory or errors in practice, without establishing positive truths. Such negative criticism would indeed be poor enough as an ultimate result; but as a means to attaining any positive knowledge or conviction worthy the name, it cannot be valued too highly; and until people are again systematically trained to it, there will be few great thinkers, and a low general average of intellect, in any but the mathematical and physical departments of speculation. On any other subject no one's opinions deserve the name of knowledge, except so far as he has either had forced upon him by others, or gone through of himself, the same mental process which would have been required of him in carrying on an active controversy with opponents. That, therefore, which when absent, it is so indispensable, but so difficult, to create, how worse than absurd is it to forego, when spontaneously offering itself! If there are any persons who contest a received opinion, or who will do so if law or opinion will let them, let us thank them for it, open our minds to listen to them, and rejoice that there is someone to do for us what we otherwise ought, if we have any regard for either the certainty or the vitality of our convictions, to do with much greater labor for ourselves.

It still remains to speak of one of the principal causes which make diversity of opinion advantageous, and will continue to do so until mankind shall have entered a stage of intellectual advancement which at present seems at an incalculable distance. We have hitherto considered only two possibilities: that the received opinion may be false, and some other opinion, consequently, true; or that, the received opinion being true, a conflict with the opposite error is essential to a clear apprehension and deep feeling of its truth. But there is a commoner case than either of these; when the conflicting doctrines, instead of being one true and the other false, share the truth between them; and the nonconforming opinion is needed to supply the remainder of the truth, of which the received doctrine embodies only a part. Popular opinions, on subjects not palpable to sense, are often true, but seldom or never the whole truth. They are a part of the truth; sometimes a greater, sometimes a smaller part, but exaggerated, distorted, and disjoined from the truths by which they ought to be accompanied and limited. Heretical opinions, on the other hand, are generally some of these suppressed and neglected truths, bursting the bonds which kept them down, and either seeking reconciliation with the truth contained in the common opinion, or fronting it as enemies, and setting themselves up, with similar exclusiveness, as the whole truth. The latter case is hitherto the most frequent, as, in the human mind, one-sidedness has always been the rule, and many-sidedness the exception. Hence, even in revolutions of opinion, one part of the truth usually sets while another rises. Even progress, which ought to super-add, for the most part only substitutes one partial and incomplete truth for another; improvement consisting chiefly in this, that the new fragment of truth is more wanted, more adapted to the needs of the time, than that which it displaces. Such being the partial character of prevailing opinions, even when resting on a true foundation; every opinion which embodies somewhat of the portion of truth which the common opinion omits, ought to be considered precious, with whatever amount of error and confusion that truth may be blended. No sober judge of human affairs will feel bound to be indignant because those who force on our notice truths which we should otherwise have overlooked, overlook some of those which we see. Rather, he will think that so long as popular truth is one-sided, it is more desirable than otherwise that unpopular truth should have one-sided asserters too; such being usually the most energetic, and the most likely to compel reluctant attention to the fragment of wisdom which they proclaim as if it were the whole.

Thus, in the eighteenth century, when nearly all the instructed, and all those of the uninstructed who were led by them, were lost in admiration of what is called civilization, and of the marvels of modern science, literature, and philosophy, and while greatly overrating the amount of unlikeness between the men of modern and those of ancient times, indulged the belief that the whole of the difference was in their own favor; with what a salutary shock did the paradoxes of Rousseau explode like bombshells in the midst, dislocating the compact mass of one-sided opinion, and forcing its elements to recombine in a better form and with additional ingredients. Not that the current opinions were on the whole farther from the truth than Rousseau's were; on the contrary, they were nearer to it; they contained more of positive truth, and very much less of error. Nevertheless there lay in Rousseau's doctrine, and has floated down the stream of opinion along with it, a considerable amount of exactly those truths which the popular opinion wanted; and these are the deposit which was left behind when the flood subsided. The superior worth of simplicity of life, the enervating and demoralizing effect of the trammels and hypocrisies of artificial society, are ideas which have never been entirely absent from cultivated minds since Rousseau wrote; and they will in time produce their due effect, though at present needing to be asserted as much as ever, and to be asserted by deeds, for words, on this subject, have nearly exhausted their power.

In politics, again, it is almost a commonplace, that a party of order or stability, and a party of progress or reform, are both necessary elements of a healthy state of political life; until the one or the other shall have so enlarged its mental grasp as to be a party equally of order and of progress, knowing and distinguishing what is fit to be preserved from what ought to be swept away. Each of these modes of thinking derives its utility from the deficiencies of the other; but it is in a great measure the opposition of the other that keeps each within the limits of reason and sanity. Unless opinions favorable to democracy and to aristocracy, to property and to equality, to co-operation and to competition, to luxury and to abstinence, to sociality and individuality, to liberty and discipline, and all the other standing antagonisms of practical life, are expressed with equal freedom, and enforced and defended with equal talent and energy, there is no chance of both elements obtaining their due; one scale is sure to go up, and the other down. Truth, in the great practical concerns of life, is so much a question of the reconciling and combining of opposites, that very few have minds sufficiently capacious and impartial to make the adjustment with an approach to correctness, and it has to be made by the rough process of a struggle between combatants fighting under hostile banners. On any of the great open questions just enumerated, if either of the two opinions has a better claim than the other, not merely to be tolerated, but to be encouraged and countenanced, it is the one which happens at the particular time and place to be in a minority. That is the opinion which, for the time being, represents the neglected interests, the side of human well-being which is in danger of obtaining less than its share. I am aware that there is not, in this country, any intolerance of differences of opinion on most of these topics. They are adduced to show, by admitted and multiplied examples, the universality of the fact, that only through diversity of opinion is there, in the existing state of human intellect, a chance of fair play to all sides of the truth. When there are persons to be found, who form an exception to the apparent unanimity of the world on any subject, even if the world is in the right, it is always probable that dissentients have something worth hearing to say for themselves, and that truth would lose something by their silence.

It may be objected, "But some received principles, especially on the highest and most vital subjects, are more than half-truths. The Christian morality, for instance, is the whole truth on that subject and if any one teaches a morality which varies from it, he is wholly in error." As this is of all cases the most important in practice, none can be fitter to test the general maxim. But before pronouncing what Christian morality is or is not, it would be desirable to decide what is meant by Christian morality. If it means the morality of the New Testament, I wonder that anyone who derives his knowledge of this from the book itself, can suppose that it was announced, or intended, as a complete doctrine of morals. The Gospel always refers to a preexisting morality, and confines its precepts to the particulars in which that morality was to be corrected, or superseded by a wider and higher; expressing itself, moreover, in terms most general, often impossible to be interpreted literally, and possessing rather the impressiveness of poetry or eloquence than the precision of legislation. To extract from it a body of ethical doctrine, has never been possible without eking it out from the Old Testament, that is, from a system elaborate indeed. . . . St. Paul, a declared enemy to this Judaic mode of interpreting the doctrine and filling up the scheme of his Master, equally assumes a preexisting morality, namely, that of the Greeks and Romans; and his advice to Christians is in a great measure a system of accommodation to that; even to the extent of giving an apparent sanction to slavery. What is called "Christian" (but should rather be termed "theological") morality, was not the work of Christ or the Apostles, but is of much later origin, having been gradually built up by the Catholic Church of the first five centuries, and though not implicitly adopted by moderns and Protestants, has been much less modified by them than might have been expected. For the most part, indeed, they have contented themselves with cutting off the additions which had been made to it in the Middle Ages, each sect supplying the place by fresh additions, adapted to its own character and tendencies. That mankind owe a great debt to this morality, and to its early teachers, I should be the last person to deny; but I do not scruple to say of it, that it is, in many important points, incomplete and one-sided, and that unless ideas and feelings, not sanctioned by it, had contributed to the formation of European life and character, human affairs would have been in a worse condition than they now are. Christian morality (so called) has all the characters of a reaction; it is, in great part, a protest against Paganism. Its ideal is negative rather than positive; passive rather than active; Innocence rather than Nobleness; Abstinence from Evil, rather than energetic Pursuit of Good: in its precepts (as has been well said) "thou shalt not" predominates unduly over "thou shalt." In its horror of sensuality, it made an idol of asceticism, which has been gradually compromised away into one of legality. It holds out the hope of heaven and the threat of hell, as the appointed and appropriate motives to a virtuous life: in this falling far below the best of the ancients, and doing what lies in it to give to human morality an essentially selfish character, by disconnecting each man's feelings of duty from the interests of his fellow-creatures, except so far as a self-interested inducement is offered to him for consulting them. It is essentially a doctrine of passive obedience; it inculcates submission to all authorities found established; who indeed are not to be actively obeyed when they command what religion forbids, but who are not to be resisted, far less rebelled against, for any amount of wrong to ourselves. And while, in the morality of the best Pagan nations, duty to the State holds even a disproportionate place, infringing on the just liberty of the individual; in purely Christian ethics that grand department of duty is scarcely noticed or acknowledged. It is in the Koran, not the New Testament, that we read the maxim—"A ruler who appoints any man to an office, when there is in his dominions another man better qualified for it, sins against God and against the State." What little recognition the idea of obligation to the public obtains in modern morality, is derived from Greek and Roman sources, not from Christian; as, even in the morality of private life, whatever exists of magnanimity, high-mindedness, personal dignity, even the sense of honor, is derived from the purely human, not the religious part of our education, and never could have grown out of a standard of ethics in which the only worth, professedly recognized, is that of obedience.

I am as far as anyone from pretending that these defects are necessarily inherent in the Christian ethics, in every manner in which it can be conceived, or that the many requisites of a complete moral doctrine which it does not contain, do not admit of being reconciled with it. Far less would I insinuate this of the doctrines and precepts of Christ himself. I believe that the sayings of Christ are all, that I can see any evidence of their having been intended to be; that they are irreconcilable with nothing which a comprehensive morality requires; that everything which is excellent in ethics may be brought within them, with no greater violence to their language than has been done to it by all who have attempted to deduce from them any practical system of conduct whatever. But it is quite consistent with this, to believe that they contain and were meant to contain, only a part of the truth; that many essential elements of the highest morality are among the things which are not provided for, nor intended to be provided for, in the recorded deliverances of the Founder of Christianity, and which have been entirely thrown aside in the system of ethics erected on the basis of those deliverances by the Christian Church. And this being so, I think it a great error to persist in attempting to find in the Christian doctrine that complete rule for our guidance, which its author intended it to sanction and enforce, but only partially to provide. I believe, too, that this narrow theory is becoming a grave practical evil, detracting greatly from the value of the moral training and instruction, which so many well-meaning persons are now at length exerting themselves to promote. I much fear that by attempting to form the mind and feelings on an exclusively religious type, and discarding those secular standards (as for want of a better name they may be called) which heretofore coexisted with and supplemented the Christian ethics, receiving some of its spirit, and infusing into it some of theirs, there will result, and is even now resulting, a low, abject, servile type of character, which, submit itself as it may to what it deems the Supreme Will, is incapable of rising to or sympathizing in the conception of Supreme Goodness. I believe that other ethics than any one which can be evolved from exclusively Christian sources, must exist side by side with Christian ethics to produce the moral regeneration of mankind; and that the Christian system is no exception to the rule that in an imperfect state of the human mind, the interests of truth require a diversity of opinions. It is not necessary that in ceasing to ignore the moral truths not contained in Christianity, men should ignore any of those which it does contain. Such prejudice, or oversight, when it occurs, is altogether an evil; but it is one from which we cannot hope to be always exempt, and must be regarded as the price paid for an inestimable good. The exclusive pretension made by a part of the truth to be the whole, must and ought to be protested against, and if a reactionary impulse should make the protestors unjust in their turn, this one-sidedness, like the other, may be lamented, but must be tolerated. If Christians would teach infidels to be just to Christianity, they should themselves be just to infidelity. It can do truth no service to blink the fact, known to all who have the most ordinary acquaintance with literary history, that a large portion of the noblest and most valuable moral teaching has been the work, not only of men who did not know, but of men who knew and rejected, the Christian faith.

I do not pretend that the most unlimited use of the freedom of enunciating all possible opinions would put an end to the evils of religious or philosophical sectarianism. Every truth which men of narrow capacity are in earnest about, is sure to be asserted, inculcated, and in many ways even acted on, as if no other truth existed in the world, or at all events none that could limit or qualify the first. I acknowledge that the tendency of all opinions to become sectarian is not cured by the freest discussion, but is often heightened and exacerbated thereby; the truth which ought to have been, but was not, seen, being rejected all the more violently because proclaimed by persons regarded as opponents. But it is not on the impassioned partisan, it is on the calmer and more disinterested bystander, that this collision of opinions works its salutary effect. Not the violent conflict between parts of the truth, but the quiet suppression of half of it, is the formidable evil: there is always hope when people are forced to listen to both sides; it is when they attend only to one that errors harden into prejudices, and truth itself ceases to have the effect of truth, by being exaggerated into falsehood. And since there are few mental attributes more rare than that judicial faculty which can sit in intelligent judgment between two sides of a question, of which only one is represented by an advocate before it, truth has no chance but in proportion as every side of it, every opinion which embodies any fraction of the truth, not only finds advocates, but is so advocated as to be listened to.

We have now recognized the necessity to the mental well-being of mankind (on which all their other well-being depends) of freedom of opinion, and freedom of the expression of opinion, on four distinct grounds; which we will now briefly recapitulate.

First, if any opinion is compelled to silence, that opinion may, for aught we can certainly know, be true. To deny this is to assume our own infallibility.

Secondly, though the silenced opinion be an error, it may, and very commonly does, contain a portion of truth; and since the general or prevailing opinion on any object is rarely or never the whole truth, it is only by the collision of adverse opinions that the remainder of the truth has any chance of being supplied.

Thirdly, even if the received opinion be not only true, but the whole truth; unless it is suffered to be, and actually is, vigorously and earnestly contested, it will, by most of those who receive it, be held in the manner of a prejudice, with little comprehension or feeling of its rational grounds. And not only this, but, *fourthly*, the meaning of the doctrine itself will be in danger of being lost, or enfeebled, and deprived of its vital effect on the character and conduct: the dogma becoming a mere formal profession, inefficacious for good, but cumbering the ground, and preventing the growth of any real and heartfelt conviction, from reason or personal experience. . . .

If the arguments of the present chapter are of any validity, there ought to exist the fullest liberty of professing and discussing, as a matter of ethical conviction, any doctrine, however immoral it may be considered. . . .

Footnote: Ample warning may be drawn from the large infusion of the passions of a persecutor, which mingled with the general display of the worst parts of our national character on the occasion of the Sepoy Insurrection [i.e., India's First War of Independence]. The ravings of fanatics or charlatans from the pulpit may be unworthy of notice; but the heads of the Evangelical party have announced as their principle, for the government of Hindus and Muslims, that no schools be supported by public money in which the Bible is not taught, and by necessary consequence that no public employment be given to any but real or pretended Christians. An Under-Secretary of State, in a speech delivered to his constituents on the 12th of November, 1857, is reported to have said: "Toleration of their faith" (the faith of a hundred millions of British subjects), "the superstition which they called religion, by the British Government, had had the effect of retarding the ascendency of the British name, and preventing the salutary growth of Christianity. . . . Toleration was the great corner-stone of the religious liberties of this country; but do not let them abuse that precious word toleration. As he understood it, it meant the complete liberty to all, freedom of worship, among Christians, who worshipped upon the same foundation. It meant toleration of all sects and denominations of Christians who believed in the one mediation." I desire to call attention to the fact, that a man who has been deemed fit to fill a high office in the government of this country, under a liberal Ministry, maintains the doctrine that all who do not believe in the divinity of Christ are beyond the pale of toleration. Who, after this imbecile display, can indulge the illusion that religious persecution has passed away, never to return?

CHAPTER III: ON INDIVIDUALITY, AS ONE OF THE ELEMENTS OF WELLBEING

Such being the reasons which make it imperative that human beings should be free to form opinions, and to express their opinions without reserve; and such the baneful consequences to the intellectual, and through that to the moral nature of man, unless this liberty is either conceded, or asserted in spite of prohibition; let us next examine whether the same reasons do not require that men should be free to act upon their opinions—to carry these out in their lives, without hindrance, either physical or moral, from their fellow-men, so long as it is at their own risk and peril. This last proviso is of course indispensable. No one pretends that actions should be as free as opinions. On the contrary, even opinions lose their immunity, when the circumstances in which they are expressed are such as to constitute their expression a positive instigation to some mischievous act. An opinion that corn-dealers are starvers of the poor, or that private property is robbery, ought to be unmolested when simply circulated through the press, but may justly incur punishment when delivered orally to an excited mob assembled before the house of a corn-dealer, or when handed about among the same mob in the form of a placard. Acts of whatever kind, which, without justifiable cause, do harm to others, may be, and in the more important cases absolutely require to be, controlled by the unfavorable sentiments, and, when needful, by the active interference of mankind. The liberty of the individual must be thus far limited; he must not make himself a nuisance to other people. But if he refrains from molesting others in what concerns them, and merely acts according to his own inclination and judgment in things which concern himself, the same reasons which show that opinion should be free, prove also that he should be allowed, without molestation, to carry his opinions into practice at his own cost. That mankind are not infallible; that their truths, for the most part, are only half-truths; that unity of opinion, unless resulting from the fullest and freest comparison of opposite opinions, is not desirable, and diversity not an evil, but a good, until mankind are much more capable than at present of recognizing all sides of the truth, are principles applicable to men's modes of action, not less than to their opinions. As it is useful that while mankind are imperfect there should be different opinions, so is it that there should be different experiments of living; that free scope should be given to varieties of character, short of injury to others; and that the worth of different modes of life should be proved practically, when anyone thinks fit to try them. It is desirable, in short, that in things which do not primarily concern others, individuality should assert itself. Where, not the person's own character, but the traditions of customs of other people are the rule of conduct, there is wanting one of the principal ingredients of human happiness, and quite the chief ingredient of individual and social progress.

In maintaining this principle, the greatest difficulty to be encountered does not lie in the appreciation of means towards an acknowledged end, but in the indifference of persons in general to the end itself. If it were felt that the free development of individuality is one of the leading essentials of well-being; that it is not only a coordinate element with all that is designated by the terms civilization, instruction, education, culture, but is itself a necessary part and condition of all those things; there would be no danger that liberty should be undervalued, and the adjustment of the boundaries between it and social control would present no extraordinary difficulty. But the evil is, that individual spontaneity is hardly recognized by the common modes of thinking as having any intrinsic worth, or deserving any regard on its own account. The majority, being satisfied with the ways of mankind as they now are (for it is they who make them what they are), cannot comprehend why those ways should not be good enough for everybody; and what is more, spontaneity forms no part of the ideal of the majority of moral and social reformers, but is rather looked on with jealousy, as a troublesome and perhaps rebellious obstruction to the general acceptance of what these reformers, in their own judgment, think would be best for mankind. Few persons, out of Germany, even comprehend the meaning of the doctrine which Wilhelm von Humboldt, so eminent both as a savant and as a politician, made the text of a treatise—that "the end of man, or that which is prescribed by the eternal or immutable dictates of reason, and not suggested by vague and transient desires, is the highest and most harmonious development of his powers to a complete and consistent whole;" that, therefore, the object "towards which every human being must ceaselessly direct his efforts, and on which especially those who design to influence their fellow-men must ever keep their eyes, is the individuality of power and development;" that for this there are two requisites, "freedom, and a variety of situations;" and that from the union of these arise "individual vigor and manifold diversity," which combine themselves in "originality."

Little, however, as people are accustomed to a doctrine like that of Von Humboldt, and surprising as it may be to them to find so high a value attached to individuality, the question, one must nevertheless think, can only be one of degree. No one's idea of excellence in conduct is that people should do absolutely nothing but copy one another. No one would assert that people ought not to put into their mode of life, and into the conduct of their concerns, any impress whatever of their own judgment, or of their own individual character. On the other hand, it would be absurd to pretend that people ought to live as if nothing whatever had been known in the world before they came into it; as if experience had as yet done nothing towards showing that one mode of existence, or of conduct, is preferable to another. Nobody denies that people should be so taught and trained in youth, as to know and benefit by the ascertained results of human experience. But it is the privilege and proper condition of a human being, arrived at the maturity of his faculties, to use and interpret experience in his own way. It is for him to find out what part of recorded experience is properly applicable to his own circumstances and character. The traditions and customs of other people are, to a certain extent, evidence of what their experience has taught them; presumptive evidence, and as such, have a claim to this deference: but, in the first place, their experience may be too narrow; or they may not have interpreted it rightly. Secondly, their interpretation of experience may be correct but unsuitable to him. Customs are made for customary circumstances, and customary characters: and his circumstances or his character may be uncustomary. Thirdly, though the customs be both good as customs, and suitable to him, yet to conform to custom, merely as custom, does not educate or develop in him any of the qualities which are the distinctive endowment of a human being. The human faculties of perception, judgment, discriminative feeling, mental activity, and even moral preference, are exercised only in making a choice. He who does anything because it is the custom, makes no choice. He gains no practice either in discerning or in desiring what is best. The mental and moral, like the muscular powers, are improved only by being used. The faculties are called into no exercise by doing a thing merely because others do it, no more than by believing a thing only because others believe it. If the grounds of an opinion are not conclusive to the person's own reason, his reason cannot be strengthened, but is likely to be weakened by his adopting it: and if the inducements to an act are not such as are consentaneous to his own feelings and character (where affection, or the rights of others are not concerned), it is so much done towards rendering his feelings and character inert and torpid, instead of active and energetic.

He who lets the world, or his own portion of it, choose his plan of life for him, has no need of any other faculty than the ape-like one of imitation. He who chooses his plan for himself, employs all his faculties. He must use observation to see, reasoning and judgment to foresee, activity to gather materials for decision, discrimination to decide, and when he has decided, firmness and self-control to hold to his deliberate decision. And these qualities he requires and exercises exactly in proportion as the part of his conduct which he determines according to his own judgment and feelings is a large one. It is possible that he might be guided in some good path, and kept out of harm's way, without any of these things. But what will be his comparative worth as a human being? It really is of importance, not only what men do, but also what manner of men they are that do it. Among the works of man, which human life is rightly employed in perfecting and beautifying, the first in importance surely is man himself. Supposing it were possible to get houses built, corn grown, battles fought, causes tried, and even churches erected and prayers said, by machinery—by automatons in human form—it would be a considerable loss to exchange for these automatons even the men and women who at present inhabit the more civilized parts of the world, and who assuredly are but starved specimens of what nature can and will produce. Human nature is not a machine to be built after a model, and set to do exactly the work prescribed for it, but a tree, which requires to grow and develop itself on all sides, according to the tendency of the inward forces which make it a living thing.

It will probably be conceded that it is desirable people should exercise their understandings, and that an intelligent following of custom, or even occasionally an intelligent deviation from custom, is better than a blind and simply mechanical adhesion to it. To a certain extent it is admitted, that our understanding should be our own: but there is not the same willingness to admit that our desires and impulses should be our own likewise; or that to possess impulses of our own, and of any strength, is anything but a peril and a snare. Yet desires and impulses are as much a part of a perfect human being, as beliefs and restraints: and strong impulses are only perilous when not properly balanced; when one set of aims and inclinations is developed into strength, while others, which ought to coexist with them, remain weak and inactive. It is not because men's desires are strong that they act ill; it is because their consciences are weak. There is no natural connection between strong impulses and a weak conscience. The natural connection is the other way. To say that one person's desires and feelings are stronger and more various than those of another, is merely to say that he has more of the raw material of human nature, and is therefore capable, perhaps of more evil, but certainly of more good. Strong impulses are but another name for energy. Energy may be turned to bad uses; but more good may always be made of an energetic nature, than of an indolent and impassive one. Those who have most natural feeling, are always those whose cultivated feelings may be made the strongest. The same strong susceptibilities which make the personal impulses vivid and powerful, are also the source from whence are generated the most passionate love of virtue, and the sternest self-control. It is through the cultivation of these, that society both does its duty and protects its interests: not by rejecting the stuff of which heroes are made, because it knows not how to make them. A person whose desires and impulses are his own—are the expression of his own nature, as it has been developed and modified by his own culture—is said to have a character. One whose desires and impulses are not his own, has no character, no more than a steam-engine has a character. If, in addition to being his own, his impulses are strong, and are under the government of a strong will, he has an energetic character. Whoever thinks that individuality of desires and impulses should not be encouraged to unfold itself, must maintain that society has no need of strong natures—is not the better for containing many persons who have much character—and that a high general average of energy is not desirable.

. . . There has been a time when the element of spontaneity and individuality was in excess, and the social principle had a hard struggle with it. The difficulty then was, to induce men of strong bodies or minds to pay obedience to any rules which required them to control their impulses. To overcome this difficulty, law and discipline, like the Popes struggling against the Emperors, asserted a power over the whole man, claiming to control all his life in order to control his character—which society had not found any other sufficient means of binding. But society has now fairly got the better of individuality; and the danger which threatens human nature is not the excess, but the deficiency, of personal impulses and preferences. Things are vastly changed, since the passions of those who were strong by station or by personal endowment were in a state of habitual rebellion against laws and ordinances, and required to be rigorously chained up to enable the persons within their reach to enjoy any particle of security. In our times, from the highest class of society down to the lowest every one lives as under the eye of a hostile and dreaded censorship. Not only in what concerns others, but in what concerns only themselves, the individual, or the family, do not ask themselves—what do I prefer? Or, what would suit my character and disposition? Or, what would allow the best and highest in me to have fair play, and enable it to grow and thrive? They ask themselves, what is suitable to my position? What is usually done by persons of my station and pecuniary circumstances? Or (worse still) what is usually done by persons of a station and circumstances superior to mine? I do not mean that they choose what is customary, in preference to what suits their own inclination. It does not occur to them to have any inclination, except for what is customary. Thus the mind itself is bowed to the yoke: even in what people do for pleasure, conformity is the first thing thought of; they like in crowds; they exercise choice only among things commonly done: peculiarity of taste, eccentricity of conduct, are shunned equally with crimes: until by dint of not following their own nature, they have no nature to follow: their human capacities are withered and starved: they become incapable of any strong wishes or native pleasures, and are generally without either opinions or feelings of home growth, or properly their own. Now is this, or is it not, the desirable condition of human nature?

It is so, on the Calvinistic theory. According to that, the one great offence of man is Self-will. All the good of which humanity is capable, is comprised in Obedience. You have no choice; thus you must do, and no otherwise; "whatever is not a duty is a sin." Human nature being radically corrupt, there is no redemption for any one until human nature is killed within him. To one holding this theory of life, crushing out any of the human faculties, capacities, and susceptibilities, is no evil: man needs no capacity, but that of surrendering himself to the will of God: and if he uses any of his faculties for any other purpose but to do that supposed will more effectually, he is better without them. That is the theory of Calvinism; and it is held, in a mitigated form, by many who do not consider themselves Calvinists; the mitigation consisting in giving a less ascetic interpretation to the alleged will of God; asserting it to be his will that mankind should gratify some of their inclinations; of course not in the manner they themselves prefer, but in the way of obedience, that is, in a way prescribed to them by authority; and, therefore, by the necessary conditions of the case, the same for all.

In some such insidious form there is at present a strong tendency to this narrow theory of life, and to the pinched and hidebound type of human character which it patronizes. Many persons, no doubt, sincerely think that human beings thus cramped and dwarfed, are as their Maker designed them to be; just as many have thought that trees are a much finer thing when clipped into pollards, or cut out into figures of animals, than as nature made them. But if it be any part of religion to believe that man was made by a good Being, it is more consistent with that faith to believe, that this Being gave all human faculties that they might be cultivated and unfolded, not rooted out and consumed, and that he takes delight in every nearer approach made by his creatures to the ideal conception embodied in them, every increase in any of their capabilities of comprehension, of action, or of enjoyment. There is a different type of human excellence from the Calvinistic; a conception of humanity as having its nature bestowed on it for other purposes than merely to be abnegated. "Pagan self-assertion" is one of the elements of human worth, as well as "Christian self-denial." There is a Greek ideal of self-development, which the Platonic and Christian ideal of self-government blends with, but does not supersede. It may be better to be a John Knox than an Alcibiades, but it is better to be a Pericles than either; nor would a Pericles, if we had one in these days, be without anything good which belonged to John Knox.

It is not by wearing down into uniformity all that is individual in themselves, but by cultivating it and calling it forth, within the limits imposed by the rights and interests of others, that human beings become a noble and beautiful object of contemplation; and as the works partake the character of those who do them, by the same process human life also becomes rich, diversified, and animating, furnishing more abundant aliment to high thoughts and elevating feelings, and strengthening the tie which binds every individual to the race, by making the race infinitely better worth belonging to. In proportion to the development of his individuality, each person becomes more valuable to himself, and is therefore capable of being more valuable to others. There is a greater fullness of life about his own existence, and when there is more life in the units there is more in the mass which is composed of them. As much compression as is necessary to prevent the stronger specimens of human nature from encroaching on the rights of others, cannot be dispensed with; but for this there is ample compensation even in the point of view of human development. The means of development which the individual loses by being prevented from gratifying his inclinations to the injury of others, are chiefly obtained at the expense of the development of other people. And even to himself there is a full equivalent in the better development of the social part of his nature, rendered possible by the restraint put upon the selfish part. To be held to rigid rules of justice for the sake of others, develops the feelings and capacities which have the good of others for their object. But to be restrained in things not affecting their good, by their mere displeasure, develops nothing valuable, except such force of character as may unfold itself in resisting the restraint. If acquiesced in, it dulls and blunts the whole nature. To give any fair play to the nature of each, it is essential that different persons should be allowed to lead different lives. In proportion as this latitude has been exercised in any age, has that age been noteworthy to posterity. Even despotism does not produce its worst effects, so long as Individuality exists under it; and whatever crushes individuality is despotism, by whatever name it may be called, and whether it professes to be enforcing the will of God or the injunctions of men.

Having said that Individuality is the same thing with development, and that it is only the cultivation of individuality which produces, or can produce, well-developed human beings, I might here close the argument: for what more or better can be said of any condition of human affairs, than that it brings human beings themselves nearer to the best thing they can be? Or what worse can be said of any obstruction to good, than that it prevents this? Doubtless, however, these considerations will not suffice to convince those who most need convincing; and it is necessary further to show, that these developed human beings are of some use to the undeveloped—to point out to those who do not desire liberty, and would not avail themselves of it, that they may be in some intelligible manner rewarded for allowing other people to make use of it without hindrance.

In the first place, then, I would suggest that they might possibly learn something from them. It will not be denied by anybody, that originality is a valuable element in human affairs. There is always need of persons not only to discover new truths, and point out when what were once truths are true no longer, but also to commence new practices, and set the example of more enlightened conduct, and better taste and sense in human life. This cannot well be gainsaid by anybody who does not believe that the world has already attained perfection in all its ways and practices. It is true that this benefit is not capable of being rendered by everybody alike: there are but few persons, in comparison with the whole of mankind, whose experiments, if adopted by others, would be likely to be any improvement on established practice. But these few are the salt of the earth; without them, human life would become a stagnant pool. Not only is it they who introduce good things which did not before exist; it is they who keep the life in those which already existed. If there were nothing new to be done, would human intellect cease to be necessary? Would it be a reason why those who do the old things should forget why they are done, and do them like cattle, not like human beings? There is only too great a tendency in the best beliefs and practices to degenerate into the mechanical; and unless there were a succession of persons whose ever-recurring originality prevents the grounds of those beliefs and practices from becoming merely traditional, such dead matter would not resist the smallest shock from anything really alive, and there would be no reason why civilization should not die out, as in the Byzantine Empire. Persons of genius, it is true, are, and are always likely to be, a small minority; but in order to have them, it is necessary to preserve the soil in which they grow. Genius can only breathe freely in an atmosphere of freedom. Persons of genius are, [by definition], more individual than any other people—less capable, consequently, of fitting themselves, without hurtful compression, into any of the small number of molds which society provides in order to save its members the trouble of forming their own character. If from timidity they consent to be forced into one of these molds, and to let all that part of themselves which cannot expand under the pressure remain unexpanded, society will be little the better for their genius. If they are of a strong character, and break their fetters they become a mark for the society which has not succeeded in reducing them to common-place, to point at with solemn warning as "wild," "erratic," and the like; much as if one should complain of the Niagara river for not flowing smoothly between its banks like a Dutch canal.

I insist thus emphatically on the importance of genius, and the necessity of allowing it to unfold itself freely both in thought and in practice, being well aware that no one will deny the position in theory, but knowing also that almost every one, in reality, is totally indifferent to it. People think genius a fine thing if it enables a man to write an exciting poem, or paint a picture. But in its true sense, that of originality in thought and action, though no one says that it is not a thing to be admired, nearly all, at heart, think they can do very well without it. Unhappily this is too natural to be wondered at. Originality is the one thing which unoriginal minds cannot feel the use of. They cannot see what it is to do for them: how should they? If they could see what it would do for them, it would not be originality. The first service which originality has to render them, is that of opening their eyes: which being once fully done, they would have a chance of being themselves original. Meanwhile, recollecting that nothing was ever yet done which some one was not the first to do, and that all good things which exist are the fruits of originality, let them be modest enough to believe that there is something still left for it to accomplish, and assure themselves that they are more in need of originality, the less they are conscious of the want.

In sober truth, whatever homage may be professed, or even paid, to real or supposed mental superiority, the general tendency of things throughout the world is to render mediocrity the ascendant power among mankind. In ancient history, in the Middle Ages, and in a diminishing degree through the long transition from feudality to the present time, the individual was a power in himself; and If he had either great talents or a high social position, he was a considerable power. At present individuals are lost in the crowd. In politics it is almost a triviality to say that public opinion now rules the world. The only power deserving the name is that of masses, and of governments while they make themselves the organ of the tendencies and instincts of masses. This is as true in the moral and social relations of private life as in public transactions. Those whose opinions go by the name of public opinion, are not always the same sort of public: in America, they are the whole white population; in England, chiefly the middle class. But they are always a mass, that is to say, collective mediocrity. And what is still greater novelty, the mass do not now take their opinions from dignitaries in Church or State, from ostensible leaders, or from books. Their thinking is done for them by men much like themselves, addressing them or speaking in their name, on the spur of the moment, through the newspapers. I am not complaining of all this. I do not assert that anything better is compatible, as a general rule, with the present low state of the human mind. But that does not hinder the government of mediocrity from being mediocre government. No government by a democracy or a numerous aristocracy, either in its political acts or in the opinions, qualities, and tone of mind which it fosters, ever did or could rise above mediocrity, except in so far as the sovereign Many have let themselves be guided (which in their best times they always have done) by the counsels and influence of a more highly gifted and instructed One or Few. The initiation of all wise or noble things, comes and must come from individuals; generally at first from some one individual. The honor and glory of the average man is that he is capable of following that initiative; that he can respond internally to wise and noble things, and be led to them with his eyes open. I am not countenancing the sort of "hero-worship" which applauds the strong man of genius for forcibly seizing on the government of the world and making it do his bidding in spite of itself. All he can claim is, freedom to point out the way. The power of compelling others into it, is not only inconsistent with the freedom and development of all the rest, but corrupting to the strong man himself. It does seem, however, that when the opinions of masses of merely average men are everywhere become or becoming the dominant power, the counterpoise and corrective to that tendency would be, the more and more pronounced individuality of those who stand on the higher eminences of thought. It is in these circumstances most especially, that exceptional individuals, instead of being deterred, should be encouraged in acting differently from the mass. In other times there was no advantage in their doing so, unless they acted not only differently, but better. In this age the mere example of non-conformity, the mere refusal to bend the knee to custom, is itself a service. Precisely because the tyranny of opinion is such as to make eccentricity a reproach, it is desirable, in order to break through that tyranny, that people should be eccentric. Eccentricity has always abounded when and where strength of character has abounded; and the amount of eccentricity in a society has generally been proportional to the amount of genius, mental vigor, and moral courage which it contained. That so few now dare to be eccentric, marks the chief danger of the time.

I have said that it is important to give the freest scope possible to uncustomary things, in order that it may in time appear which of these are fit to be converted into customs. But independence of action, and disregard of custom are not solely deserving of encouragement for the chance they afford that better modes of action, and customs more worthy of general adoption, may be struck out; nor is it only persons of decided mental superiority who have a just claim to carry on their lives in their own way. There is no reason that all human existences should be constructed on someone, or some small number of patterns. If a person possesses any tolerable amount of common sense and experience, his own mode of laying out his existence is the best, not because it is the best in itself, but because it is his own mode. Human beings are not like sheep; and even sheep are not undistinguishably alike. A man cannot get a coat or a pair of boots to fit him, unless they are either made to his measure, or he has a whole warehouse-full to choose from: and is it easier to fit him with a life than with a coat, or are human beings more like one another in their whole physical and spiritual conformation than in the shape of their feet? If it were only that people have diversities of taste that is reason enough for not attempting to shape them all after one model. But different persons also require different conditions for their spiritual development; and can no more exist healthily in the same moral, than all the variety of plants can in the same physical atmosphere and climate. The same things which are helps to one person towards the cultivation of his higher nature, are hindrances to another. The same mode of life is a healthy excitement to one, keeping all his faculties of action and enjoyment in their best order, while to another it is a distracting burden, which suspends or crushes all internal life. Such are the differences among human beings in their sources of pleasure, their susceptibilities of pain, and the operation on them of different physical and moral agencies, that unless there is a corresponding diversity in their modes of life, they neither obtain their fair share of happiness, nor grow up to the mental, moral, and aesthetic stature of which their nature is capable. Why then should tolerance, as far as the public sentiment is concerned, extend only to tastes and modes of life which extort acquiescence by the multitude of their adherents? Nowhere (except in some monastic institutions) is diversity of taste entirely unrecognized; a person may without blame, either like or dislike rowing, or smoking, or music, or athletic exercises, or chess, or cards, or study, because both those who like each of these things, and those who dislike them, are too numerous to be put down. But the man, and still more the woman, who can be accused either of doing "what nobody does," or of not doing "what everybody does," is the subject of as much depreciatory remark as if he or she had committed some grave moral delinquency. Persons require to possess a title, or some other badge of rank, or the consideration of people of rank, to be able to indulge somewhat in the luxury of doing as they like without detriment to their estimation. To indulge somewhat, I repeat: for whoever allow themselves much of that indulgence, incur the risk of something worse than disparaging speeches—they are in peril of a commission *de lunatico*, and of having their property taken from them and given to their relations.

There is one characteristic of the present direction of public opinion, peculiarly calculated to make it intolerant of any marked demonstration of individuality. The general average of mankind are not only moderate in intellect, but also moderate in inclinations: they have no tastes or wishes strong enough to incline them to do anything unusual, and they consequently do not understand those who have, and class all such with the wild and intemperate whom they are accustomed to look down upon. Now, in addition to this fact which is general, we have only to suppose that a strong movement has set in towards the improvement of morals, and it is evident what we have to expect. In these days such a movement has set in; much has actually been effected in the way of increased regularity of conduct, and discouragement of excesses; and there is a philanthropic spirit abroad, for the exercise of which there is no more inviting field than the moral and prudential improvement of our fellow-creatures. These tendencies of the times cause the public to be more disposed than at most former periods to prescribe general rules of conduct, and endeavor to make every one conform to the approved standard. And that standard, express or tacit, is to desire nothing strongly. Its ideal of character is to be without any marked character; to maim by compression . . . every part of human nature which stands out prominently, and tends to make the person markedly dissimilar in outline to commonplace humanity.

As is usually the case with ideals which exclude one half of what is desirable, the present standard of approbation produces only an inferior imitation of the other half. Instead of great energies guided by vigorous reason, and strong feelings strongly controlled by a conscientious will, its result is weak feelings and weak energies, which therefore can be kept in outward conformity to rule without any strength either of will or of reason. Already energetic characters on any large scale are becoming merely traditional. There is now scarcely any outlet for energy in this country except business. The energy expended in that may still be regarded as considerable. What little is left from that employment, is expended on some hobby; which may be a useful, even a philanthropic hobby, but is always some one thing, and generally a thing of small dimensions. The greatness of England is now all collective: individually small, we only appear capable of anything great by our habit of combining; and with this our moral and religious philanthropists are perfectly contented. But it was men of another stamp than this that made England what it has been; and men of another stamp will be needed to prevent its decline.

The despotism of custom is everywhere the standing hindrance to human advancement, being in unceasing antagonism to that disposition to aim at something better than customary, which is called, according to circumstances, the spirit of liberty, or that of progress or improvement. The spirit of improvement is not always a spirit of liberty, for it may aim at forcing improvements on an unwilling people; and the spirit of liberty, in so far as it resists such attempts, may ally itself locally and temporarily with the opponents of improvement; but the only unfailing and permanent source of improvement is liberty, since by it there are as many possible independent centers of improvement as there are individuals. The progressive principle, however, in either shape, whether as the love of liberty or of improvement, is antagonistic to the sway of Custom, involving at least emancipation from that yoke; and the contest between the two constitutes the chief interest of the history of mankind. The greater part of the world has, properly speaking, no history, because the despotism of Custom is complete.

. . . What is it that has hitherto preserved Europe from this lot? What has made the European family of nations an improving, instead of a stationary portion of mankind? Not any superior excellence in them, which when it exists, exists as the effect, not as the cause; but their remarkable diversity of character and culture. Individuals, classes, nations, have been extremely unlike one another: they have struck out a great variety of paths, each leading to something valuable; and although at every period those who travelled in different paths have been intolerant of one another, and each would have thought it an excellent thing if all the rest could have been compelled to travel his road, their attempts to thwart each other's development have rarely had any permanent success, and each has in time endured to receive the good which the others have offered. Europe is, in my judgment, wholly indebted to this plurality of paths for its progressive and many-sided development. But it already begins to possess this benefit in a considerably less degree. It is decidedly advancing towards the . . . ideal of making all people alike. . . . In a passage already quoted from Wilhelm von Humboldt, he points out two things as necessary conditions of human development, because necessary to render people unlike one another; namely, freedom, and variety of situations. The second of these two conditions is in this country every day diminishing. The circumstances which surround different classes and individuals, and shape their characters, are daily becoming more assimilated. Formerly, different ranks, different neighborhoods, different trades and professions lived in what might be called different worlds; at present, to a great degree, in the same. Comparatively speaking, they now read the same things, listen to the same things, see the same things, go to the same places, have their hopes and fears directed to the same objects, have the same rights and liberties, and the same means of asserting them. Great as are the differences of position which remain, they are nothing to those which have ceased. And the assimilation is still proceeding. All the political changes of the age promote it, since they all tend to raise the low and to lower the high. Every extension of education promotes it, because education brings people under common influences, and gives them access to the general stock of facts and sentiments. Improvements in the means of communication promote it, by bringing the inhabitants of distant places into personal contact, and keeping up a rapid flow of changes of residence between one place and another. The increase of commerce and manufactures promotes it, by diffusing more widely the advantages of easy circumstances, and opening all objects of ambition, even the highest, to general competition, whereby the desire of rising becomes no longer the character of a particular class, but of all classes. A more powerful agency than even all these, in bringing about a general similarity among mankind, is the complete establishment, in this and other free countries, of the ascendancy of public opinion in the State. As the various social eminences which enabled persons entrenched on them to disregard the opinion of the multitude, gradually became levelled; as the very idea of resisting the will of the public, when it is positively known that they have a will, disappears more and more from the minds of practical politicians; there ceases to be any social support for nonconformity—any substantive power in society, which, itself opposed to the ascendancy of numbers, is interested in taking under its protection opinions and tendencies at variance with those of the public.

The combination of all these causes forms so great a mass of influences hostile to Individuality, that it is not easy to see how it can stand its ground. It will do so with increasing difficulty, unless the intelligent part of the public can be made to feel its value—to see that it is good there should be differences, even though not for the better, even though, as it may appear to them, some should be for the worse. If the claims of Individuality are ever to be asserted, the time is now, while much is still wanting to complete the enforced assimilation. It is only in the earlier stages that any stand can be successfully made against the encroachment. The demand that all other people shall resemble ourselves, grows by what it feeds on. If resistance waits till life is reduced nearly to one uniform type, all deviations from that type will come to be considered impious, immoral, even monstrous and contrary to nature. Mankind speedily become unable to conceive diversity, when they have been for some time unaccustomed to see it.

CHAPTER IV: OF THE LIMITS TO THE AUTHORITY OF SOCIETY OVER THE INDIVIDUAL

What, then, is the rightful limit to the sovereignty of the individual over himself? Where does the authority of society begin? How much of human life should be assigned to individuality, and how much to society?

Each will receive its proper share, if each has that which more particularly concerns it. To individuality should belong the part of life in which it is chiefly the individual that is interested; to society, the part which chiefly interests society.

Though society is not founded on a contract, and though no good purpose is answered by inventing a contract in order to deduce social obligations from it, everyone who receives the protection of society owes a return for the benefit, and the fact of living in society renders it indispensable that each should be bound to observe a certain line of conduct towards the rest. This conduct consists, first, in not injuring the interests of one another; or rather certain interests, which, either by express legal provision or by tacit understanding, ought to be considered as rights; and secondly, in each person's bearing his share (to be fixed on some equitable principle) of the labors and sacrifices incurred for defending the society or its members from injury and molestation. These conditions society is justified in enforcing, at all costs to those who endeavor to withhold fulfilment. Nor is this all that society may do. The acts of an individual may be hurtful to others, or wanting in due consideration for their welfare, without going the length of violating any of their constituted rights. The offender may then be justly punished by opinion, though not by law. As soon as any part of a person's conduct affects prejudicially the interests of others, society has jurisdiction over it, and the question whether the general welfare will or will not be promoted by interfering with it, becomes open to discussion. But there is no room for entertaining any such question when a person's conduct affects the interests of no persons besides himself, or needs not affect them unless they like (all the persons concerned being of full age, and the ordinary amount of understanding). In all such cases there should be perfect freedom, legal and social, to do the action and stand the consequences.

It would be a great misunderstanding of this doctrine, to suppose that it is one of selfish indifference, which pretends that human beings have no business with each other's conduct in life, and that they should not concern themselves about the well-doing or well-being of one another, unless their own interest is involved. Instead of any diminution, there is need of a great increase of disinterested exertion to promote the good of others. But disinterested benevolence can find other instruments to persuade people to their good, than whips and scourges, either of the literal or the metaphorical sort. I am the last person to undervalue the self-regarding virtues; they are only second in importance, if even second, to the social. It is equally the business of education to cultivate both. But even education works by conviction and persuasion as well as by compulsion, and it is by the former only that, when the period of education is past, the self-regarding virtues should be inculcated. Human beings owe to each other help to distinguish the better from the worse, and encouragement to choose the former and avoid the latter. They should be forever stimulating each other to increased exercise of their higher faculties, and increased direction of their feelings and aims towards wise instead of foolish, elevating instead of degrading, objects and contemplations. But neither one person, nor any number of persons, is warranted in saying to another human creature of ripe years, that he shall not do with his life for his own benefit what he chooses to do with it. He is the person most interested in his own well-being, the interest which any other person, except in cases of strong personal attachment, can have in it, is trifling, compared with that which he himself has; the interest which society has in him individually (except as to his conduct to others) is fractional, and altogether indirect: while, with respect to his own feelings and circumstances, the most ordinary man or woman has means of knowledge immeasurably surpassing those that can be possessed by any one else. The interference of society to overrule his judgment and purposes in what only regards himself, must be grounded on general presumptions; which may be altogether wrong, and even if right, are as likely as not to be misapplied to individual cases, by persons no better acquainted with the circumstances of such cases than those are who look at them merely from without. In this department, therefore, of human affairs, Individuality has its proper field of action. In the conduct of human beings towards one another, it is necessary that general rules should for the most part be observed, in order that people may know what they have to expect; but in each person's own concerns, his individual spontaneity is entitled to free exercise. Considerations to aid his judgment, exhortations to strengthen his will, may be offered to him, even obtruded on him, by others; but he, himself, is the final judge. All errors which he is likely to commit against advice and warning, are far outweighed by the evil of allowing others to constrain him to what they deem his good.

I do not mean that the feelings with which a person is regarded by others, ought not to be in any way affected by his self-regarding qualities or deficiencies. This is neither possible nor desirable. If he is eminent in any of the qualities which conduce to his own good, he is, so far, a proper object of admiration. He is so much the nearer to the ideal perfection of human nature. If he is grossly deficient in those qualities, a sentiment the opposite of admiration will follow. There is a degree of folly, and a degree of what may be called (though the phrase is not unobjectionable) lowness or depravation of taste, which, though it cannot justify doing harm to the person who manifests it, renders him necessarily and properly a subject of distaste, or, in extreme cases, even of contempt: a person could not have the opposite qualities in due strength without entertaining these feelings. Though doing no wrong to any one, a person may so act as to compel us to judge him, and feel to him, as a fool, or as a being of an inferior order: and since this judgment and feeling are a fact which he would prefer to avoid, it is doing him a service to warn him of it beforehand, as of any other disagreeable consequence to which he exposes himself. It would be well, indeed, if this good office were much more freely rendered than the common notions of politeness at present permit, and if one person could honestly point out to another that he thinks him in fault, without being considered unmannerly or presuming. We have a right, also, in various ways, to act upon our unfavorable opinion of any one, not to the oppression of his individuality, but in the exercise of ours. We are not bound, for example, to seek his society; we have a right to avoid it (though not to parade the avoidance), for we have a right to choose the society most acceptable to us. We have a right, and it may be our duty, to caution others against him, if we think his example or conversation likely to have a pernicious effect on those with whom he associates. We may give others a preference over him in optional good offices, except those which tend to his improvement. In these various modes a person may suffer very severe penalties at the hands of others, for faults which directly concern only himself; but he suffers these penalties only in so far as they are the natural, and, as it were, the spontaneous consequences of the faults themselves, not because they are purposely inflicted on him for the sake of punishment. A person who shows rashness, obstinacy, self-conceit—who cannot live within moderate means—who cannot restrain himself from hurtful indulgences—who pursues animal pleasures at the expense of those of feeling and intellect—must expect to be lowered in the opinion of others, and to have a less share of their favorable sentiments, but of this he has no right to complain, unless he has merited their favor by special excellence in his social relations, and has thus established a title to their good offices, which is not affected by his demerits towards himself.

What I contend for is, that the inconveniences which are strictly inseparable from the unfavorable judgment of others, are the only ones to which a person should ever be subjected for that portion of his conduct and character which concerns his own good, but which does not affect the interests of others in their relations with him. Acts injurious to others require a totally different treatment. Encroachment on their rights; infliction on them of any loss or damage not justified by his own rights; falsehood or duplicity in dealing with them; unfair or ungenerous use of advantages over them; even selfish abstinence from defending them against injury—these are fit objects of moral reprobation, and, in grave cases, of moral retribution and punishment. And not only these acts, but the dispositions which lead to them, are properly immoral, and fit subjects of disapprobation which may rise to abhorrence. Cruelty of disposition; malice and ill-nature; that most anti-social and odious of all passions, envy; dissimulation and insincerity, irascibility on insufficient cause, and resentment disproportioned to the provocation; the love of domineering over others; the desire to engross more than one's share of advantages; the pride which derives gratification from the abasement of others; the egotism which thinks self and its concerns more important than everything else, and decides all doubtful questions in his own favor;—these are moral vices, and constitute a bad and odious moral character: unlike the self-regarding faults previously mentioned, which are not properly immoralities, and to whatever pitch they may be carried, do not constitute wickedness. They may be proofs of any amount of folly, or want of personal dignity and self-respect; but they are only a subject of moral reprobation when they involve a breach of duty to others, for whose sake the individual is bound to have care for himself. What are called duties to ourselves are not socially obligatory, unless circumstances render them at the same time duties to others. The term duty to oneself, when it means anything more than prudence, means self-respect or self-development; and for none of these is any one accountable to his fellow-creatures, because for none of them is it for the good of mankind that he be held accountable to them.

The distinction between the loss of consideration which a person may rightly incur by defect of prudence or of personal dignity, and the reprobation which is due to him for an offence against the rights of others, is not a merely nominal distinction. It makes a vast difference both in our feelings and in our conduct towards him, whether he displeases us in things in which we think we have a right to control him, or in things in which we know that we have not. If he displeases us, we may express our distaste, and we may stand aloof from a person as well as from a thing that displeases us; but we shall not therefore feel called on to make his life uncomfortable. We shall reflect that he already bears, or will bear, the whole penalty of his error; if he spoils his life by mismanagement, we shall not, for that reason, desire to spoil it still further: instead of wishing to punish him, we shall rather endeavor to alleviate his punishment, by showing him how he may avoid or cure the evils his conduct tends to bring upon him. He may be to us an object of pity, perhaps of dislike, but not of anger or resentment; we shall not treat him like an enemy of society: the worst we shall think ourselves justified in doing is leaving him to himself, if we do not interfere benevolently by showing interest or concern for him. It is far otherwise if he has infringed the rules necessary for the protection of his fellow-creatures, individually or collectively. The evil consequences of his acts do not then fall on himself, but on others; and society, as the protector of all its members, must retaliate on him; must inflict pain on him for the express purpose of punishment, and must take care that it be sufficiently severe. In the one case, he is an offender at our bar, and we are called on not only to sit in judgment on him, but, in one shape or another, to execute our own sentence: in the other case, it is not our part to inflict any suffering on him, except what may incidentally follow from our using the same liberty in the regulation of our own affairs, which we allow to him in his.

The distinction here pointed out between the part of a person's life which concerns only himself, and that which concerns others, many persons will refuse to admit. How (it may be asked) can any part of the conduct of a member of society be a matter of indifference to the other members? No person is an entirely isolated being; it is impossible for a person to do anything seriously or permanently hurtful to himself, without mischief reaching at least to his near connections, and often far beyond them. If he injures his property, he does harm to those who directly or indirectly derived support from it, and usually diminishes, by a greater or less amount, the general resources of the community. If he deteriorates his bodily or mental faculties, he not only brings evil upon all who depended on him for any portion of their happiness, but disqualifies himself for rendering the services which he owes to his fellow-creatures generally; perhaps becomes a burden on their affection or benevolence; and if such conduct were very frequent, hardly any offence that is committed would detract more from the general sum of good. Finally, if by his vices or follies a person does no direct harm to others, he is nevertheless (it may be said) injurious by his example; and ought to be compelled to control himself, for the sake of those whom the sight or knowledge of his conduct might corrupt or mislead.

And even (it will be added) if the consequences of misconduct could be confined to the vicious or thoughtless individual, ought society to abandon to their own guidance those who are manifestly unfit for it? If protection against themselves is confessedly due to children and persons under age, is not society equally bound to afford it to persons of mature years who are equally incapable of self-government? If gambling, or drunkenness, or incontinence, or idleness, or uncleanliness, are as injurious to happiness, and as great a hindrance to improvement, as many or most of the acts prohibited by law, why (it may be asked) should not law, so far as is consistent with practicability and social convenience, endeavor to repress these also? And as a supplement to the unavoidable imperfections of law, ought not opinion at least to organize a powerful police against these vices, and visit rigidly with social penalties those who are known to practice them? There is no question here (it may be said) about restricting individuality, or impeding the trial of new and original experiments in living. The only things it is sought to prevent are things which have been tried and condemned from the beginning of the world until now; things which experience has shown not to be useful or suitable to any person's individuality. There must be some length of time and amount of experience, after which a moral or prudential truth may be regarded as established, and it is merely desired to prevent generation after generation from falling over the same precipice which has been fatal to their predecessors.

I fully admit that the mischief which a person does to himself, may seriously affect, both through their sympathies and their interests, those nearly connected with him, and in a minor degree, society at large. When, by conduct of this sort, a person is led to violate a distinct and assignable obligation to any other person or persons, the case is taken out of the self-regarding class, and becomes amenable to moral disapprobation in the proper sense of the term. If, for example, a man, through intemperance or extravagance, becomes unable to pay his debts, or, having undertaken the moral responsibility of a family, becomes from the same cause incapable of supporting or educating them, he is deservedly reprobated, and might be justly punished; but it is for the breach of duty to his family or creditors, not for the extravagance. If the resources which ought to have been devoted to them, had been diverted from them for the most prudent investment, the moral culpability would have been the same. George Barnwell murdered his uncle to get money for his mistress, but if he had done it to set himself up in business, he would equally have been hanged. Again, in the frequent case of a man who causes grief to his family by addiction to bad habits, he deserves reproach for his unkindness or ingratitude; but so he may for cultivating habits not in themselves vicious, if they are painful to those with whom he passes his life, or who from personal ties are dependent on him for their comfort. Whoever fails in the consideration generally due to the interests and feelings of others, not being compelled by some more imperative duty, or justified by allowable self-preference, is a subject of moral disapprobation for that failure, but not for the cause of it, nor for the errors, merely personal to himself, which may have remotely led to it. In like manner, when a person disables himself, by conduct purely self-regarding, from the performance of some definite duty incumbent on him to the public, he is guilty of a social offence. No person ought to be punished simply for being drunk; but a soldier or a policeman should be punished for being drunk on duty. Whenever, in short, there is a definite damage, or a definite risk of damage, either to an individual or to the public, the case is taken out of the province of liberty, and placed in that of morality or law.

But with regard to the merely contingent or, as it may be called, constructive injury which a person causes to society, by conduct which neither violates any specific duty to the public, nor occasions perceptible hurt to any assignable individual except himself; the inconvenience is one which society can afford to bear, for the sake of the greater good of human freedom. If grown persons are to be punished for not taking proper care of themselves, I would rather it were for their own sake, than under pretense of preventing them from impairing their capacity of rendering to society benefits which society does not pretend it has a right to exact. But I cannot consent to argue the point as if society had no means of bringing its weaker members up to its ordinary standard of rational conduct, except waiting till they do something irrational, and then punishing them, legally or morally, for it. Society has had absolute power over them during all the early portion of their existence: it has had the whole period of childhood and nonage in which to try whether it could make them capable of rational conduct in life. The existing generation is master both of the training and the entire circumstances of the generation to come; it cannot indeed make them perfectly wise and good, because it is itself so lamentably deficient in goodness and wisdom; and its best efforts are not always, in individual cases, its most successful ones; but it is perfectly well able to make the rising generation, as a whole, as good as, and a little better than, itself. If society lets any considerable number of its members grow up mere children, incapable of being acted on by rational consideration of distant motives, society has itself to blame for the consequences. Armed not only with all the powers of education, but with the ascendency which the authority of a received opinion always exercises over the minds who are least fitted to judge for themselves; and aided by the natural penalties which cannot be prevented from falling on those who incur the distaste or the contempt of those who know them; let not society pretend that it needs, besides all this, the power to issue commands and enforce obedience in the personal concerns of individuals, in which, on all principles of justice and policy, the decision ought to rest with those who are to abide the consequences. Nor is there anything which tends more to discredit and frustrate the better means of influencing conduct, than a resort to the worse. If there be among those whom it is attempted to coerce into prudence or temperance, any of the material of which vigorous and independent characters are made, they will infallibly rebel against the yoke. No such person will ever feel that others have a right to control him in his concerns, such as they have to prevent him from injuring them in theirs; and it easily comes to be considered a mark of spirit and courage to fly in the face of such usurped authority, and do with ostentation the exact opposite of what it enjoins; as in the fashion of grossness which succeeded, in the time of Charles II, to the fanatical moral intolerance of the Puritans. With respect to what is said of the necessity of protecting society from the bad example set to others by the vicious or the self-indulgent; it is true that bad example may have a pernicious effect, especially the example of doing wrong to others with impunity to the wrong-doer. But we are now speaking of conduct which, while it does no wrong to others, is supposed to do great harm to the agent himself: and I do not see how those who believe this, can think otherwise than that the example, on the whole, must be more salutary than hurtful, since, if it displays the misconduct, it displays also the painful or degrading consequences which, if the conduct is justly censured, must be supposed to be in all or most cases attendant on it.

But the strongest of all the arguments against the interference of the public with purely personal conduct, is that when it does interfere, the odds are that it interferes wrongly, and in the wrong place. On questions of social morality, of duty to others, the opinion of the public, that is, of an overruling majority, though often wrong, is likely to be still oftener right; because on such questions they are only required to judge of their own interests; of the manner in which some mode of conduct, if allowed to be practiced, would affect themselves. But the opinion of a similar majority, imposed as a law on the minority, on questions of self-regarding conduct, is quite as likely to be wrong as right; for in these cases public opinion means, at the best, some people's opinion of what is good or bad for other people; while very often it does not even mean that; the public, with the most perfect indifference, passing over the pleasure or convenience of those whose conduct they censure, and considering only their own preference. There are many who consider as an injury to themselves any conduct which they have a distaste for, and resent it as an outrage to their feelings; as a religious bigot, when charged with disregarding the religious feelings of others, has been known to retort that they disregard his feelings, by persisting in their abominable worship or creed. But there is no parity between the feeling of a person for his own opinion, and the feeling of another who is offended at his holding it; no more than between the desire of a thief to take a purse, and the desire of the right owner to keep it. And a person's taste is as much his own peculiar concern as his opinion or his purse. It is easy for anyone to imagine an ideal public, which leaves the freedom and choice of individuals in all uncertain matters undisturbed, and only requires them to abstain from modes of conduct which universal experience has condemned. But where has there been seen a public which set any such limit to its censorship? Or when does the public trouble itself about universal experience. In its interferences with personal conduct it is seldom thinking of anything but the enormity of acting or feeling differently from itself; and this standard of judgment, thinly disguised, is held up to mankind as the dictate of religion and philosophy, by nine tenths of all moralists and speculative writers. These teach that things are right because they are right; because we feel them to be so. They tell us to search in our own minds and hearts for laws of conduct binding on ourselves and on all others. What can the poor public do but apply these instructions, and make their own personal feelings of good and evil, if they are tolerably unanimous in them, obligatory on all the world?

The evil here pointed out is not one which exists only in theory; and it may perhaps be expected that I should specify the instances in which the public of this age and country improperly invests its own preferences with the character of moral laws. I am not writing an essay on the aberrations of existing moral feeling. That is too weighty a subject to be discussed parenthetically, and by way of illustration. Yet examples are necessary, to show that the principle I maintain is of serious and practical moment, and that I am not endeavoring to erect a barrier against imaginary evils. And it is not difficult to show, by abundant instances, that to extend the bounds of what may be called moral police, until it encroaches on the most unquestionably legitimate liberty of the individual, is one of the most universal of all human propensities.

As a first instance, consider the antipathies which men cherish on no better grounds than that persons whose religious opinions are different from theirs, do not practice their religious observances, especially their religious abstinences. . . .

To come somewhat nearer home: the majority of Spaniards consider it a gross impiety, offensive in the highest degree to the Supreme Being, to worship him in any other manner than the Roman Catholic; and no other public worship is lawful on Spanish soil. The people of all Southern Europe look upon a married clergy as not only irreligious, but unchaste, indecent, gross, disgusting. What do Protestants think of these perfectly sincere feelings, and of the attempt to enforce them against non-Catholics? Yet, if mankind are justified in interfering with each other's liberty in things which do not concern the interests of others, on what principle is it possible consistently to exclude these cases? Or who can blame people for desiring to suppress what they regard as a scandal in the sight of God and man?

No stronger case can be shown for prohibiting anything which is regarded as a personal immorality, than is made out for suppressing these practices in the eyes of those who regard them as impieties; and unless we are willing to adopt the logic of persecutors, and to say that we may persecute others because we are right, and that they must not persecute us because they are wrong, we must beware of admitting a principle of which we should resent as a gross injustice the application to ourselves.

The preceding instances may be objected to, although unreasonably, as drawn from contingencies impossible among us: opinion, in this country, not being likely to enforce abstinence from meats, or to interfere with people for worshipping, and for either marrying or not marrying, according to their creed or inclination. The next example, however, shall be taken from an interference with liberty which we have by no means passed all danger of. Wherever the Puritans have been sufficiently powerful, as in New England, and in Great Britain at the time of the Commonwealth, they have endeavored, with considerable success, to put down all public, and nearly all private, amusements: especially music, dancing, public games, or other assemblages for purposes of diversion, and the theatre. There are still in this country large bodies of persons by whose notions of morality and religion these recreations are condemned; and those persons belonging chiefly to the middle class, who are the ascendant power in the present social and political condition of the kingdom, it is by no means impossible that persons of these sentiments may at some time or other command a majority in Parliament. How will the remaining portion of the community like to have the amusements that shall be permitted to them regulated by the religious and moral sentiments of the stricter Calvinists and Methodists? Would they not, with considerable peremptoriness, desire these intrusively pious members of society to mind their own business? This is precisely what should be said to every government and every public, who have the pretension that no person shall enjoy any pleasure which they think wrong. But if the principle of the pretension be admitted, no one can reasonably object to its being acted on in the sense of the majority, or other preponderating power in the country; and all persons must be ready to conform to the idea of a Christian commonwealth, as understood by the early settlers in New England, if a religious profession similar to theirs should ever succeed in regaining its lost ground, as religions supposed to be declining have so often been known to do.

To imagine another contingency, perhaps more likely to be realized than the one last mentioned. There is confessedly a strong tendency in the modern world towards a democratic constitution of society, accompanied or not by popular political institutions. It is affirmed that in the country where this tendency is most completely realized—where both society and the government are most democratic—the United States—the feeling of the majority, to whom any appearance of a more showy or costly style of living than they can hope to rival is disagreeable, operates as a tolerably effectual sumptuary law, and that in many parts of the Union it is really difficult for a person possessing a very large income, to find any mode of spending it, which will not incur popular disapprobation. Though such statements as these are doubtless much exaggerated as a representation of existing facts, the state of things they describe is not only a conceivable and possible, but a probable result of democratic feeling, combined with the notion that the public has a right to a veto on the manner in which individuals shall spend their incomes. We have only further to suppose a considerable diffusion of Socialist opinions, and it may become infamous in the eyes of the majority to possess more property than some very small amount, or any income not earned by manual labor. Opinions similar in principle to these, already prevail widely among the artisan class, and weigh oppressively on those who are amenable to the opinion chiefly of that class, namely, its own members. It is known that the bad workmen who form the majority of the operatives in many branches of industry, are decidedly of opinion that bad workmen ought to receive the same wages as good, and that no one ought to be allowed, through piecework or otherwise, to earn by superior skill or industry more than others can without it. And they employ a moral police, which occasionally becomes a physical one, to deter skilful workmen from receiving, and employers from giving, a larger remuneration for a more useful service. If the public have any jurisdiction over private concerns, I cannot see that these people are in fault, or that any individual's particular public can be blamed for asserting the same authority over his individual conduct, which the general public asserts over people in general.

But, without dwelling upon supposititious cases, there are, in our own day, gross usurpations upon the liberty of private life actually practiced, and still greater ones threatened with some expectation of success, and opinions proposed which assert an unlimited right in the public not only to prohibit by law everything which it thinks wrong, but in order to get at what it thinks wrong, to prohibit any number of things which it admits to be innocent.

Under the name of preventing intemperance the people of one English colony, and of nearly half the United States, have been interdicted by law from making any use whatever of fermented drinks, except for medical purposes: for prohibition of their sale is in fact, as it is intended to be, prohibition of their use. And though the impracticability of executing the law has caused its repeal in several of the States which had adopted it, including the one from which it derives its name, an attempt has notwithstanding been commenced, and is prosecuted with considerable zeal by many of the professed philanthropists, to agitate for a similar law in this country. The association, or "Alliance" as it terms itself, which has been formed for this purpose, has acquired some notoriety through the publicity given to a correspondence between its Secretary and one of the very few English public men who hold that a politician's opinions ought to be founded on principles. Lord Stanley's share in this correspondence is calculated to strengthen the hopes already built on him, by those who know how rare such qualities as are manifested in some of his public appearances, unhappily are among those who figure in political life. The organ of the Alliance, who would "deeply deplore the recognition of any principle which could be wrested to justify bigotry and persecution," undertakes to point out the "broad and impassable barrier" which divides such principles from those of the association. "All matters relating to thought, opinion, conscience, appear to me," he says, "to be without the sphere of legislation; all pertaining to social act, habit, relation, subject only to a discretionary power vested in the State itself, and not in the individual, to be within it." No mention is made of a third class, different from either of these, viz., acts and habits which are not social, but individual; although it is to this class, surely, that the act of drinking fermented liquors belongs. Selling fermented liquors, however, is trading, and trading is a social act. But the infringement complained of is not on the liberty of the seller, but on that of the buyer and consumer; since the State might just as well forbid him to drink wine, as purposely make it impossible for him to obtain it. The Secretary, however, says, "I claim, as a citizen, a right to legislate whenever my social rights are invaded by the social act of another." And now for the definition of these "social rights." "If anything invades my social rights, certainly the traffic in strong drink does. It destroys my primary right of security, by constantly creating and stimulating social disorder. It invades my right of equality, by deriving a profit from the creation of a misery, I am taxed to support. It impedes my right to free moral and intellectual development, by surrounding my path with dangers, and by weakening and demoralizing society, from which I have a right to claim mutual aid and intercourse." A theory of "social rights," the like of which probably never before found its way into distinct language—being nothing short of this—that it is the absolute social right of every individual, that every other individual shall act in every respect exactly as he ought; that whosoever fails thereof in the smallest particular, violates my social right, and entitles me to demand from the legislature the removal of the grievance. So monstrous a principle is far more dangerous than any single interference with liberty; there is no violation of liberty which it would not justify; it acknowledges no right to any freedom whatever, except perhaps to that of holding opinions in secret, without ever disclosing them; for the moment an opinion which I consider noxious, passes any one's lips, it invades all the "social rights" attributed to me by the Alliance. The doctrine ascribes to all mankind a vested interest in each other's moral, intellectual, and even physical perfection, to be defined by each claimant according to his own standard.

Another important example of illegitimate interference with the rightful liberty of the individual, not simply threatened, but long since carried into triumphant effect, is Sabbatarian legislation. Without doubt, abstinence on one day in the week, so far as the exigencies of life permit, from the usual daily occupation, though in no respect religiously binding on any except Jews, is a highly beneficial custom. And inasmuch as this custom cannot be observed without a general consent to that effect among the industrious classes, therefore, in so far as some persons by working may impose the same necessity on others, it may be allowable and right that the law should guarantee to each, the observance by others of the custom, by suspending the greater operations of industry on a particular day. But this justification, grounded on the direct interest which others have in each individual's observance of the practice, does not apply to the self-chosen occupations in which a person may think fit to employ his leisure; nor does it hold good, in the smallest degree, for legal restrictions on amusements. It is true that the amusement of some is the day's work of others; but the pleasure, not to say the useful recreation, of many, is worth the labor of a few, provided the occupation is freely chosen, and can be freely resigned. The operatives are perfectly right in thinking that if all worked on Sunday, seven days' work would have to be given for six days' wages: but so long as the great mass of employments are suspended, the small number who for the enjoyment of others must still work, obtain a proportional increase of earnings; and they are not obliged to follow those occupations, if they prefer leisure to emolument. If a further remedy is sought, it might be found in the establishment by custom of a holiday on some other day of the week for those particular classes of persons. The only ground, therefore, on which restrictions on Sunday amusements can be defended, must be that they are religiously wrong; a motive of legislation which never can be too earnestly protested against. "*Deorum injuriae Diis curae*." It remains to be proved that society or any of its officers holds a commission from on high to avenge any supposed offence to Omnipotence, which is not also a wrong to our fellow-creatures. The notion that it is one man's duty that another should be religious, was the foundation of all the religious persecutions ever perpetrated, and if admitted, would fully justify them. Though the feeling which breaks out in the repeated attempts to stop railway travelling on Sunday, in the resistance to the opening of Museums, and the like, has not the cruelty of the old persecutors, the state of mind indicated by it is fundamentally the same. It is a determination not to tolerate others in doing what is permitted by their religion, because it is not permitted by the persecutor's religion. It is a belief that God not only abominates the act of the misbeliever, but will not hold us guiltless if we leave him unmolested. . . .

CHAPTER V: APPLICATIONS

The principles asserted in these pages must be more generally admitted as the basis for discussion of details, before a consistent application of them to all the various departments of government and morals can be attempted with any prospect of advantage. The few observations I propose to make on questions of detail, are designed to illustrate the principles, rather than to follow them out to their consequences. I offer, not so much applications, as specimens of application; which may serve to bring into greater clearness the meaning and limits of the two maxims which together form the entire doctrine of this Essay and to assist the judgment in holding the balance between them, in the cases where it appears doubtful which of them is applicable to the case.

The maxims are, first, that the individual is not accountable to society for his actions, in so far as these concern the interests of no person but himself. Advice, instruction, persuasion, and avoidance by other people, if thought necessary by them for their own good, are the only measures by which society can justifiably express its dislike or disapprobation of his conduct. Secondly, that for such actions as are prejudicial to the interests of others, the individual is accountable, and may be subjected either to social or to legal punishments, if society is of opinion that the one or the other is requisite for its protection.

In the first place, it must by no means be supposed, because damage, or probability of damage, to the interests of others, can alone justify the interference of society, that therefore it always does justify such interference. In many cases, an individual, in pursuing a legitimate object, necessarily and therefore legitimately causes pain or loss to others, or intercepts a good which they had a reasonable hope of obtaining. Such oppositions of interest between individuals often arise from bad social institutions, but are unavoidable while those institutions last; and some would be unavoidable under any institutions. Whoever succeeds in an overcrowded profession, or in a competitive examination; whoever is preferred to another in any contest for an object which both desire, reaps benefit from the loss of others, from their wasted exertion and their disappointment. But it is, by common admission, better for the general interest of mankind, that persons should pursue their objects undeterred by this sort of consequences. In other words, society admits no right, either legal or moral, in the disappointed competitors, to immunity from this kind of suffering; and feels called on to interfere, only when means of success have been employed which it is contrary to the general interest to permit—namely, fraud or treachery, and force.

Again, trade is a social act. Whoever undertakes to sell any description of goods to the public, does what affects the interest of other persons, and of society in general; and thus his conduct, in principle, comes within the jurisdiction of society: accordingly, it was once held to be the duty of governments, in all cases which were considered of importance, to fix prices, and regulate the processes of manufacture. But it is now recognized, though not till after a long struggle, that both the cheapness and the good quality of commodities are most effectually provided for by leaving the producers and sellers perfectly free, under the sole check of equal freedom to the buyers for supplying themselves elsewhere. This is the so-called doctrine of Free Trade, which rests on grounds different from, though equally solid with, the principle of individual liberty asserted in this essay. Restrictions on trade, or on production for purposes of trade, are indeed restraints; and all restraint, qua restraint, is an evil: but the restraints in question affect only that part of conduct which society is competent to restrain, and are wrong solely because they do not really produce the results which it is desired to produce by them. As the principle of individual liberty is not involved in the doctrine of Free Trade so neither is it in most of the questions which arise respecting the limits of that doctrine: as for example, what amount of public control is admissible for the prevention of fraud by adulteration; how far sanitary precautions, or arrangements to protect work-people employed in dangerous occupations, should be enforced on employers. Such questions involve considerations of liberty, only in so far as leaving people to themselves is always better, *caeteris paribus* [i.e., all things being equal], than controlling them: but that they may be legitimately controlled for these ends, is in principle undeniable. On the other hand, there are questions relating to interference with trade which are essentially questions of liberty; such as the Maine Law, already touched upon; the prohibition of the importation of opium into China; the restriction of the sale of poisons; all cases, in short, where the object of the interference is to make it impossible or difficult to obtain a particular commodity. These interferences are objectionable, not as infringements on the liberty of the producer or seller, but on that of the buyer.

One of these examples, that of the sale of poisons, opens a new question; the proper limits of what may be called the functions of police; how far liberty may legitimately be invaded for the prevention of crime, or of accident. It is one of the undisputed functions of government to take precautions against crime before it has been committed, as well as to detect and punish it afterwards. The preventive function of government, however, is far more liable to be abused, to the prejudice of liberty, than the punitive function; for there is hardly any part of the legitimate freedom of action of a human being which would not admit of being represented, and fairly too, as increasing the facilities for some form or other of delinquency. Nevertheless, if a public authority, or even a private person, sees any one evidently preparing to commit a crime, they are not bound to look on inactive until the crime is committed, but may interfere to prevent it. If poisons were never bought or used for any purpose except the commission of murder, it would be right to prohibit their manufacture and sale. They may, however, be wanted not only for innocent but for useful purposes, and restrictions cannot be imposed in the one case without operating in the other. Again, it is a proper office of public authority to guard against accidents. If either a public officer or anyone else saw a person attempting to cross a bridge which had been ascertained to be unsafe, and there were no time to warn him of his danger, they might seize him and turn him back without any real infringement of his liberty; for liberty consists in doing what one desires, and he does not desire to fall into the river. Nevertheless, when there is not a certainty, but only a danger of mischief, no one but the person himself can judge of the sufficiency of the motive which may prompt him to incur the risk: in this case, therefore, (unless he is a child, or delirious, or in some state of excitement or absorption incompatible with the full use of the reflecting faculty,) he ought, I conceive, to be only warned of the danger; not forcibly prevented from exposing himself to it. Similar considerations, applied to such a question as the sale of poisons, may enable us to decide which among the possible modes of regulation are or are not contrary to principle. Such a precaution, for example, as that of labelling the drug with some word expressive of its dangerous character, may be enforced without violation of liberty: the buyer cannot wish not to know that the thing he possesses has poisonous qualities. But to require in all cases the certificate of a medical practitioner, would make it sometimes impossible, always expensive, to obtain the article for legitimate uses. The only mode apparent to me, in which difficulties may be thrown in the way of crime committed through this means, without any infringement, worth taking into account, upon the liberty of those who desire the poisonous substance for other purposes, consists in providing what, in the apt language of Bentham, is called "pre-appointed evidence." This provision is familiar to everyone in the case of contracts. It is usual and right that the law, when a contract is entered into, should require as the condition of its enforcing performance, that certain formalities should be observed, such as signatures, attestation of witnesses, and the like, in order that in case of subsequent dispute, there may be evidence to prove that the contract was really entered into, and that there was nothing in the circumstances to render it legally invalid: the effect being, to throw great obstacles in the way of fictitious contracts, or contracts made in circumstances which, if known, would destroy their validity. Precautions of a similar nature might be enforced in the sale of articles adapted to be instruments of crime. The seller, for example, might be required to enter in a register the exact time of the transaction, the name and address of the buyer, the precise quality and quantity sold; to ask the purpose for which it was wanted, and record the answer he received. When there was no medical prescription, the presence of some third person might be required, to bring home the fact to the purchaser, in case there should afterwards be reason to believe that the article had been applied to criminal purposes. Such regulations would in general be no material impediment to obtaining the article, but a very considerable one to making an improper use of it without detection.

The right inherent in society, to ward off crimes against itself by antecedent precautions, suggests the obvious limitations to the maxim, that purely self-regarding misconduct cannot properly be meddled with in the way of prevention or punishment. Drunkennesses, for example, in ordinary cases, is not a fit subject for legislative interference; but I should deem it perfectly legitimate that a person, who had once been convicted of any act of violence to others under the influence of drink, should be placed under a special legal restriction, personal to himself; that if he were afterwards found drunk, he should be liable to a penalty, and that if when in that state he committed another offence, the punishment to which he would be liable for that other offence should be increased in severity. The making himself drunk, in a person whom drunkenness excites to do harm to others, is a crime against others. So, again, idleness, except in a person receiving support from the public, or except when it constitutes a breach of contract, cannot without tyranny be made a subject of legal punishment; but if either from idleness or from any other avoidable cause, a man fails to perform his legal duties to others, as for instance to support his children, it is no tyranny to force him to fulfil that obligation, by compulsory labor, if no other means are available.

Again, there are many acts which, being directly injurious only to the agents themselves, ought not to be legally interdicted, but which, if done publicly, are a violation of good manners, and coming thus within the category of offences against others, may rightfully be prohibited. Of this kind are offences against decency; on which it is unnecessary to dwell, the rather as they are only connected indirectly with our subject, the objection to publicity being equally strong in the case of many actions not in themselves condemnable, nor supposed to be so.

There is another question to which an answer must be found, consistent with the principles which have been laid down. In cases of personal conduct supposed to be blameworthy, but which respect for liberty precludes society from preventing or punishing, because the evil directly resulting falls wholly on the agent; what the agent is free to do, ought other persons to be equally free to counsel or instigate? This question is not free from difficulty. The case of a person who solicits another to do an act, is not strictly a case of self-regarding conduct. To give advice or offer inducements to any one, is a social act, and may therefore, like actions in general which affect others, be supposed amenable to social control. But a little reflection corrects the first impression, by showing that if the case is not strictly within the definition of individual liberty, yet the reasons on which the principle of individual liberty is grounded, are applicable to it. If people must be allowed, in whatever concerns only themselves, to act as seems best to themselves at their own peril, they must equally be free to consult with one another about what is fit to be so done; to exchange opinions, and give and receive suggestions. Whatever it is permitted to do, it must be permitted to advise to do. The question is doubtful, only when the instigator derives a personal benefit from his advice; when he makes it his occupation, for subsistence, or pecuniary gain, to promote what society and the State consider to be an evil. Then, indeed, a new element of complication is introduced; namely, the existence of classes of persons with an interest opposed to what is considered as the public weal, and whose mode of living is grounded on the counteraction of it. Ought this to be interfered with, or not? Fornication, for example, must be tolerated, and so must gambling; but should a person be free to be a pimp, or to keep a gambling-house? The case is one of those which lie on the exact boundary line between two principles, and it is not at once apparent to which of the two it properly belongs. There are arguments on both sides. On the side of toleration it may be said, that the fact of following anything as an occupation, and living or profiting by the practice of it, cannot make that criminal which would otherwise be admissible; that the act should either be consistently permitted or consistently prohibited; that if the principles which we have hitherto defended are true, society has no business, as society, to decide anything to be wrong which concerns only the individual; that it cannot go beyond dissuasion, and that one person should be as free to persuade, as another to dissuade. In opposition to this it may be contended, that although the public, or the State, are not warranted in authoritatively deciding, for purposes of repression or punishment, that such or such conduct affecting only the interests of the individual is good or bad, they are fully justified in assuming, if they regard it as bad, that its being so or not is at least a disputable question: That, this being supposed, they cannot be acting wrongly in endeavoring to exclude the influence of solicitations which are not disinterested, of instigators who cannot possibly be impartial—who have a direct personal interest on one side, and that side the one which the State believes to be wrong, and who confessedly promote it for personal objects only. There can surely, it may be urged, be nothing lost, no sacrifice of good, by so ordering matters that persons shall make their election, either wisely or foolishly, on their own prompting, as free as possible from the arts of persons who stimulate their inclinations for interested purposes of their own. Thus (it may be said) though the statutes respecting unlawful games are utterly indefensible—though all persons should be free to gamble in their own or each other's houses, or in any place of meeting established by their own subscriptions, and open only to the members and their visitors—yet public gambling-houses should not be permitted. It is true that the prohibition is never effectual, and that whatever amount of tyrannical power is given to the police, gambling-houses can always be maintained under other pretenses; but they may be compelled to conduct their operations with a certain degree of secrecy and mystery, so that nobody knows anything about them but those who seek them; and more than this society ought not to aim at. There is considerable force in these arguments. I will not venture to decide whether they are sufficient to justify the moral anomaly of punishing the accessary, when the principal is (and must be) allowed to go free; of fining or imprisoning the procurer, but not the fornicator, the gambling-house keeper, but not the gambler. Still less ought the common operations of buying and selling to be interfered with on analogous grounds. Almost every article which is bought and sold may be used in excess, and the sellers have a pecuniary interest in encouraging that excess; but no argument can be founded on this, in favor, for instance, of the Maine Law; because the class of dealers in strong drinks, though interested in their abuse, are indispensably required for the sake of their legitimate use. The interest, however, of these dealers in promoting intemperance is a real evil, and justifies the State in imposing restrictions and requiring guarantees, which but for that justification would be infringements of legitimate liberty.

A further question is, whether the State while it permits, should nevertheless indirectly discourage conduct which it deems contrary to the best interests of the agent; whether, for example, it should take measures to render the means of drunkenness more costly, or add to the difficulty of procuring them, by limiting the number of the places of sale. On this as on most other practical questions, many distinctions require to be made. To tax stimulants for the sole purpose of making them more difficult to be obtained, is a measure differing only in degree from their entire prohibition; and would be justifiable only if that were justifiable. Every increase of cost is a prohibition, to those whose means do not come up to the augmented price; and to those who do, it is a penalty laid on them for gratifying a particular taste. Their choice of pleasures, and their mode of expending their income, after satisfying their legal and moral obligations to the State and to individuals, are their own concern, and must rest with their own judgment. These considerations may seem at first sight to condemn the selection of stimulants as special subjects of taxation for purposes of revenue. But it must be remembered that taxation for fiscal purposes is absolutely inevitable; that in most countries it is necessary that a considerable part of that taxation should be indirect; that the State, therefore, cannot help imposing penalties, which to some persons may be prohibitory, on the use of some articles of consumption. It is hence the duty of the State to consider, in the imposition of taxes, what commodities the consumers can best spare; and a fortiori, to select in preference those of which it deems the use, beyond a very moderate quantity, to be positively injurious. Taxation, therefore, of stimulants, up to the point which produces the largest amount of revenue (supposing that the State needs all the revenue which it yields) is not only admissible, but to be approved of.

The question of making the sale of these commodities a more or less exclusive privilege, must be answered differently, according to the purposes to which the restriction is intended to be subservient. All places of public resort require the restraint of a police, and places of this kind peculiarly, because offences against society are especially apt to originate there. It is, therefore, fit to confine the power of selling these commodities (at least for consumption on the spot) to persons of known or vouched-for respectability of conduct; to make such regulations respecting hours of opening and closing as may be requisite for public surveillance, and to withdraw the license if breaches of the peace repeatedly take place through the connivance or incapacity of the keeper of the house, or if it becomes a rendezvous for concocting and preparing offences against the law. Any further restriction I do not conceive to be, in principle, justifiable. The limitation in number, for instance, of beer and spirit-houses, for the express purpose of rendering them more difficult of access, and diminishing the occasions of temptation, not only exposes all to an inconvenience because there are some by whom the facility would be abused, but is suited only to a state of society in which the laboring classes are avowedly treated as children or savages, and placed under an education of restraint, to fit them for future admission to the privileges of freedom. This is not the principle on which the laboring classes are professedly governed in any free country; and no person who sets due value on freedom will give his adhesion to their being so governed, unless after all efforts have been exhausted to educate them for freedom and govern them as freemen, and it has been definitively proved that they can only be governed as children. The bare statement of the alternative shows the absurdity of supposing that such efforts have been made in any case which needs be considered here. It is only because the institutions of this country are a mass of inconsistencies, that things find admittance into our practice which belong to the system of despotic, or what is called paternal, government, while the general freedom of our institutions precludes the exercise of the amount of control necessary to render the restraint of any real efficacy as a moral education. . . .

[*On Liberty* (London: Parker, 1859).]

CHAPTER ELEVEN

Marx and Engels on Capitalism and Its Discontents

© Nicku/Shutterstock.com

Karl Marx (1818–1883)

© Georgios Kollidas/Shutterstock.com

Friedrich Engels (1820–1895)

SELECTED READINGS

▶ *Manifesto of the Communist Party*—Karl Marx and Friedrich Engels

Manifesto of the Communist Party

Karl Marx and Friedrich Engels

A specter is haunting Europe—the specter of Communism. All the Powers of old Europe have entered into a holy alliance to exorcise this specter: Pope and Czar, Metternich and Guizot, French Radicals and German police-spies.

Where is the party in opposition that has not been decried as Communistic by its opponents in power? Where is the Opposition that has not hurled back the branding reproach of Communism, against the more advanced opposition parties, as well as against its reactionary adversaries?

Two things result from this fact.

I. Communism is already acknowledged by all European Powers to be itself a Power.

II. It is high time that Communists should openly, in the face of the whole world, publish their views, their aims, their tendencies, and meet this nursery tale of the Specter of Communism with a Manifesto of the party itself.

To this end, Communists of various nationalities have assembled in London, and sketched the following Manifesto, to be published in the English, French, German, Italian, Flemish and Danish languages.

I. BOURGEOIS AND PROLETARIANS

The history of all hitherto existing societies is the history of class struggles.

Freeman and slave, patrician and plebeian, lord and serf, guild-master and journeyman, in a word, oppressor and oppressed, stood in constant opposition to one another, carried on an uninterrupted, now hidden, now open fight, a fight that each time ended, either in a revolutionary re-constitution of society at large, or in the common ruin of the contending classes.

In the earlier epochs of history, we find almost everywhere a complicated arrangement of society into various orders, a manifold gradation of social rank. In ancient Rome we have patricians, knights, plebeians, slaves; in the Middle Ages, feudal lords, vassals, guild-masters, journeymen, apprentices, serfs; in almost all of these classes, again, subordinate gradations.

The modern bourgeois society that has sprouted from the ruins of feudal society has not done away with class antagonisms. It has but established new classes, new conditions of oppression, new forms of struggle in place of the old ones. Our epoch, the epoch of the bourgeoisie, possesses, however, this distinctive feature: it has simplified the class antagonisms. Society as a whole is more and more splitting up into two great hostile camps, into two great classes, directly facing each other: Bourgeoisie and Proletariat.

From the serfs of the Middle Ages sprang the chartered burghers of the earliest towns. From these burgesses the first elements of the bourgeoisie were developed.

The discovery of America, the rounding of the Cape, opened up fresh ground for the rising bourgeoisie. The East-Indian and Chinese markets, the colonization of America, trade with the colonies, the increase in the means of exchange and in commodities generally, gave to commerce, to navigation, to industry, an impulse never before known, and thereby, to the revolutionary element in the tottering feudal society, a rapid development.

The feudal system of industry, under which industrial production was monopolized by closed guilds, now no longer sufficed for the growing wants of the new markets. The manufacturing system took its place. The guild-masters were pushed on one side by the manufacturing middle class; division of labor between the different corporate guilds vanished in the face of division of labor in each single workshop.

Meantime the markets kept ever growing, the demand ever rising. Even manufacture no longer sufficed. Thereupon, steam and machinery revolutionized industrial production. The place of manufacture was taken by the giant, Modern Industry, the place of the industrial middle class, by industrial millionaires, the leaders of whole industrial armies, the modern bourgeois.

Modern industry has established the world-market, for which the discovery of America paved the way. This market has given an immense development to commerce, to navigation, to communication by land. This development has, in its time, reacted on the extension of industry; and in proportion as industry, commerce, navigation, railways extended, in the same proportion the bourgeoisie developed, increased its capital, and pushed into the background every class handed down from the Middle Ages.

We see, therefore, how the modern bourgeoisie is itself the product of a long course of development, of a series of revolutions in the modes of production and of exchange.

Each step in the development of the bourgeoisie was accompanied by a corresponding political advance of that class. An oppressed class under the sway of the feudal nobility, an armed and self-governing association in the mediaeval commune; here independent urban republic (as in Italy and Germany), there taxable "third estate" of the monarchy (as in France), afterwards, in the period of manufacture proper, serving either the semi-feudal or the absolute monarchy as a counterpoise against the nobility, and, in fact, cornerstone of the great monarchies in general, the bourgeoisie has at last, since the establishment of Modern Industry and of the world-market, conquered for itself, in the modern representative State, exclusive political sway. The executive of the modern State is but a committee for managing the common affairs of the whole bourgeoisie.

The bourgeoisie, historically, has played a most revolutionary part.

The bourgeoisie, wherever it has got the upper hand, has put an end to all feudal, patriarchal, idyllic relations. It has pitilessly torn asunder the motley feudal ties that bound man to his "natural superiors," and has left remaining no other nexus between man and man than naked self-interest, than callous "cash payment." It has drowned the most heavenly ecstasies of religious fervor, of chivalrous enthusiasm, of philistine sentimentalism, in the icy water of egotistical calculation. It has resolved personal worth into exchange value, and in place of the numberless and indefeasible chartered freedoms, has set up that single, unconscionable freedom—Free Trade. In one word, for exploitation, veiled by religious and political illusions, naked, shameless, direct, brutal exploitation.

The bourgeoisie has stripped of its halo every occupation hitherto honored and looked up to with reverent awe. It has converted the physician, the lawyer, the priest, the poet, the man of science, into its paid wage laborers.

The bourgeoisie has torn away from the family its sentimental veil, and has reduced the family relation to a mere money relation.

The bourgeoisie has disclosed how it came to pass that the brutal display of vigor in the Middle Ages, which Reactionists so much admire, found its fitting complement in the most slothful indolence. It has been the first to show what man's activity can bring about. It has accomplished wonders far surpassing Egyptian pyramids, Roman aqueducts, and Gothic cathedrals; it has conducted expeditions that put in the shade all former Exoduses of nations and crusades.

The bourgeoisie cannot exist without constantly revolutionizing the instruments of production, and thereby the relations of production, and with them the whole relations of society. Conservation of the old modes of production in unaltered form, was, on the contrary, the first condition of existence for all earlier industrial classes. Constant revolutionizing of production, uninterrupted disturbance of all social conditions, everlasting uncertainty and agitation distinguish the bourgeois epoch from all earlier ones. All fixed, fast-frozen relations, with their train of ancient and venerable prejudices and opinions, are swept away, all new-formed ones become antiquated before they can ossify. All that is solid melts into air, all that is holy is profaned, and man is at last compelled to face with sober senses, his real conditions of life, and his relations with his kind.

The need of a constantly expanding market for its products chases the bourgeoisie over the whole surface of the globe. It must nestle everywhere, settle everywhere, establish connections everywhere.

The bourgeoisie has through its exploitation of the world-market given a cosmopolitan character to production and consumption in every country. To the great chagrin of Reactionists, it has drawn from under the feet of industry the national ground on which it stood. All old-established national industries have been destroyed or are daily being destroyed. They are dislodged by new industries, whose introduction becomes a life and death question for all civilized nations, by industries that no longer work up indigenous raw material, but raw material drawn from the remotest zones; industries whose products are consumed, not only at home, but in every quarter of the globe. In place of the old wants, satisfied by the productions of the country, we find new wants, requiring for their satisfaction the products of distant lands and climes. In place of the old local and national seclusion and self-sufficiency, we have intercourse in every direction, universal interdependence of nations. And as in material, so also in intellectual production. The intellectual creations of individual nations become common property. National one-sidedness and narrow-mindedness become more and more impossible, and from the numerous national and local literatures, there arises a world literature.

The bourgeoisie, by the rapid improvement of all instruments of production, by the immensely facilitated means of communication, draws all, even the most barbarian, nations into civilization. The cheap prices of its commodities are the heavy artillery with which it batters down all Chinese walls, with which it forces the barbarians' intensely obstinate hatred of foreigners to capitulate. It compels all nations, on pain of extinction, to adopt the bourgeois mode of production; it compels them to introduce what it calls civilization into their midst, i.e., to become bourgeois themselves. In one word, it creates a world after its own image.

The bourgeoisie has subjected the country to the rule of the towns. It has created enormous cities, has greatly increased the urban population as compared with the rural, and has thus rescued a considerable part of the population from the idiocy of rural life. Just as it has made the country dependent on the towns, so it has made barbarian and semi-barbarian countries dependent on the civilized ones, nations of peasants on nations of bourgeois, the East on the West.

The bourgeoisie keeps more and more doing away with the scattered state of the population, of the means of production, and of property. It has agglomerated production, and has concentrated property in a few hands. The necessary consequence of this was political centralization. Independent, or but loosely connected provinces, with separate interests, laws, governments and systems of taxation, became lumped together into one nation, with one government, one code of laws, one national class-interest, one frontier and one customs-tariff. The bourgeoisie, during its rule of scarce one hundred years, has created more massive and more colossal productive forces than have all preceding generations together. Subjection of Nature's forces to man, machinery, application of chemistry to industry and agriculture, steam-navigation, railways, electric telegraphs, clearing of whole continents for cultivation, canalization of rivers, whole populations conjured out of the ground—what earlier century had even a presentiment that such productive forces slumbered in the lap of social labor?

We see then: the means of production and of exchange, on whose foundation the bourgeoisie built itself up, were generated in feudal society. At a certain stage in the development of these means of production and of exchange, the conditions under which feudal society produced and exchanged, the feudal organization of agriculture and manufacturing industry, in one word, the feudal relations of property became no longer compatible with the already developed productive forces; they became so many fetters. They had to be burst asunder; they were burst asunder.

Into their place stepped free competition, accompanied by a social and political constitution adapted to it, and by the economical and political sway of the bourgeois class.

A similar movement is going on before our own eyes. Modern bourgeois society with its relations of production, of exchange and of property, a society that has conjured up such gigantic means of production and of exchange, is like the sorcerer, who is no longer able to control the powers of the nether world whom he has called up by his spells. For many a decade past the history of industry and commerce is but the history of the revolt of modern productive forces against modern conditions of production, against the property relations that are the conditions for the existence of the bourgeoisie and of its rule. It is enough to mention the commercial crises that by their periodical return put on its trial, each time more threateningly, the existence of the entire bourgeois society. In these crises a great part not only of the existing products, but also of the previously created productive forces, are periodically destroyed. In these crises there breaks out an epidemic that, in all earlier epochs, would have seemed an absurdity—the epidemic of over-production. Society suddenly finds itself put back into a state of momentary barbarism; it appears as if a famine, a universal war of devastation had cut off the supply of every means of subsistence; industry and commerce seem to be destroyed; and why? Because there is too much civilization, too much means of subsistence, too much industry, too much commerce. The productive forces at the disposal of society no longer tend to further the development of the conditions of bourgeois property; on the contrary, they have become too powerful for these conditions, by which they are fettered, and so soon as they overcome these fetters, they bring disorder into the whole of bourgeois society, endanger the existence of bourgeois property. The conditions of bourgeois society are too narrow to comprise the wealth created by them. And how does the bourgeoisie get over these crises? On the one hand enforced destruction of a mass of productive forces; on the other, by the conquest of new markets, and by the more thorough exploitation of the old ones. That is to say, by paving the way for more extensive and more destructive crises, and by diminishing the means whereby crises are prevented.

The weapons with which the bourgeoisie felled feudalism to the ground are now turned against the bourgeoisie itself.

But not only has the bourgeoisie forged the weapons that bring death to itself; it has also called into existence the men who are to wield those weapons—the modern working class—the proletarians.

In proportion as the bourgeoisie, i.e., capital, is developed, in the same proportion is the proletariat, the modern working class, developed—a class of laborers, who live only so long as they find work, and who find work only so long as their labor increases capital. These laborers, who must sell themselves piece-meal, are a commodity, like every other article of commerce, and are consequently exposed to all the vicissitudes of competition, to all the fluctuations of the market.

Owing to the extensive use of machinery and to division of labor, the work of the proletarians has lost all individual character, and consequently, all charm for the workman. He becomes an appendage of the machine, and it is only the most simple, most monotonous, and most easily acquired knack, that is required of him. Hence, the cost of production of a workman is restricted, almost entirely, to the means of subsistence that he requires for his maintenance, and for the propagation of his race. But the price of a commodity, and therefore also of labor, is equal to its cost of production. In proportion therefore, as the repulsiveness of the work increases, the wage decreases. Nay more, in proportion as the use of machinery and division of labor increases, in the same proportion the burden of toil also increases, whether by prolongation of the working hours, by increase of the work exacted in a given time or by increased speed of the machinery, etc.

Modern industry has converted the little workshop of the patriarchal master into the great factory of the industrial capitalist. Masses of laborers, crowded into the factory, are organised like soldiers. As privates of the industrial army they are placed under the command of a perfect hierarchy of officers and sergeants. Not only are they slaves of the bourgeois class, and of the bourgeois State; they are daily and hourly enslaved by the machine, by the over-looker, and, above all, by the individual bourgeois manufacturer himself. The more openly this despotism proclaims gain to be its end and aim, the more petty, the more hateful and the more embittering it is.

The less the skill and exertion of strength implied in manual labor, in other words, the more modern industry becomes developed, the more is the labor of men superseded by that of women. Differences of age and sex have no longer any distinctive social validity for the working class. All are instruments of labor, more or less expensive to use, according to their age and sex.

No sooner is the exploitation of the laborer by the manufacturer, so far at an end, that he receives his wages in cash, than he is set upon by the other portions of the bourgeoisie, the landlord, the shopkeeper, the pawnbroker, etc.

The lower strata of the middle class—the small tradespeople, shopkeepers, retired tradesmen generally, the handicraftsmen and peasants—all these sink gradually into the proletariat, partly because their diminutive capital does not suffice for the scale on which Modern Industry is carried on, and is swamped in the competition with the large capitalists, partly because their specialized skill is rendered worthless by the new methods of production. Thus the proletariat is recruited from all classes of the population.

The proletariat goes through various stages of development. With its birth begins its struggle with the bourgeoisie. At first the contest is carried on by individual laborers, then by the workpeople of a factory, then by the operatives of one trade, in one locality, against the individual bourgeois who directly exploits them. They direct their attacks not against the bourgeois conditions of production, but against the instruments of production themselves; they destroy imported wares that compete with their labor, they smash to pieces machinery, they set factories ablaze, they seek to restore by force the vanished status of the workman of the Middle Ages.

At this stage the laborers still form an incoherent mass scattered over the whole country, and broken up by their mutual competition. If anywhere they unite to form more compact bodies, this is not yet the consequence of their own active union, but of the union of the bourgeoisie, which class, in order to attain its own political ends, is compelled to set the whole proletariat in motion, and is moreover yet, for a time, able to do so. At this stage, therefore, the proletarians do not fight their enemies, but the enemies of their enemies, the remnants of absolute monarchy, the landowners, the non-industrial bourgeois, the petty bourgeoisie. Thus the whole historical movement is concentrated in the hands of the bourgeoisie; every victory so obtained is a victory for the bourgeoisie.

But with the development of industry the proletariat not only increases in number; it becomes concentrated in greater masses, its strength grows, and it feels that strength more. The various interests and conditions of life within the ranks of the proletariat are more and more equalized, in proportion as machinery obliterates all distinctions of labor, and nearly everywhere reduces wages to the same low level. The growing competition among the bourgeois, and the resulting commercial crises, make the wages of the workers ever more fluctuating. The unceasing improvement of machinery, ever more rapidly developing, makes their livelihood more and more precarious; the collisions between individual workmen and individual bourgeois take more and more the character of collisions between two classes. Thereupon the workers begin to form combinations (Trades Unions) against the bourgeois; they club together in order to keep up the rate of wages; they found permanent associations in order to make provision beforehand for these occasional revolts. Here and there the contest breaks out into riots.

Now and then the workers are victorious, but only for a time. The real fruit of their battles lies, not in the immediate result, but in the ever-expanding union of the workers. This union is helped on by the improved means of communication that are created by modern industry and that place the workers of different localities in contact with one another. It was just this contact that was needed to centralize the numerous local struggles, all of the same character, into one national struggle between classes. But every class struggle is a political struggle. And that union, to attain which the burghers of the Middle Ages, with their miserable highways, required centuries, the modern proletarians, thanks to railways, achieve in a few years.

This organization of the proletarians into a class, and consequently into a political party, is continually being upset again by the competition between the workers themselves. But it ever rises up again, stronger, firmer, mightier. It compels legislative recognition of particular interests of the workers, by taking advantage of the divisions among the bourgeoisie itself. Thus the ten-hours' bill in England was carried.

Altogether collisions between the classes of the old society further, in many ways, the course of development of the proletariat. The bourgeoisie finds itself involved in a constant battle. At first with the aristocracy; later on, with those portions of the bourgeoisie itself, whose interests have become antagonistic to the progress of industry; at all times, with the bourgeoisie of foreign countries. In all these battles it sees itself compelled to appeal to the proletariat, to ask for its help, and thus, to drag it into the political arena. The bourgeoisie itself, therefore, supplies the proletariat with its own instruments of political and general education, in other words, it furnishes the proletariat with weapons for fighting the bourgeoisie.

Further, as we have already seen, entire sections of the ruling classes are, by the advance of industry, precipitated into the proletariat, or are at least threatened in their conditions of existence. These also supply the proletariat with fresh elements of enlightenment and progress.

Finally, in times when the class struggle nears the decisive hour, the process of dissolution going on within the ruling class, in fact within the whole range of society, assumes such a violent, glaring character, that a small section of the ruling class cuts itself adrift, and joins the revolutionary class, the class that holds the future in its hands. Just as, therefore, at an earlier period, a section of the nobility went over to the bourgeoisie, so now a portion of the bourgeoisie goes over to the proletariat, and in particular, a portion of the bourgeois ideologists, who have raised themselves to the level of comprehending theoretically the historical movement as a whole.

Of all the classes that stand face to face with the bourgeoisie today, the proletariat alone is a really revolutionary class. The other classes decay and finally disappear in the face of Modern Industry; the proletariat is its special and essential product. The lower middle class, the small manufacturer, the shopkeeper, the artisan, the peasant, all these fight against the bourgeoisie, to save from extinction their existence as fractions of the middle class. They are therefore not revolutionary, but conservative. Nay more, they are reactionary, for they try to roll back the wheel of history. If by chance they are revolutionary, they are so only in view of their impending transfer into the proletariat, they thus defend not their present, but their future interests, they desert their own standpoint to place themselves at that of the proletariat.

The "dangerous class," the social scum, that passively rotting mass thrown off by the lowest layers of old society, may, here and there, be swept into the movement by a proletarian revolution; its conditions of life, however, prepare it far more for the part of a bribed tool of reactionary intrigue.

In the conditions of the proletariat, those of old society at large are already virtually swamped. The proletarian is without property; his relation to his wife and children has no longer anything in common with the bourgeois family-relations; modern industrial labor, modern subjection to capital, the same in England as in France, in America as in Germany, has stripped him of every trace of national character. Law, morality, religion, are to him so many bourgeois prejudices, behind which lurk in ambush just as many bourgeois interests.

All the preceding classes that got the upper hand, sought to fortify their already acquired status by subjecting society at large to their conditions of appropriation. The proletarians cannot become masters of the productive forces of society, except by abolishing their own previous mode of appropriation, and thereby also every other previous mode of appropriation. They have nothing of their own to secure and to fortify; their mission is to destroy all previous securities for, and insurances of, individual property.

All previous historical movements were movements of minorities, or in the interests of minorities. The proletarian movement is the self-conscious, independent movement of the immense majority, in the interests of the immense majority. The proletariat, the lowest stratum of our present society, cannot stir, cannot raise itself up, without the whole superincumbent strata of official society being sprung into the air.

Though not in substance, yet in form, the struggle of the proletariat with the bourgeoisie is at first a national struggle. The proletariat of each country must, of course, first of all settle matters with its own bourgeoisie.

In depicting the most general phases of the development of the proletariat, we traced the more or less veiled civil war, raging within existing society, up to the point where that war breaks out into open revolution, and where the violent overthrow of the bourgeoisie lays the foundation for the sway of the proletariat.

Hitherto, every form of society has been based, as we have already seen, on the antagonism of oppressing and oppressed classes. But in order to oppress a class, certain conditions must be assured to it under which it can, at least, continue its slavish existence. The serf, in the period of serfdom, raised himself to membership in the commune, just as the petty bourgeois, under the yoke of feudal absolutism, managed to develop into a bourgeois. The modern laborer, on the contrary, instead of rising with the progress of industry, sinks deeper and deeper below the conditions of existence of his own class. He becomes a pauper, and pauperism develops more rapidly than population and wealth. And here it becomes evident, that the bourgeoisie is unfit any longer to be the ruling class in society, and to impose its conditions of existence upon society as an over-riding law. It is unfit to rule because it is incompetent to assure an existence to its slave within his slavery, because it cannot help letting him sink into such a state, that it has to feed him, instead of being fed by him. Society can no longer live under this bourgeoisie, in other words, its existence is no longer compatible with society.

The essential condition for the existence, and for the sway of the bourgeois class, is the formation and augmentation of capital; the condition for capital is wage-labor. Wage-labor rests exclusively on competition between the laborers. The advance of industry, whose involuntary promoter is the bourgeoisie, replaces the isolation of the laborers, due to competition, by their revolutionary combination, due to association. The development of Modern Industry, therefore, cuts from under its feet the very foundation on which the bourgeoisie produces and appropriates products. What the bourgeoisie, therefore, produces, above all, is its own grave-diggers. Its fall and the victory of the proletariat are equally inevitable.

II. PROLETARIANS AND COMMUNISTS

In what relation do the Communists stand to the proletarians as a whole?

The Communists do not form a separate party opposed to other working-class parties.

They have no interests separate and apart from those of the proletariat as a whole.

They do not set up any sectarian principles of their own, by which to shape and mold the proletarian movement.

The Communists are distinguished from the other working-class parties by this only: (1) In the national struggles of the proletarians of the different countries, they point out and bring to the front the common interests of the entire proletariat, independently of all nationality. (2) In the various stages of development which the struggle of the working class against the bourgeoisie has to pass through, they always and everywhere represent the interests of the movement as a whole.

The Communists, therefore, are on the one hand, practically, the most advanced and resolute section of the working-class parties of every country, that section which pushes forward all others; on the other hand, theoretically, they have over the great mass of the proletariat the advantage of clearly understanding the line of march, the conditions, and the ultimate general results of the proletarian movement.

The immediate aim of the Communist is the same as that of all the other proletarian parties: formation of the proletariat into a class, overthrow of the bourgeois supremacy, conquest of political power by the proletariat.

The theoretical conclusions of the Communists are in no way based on ideas or principles that have been invented, or discovered, by this or that would-be universal reformer. They merely express, in general terms, actual relations springing from an existing class struggle, from a historical movement going on under our very eyes. The abolition of existing property relations is not at all a distinctive feature of Communism.

All property relations in the past have continually been subject to historical change consequent upon the change in historical conditions.

The French Revolution, for example, abolished feudal property in favor of bourgeois property.

The distinguishing feature of Communism is not the abolition of property generally, but the abolition of bourgeois property. But modern bourgeois private property is the final and most complete expression of the system of producing and appropriating products, that is based on class antagonisms, on the exploitation of the many by the few.

In this sense, the theory of the Communists may be summed up in the single sentence: Abolition of private property.

We Communists have been reproached with the desire of abolishing the right of personally acquiring property as the fruit of a man's own labor, which property is alleged to be the groundwork of all personal freedom, activity and independence.

Hard-won, self-acquired, self-earned property! Do you mean the property of the petty artisan and of the small peasant, a form of property that preceded the bourgeois form? There is no need to abolish that; the development of industry has to a great extent already destroyed it, and is still destroying it daily.

Or do you mean modern bourgeois private property?

But does wage-labor create any property for the laborer? Not a bit. It creates capital, i.e., that kind of property which exploits wage-labor, and which cannot increase except upon condition of begetting a new supply of wage-labor for fresh exploitation. Property, in its present form, is based on the antagonism of capital and wage-labor. Let us examine both sides of this antagonism.

To be a capitalist, is to have not only a purely personal, but a social status in production. Capital is a collective product, and only by the united action of many members, nay, in the last resort, only by the united action of all members of society, can it be set in motion.

Capital is, therefore, not a personal, it is a social power.

When, therefore, capital is converted into common property, into the property of all members of society, personal property is not thereby transformed into social property. It is only the social character of the property that is changed. It loses its class-character.

Let us now take wage-labor.

The average price of wage-labor is the minimum wage, i.e., that quantum of the means of subsistence, which is absolutely requisite in bare existence as a laborer. What, therefore, the wage-laborer appropriates by means of his labor, merely suffices to prolong and reproduce a bare existence. We by no means intend to abolish this personal appropriation of the products of labor, an appropriation that is made for the maintenance and reproduction of human life, and that leaves no surplus wherewith to command the labor of others. All that we want to do away with, is the miserable character of this appropriation, under which the laborer lives merely to increase capital, and is allowed to live only in so far as the interest of the ruling class requires it.

In bourgeois society, living labor is but a means to increase accumulated labor. In Communist society, accumulated labor is but a means to widen, to enrich, to promote the existence of the laborer.

In bourgeois society, therefore, the past dominates the present; in Communist society, the present dominates the past. In bourgeois society capital is independent and has individuality, while the living person is dependent and has no individuality.

And the abolition of this state of things is called by the bourgeois, abolition of individuality and freedom! And rightly so. The abolition of bourgeois individuality, bourgeois independence, and bourgeois freedom is undoubtedly aimed at.

By freedom is meant, under the present bourgeois conditions of production, free trade, free selling and buying.

But if selling and buying disappears, free selling and buying disappears also. This talk about free selling and buying, and all the other "brave words" of our bourgeoisie about freedom in general, have a meaning, if any, only in contrast with restricted selling and buying, with the fettered traders of the Middle Ages, but have no meaning when opposed to the Communistic abolition of buying and selling, of the bourgeois conditions of production, and of the bourgeoisie itself.

You are horrified at our intending to do away with private property. But in your existing society, private property is already done away with for nine-tenths of the population; its existence for the few is solely due to its non-existence in the hands of those nine-tenths. You reproach us, therefore, with intending to do away with a form of property, the necessary condition for whose existence is the non-existence of any property for the immense majority of society.

In one word, you reproach us with intending to do away with your property. Precisely so; that is just what we intend.

From the moment when labor can no longer be converted into capital, money, or rent, into a social power capable of being monopolized, i.e., from the moment when individual property can no longer be transformed into bourgeois property, into capital, from that moment, you say individuality vanishes.

You must, therefore, confess that by "individual" you mean no other person than the bourgeois, than the middle-class owner of property. This person must, indeed, be swept out of the way, and made impossible.

Communism deprives no man of the power to appropriate the products of society; all that it does is to deprive him of the power to subjugate the labor of others by means of such appropriation.

It has been objected that upon the abolition of private property all work will cease, and universal laziness will overtake us.

According to this, bourgeois society ought long ago to have gone to the dogs through sheer idleness; for those of its members who work, acquire nothing, and those who acquire anything, do not work. The whole of this objection is but another expression of the tautology: that there can no longer be any wage-labor when there is no longer any capital.

All objections urged against the Communistic mode of producing and appropriating material products, have, in the same way, been urged against the Communistic modes of producing and appropriating intellectual products. Just as, to the bourgeois, the disappearance of class property is the disappearance of production itself, so the disappearance of class culture is to him identical with the disappearance of all culture.

That culture, the loss of which he laments, is, for the enormous majority, a mere training to act as a machine.

But don't wrangle with us so long as you apply, to our intended abolition of bourgeois property, the standard of your bourgeois notions of freedom, culture, law, etc. Your very ideas are but the outgrowth of the conditions of your bourgeois production and bourgeois property, just as your jurisprudence is but the will of your class made into a law for all, a will, whose essential character and direction are determined by the economical conditions of existence of your class.

The selfish misconception that induces you to transform into eternal laws of nature and of reason, the social forms springing from your present mode of production and form of property—historical relations that rise and disappear in the progress of production—this misconception you share with every ruling class that has preceded you. What you see clearly in the case of ancient property, what you admit in the case of feudal property, you are of course forbidden to admit in the case of your own bourgeois form of property.

Abolition of the family! Even the most radical flare up at this infamous proposal of the Communists.

On what foundation is the present family, the bourgeois family, based? On capital, on private gain. In its completely developed form this family exists only among the bourgeoisie. But this state of things finds its complement in the practical absence of the family among the proletarians, and in public prostitution.

The bourgeois family will vanish as a matter of course when its complement vanishes, and both will vanish with the vanishing of capital.

Do you charge us with wanting to stop the exploitation of children by their parents? To this crime we plead guilty.

But, you will say, we destroy the most hallowed of relations, when we replace home education by social.

And your education! Is not that also social, and determined by the social conditions under which you educate, by the intervention, direct or indirect, of society, by means of schools, etc.? The Communists have not invented the intervention of society in education; they do but seek to alter the character of that intervention, and to rescue education from the influence of the ruling class.

The bourgeois clap-trap about the family and education, about the hallowed co-relation of parent and child, becomes all the more disgusting, the more, by the action of Modern Industry, all family ties among the proletarians are torn asunder, and their children transformed into simple articles of commerce and instruments of labor.

But you Communists would introduce community of women, screams the whole bourgeoisie in chorus.

The bourgeois sees in his wife a mere instrument of production. He hears that the instruments of production are to be exploited in common, and, naturally, can come to no other conclusion than that the lot of being common to all will likewise fall to the women.

He has not even a suspicion that the real point is to do away with the status of women as mere instruments of production.

For the rest, nothing is more ridiculous than the virtuous indignation of our bourgeois at the community of women which, they pretend, is to be openly and officially established by the Communists. The Communists have no need to introduce community of women; it has existed almost from time immemorial.

Our bourgeois, not content with having the wives and daughters of their proletarians at their disposal, not to speak of common prostitutes, take the greatest pleasure in seducing each other's wives.

Bourgeois marriage is in reality a system of wives in common and thus, at the most, what the Communists might possibly be reproached with, is that they desire to introduce, in substitution for a hypocritically concealed, an openly legalized community of women. For the rest, it is self-evident that the abolition of the present system of production must bring with it the abolition of the community of women springing from that system, i.e., of prostitution both public and private.

The Communists are further reproached with desiring to abolish countries and nationality.

The working men have no country. We cannot take from them what they have not got. Since the proletariat must first of all acquire political supremacy, must rise to be the leading class of the nation, must constitute itself the nation, it is, so far, itself national, though not in the bourgeois sense of the word.

National differences and antagonisms between peoples are daily more and more vanishing, owing to the development of the bourgeoisie, to freedom of commerce, to the world-market, to uniformity in the mode of production and in the conditions of life corresponding thereto.

The supremacy of the proletariat will cause them to vanish still faster. United action, of the leading civilized countries at least, is one of the first conditions for the emancipation of the proletariat.

In proportion as the exploitation of one individual by another is put an end to, the exploitation of one nation by another will also be put an end to. In proportion as the antagonism between classes within the nation vanishes, the hostility of one nation to another will come to an end.

The charges against Communism made from a religious, a philosophical, and, generally, from an ideological standpoint, are not deserving of serious examination.

Does it require deep intuition to comprehend that man's ideas, views and conceptions, in one word, man's consciousness, changes with every change in the conditions of his material existence, in his social relations and in his social life?

What else does the history of ideas prove, than that intellectual production changes its character in proportion as material production is changed? The ruling ideas of each age have ever been the ideas of its ruling class.

When people speak of ideas that revolutionize society, they do but express the fact, that within the old society, the elements of a new one have been created, and that the dissolution of the old ideas keeps even pace with the dissolution of the old conditions of existence.

When the ancient world was in its last throes, the ancient religions were overcome by Christianity. When Christian ideas succumbed in the 18th century to rationalist ideas, feudal society fought its death battle with the then revolutionary bourgeoisie. The ideas of religious liberty and freedom of conscience merely gave expression to the sway of free competition within the domain of knowledge.

"Undoubtedly," it will be said, "religious, moral, philosophical and juridical ideas have been modified in the course of historical development. But religion, morality philosophy, political science, and law, constantly survived this change."

"There are, besides, eternal truths, such as Freedom, Justice, etc. that are common to all states of society. But Communism abolishes eternal truths, it abolishes all religion, and all morality, instead of constituting them on a new basis; it therefore acts in contradiction to all past historical experience."

What does this accusation reduce itself to? The history of all past society has consisted in the development of class antagonisms, antagonisms that assumed different forms at different epochs.

But whatever form they may have taken, one fact is common to all past ages, *viz*., the exploitation of one part of society by the other. No wonder, then, that the social consciousness of past ages, despite all the multiplicity and variety it displays, moves within certain common forms, or general ideas, which cannot completely vanish except with the total disappearance of class antagonisms.

The Communist revolution is the most radical rupture with traditional property relations; no wonder that its development involves the most radical rupture with traditional ideas.

But let us have done with the bourgeois objections to Communism.

We have seen above, that the first step in the revolution by the working class, is to raise the proletariat to the position of ruling as to win the battle of democracy.

The proletariat will use its political supremacy to wrest, by degrees, all capital from the bourgeoisie, to centralize all instruments of production in the hands of the State, i.e., of the proletariat organized as the ruling class; and to increase the total of productive forces as rapidly as possible.

Of course, in the beginning, this cannot be effected except by means of despotic inroads on the rights of property, and on the conditions of bourgeois production; by means of measures, therefore, which appear economically insufficient and untenable, but which, in the course of the movement, outstrip themselves, necessitate further inroads upon the old social order, and are unavoidable as a means of entirely revolutionizing the mode of production.

These measures will of course be different in different countries.

Nevertheless in the most advanced countries, the following will be pretty generally applicable.

1. Abolition of property in land and application of all rents of land to public purposes.
2. A heavy progressive or graduated income tax.
3. Abolition of all right of inheritance.
4. Confiscation of the property of all emigrants and rebels.
5. Centralization of credit in the hands of the State, by means of a national bank with State capital and an exclusive monopoly.
6. Centralization of the means of communication and transport in the hands of the State.
7. Extension of factories and instruments of production owned by the State; the bringing into cultivation of waste-lands, and the improvement of the soil generally in accordance with a common plan.
8. Equal liability of all to labor. Establishment of industrial armies, especially for agriculture.
9. Combination of agriculture with manufacturing industries; gradual abolition of the distinction between town and country, by a more equable distribution of the population over the country.
10. Free education for all children in public schools. Abolition of children's factory labor in its present form. Combination of education with industrial production, etc., etc.

When, in the course of development, class distinctions have disappeared, and all production has been concentrated in the hands of a vast association of the whole nation, the public power will lose its political character.

Political power, properly so called, is merely the organized power of one class for oppressing another. If the proletariat during its contest with the bourgeoisie is compelled, by the force of circumstances, to organize itself as a class, if, by means of a revolution, it makes itself the ruling class, and, as such, sweeps away by force the old conditions of production, then it will, along with these conditions, have swept away the conditions for the existence of class antagonisms and of classes generally, and will thereby have abolished its own supremacy as a class.

In place of the old bourgeois society, with its classes and class antagonisms, we shall have an association, in which the free development of each is the condition for the free development of all. . . .

IV. POSITION OF THE COMMUNISTS IN RELATION TO THE VARIOUS EXISTING OPPOSITION PARTIES

Section II has made clear the relations of the Communists to the existing working-class parties, such as the Chartists in England and the Agrarian Reformers in America.

The Communists fight for the attainment of the immediate aims, for the enforcement of the momentary interests of the working class; but in the movement of the present, they also represent and take care of the future of that movement. In France the Communists ally themselves with the Social-Democrats, against the conservative and radical bourgeoisie, reserving, however, the right to take up a critical position in regard to phrases and illusions traditionally handed down from the great Revolution.

In Switzerland they support the Radicals, without losing sight of the fact that this party consists of antagonistic elements, partly of Democratic Socialists, in the French sense, partly of radical bourgeois.

In Poland they support the party that insists on an agrarian revolution as the prime condition for national emancipation, that party which fomented the insurrection of Cracow in 1846.

In Germany they fight with the bourgeoisie whenever it acts in a revolutionary way, against the absolute monarchy, the feudal "squirearchy," and the petty bourgeoisie.

But they never cease, for a single instant, to instil into the working class the clearest possible recognition of the hostile antagonism between bourgeoisie and proletariat, in order that the German workers may straightaway use, as so many weapons against the bourgeoisie, the social and political conditions that the bourgeoisie must necessarily introduce along with its supremacy, and in order that, after the fall of the reactionary classes in Germany, the fight against the bourgeoisie itself may immediately begin.

The Communists turn their attention chiefly to Germany, because that country is on the eve of a bourgeois revolution that is bound to be carried out under more advanced conditions of European civilization, and with a much more developed proletariat, than that of England was in the seventeenth, and of France in the eighteenth century, and because the bourgeois revolution in Germany will be but the prelude to an immediately following proletarian revolution.

In short, the Communists everywhere support every revolutionary movement against the existing social and political order of things.

In all these movements they bring to the front, as the leading question in each, the property question, no matter what its degree of development at the time.

Finally, they labor everywhere for the union and agreement of the democratic parties of all countries.

The Communists disdain to conceal their views and aims. They openly declare that their ends can be attained only by the forcible overthrow of all existing social conditions.

Let the ruling classes tremble at a Communistic revolution. The proletarians have nothing to lose but their chains. They have a world to win.

WORKING MEN OF ALL COUNTRIES, UNITE!

[*Manifesto of the Communist Party* from the English edition of 1888, edited by Friedrich Engels]

Appendix: An Introduction to Logical Argument

Logic is the branch of philosophy dedicated to the study of correct reasoning and the rules and principles that govern proper logical argument. It is important to note that, in this context, an *argument* is not to be confused with merely *arguing* with someone over some matter. A logical argument is not the same thing as a dispute. Put simply, a logical argument involves the attempt to support the truth of *one* proposition (i.e., belief, opinion, claim, etc.) by appealing to the truth of *other*, logically related, propositions. We call the proposition whose truth we seek to support a **conclusion**. We call any proposition cited to support the truth of the conclusion a **premise**. You can think of the conclusion of an argument as its main point, while its premises are reasons to accept the truth of the main point.

Often, the author of an argument will flag the premise(s) and/or conclusion of their argument with **indicator words** or **phrases**. These are word or phrases used to distinguish the conclusion of an argument from its premise(s). Please note the list of some commonly occurring indicators, below.

Conclusion Indicators: therefore / wherefore / accordingly / we may conclude / entails that / hence / thus / consequently / we may infer / it must be that / whence / so / it follows that / implies that / as a result / etc.

Premise Indicators: since / as / insofar as / in that / because / for / given that / for the reason that / owing to / inasmuch as / etc.

It is also important to note that a proper logical argument requires *both* a conclusion and one or more premises. A single, stand-alone "conclusion" is not an argument; in fact, it's not even a proper conclusion. A lone proposition is called an **assertion**. Assertions may very well be true, but without any further reasons "backing them up," we have no good reason for accepting them as true. For example, I may assert: "The Detroit Tigers are the best team in baseball," but if I don't provide further reasons to back up my claim, it remains a mere assertion. If, instead, I bolster my claim by pointing to the team's win-loss record, their superior statistics in pitching and hitting compared with other teams, and so forth, my assertion becomes a proper argument.

Assertion: "The Detroit Tigers are the best team in baseball."

Argument: "The best team in baseball is the team with the best record. The Detroit Tigers have the best record. Therefore, the Detroit Tigers are the best team in baseball."

However, not all propositions are relevant to the truth of a particular conclusion, logically speaking. Consider:

"The best team in baseball is any team with white and blue jerseys. The Detroit Tigers have white and blue jerseys. Therefore, the Detroit Tigers are the best team in baseball."

There is something logically suspect about this reasoning, and you do not have to be a fan of baseball (or its sartorial conventions) to spot it. Of what logical *relevance* is a team's colors to that team's performance? Thus, in assessing the quality of a logical argument, we need to do more than merely assess the truth of its premise(s) and/or its conclusion. We also need to assess the quality of the underlying logical *structure* of an argument: that is, the logical connections (or lack thereof) between the premise(s) and the conclusion. In logic, we employ the concept of **validity** to describe the structure or form of an argument. An argument is logically valid when the truth of the premise(s) would conclusively guarantee the truth of the conclusion. In other words, a valid argument is an argument whose conclusion *must* be true if its premise(s) were true. We may very well use the word "valid" in a looser sense in casual conversation (e.g., "You make a valid point!"), but, in logic, "valid" is a more precise term of art. Individual propositions (e.g., premises and conclusions) are either *true* or *false*, not valid or invalid. Logical arguments, on the other hand, are never true or false, but *valid* or *invalid*. Validity is a formal or structural property of logical arguments. This means that, as odd as it may seem, an argument with a false premise—or even a false conclusion!—may nonetheless be valid. Let's see why.

Premise 1: All men are mortal.

Premise 2: Socrates is a man.

Conclusion: Socrates is mortal.

The above is a (classic) example of a logically valid argument. *If* it is true that all men are mortal, and *if* it is true that Socrates is a man, then it would follow logically that Socrates is mortal. Moreover, the truth of the conclusion of any logically valid argument follows with strict logical necessity. That is, there is no possible way for a valid argument to have true premises and a false conclusion. In logic, we say the truth of the conclusion of a valid argument *follow from* the truth of its premises. But compare:

Premise 1: All fnorbs are conbloozable.

Premise 2: Bsnord is a fnorb.

Conclusion: Bsnord is conbloozable.

It may seem bizarre to describe the above (intentionally obscure) argument as valid, but it is. Remember: validity is a structural or formal property of logical arguments, and thus does not depend on the actual truth of any particular premise. *If* it were true that all fnorbs are conbloozable, and *if* it were true that Bsnord is a fnorb, then it would follow logically that Bsnord is conbloozable – whatever any of that might mean! Just as a valid argument may nonetheless have false premises, it is also possible for a valid argument to have a false conclusion:

Premise 1: All dogs are cats.

Premise 2: Professor Kirkland is a dog.

Conclusion: Professor Kirkland is a cat.

Here we have an argument with false premises *and* a false conclusion that, nevertheless, is valid. *If* it were true that all dogs are cats, and *if* it were true that Professor Kirkland is a dog, then it would follow logically that Professor Kirkland is a cat. Clearly, then, we need an additional concept to describe those arguments with a valid structure whose premises are *in fact* true. This is the concept of **soundness**. A logically sound argument is a logically valid argument whose premises are *actually* (not just presumably) true. In logic, it does not get any better than a sound argument. For, with a sound argument, we can confidently conclude that its conclusion is *necessarily true*:

Premise 1: All circles are round.

Premise 2: No squares are round.

Conclusion: No squares are circles.

As you might imagine, logically sound arguments are relatively rare in discourse. It is often the case that we cannot provide the sort of *conclusive* proof that sound arguments both require and guarantee. Fortunately, we have other options, logically speaking.

Deduction and Induction

In logic, it is useful to distinguish between **deductive** and **inductive** reasoning. In the case of deductive reasoning, we attempt to construct an argument that is both valid and sound—that is, an argument with a structure such that the actual truth of its premises guarantees the actual truth of its conclusion. Any logical argument that fails to meet this high bar can be classified as inductive. In an inductive argument, the truth of the premise(s) provides less-than-definitive reasons for accepting the truth of the conclusion. We may think of the concepts of probability or likelihood, here. An inductive argument that is well-constructed gives us good reasons for accepting the *probable* or *likely* truth of the conclusion. For example, if you developed heartburn shortly after every time you happened to drink a cup of coffee to-date, it is reasonable to conclude that the coffee may have something to do with your symptoms. From this may we *definitively* conclude that *every* time you drink a cup of coffee in the future you will develop heartburn? We may not. Is it possible? Sure. Is it necessary, in the logical sense? It is not. Philosopher Bertrand Russell was fond of the following anecdote to illustrate this aspect of inductive reasoning. Every morning a chicken sees the screen of the chicken coop slide open as the farmer deposits the chicken's feed into the coop. This happens without fail, every morning, for years. In fact, the chicken comes to associate the opening of the screen with the pleasant experience of being fed. It is reasonable to infer that when the screen swings open tomorrow morning the chicken will be fed? Sure. Unless, of course, tomorrow is the ill-fated day that chicken soup is on the farmhouse menu!

Since the truth of the conclusion of an inductive argument is never guaranteed, we will need a different concept to evaluate the relative quality of inductive arguments. The concepts of validity and soundness are reserved for deductive arguments. With respect to inductive arguments, then, we speak of their relative **strength**. Any particular inductive argument is either more or less strong (or weak). The way to improve the strength of an inductive argument is to provide premises that increase the likelihood that the conclusion is true. But note: the moment that the truth of an argument's premises actually *guarantees* the truth of its conclusion it is no longer an inductive argument but a deductively sound one. Thus, when it comes to induction, it is always possible for an inductive argument to have true premises and a very strong structure, but with a false conclusion all the same. A helpful analogy here can be drawn from the sphere of justice and criminal law. In a criminal courtroom, the prosecutor may try to prove the guilt of a defendant beyond all reasonable doubt by introducing evidence that bolsters her claim that the defendant is, in fact, guilty. That said, no matter how much evidence a prosecutor cites in making her case, it always remains logically possible that the defendant is not, in fact, guilty. Maybe it's a case of mistaken identity. Maybe his evil twin did it! When it comes to inductive reasoning, the most we can strive for are highly probable or likely conclusions. Certain truth is the province of deduction, not induction.

Logical Fallacies

In logic, a **fallacy** is an error in reasoning. Thus, a fallacious argument is a logical argument that suffers from one or more serious defects. Logical fallacies are therefore best avoided wherever possible in our reasoning. Logical fallacies may be *intentional*—that is, deliberately committed, perhaps as a rhetorical tactic to "win" a dispute by whatever means necessary, logical or not—or *unintentional* in nature. Intentional or otherwise, we should avoid fallacious reasoning in our own arguments, and we should be attentive to fallacious reasoning in the arguments of others. Provided below is a list of some unfortunately common informal logical fallacies. This is far from a complete list, but it can serve as a useful reference for when we encounter an aspect of someone's argument that seems suspect for reasons we perhaps cannot initially put our finger on.

Straw Man: When a person's position or claims are mischaracterized in an uncharitable fashion so as to make them easier to address and/or refute. It takes its name from the image of a scarecrow. Just as a scarecrow is easier to topple than an actual person, a caricatured version of one's views can be easier to "knock over," as well. This is fallacious because the straw man fallacy amounts to changing the subject to a different, and therefore irrelevant, claim or set of claims.

> *"Anyone who supports a raise in the minimum wage hates capitalism and thus is a Communist."*

Slippery Slope: When it is erroneously claimed that a particular position, policy, etc., (A) will inexorably lead to terrible and/or unacceptable consequences in the future (X, Y, Z). Not all invocations of a "slippery slope" are fallacious, however, as it is possible that A will in fact make it more likely that X, Y, and/or Z will occur. The invocation of a slippery slope is fallacious when it is unclear or unlikely that A will in fact lead to X, Y, and Z.

> *"If we lower the legal voting age to 18, then eventually babies will demand the right to vote!"*

Post hoc ergo propter hoc: From the Latin: "After this, therefore because of this." When one event is assumed to be the effect of another, prior event on insufficient causal evidence. Just because event A precedes event B in time does not necessarily mean that A was the cause of B. The likely source of many superstitious beliefs.

> *"A black cat crossed my path and then I received a phone call with bad news. Black cats are bad luck."*

Circular Argument: When an argument merely asserts the truth of the conclusion it is supposed to prove instead of providing premises that actually support the truth of the conclusion. Also known as "begging the question."

> *"There ought to be a law against gambling because gambling should be illegal."*

Argumentum ad Hominem: From the Latin: "Against the man." An irrelevant personal attack, critiquing some aspect of the person espousing a position instead of their position itself. If someone's character or personal history is in fact relevant to a discussion, then invocations of the same are not irrelevant and therefore not fallacious. However, the Argumentum ad Hominem fallacy is comparable to the Straw Man fallacy in that it effectively changes the subject and can be construed as a gesture of argumentative surrender.

> *"Professor Kirkland supports a raise for adjunct lecturers, but of course he would. Have you seen his stupid hat? Only an idiot would wear a hat like that, so we can safely ignore his concerns."*

Argumentum ad Populum: An irrelevant appeal to the popularity of a position, view, or practice; that is, an appeal to the majority. This appeal can be fallacious insofar as the truth does not always reside with the majority.

> *"More Americans smoke Marlboros than any other brand. Smoking Marlboros is good for you!"*

False Dilemma: When one presumes that there are only two mutually exclusive options in a particular scenario, when in fact there are more than two. Not all dilemmas are false: when you flip a coin, it's going to turn up either heads or tails. A dilemma becomes fallacious when there are legitimately more than two possible outcomes (i.e., possibilities, options, etc.) but the author or speaker in question unreasonably insists there are not.

> *"America: Love it or leave it!"*

Fallacy of Composition: When one presumes that something true of one part of a whole must also be true of the whole itself.

> *"Students are an important part of the University. Students have arms and legs. Therefore, the University has arms and legs."*

Fallacy of Division: When one presumes that something true of the whole must also be true of parts of the whole.

> *"Water is wet, and water consists of hydrogen and oxygen. Thus, hydrogen and oxygen are wet."*

Appeal to Authority: When no further reasons to support the truth of a conclusion are provided, save for the invocation of one's authority. Not all appeals to authority are fallacious, as some people do in fact have more expertise than others in certain areas. However, any non-fallacious appeal to authority will feature additional reasons justifying *why* a given authority accepts a particular claim. Be on guard for authorities in one area claiming to speak as authorities in another area unrelated to their expertise (e.g., celebrity endorsements in advertising).

> *"Because I said so."*

Logical Exercises

Name: ______________________________

For each of the following logical arguments, indicate whether they are valid and/or sound. If an argument is invalid and/or unsound, explain why in the space provided.

1. All whales are mammals, and Shamu is a whale. Thus, Shamu is a mammal.

2. If it rains, then the sidewalks will be wet. Since the sidewalks are wet, we can infer that it rained.

3. Because it rained, we can conclude that the sidewalks are wet. That's because, if it rains then the sidewalks will be wet.

4. Most people are right handed and Kurt Cobain was a person, so we can infer that Kurt Cobain was right handed.

5. All people are left handed and Kurt Cobain was a person, so we can conclude that Kurt Cobain was left handed.

6. Insofar as all unicorns have horns and all bulls have horns, then it follows that all bulls are unicorns.

7. Eighty-two percent of all Americans who have died from liver complications consumed tomatoes at some point in their life. From this we may conclude that eating tomatoes causes liver damage.

8. The Bible claims that God exists, and the Bible is true because it was inspired by God. Therefore, God exists.

9. If we legalize marijuana for recreational use, then what's stopping us from repealing the laws prohibiting theft and murder? Hence, legalizing marijuana for recreational use is a terrible idea.

10. Either you love chocolate ice cream or you love vanilla ice cream. You do not love vanilla ice cream, therefore we can infer that you love chocolate ice cream.

Homework Assignment: Appendix

Name: ______________________________ Section: ______________________________

Explain the main difference between *deductive arguments* and *inductive arguments*. Provide your own examples of each kind of argument that illustrate this difference.

Homework Assignment: Appendix

Name: ______________________________ Section: ______________________________

Provide your own examples of the following logical fallacies:

Straw Man Fallacy:

Slippery Slope Fallacy:

Circular Argument (i.e., "Begging the Question"):

False Dilemma: